Biographical Dictionary
OF
THE Youngs
(Born circa 1625-1870)
From Towns Under the
Jurisdiction of York
County, Maine

Louise Ryder Young

HERITAGE BOOKS
2007

HERITAGE BOOKS

AN IMPRINT OF HERITAGE BOOKS, INC.

Books, CDs, and more—Worldwide

For our listing of thousands of titles see our website
at
www.HeritageBooks.com

Published 2007 by
HERITAGE BOOKS, INC.
Publishing Division
65 East Main Street
Westminster, Maryland 21157-5026

Other books by the author:

Dictionary of The Youngs (Born circa 1600-1870): From Essex and Old Norfolk Counties, Massachusetts Bay Colony, Which Once Contained Parts of Rockingham County, New Hampshire

International Standard Book Number: 978-0-7884-0565-5

CONTENTS

Addenda: Corrections and Additions to *Biographical Dictionary of Strafford County, New Hampshire*; and *Biographical Dictionary of Essex and Old Norfolk Counties, Massachusetts Bay Colony.*

PREFACE

The two major efforts on the Youngs of Strafford County, N.H. (1989) and the Youngs of Essex County, Massachusetts which included parts of Rockingham County, N.H., (1994), inevitably raised more questions on those Youngs than could be answered and inevitably led me to consider going beyond those borders into the lower part of Maine that contains York County for some of the answers. Ironically enough, this was where I had spent four summers as a teenager. So the decision to research York County was made not only for practical reasons, but for sentimental ones also. Begun approximately four years ago as idle thoughts, the Youngs of York County, Maine have helped to add another dimension to the histories already in.

I am so grateful to my family and friends for their encouragement over the years on this on-going project, but my special thanks go to:

My husband Richard who is untiring in his technical assistance on the computers and printers. He utilized the Graphics Program from Windows 3.1 in order to develop two maps, the first of Old York County, the second, of present-day York County.

The staff of the Latter Day Saints Family History Library, Columbia, Maryland. Their assistance and encourage-ment over the years certainly helped to make the project feasible.

Special words of thanks and appreciation are extended to these publishers and authors who have granted me permission to use their materials (please see Bibliography for full citation on each one):

(1) Boyle, Frederick R.: Early Families of Sanford-Springvale, Maine, Publisher: Peter E. Randall, Portsmouth, NH.

(2) Picton Press, Rockport, Maine: spokeswoman Candy McMahan's authorizations relative to the following four reference books: Gray's Maine Families in 1790, Vol. 1, p261 (1992); Maine Cemetery Inscriptions, Vols. 1-4; John L. M. Willis' Old Eliot, ME, reprint 1985; Lester M. Bragdon & John E. Frost's Vital Records of York, Maine, (1982).

(3) Genealogical Publishing Co., Inc, Baltimore, MD: spokeswoman Lorie Szarek stated that the six works mentioned in my list are now in the public domain: List of Freemen of Massachusetts, 1630-1691 by Paige; Genealogical Dictionary of Maine and New Hampshire by Noyes et al; The Pioneers of Maine and New Hampshire, 1623 to 1660 by Pope; A Genealogical Dictionary of the First Settlements of New England by Savage; Maine Wills by Sargent; and Heads of Families at the First Census of the United States Taken in the Year 1790, Maine.

iv

However, Genealogical Publishing Co., Inc. holds the copyright on Torrey's New England Marriages Prior to 1700; his permission was granted on this publication.

(4) Heritage Books, Inc., Bowie, MD, spokeswoman Leslie Towle. Both references used are now in the public domain: George Folsom's History of Saco and Biddeford, with Notices of Other Early Settlements, and of the Proprietary Governments in Maine, including the Provinces of New Somersetshire and Lygonia (Reprint 1984); George J. Varney's A Gazetteer of the State of Maine (Reprint 1991).

I am also very appreciative of the interest shown and of the contributions made by the following individuals responding to my ad in 1995 in the New England Historic and Genealogical Society NEXUS: Charles D. Young of Oswego, N.Y.; Ms. Nancy W. Bollenbach, Ajijic, Jalisco, Mexico; Mrs. Douglas M. Crawford, Santa Barbara, CA; Robert W. Townsend, Honolulu, HI; Charles Hitchcock, Jr., Hingham, MA; Joan Reed Miller, York, PA; Mrs. Anne Smith, West Danville, VT; Mrs. James A. Young, Albuquerque, N.Mex; Professor F. L. Dixon Yard, Assonet, MA; John G. Holyoke, Dayton, Ohio; Mrs. Nancy Porter, West Farmington, ME; Forest G. Hicks, Oxnard, CA; David Young, Melbourne, FL; and Robert M. Young, Essex, MA.

Louise R. Young

Finksburg, Maryland
May 1996

LIST OF ABBREVIATIONS

Admin.	Administration	n.d.	no date given
	Administrator	n.p.	no page given
	Administratrix	N.E.	north east, northeastern
aka	also known as	N.W.	north west, northwestern
Assoc.	Association	N.S.	Nova Scotia
b	born	p, pp	page/pages
bp	baptized	PA	Pennsylvania
ca	circa	poss.	possibly
cem.	cemetery	poss.	possible
cert.	certified, certificate	prob.	probable
ch.	child, children	Prov.	Provincial
CR	church records	rec'd	received, recorded
Co.	company, county	Recs.	records
cont.	continued	Reg.	register, registered
d	died	Regt.	regiment
d/o	daughter of	res.	resident, resided
DAR	Daughters of the American Revolution	s/o	son of
dau.	daughter	S.E.	southeast, southeastern
d-o-b	date of birth	S.W.	southwest, southwestern
d-o-d	date of death	TMs	typed manuscript
d.y.	died young	TR	Town Records
Exec.	Executor/Executrix	V	Virginia
fam.	family	R	Vital Records
gen.	genealogy, genealogical	V	volume
gr.d/o	granddaughter of	VT	Vermont
gr.s/o	grandson of	y-o-b	year of birth
I.G.I.	International Genealogical Index	y-o-d	year of death
LDA	Latter Day Saints		
m, marr	married		
MA	Massachusetts		
Mil.	military		
ME	Maine		
Nat'l	national		
N.B.	New Brunswick		
N.E.	New England		
N.H.	New Hampshire		
NHVR	New Hampshire Vital Records		

Brackets [ ] were used: (1) to enclose citation of a document; (2) to enclose interjectory comments believed to be true on statements found within documents.

TOPOGRAPHY OF YORK COUNTY, MAINE

(For sources of historical background, grateful acknowledgement is made to George J. Varney's "A Gazetteer of the State of Maine With Numerous Illustrations, Vols. I and II, Reprint, 1991)

ARUNDEL. For full background, please see Kennebunk Port. The town name of Arundel appeared in Revolutionary War records: John Young and sibling Hezekiah, both of Saco, joined a company being raised February 1776, commanded by Capt. John Elden of Buxton, from the towns of Buxton, Arundel, Biddeford and Saco, for a short term of service in the Continental Army. The company belonged to the regiment of militia under Col. Lemuel Robinson, and was assigned the task of fortifying Dorchester Heights on the night of March 4th.

ACTON. The New Hampshire border abuts this town on its western boundary, and the Salmon Falls River forms the boundary for three-fourths of this distance. The town is bounded by Newfield on the north, Lebanon on the south and by Shapleigh on the east, from which it was incorporated in 1830.

ALFRED. The shire town of York County is located practically in the geographical center of the county. It is surrounded by Waterboro on the north and north east, Lyman on the east, Shapleigh and Sanford on the west, and Kennebunk and Sanford on the south. The early history of the town is de

rived from that of Sanford. It was incorporated in 1794, to become a half-shire town in 1802.

BERWICK. Was originally the ninth town of the state, incorporated in 1713, from which North and South Berwick were derived. Its boundaries are Lebanon on the north, North Berwick on the east, South Berwick on the south, and New Hampshire on its western side. Salmon Falls river forms the boundary line with New Hampshire. See also Kittery for Berwick's early history.

BIDDEFORD. The town is situated upon the southern bank of Saco River, by which stream it is separated from Saco, of which it was formerly a part. It is bounded easterly by the sea. Kennebunkport lies on the south and south west, and Dayton on the north west. Biddeford's history is much intertwined with that of the town of Saco on the south. Varney's **Maine Gazetteer** stated: "It was included with the other side of the river in a corporation under the name of Saco from 1653 to 1718, when it was incorporated by itself, receiving the name of Biddeford, a town in England whence some of the inhabitants had emigrated."

It received a city charter in 1855. For many years these twin cities on the Saco River formed the foremost community while Maine was a province.

BUXTON. The town was incorporated in 1772 after an English town of the same name. There are four villages in the town, Salmon Falls, Bar Mills, West Buxton and Buxton Center. An attempt to settle the town was made in 1740, but further settlement of the town was precluded due to the French and Indian Wars.

CAPE NEDDOCK. The name of one of two notable headlands, the other being Bald Head Cliff. Cape Neddock aka Cape Neddick was quite often a point of reference in land deeds researched on the Youngs in the York area.

CORNISH. Incorporated in 1794, the town is located where the Ossipee and Saco Rivers join at the extreme north of York County. It abuts Limington on the east, Limerick on the south, Parsonsfield on the west, and Baldwin and Hiram, both in Cumberland County, on the north.

CUMBERLAND COUNTY. This neighboring county is located in the S.W. part of the State, directly N.E. of York County. After the purchase of the province by Massachusetts in 1677, it came under the jurisdiction of that commonwealth, being included in the county of Yorkshire until its organization under its present name of York in 1760.

DAYTON. Originally the town was part of Hollis up through 1854, when it was incorporated as a distinct entity. Its boundaries are the Saco River on its eastern line, Biddeford on its south eastern boundary, Lyman on the south west, and a portion of Hollis on the west. For Dayton's early history, please see Hollis.

ELIOT. Incorporated under its present name in 1810 and is found on the eastern bank of Piscataqua River in the northwestern part of York County. Previous to this it was known as the north parish of Kittery and bore the name of Sturgeon Creek.

FALMOUTH. Originally a town of York County, it was incorporated in 1718, but has since become a part of Cumberland County. Early on, it included the present towns of Cape Elizabeth, Westbrook, Deering and Portland. A land deed between Moses Young and Josiah Noyes, both of Falmouth, was dated 14 July 1758.

GREAT WORKS. Not to be confused with a town of the same name in Penobscot County; see South Berwick.

HOLLIS. The township was originally a part of Little Falls Plantation, a tract of land that had been purchased of the Indians, where settlements began as early as 1753 along the Saco River. It was incorporated in 1798 under the name of Phillipsburg, but the name was changed to Hollis in 1811. The town of Dayton was derived from Hollis in 1854. Towns adjoining Hollis today are Buxton across the river on the east, Dayton on the south, Waterborough on the west, and Limington on the north.

ISLES OF SHOALS. The Shoals lie about nine miles south of Kittery Point, and are divided by the line between Maine and New Hampshire, by which the larger number belong to Kittery. One of the earliest known settlers there was Rowland Young Jr. and spouse Susanna nee Matthews, recipients of land according to a deed of gift dated 25 Aug 1685.

KENNEBUNK. In its early days, this town was part of Wells. Incorporated in 1820, it abuts Kennebunk Port and Kennebunk River on the east, the ocean on the south, Wells on the west and the towns of Sanford, Alfred and Lyman on the north.

KENNEBUNKPORT. This lies in the eastern part of York County, bounded on the east by Biddeford, west by Kennebunk, north by Lyman, and south by the sea. The town was originally known as Cape Porpoise in 1653 by the Massachusetts Commissioners. In 1718 it was reorganized under the name of Arundel. In 1820 the name was changed again, this time to its present-day cognomen. It possesses two or three small but deep bays known as Cape Porpoise Harbor. Its principal businesses are fisheries and shipbuilding.

KITTERY. This town's territory, located on the extreme southwestern part of York County and of Maine, at one time included Eliot, Berwick, South Berwick and North Berwick. It was incorporated in 1647 as the plantation known as Pisca-taqua. Its history will show it was one of the oldest towns in Maine and the first to be incorporated, set off in 1713, and Eliot in 1810. Kittery's bounds are Eliot on the northwest, Eliot and York on the north, Piscataqua River and its harbor on the southwest and south, and by the sea, southeast. Ship building and sea faring became the principal occupations, not to mention in later years the proliferation of summer resorts.

LEBANON. Situated up in the north of York County, bordering New Hampshire, and separated from it by the Salmon Falls River. Its boundaries are Acton on the north, Sanford on the east, and North Berwick and Berwick on the south.

LIMERICK. The town is located in the northern part of York County. It is bounded by Cornish on the north, Limington on the east, Little Ossipee River on the south, and Newfield and Parsonsfield on the west. First settled in 1775, it is noteworthy that the settlers came from seaboard towns of York County, Maine, Newbury, Mass., and a few from Limerick, Ireland; the town was incorporated in 1787.

LIMINGTON. One of the most northerly towns in York County, it is bounded on the north by Baldwin, on the east by Standish, on the south by Hollis and Waterborough, and by Limerick and Cornish on the west. The town was incorporated in 1792; previous to that it was known as Little Ossipee Plantation.

LITTLE FALLS PLANTATION.
Please see Hollis.

LITTLE OSSIPEE PLANTATION. Please see Limington.

LYMAN. The township abuts Alfred on the northwest, Kennebunkport on the southeast, Sanford on the southwest, and Waterborough on the northwest. Lyman was first incorporated in 1778 by the name of Coxhall, but was changed to its present-day name in 1803.

NEWFIELD. **Varney's Maine Gazetteer** spoke of Newfield as "a part of the tract conveyed to Francis Small of Kittery, Indian trader, by Captain Sunday, a sagamore in the region in 1668. The tract lay between the Ossipee and Little Ossipee rivers, which when laid out into townships were generally spoken of as the five Ossipee towns." The name of Newfield was adopted when the town was incorporated in 1794. In 1844, a portion of the northwest corner of Shapleigh was annexed to Newfield.

OLD ORCHARD BEACH. Township is situated between Wood Island Light at the mouth of the Saco River and Prout's Neck in Scarborough. This beach that forms part of Maine's coastline of surpassing beauty received its name from an orchard set by Thomas Rogers who settled here in 1638.

PARSONSFIELD. The town is bounded on its western side by New Hampshire, on the north by Porter and Hiram, on the east by Cornish and Limerick, and on the south by Newfield. The Ossipee River forms the northern boundary line and provides at Kezar Falls the principal water power of the town. It was incorporated in 1785, deriving its name from Thomas Parsons, one of the earliest proprietors.

PEPPERRELLBOROUGH. Name originally given to Saco, in honor of Sir William Pepperrell [b 1696, Kittery Point, d 1759]. He and his father built up the largest mercantile house in New England, and he himself ultimately became sole owner of most of the towns of Saco and Scarboro, holding large properties as well in Portsmouth and Hampton, New Hampshire. He went on to become a powerful figure in government and the military. See Saco for statistics of the town.

PHILLIPSBURG, PHILLIPSTOWN. Please see Hollis.

SACO. Saco is situated on the Saco River, opposite Biddeford, with which it is connected not only by bridges and a federal highway, but also by their histories to this extent: they were both founded in 1630, and were called Saco until 1718; it was incorporated as Biddeford in 1719, being the fourth town in Maine. In 1762, it received a separate incorporation, with all the rights of a town except that of sending a representative to the General Assembly, it then being renamed Pepperellborough. In 1805, it resumed its original name of Saco, to receive its city charter in 1867. See also Biddeford.

SACO RIVER. This rises in New Hampshire in the White

Mountains, and flows southward through Maine into the Atlantic Ocean.

SANFORD. First called Phillipstown, its settlement began in 1740. It derived its present-day name from an interesting twist of history: In 1661 Major William Phillips purchased from the Indian chiefs a tract of land, the western portion of which was willed to Major Phillips wife. In 1696 she willed it to her former husband's son, Peleg Sanford, by which name the town became known. The town is adjacent to Alfred and Kennebunk on the east, Alfred and Shapleigh on the north, Wells and North Berwick on the south, and Lebanon and North Berwick on the west.

SHAPLEIGH. The township was formerly known as Hubbardstown, but derived its name from Nicholas Shapleigh who purchased it from Francis Small, who in turn derived his claim by his purchase of this and adjoining territory from the Indian sagamores. The town was incorporated in 1785. At that time it included Acton which was set off in 1830, and the northwest corner was annexed to Newfield in 1844.

SOUTH BERWICK. The first settlement of the town was at the Quampheagan Falls about 1624. South Berwick was included in Berwick when in 1700 that town was separated from Kittery. It was then taken from Berwick and incorporated in its own name in 1814. The town is bounded by the towns of Eliot and York on the south and southeast, Rollingsford, N.H. on

the west, Berwick, North Berwick and Wells on the northwest, and Wells on the north and northeast.

WATERBOROUGH. The perimeters of the township are Hollis for most of its eastern boundary, Limerick and Limington on the north, Alfred and Lyman on the south, and Alfred, Shapleigh and Newfield on the west. Before it was incorporated in 1787, the town was included with the northern part of Alfred under the tongue twister of Massabesic Plantation. The Little Ossipee River bounds the town on the north and furnishes several good water powers.

WELLS. Situated upon the sea coast, the town was settled by persons from Wells, England, immigrating by way of Exeter, N.H., circa 1840. Wells was incorporated in 1653, becoming the third town in Maine. Originally it included Kennebunk up until 1820, when that section was set off. Its present boundaries are Sanford and Kennebunk on the north, then Kennebunk and the ocean on the east and southeast, York and South Berwick on the south, and South and North Berwick on the west.

YORK. This sea coast town, originally known as Agamenticus, has a long and multi-hued history. Here was established the first English city in America in the early 1640s, situated twenty-five miles S.S.W. of Biddeford. In 1652 its name was changed to York, and that of the province to Yorkshire to avoid the city charter. Today the town which includes

York Beach and York Harbor is
generally known as Old York.
Its limits were seven miles
inland from the sea by three
in breadth, and the York
River formed its southwestern
boundary. The boundaries of
the present town are about as
they were in 1652: the sea
on the east, Wells on the
north, South Berwick on the
west, and Eliot and Kittery
on the south. Its principal
occupations are fishing, sea-
faring and agriculture;
summer tourism would come in
a close fourth, one would
imagine.

INTRODUCTION

Even before the completion of the Youngs of Essex County, Massachusetts, Vol. II, several years ago, I had begun to turn my thoughts more and more to York County, Maine as a new field of endeavor bearing upon the Youngs just studied. For in my mind, there was the likelihood of a great many interrelationships and indeed that proved to be the case.

1. The Biographical Dictionary

The presentation of the Youngs in alphabetical listings was derived from Freemont Rider's "trace system" of cross-indexing as presented in his encyclopedic biographical dictionary entitled: <u>Preliminary Materials for a Genealogy of the Rider (Ryder) Families in the United States, Arranged According to the "Rider Trace" System of Presentation</u>. Godfrey Memorial Library, Middletown, Connecticut (1959), 3 Vols.

Two distinct methods of research were used, which blended easily one with the other.

A. **The Whole Family Approach.** This approach can be described as testing anyone and everyone having the same family name within a given area such as a town or city, or county-wide, which can only generate a preponderance of evidence.

B. **Preliminary Materials Approach.** The above approach was balanced, I felt, with this approach as set forth by Freemont Rider in his biographical dictionary previously cited. What this second approach allowed for, in contrast to the other, was that all Young data was to be considered "preliminary" or inconclusive until other data was found to prove or disapprove. Thus it put one at ease to make a judgment call when necessary, rather than have them sound as statements of fact.

2. York County, Maine.

York County forms the southwestern portion of the state, adjacent to the northern boundaries of Massachusetts, and westerly, the borders of New Hampshire. It did not grow into its present-day size or influence upon bordering state lines, its counties or its country over night! It was a long process of growth from its status as Province of Maine in 1640, to living under the control of Massachusetts up through 1820. That was when it was voted by the United States Congress to grant Maine statehood.

In 1790, when census reports started, the county held twenty-six towns, thirteen of which either became hardly heard of again or the name of the town had changed. Today the county holds twenty-four towns and two major cities, with Old York as the county seat. Please see Topography for details on the ancient and present-day towns of York County.

3.   **The Main Entry, Who Qualifies.** A male Young earned a main entry when he was born no later than 1870, generally was an adult over twenty-one years of age, and was at least one of the following--native son, proprietor, land owner, head of family or taxpayer, soldier or sailor. Whether he was single or married was immaterial. A female Young earned her own entry when she was born no later than 1870, was a married daughter provided that date of marriage was known, widow of a male Young who could not be identified, or a single, working woman. Orphans were treated on a case-by-case basis, depending upon the amount of material known, but were put preferably under their father's entry. Titles such as Jr., 2nd, II, 3rd, Gent., Esq., etc., are seemingly of a transitory nature and were not a factor in the alphabetical listings of entries.

4.   **Who and What Get Cross-Indexed or Cross-Referenced.**
Dates of birth and parentage were fully cross-indexed in accordance with Freemont Rider's trace system. Another clue to the existence of a main entry is plus sign + placed beside the names of married children under the parents' entry. In the case of citations of land deeds between Young grantors and Young grantees, the full citation goes to the grantor; citation for the Young grantee is limited just to the dates of signing and recordation. Likewise, in citing probate papers, especially wills, the complete citation goes to the one who created the will. Entries on the heirs-at-law would have simply the date of signing and date of when it was proved in court. Census returns were only cited under the father's or widower's entry.

5.   **Identities of the Earliest Inhabitants, Landowners and/or Progenitors of the Youngs from York County.**
The fact that certain townships were not included indicated merely that no Young lived there for any length of time to make his mark.

Acton: Jonathan Young, Esq., b 12 Dec 1773, landowner, most likely progenitor with his large family. Three of his four sons carried on the line, Peter, William M. and Edmund J. Acton has many connections with Sanford.

Berwick: Stephen Young, b ca 1795, inhabitant, spouse of Abigail Ricker.

Biddeford: David Young, b ca 1695, resident and land-owner, most likely progenitor of David Young and Thomas Young, both b ca 1725. Another off-shoot, not related to the above, was Lewis Young, b 7 Jan 1773, native of Barnstable County, MA, landowner.

Buxton: Francis Young, b 14 Jul 1788, Buxton, prob. landowner, spouse of Fanny Bacon.

Hollis: Hezekiah Young, bp 24 Jun 1753, originally of Biddeford/Saco, s/o Thomas and Eunice (   ) Young of Saco, later resident of Hollis/Dayton. He was progenitor of a large and long-lived branch of Youngs in that area.

Kittery: Stephen H. Young, b 1794, listed on 1840 federal census, lived with spouse Eunice Fernald Young; early and long-time inhabitant of Kittery and progenitor.

Lebanon: Eliphalet Young, b ca 1760, spouse of Susanna Wallingford Young, early inhabitant of Lebanon, and progenitor.

Limington: David Young, bp 1763, Saco, came to Limington with his father [unknown]; David and spouse Elizabeth Smith Young became residents of Limington and raised ten children there. He was inhabitant and progenitor.

Saco: formerly Biddeford, see David Young of that town.

Sanford: Joseph, b ca 1680, originally of York, s/o Robert and Mary (Sayward) Young, spouse of Sarah King Young, progenitor of a very large family, by way of son Daniel, stemming from Sanford.

Shapleigh: Jonathan Young, Lt., aka Gent., b ca 1775, originally of Wells, later of Shapleigh, progenitor and landowner.

Waterboro: John Young, b 1787, spouse of Nancy Horn Young, should be considered the Young progenitor of this town.

York: Rowland Young, Sr., b ca 1620, England, spouse of Joan Knight Young, settled early in York; undoubtedly, Rowland was the earliest inhabitant and progenitor, bar none, of a prolific family stemming from Old York.

BIOGRAPHICAL DICTIONARY OF THE YOUNGS
(BORN 1625-1870) FROM
YORK COUNTY, MAINE

AARON, b ca 1775, of Sanford, laborer, most likely s/o Daniel and Anna (Johnson) Young; filed (Ints.) 9 Jul 1802, Sanford, Mary Cram [b 9 Mar 1781, Sanford, d/o John S. and Peace (Nason) Cram]. Aaron was listed as resident of Sanford in the 1810 census, age 26-45, with a spousal figure of the same age bracket, and two males under 10 years of age. Identities of the sons were not discovered.

Between 1807-1809 three deeds were found for Aaron of Sanford, the first two, deeds of purchase. His earliest land deed was signed 27 Feb 1807, rec'd 25 Nov 1807, for acreage he bought from Stephen Johnson of Sanford for $17.00, situated at the N.W. corner of the school lot which Johnson had purchased from John Parsons of York; Stephen Johnson's wife Abigail ceded dower rights, witnesses James Raker, Daniel Young [York Co. Deed 77:152]. His second deed was dated 1 Oct 1807, rec'd 25 Nov 1809, as resident of Sanford: Purchase from Daniel Young of Avon, Kennebunk County, yeoman, for $50.00, a one-fourth lot in No. 5 in the Middle Range of lots in Sanford, "being the same I bought from Benjamin Estes where my house now stands, by lands of Joseph Young and Hunken Dennett"; witnesses John L. Cram, William Nason [York Deed 81:149].

Aaron's third deed was signed 18 Sep 1809, rec'd 25 Nov 1809 in which he sold to Elisha Allen of Sanford for $42.00, eight acres land in Sanford, adjacent to lands of Joseph Young, Samuel Tripe and Daniel W. Nowell, and by Lot No. 7 and the county road, deed signed 18 Sep 1809, rec'd 25 Nov 1809; witness Caleb Emery, J.P. [York Deed 81:149]. (F. R. Boyle's Sanford, p330; Mormon/ME V.R., Wright-Zitkov; Census York Co., 1810, p1014)

AARON, b ca 1820, of York; m 13 Nov 1845, Alfred, Susan J. aka Sarah J. Griffin [b ca 1825, of Alfred]. (ME I.G.I.; MH&G Rec., V4, p268)

AARON, b 1846, of Saco, adopted s/o Thomas and Lydia Dyer, who were listed as residents of Saco in the 1860 census, their real estate valued at $5,000. Thomas Dyer was farmer, b 1802, Lydia Dyer, b 1804. (Census York Co., 1860, Reel C, p779)

ABBIE A., b 26 Nov 1834, Kittery, d/o Stephen H. and Eunice L. (Fernald) Young, d 26 Feb 1918, native town, single, age 78-3-0, buried at Orchard Grove on Rogers Road, Kittery.

In 1900 she lived at the home of her sister Maria E. (Young) Tilton [n.d. nor main entry]. (1900 ME Soundex; Hale's Cems., Series I, n.p.)

ABIGAIL (   ), b pre 1775, of Waterboro, widow and head of household as listed in the 1820 census for Waterboro, age 45 plus. Residing with her was one male age 10-16 and one female age 16-26. (Census York Co., 1820, p670)

ABIGAIL, b 22 Aug 1699, York, d/o Lt. Joseph and Abigail (Donnell) Young; m ca 1721, York, Judge John Bradbury Jr., [b ca 1695, York, s/o Wymond and Maria (Cotton) Bradbury]. Abigail's father Joseph made deed of gift to her when she was known as Abigail Bradbury, wife of John Bradbury, dated 13 Apr 1734, rec'd 20 May 1734: for ten pounds current money, two acres land in York, beginning at the S.W. corner of the land John Bradbury bought of Joseph Jr. and by land of Alexander Junkins bought of Joseph, which Joseph's honored father devised to him in his last will. John Bradbury was named Co-Exec. in his father-in-law's will signed 1 May 1734, proved 4 Jun 1734, wherein Abigail Bradbury was named married daughter and heir-at-law of Joseph.

Bradbury ch. b York: Cotton Bradbury, b 4 Oct 1722; Lucy Bradbury, b 18 Jan 1724/5; Bethulah Bradbury, b 20 Mar 1726/7; Maria Bradbury, b 5 Apr 1729; Abigail Bradbury, b 12 Aug 1731; Elizabeth Bradbury, b 5 Jan 1733/4; John Bradbury, Jr., b 18 Sep 1736; Joseph Bradbury, b 23 Oct 1740; Anne Bradbury, b 2 Jun 1743. (ME I.G.I.; Noyes et al, p776; Bragdon & Frost's York V.R., p320; Marshall's Buxton, ME, pp 234-235)

ABIGAIL, b 30 Jun 1727, York, d/o Samuel and Mehitable (Beane) Young, alive May 1765, native town; m 20 Feb 1754, York, Henry Grow [b ca 1725, of same town]. As a young child, Abigail was remembered in her grandfather Joseph Young's will that was signed 1 May 1734, probated 4 Jun 1734, her father Samuel having predeceased his father Joseph. Before she married, she was mentioned also as a single person in probate papers on her brother Joseph Jr.'s estate under administration by her mother Mehitable, dated 16 Oct 1753. Distribution of sibling Joseph's estate included payments to Abigail and four step-sisters.

A dual marriage took place on date cited above in York, between Henry Grow and Abigail Young, d/o Samuel Young, and William Grow and Abigail Young, d/o Jonathan Young Jr. Most likely Henry and William Grow were siblings, but the brides were indeed related; they were first cousins, granddaughters of Rowland and Susanna (Matthews) Young.

By deed signed 8 May 1765, rec'd the day after, Abigail Young Grow sold to Thomas Haines, mariner, of York for seven pounds, ten shillings, five acres land in York, bounded S.W. by York River, N.W. by lands of John Bradbury Esq., N.E. by lands of Jeremiah Boulton, and S.E. by Benaiah Young; received as the right and inheritance of Abigail Young of York when she was single, the property having the incumbrance of the Right of Dower of her mother Mehitable Bean Young Haines, the widow of Samuel and recent spouse of Acquilla Haines; witnesses Daniel Moulton Jr. and spouse Hannah [York Deed 38:130].

It is noteworthy that neither probate nor land deed nor vital record was found to indicate that there were heirs-at-law of Abigail and Henry Grow! (ME I.G.I.)

ABIGAIL, b 11 Jul 1729, York, twin, d/o Jonathan Jr. and Abigail (Came) Young, alive 1766, native town; filed (Ints.) 26 Jan 1754, m 20 Feb 1754, York, William Grow [b ca 1730, of York]. Abigail Grow and married sisters Eunice Junkins and Patience Stover, with husbands co-signing, sold their shares in their father's estate in York to brother Samuel Young of York for 80 pounds lawful money. The only exception was that part of the real estate belonging to their mother Abigail Young as her right of Thirds; by deed signed 9 Jul 1766, rec'd 24 Oct 1772; witnesses Abraham Nowell, Anna Tappan [York Deed 42:135]. Abigail and husband William Grow and son Timothy and his wife Hannah were buried at the family plot at York Cemetery.

Grow ch. b York: William Grow Jr., b 9 Mar 1755; Eunice Grow, b 12 Jan 1757; Abigail Grow, b 2 Dec 1760; Dorcas Grow, b 18 Jul 1763; Joseph Grow, b 25 Apr 1765; John Grow, b 14 Jul 1767; Timothy Grow, b 13 Jul 1769, d 14 Jun 1821, age 52. (Bragdon & Frost's York V.R., pp76, 139; ME I.G.I.; Picton's ME Cem. Inscrips., V3, p2358)

ABIGAIL, b ca 1750, of York, m 31 Jul 1772 at First Parish Church, York, Ichabod Jellison [b ca 1745, of same town]. (Bragdon & Frost's York V.R., p358)

ABIGAIL, b ca 1755, of York, m 10 Feb 1780, York, Ebenezer Cleaves [b ca 1750, of same town]. (ME I.G.I.)

ABIGAIL, b ca 1764, York, relative of James Heber Moulton. (ME I.G.I.)

ABIGAIL, b ca 1775, of Alfred, filed (Ints.) 20 Dec 1794, m 23 Dec 1795, Alfred, Aaron Day [b ca 1770, of Alfred]. (ME I.G.I.; MH&G Rec., V4, p59)

ABIGAIL, b ca 1776, of York, filed (Ints.) 16 Dec 1796, m 23 Jan 1797, York, Daniel Moulton Jr. [b ca 1770, of York]. (ME I.G.I.; Bragdon & Frost's York V.R., p181)

ABIGAIL, b ca 1780, of York, poss. d/o Rowland and Mary (Norton) Young, filed (Ints.) 7 Oct 1802, York, William Hutchins [b ca 1775, of same town]. (Bragdon & Frost's York V.R., p186)

ABIGAIL, b ca 1790, of Parsonsfield, m 26 Oct 1809, Parsonsfield, Jacob Peare [b ca 1780, of same town]. (Parsonsfield V.R., Town Clerk, p6)

ABIGAIL, b ca 1795, of Buxton, believed to be d/o Daniel and Abigail (Dyer) Young of Hollis, d 3 Jun 1827; m Nov 1815, Buxton, Amos Kimball [b 18 Aug 1790, of Buxton, d 23 Sep 1863, same town]. Abigail Kimball was named a deceased married daughter of Daniel Young of Hollis by his will signed 8 Jan 1848, probated 6 Mar 1848, and her children were thus named Daniel's heirs-at-law. Kimball ch. b Buxton: Daniel Kimball, b ca 1816; Martha Kimball, b ca 1818. (ME I.G.I.; Marshall's Buxton, ME, p147)

ABIGAIL, b ca 1800, of York, prob. d/o Jotham and Hannah (Sherman) Young; filed (Ints.) 9 Jan 1818, Hollis, cert. 3 Apr 1819, same town, George Goodwin [b ca 1795, of same town]. (V.R. of Hollis, Town Clerk, n.p.)

ABIGAIL, b ca 1800, of York, double filing (Ints.) 10 Apr 1822, (Ints.) 8 May 1822, York, m 19 May 1822, York, Abner Goodale [b ca 1795, of Wells]. (ME I.G.I.; Bragdon & Frost's York V.R., p215; Kittery V.R., p284)

ABIJAH aka HABIJAH, b 10 Aug 1720, York, s/o Jonathan and Margaret (Stackpole) Young, d pre 8 Apr 1758, native town; m 3 Sep 1747, Mary McInnes [b ca 1725, of Merriconeag, d/o William McInnes, alive 1758. Jonathan Young of York, husbandman, made deed of gift to daughter-in-law Mary Young, widow of Habijah Young, costing her a mere five shillings for fifty acres land in York which "lately belonged to my son Habijah and which he purchased from his father-in-law William McInnes," by deed signed and rec'd 8 Apr 1758; witnesses Daniel Moulton, Samuel Black [York Deed 33:185]. (ME I.G.I.; Noyes et al, p777; Bragdon & Frost's York V.R., p7)

ABNER, b ca 1730, of Somersworth, N.H., head of household in Berwick per 1790 census, with two females in the family. Five land deeds helped to shed light on Abner's background and family status. The first of these was signed 10 Oct 1780, rec'd 24 May 1785, in which Abner of Berwick bought from Mary Wallingford, widow of Ebenezer, for 30 pounds lawful money, 97 acres in Lot No. 1, 1st Range in the division of Berwick Common Lands which had been set off to Ebenezer Wallingford, deceased, as part of the estate of Thomas Wallingford, Esq., deceased; witnesses Susanna and Joanna Wentworth [York Deed 48:179].

A warrant was issued by the court against Abner Young who was then of Lebanon, for the recovery of 88-1-4, plus damages, in favor of creditor Stephen Evans of Dover, N.H., by deed dated the 2nd Tuesday of April 1783, rec'd 11 Jul 1783 [York Deed 48:202]. It will be noted, however, that Abner's first land deed was not recorded until 1785--only "after the fact" when Abner's son George of Berwick bought this self-same property in Berwick which Abner had intended to buy in 1780. Please see main entry on son George.

Another deed, dated 26 Oct 1790, rec'd the day after, showed that Abner of Berwick bought from the Berwick proprietors for 13-10-0 lawful money, 18 acres land in Berwick, "it being the whole of that piece of land which said Young had possessed and improved for many years," bounded north by Lebanon, and west of Salmon Falls River; witnesses Dominicus Goodwin, Moses Wingate of Rochester, N.H. [York Deed 53:78]. Simultaneously with this deed, Abner of Berwick sold to Moses Wingate for 20 pounds lawful money, these same 18 acres in Berwick that Abner bought from the Proprietors of Berwick; witnesses John Hill, Dominicus Goodwin [York Deed 53:78].

4

Ch. b prob. Berwick: George+, b ca 1755. (Census York Co., 1790, p56)

ABRAHAM, b ca 1740, of York, most likely b 8 Jan 1742, York, as s/o Joseph and Susannah (Johnson) Young; filed (Ints.) 18 May 1763, m 14 Nov 1763, York, Phebe Young [b 8 May 1744, York, d/o Job and Patience (King) Young]. Ch. b York: Susannah, b 9 Aug 1764. (ME I.G.I.; York V.R., pp65, 146)

ABRAHAM, b Jul 1851, resident of Sanford in 1900, age 48. At home were spouse Lizzie A. (   ), age 46 [Jan 1854, of Sanford], and young Hazel Gowen, age 7 [b Sep 1892]. (1900 ME Soundex)

ALBERT, b 1822, Limington, s/o James and 2nd wife Polly (Small) Coffin Young, gr.s/o David and Elizabeth (Smith) Young; filed (Ints.) 10 May 1846, m 31 May 1846, Limington, Martha A. Thomas [b ca 1825, of Limington]. (Taylor's Limington, TMs, pp112, 152)

ALBERT, b Apr 1826, York, s/o Joel and Susan (Sayward) Young, d 1914, native town, age 88, apparently single. In 1850 Albert lived at home, age 24. By his father's will signed 27 Jun 1855, probated 6 Apr 1869, Albert was named sole Exec. and residuary legatee of his father's estate at age 29, his bequest, $275.00. In 1900 Albert was listed as head of household in York, family including his sister Julia M.+ Young [b Sep 1829], age 70, and nephew Alfred M. Young [b Sep 1857]. (1900 ME Soundex)

ALBINA, b 1843, operative, single, lived in Biddeford at boarding house per the 1860 census for Biddeford. (Census York Co., 1860, Reel A, p252)

ALFRED, b ca 1840, of Biddeford, m 4 Mar 1867, Biddeford, Mary Peabel aka Preble [b ca 1845, of same town]. (ME I.G.I.; Mormon/ME V.R., Wright-Zitkov)

ALFRED C., b 1854, of Eliot, d 1933, same town, widower, age 79; spouse was Coral O. (   ) [b 1857, d 1918, married, age 61, of same town]. Both were buried at Mt. Pleasant Cemetery, Bolt Hill Road, Eliot. (Hale's Cems., n.p.; Picton's ME Cem. Inscrips., V1, p643)

ALICE, b ca 1818, of North Berwick, filed (Ints.) 2 Apr 1838, Lebanon, Henry Wallingford [b ca 1815, of North Berwick]. (Lebanon Marr., p223)

ALICE, b 21 Apr 1859, Biddeford, d 13 Sep 1935, Saco, age 76, widow; her spouse was Fred H. Goodwin [b 2 Aug 1858, of Saco, d 8 Aug 1886, same town, age 28-0-6, married. Alice and Fred Goodwin were buried at Laurel Hill Cem., Beach St., Saco. (Picton's ME Cem. Inscrips., V2, p1491; Mormon/ME V.R., Wright-Zitkov)

ALMIRA, b 1842, resident of Saco per the 1860 census, her occupation, operative in mill. She was single and lived at a boarding home. (Census York Co., 1860, Reel C, p719)

AMAZIAH (   ), b ca 1765, of Kennebunk, widow of ____ Young and head of household in the 1830 census report for Kennebunk. Her family contained four males, one each in age

5

brackets 10-15, 15-20, 20-30 and 30-40. (Census York Co., 1830, p120)

AMMI, b 1800, of Kennebunk; on one Sunday afternoon died 1 Jun 1839, Kennebunk, male, age 39. (Thompson's Recs. of York Co., TMs, p416)

AMOS, b 1828, of York, d 29 May, 1829, age 21, buried at the Young Lot on Scituate Pond Road, York, in a cemetery plot headed by John Young [b 1815} and his two wives Mary A. and Adeline P. Young. No further identification was made. (Frost's York Cem., p633)

AMOS, b 1831, York, s/o George and Eliza (Roberts) Young; filed (Ints.) 21 Nov 1854, m 26 Nov 1854, York, Caroline A. Chadbourne [b ca 1835, of York]. Amos lived at home in 1850, age 19, per the census that year. Ch. b York: Amos Jr., b 1861, d 25 Jun 1867, age 5-0-24. (ME I.G.I.; Bragdon & Frost's York V.R., p280; Hale's Cems., n.p.)

ANN, b ca 1720, of Biddeford, co-grantor with Moses and Joan Wadlen of same town in the sale to John Racklief of Scarborough, the one-half part of 100 acres in Scarborough that was granted to Roger Perry by the Proprietors of the town, 22 Jun 1720, situated at the head of Samuel Oakman's land; the lot was 160 rods by 100 rods square, deed signed 1 Dec 1743, rec'd 1 Nov 1744; witnesses John Davis, Andrew Stackpole [York Deed 24:234]. This deed did not disclose whether Ann was single or widowed, but had she been married, her husband's signature would have most certainly appeared.

ANN, b 1801, of South Berwick, d 1890, same town, widow of Alexander Watt of South Berwick [b 1797, d 1871, married]. (Picton's ME Cem. Inscrips., V3, p2065)

ANN L., b 1853, N.H., minor, living in Sanford per 1860 census, age 7, at the home of John Stephens, brick mason [b 1798] and spouse Mary J. Stephens [b 1808]. A daughter living at home was Almyra L. Stephens, domestic [b 1839]. (Census York Co., 1860, Reel A, p389)

ANNA (   ), b 1715, of York, d Jun 1812, Eliot, married. (Thompson's Recs. of York Co., TMs, p416)

ANNA, b ca 1728, Saco, filed (Ints.) 15 Mar 1748, Saco, m 4 Apr 1749, at First Congregational Church, Biddeford, Bryant aka Brian Fletcher [b ca 1725, of same town]. (Ridlon's Saco V.R., p103; ME I.G.I.; MH&G Rec., V6, p295)

ANNA, b ca 1760, Saco, prob. d/o Thomas and Eunice (   ) Young of Biddeford, m 1780, Hollis, Joshua Warren [b 14 Apr 1758, of Saco, 27 Feb 1849, age 91 years]. Thomas' daughter Anna was bp 10 Jun 1759 at First Congregational Church, Biddeford. Joshua and Anna settled at "Deerwander" in the plantation of Littlefalls, now known as Hollis, where they raised their family. Ridlon's Saco stated, "Joshua Warren served in the Revolutionary Army as a member of the 16th Mass. Continentals, was at the surrender of Burgoyne and at Trenton, where, when the engagement began, he was 'on picket' and captured the first Hessian taken in the war."

Warren ch. b Hollis: Joshua Warren Jr., b 1781; Dominicus Warren, b 1782; Hezekiah Warren, b 1785; Thomas Warren, b 16 Jul 1788; Joseph Warren, b 18 Sep 1797; Edmund Warren, b 1800; Weymouth Warren, b 6 Jul 1803. (ME I.G.I.; Ridlon's **Saco**, pp1203-1205)

ANNA, b 23 Feb 1775, Kittery, relative of Brigham Young. (ME I.G.I.)

ANNIE M., b ca 1835, York, d/o Samuel and Martha Ann (Crosby) Young, alive 1885, native town, married; filed (Ints.) 18 Sep 1857, m 5 Oct 1857, York, John P. Grant [b ca 1830, of same town]. The 1850 census for York indicated that Annie did not then live at home. However, Annie M. Grant was named married daughter and heir-at-law of widower Samuel Young of York by his will written 19 May 1885, probated 6 Oct 1885; her father's bequest to her, one thousand dollars.

Annie M.'s daughter was Mirabah A. (Grant) Staples, b 1860, w/o Robert F. Staples of North Berwick. Her son George Samuel Grant, b ca 1860, was named gr.s/o Samuel Young of York in will cited above; he was to receive all the money deposited in the East Boston Savings Bank by Samuel's son George S. Young, then deceased. (ME I.G.I.; Bragdon & Frost's York V.R., pp287, 350)

ANTHONY, b ca 1680, of York, relative of Brigham Young, m 30 Jun 1702, York, Rachel Wheeler [b ca 1685, York]. By courtesy of family papers sent by Robert M. Young, Jr. of Essex, MA in the Spring of 1996, we learn, and are indebted for the correction on these records, that "the I.G.I. has erroneously identified both his [Anthony's] birth and marriage as being in York, Maine. This may be partly due to an 'inferred lineage' reportedly prepared around 1937 by Mr. Archibald F. Bennett, which lists Anthony Young as the eldest of eleven 'probable children' of William Young, Sr., the 'probable grandson of Rowland Young, Sr. of York.'" (ME I.G.I.)

ASENITH D., b ca 1825, of Somersworth, N.H.; m 11 Jan 1844, Lebanon, by Elder D. B. Cowell, Nathaniel Wentworth [b ca 1820, of Somersworth]. (ME I.G.I.; Lebanon Marr, p224)

AUGUSTA, b 1835, resident of South Berwick at age 15, living with the family of Joshua Walker [b 1800] and spouse Susan Walker [b 1803]. (Census York Co., 1850, Reel C, p328)

AUGUSTUS D., b 6 Jan 1841, Kittery, s/o Stephen H. and Eunice L. (Fernald) Young, d 24 Mar 1877, native town, age 36-3-18, of yellow fever, buried at Orchard Grove, Kittery; m 25 Dec 1865, Kittery, Frances A. Williams [b ca 1845, of same town]. The 1860 census for Kittery did not indicate that Augustus D. then lived with his parents. Augustus enlisted in the Army 10 Sep 1862, was mustered in 30 Sep 1862 at Kittery, served as Pvt. in Co. G., 27th Reg. Maine Volunteers, and was discharged 17 Jul 1873. The 1890 ME Vets, Census Index of Civil War Vets, included Augustus' name for Kittery, District SD#1, Enum. ED#217. (Kittery V.R., pp420, 451; Picton's ME

Cem. Inscrips., V2, p1106; Civil War Recs. res. by Thelma E.
Brooks of Maine)

BENAIAH, b late 1670s, York, 2nd s/o Rowland and Susanna
(Matthews) Young, d pre 27 Jan 1779, testate, native town,
married; m1 ca 1714, York, Ruth Johnson [b ca 1795, York, d/o
Samuel and Elizabeth (Adams) Johnson, d pre 1779, native
town]; m2 Dorcas (   ) [b 1700s, of York, alive Apr 1779,
widow].

Benaiah, sibling Joseph and neighbor Henry Donnell were
witnesses to father Rowland's exchange of land between
neighbor John Pickering of Portsmouth, N.H. and himself in Nov
1718, rec'd 15 May 1719. Young and Pickering preferred to
swap the acreage: Rowland had 24 acres and Pickering had the
same quantity of land adjoining Rowland's, granted to each one
by the town of York.

Benaiah's father Rowland had his will drawn 14 Sep 1719,
proved 2 Jan 1721/2, in which Benaiah was named co-residuary
legatee with eldest brother Joseph. He was devised a moiety
of the little pasture adjoining the house and the twenty-six
acres adjoining York River, on which Benaiah dwelt, plus
another moiety of the two acres of salt marsh in the western
cove. Inasmuch as Joseph was to receive the home place where
they then lived, one half of the little pasture adjoining it
with the housing and orchard, as well as one acre more or less
of salt marsh that lies next to Kittery, Benaiah was devised
the other half of the little pasture and all the twenty-six
acres of land which adjoined on York River upon which he dwelt
[just cited above], plus one half of the two acres of salt
marsh in the western cove. Lastly, Joseph and Benaiah were to
pay six pounds apiece to their sisters Mary, Susanna, Elizabeth, Sarah and Mercy.

In the settlement of the estate of Ruth Johnson's father
Samuel, a deed was signed and rec'd on same date of 30 May
1721, by all his heirs-at-law, the widow Elizabeth Johnson,
John Wilson, husband of Mary Johnson, Benaiah Young, husband
of Ruth Johnson, and single women Sarah Johnson and Kezia
Johnson, wherein the sum of 24 pounds money was paid by their
brother Samuel Johnson [Jr.]. to the heirs-at-law who sold
their shares in the estate in favor of said Samuel Johnson,
the son: John Wilson, six pounds; Benaiah Young, six pounds;
Sarah Johnson, six pounds, and Keziah Johnson, six pounds;
witnesses Benjamin Stone, Abraham Preble [York Deed 10:173-
174].

The following year Benaiah of York bought from his eldest
brother Joseph for seven pounds money, one-1/2 acres of fresh
marsh or meadow ground in York, situated upon the north side
of York River adjacent to the north side of Benaiah's land and
the S.W. side of Joseph's land given him by his father
"Roland" Young, late of York, by deed signed 18 Feb 1722,
rec'd 3 Jan 1723/4.

Almost twenty years later by deed signed 22 Jun 1739,
rec'd 8 Mar 1741, final settlement on the estate of Samuel

Johnson [Sr.] was made by Henry Simpson and wife Sarah, John Wilson of Falmouth, Mary and Benjamin Johnson, Ruth Johnson Young and spouse Benaiah Young, the said Sarah, Ruth, Mary and Benjamin Johnson, being heirs-at-law of Samuel Johnson and wife Elizabeth, late of York, and grandchildren of Philip and Elizabeth Adams: They jointly sold all the rights and interest in Samuel Johnson's estate to Hezekiah and Thomas Adams, the heirs of Philip and Elizabeth Adams, for twenty-two pounds money; witnesses Benjamin Johnson, Daniel Moulton [York Deed 23:15].

Benaiah made another purchase of land by deed dated 5 Apr 1743 and rec'd 5 Apr 1744, from Abraham and Sarah Batten and Henry Wright, one of the heirs of Thomas Start of York, for fifteen pounds bills of credit, Old tenor, all that part of the 18 acres in York sold by Richard Burgess to Thomas Start on 24 Feb 1673; witnesses Daniel and Hannah Moulton [York Deed 24:143].

A deed of gift was made by Benaiah to his son and namesake Benaiah Jr., mariner, signed and rec'd 7 Jan 1752, of one acre land in York where he had lately erected a house at his own cost, "being part of my homestead at the eastern corner of my land and by the southern corner of Mehitable Haine's land; witnesses Amos Greeley, Jeremiah Moulton [York Deed 29:125]. That same year Benaiah conveyed to Daniel Moulton, Esq. of York for 6-2-8 lawful money, five shares in Lot No. 3, 12th range of the Div., in the York Outer Commons granted to Benaiah by the Proprietors, by deed signed 1 Jun 1752, rec'd 8 Jun 1752; witnesses Ruth Young, Hannah Young [York Deed 29:211].

Benaiah and Nathan Donnell of York worked out an even and satisfactory exchange of their shares in the Common Lands in York five days later: on the same dates of 6 Jun 1752, rec'd 8 Jun 1752, Benaiah sold to Donnell his five shares in Lot No. 4, 2nd Div., and "as his consideration" received three shares of Lot No. 4, 1st Div., two of which were originally granted to Ichabod Linscot, the other one to Job Young Jr., of whom Donnell purchased the same, and two shares in Lot No. 4, 2nd Div.; witnesses Joseph Simpson Jr., Daniel Moulton [York Deed 29:212].

The following two land transactions with the Moulton brothers Jeremiah and Daniel of York depicted an even exchange also. By deed signed 8 Jun 1752, rec'd 16 May 1753, Benaiah conveyed to the Moulton brothers three shares in Lot No. 4, 1st Div., two of which had originally been granted to Ichabod Linscot, the other one to Job Young Jr. who conveyed the same to Nathaniel Donnell, Esq., of whom Benaiah purchased the same; also conveyed were two shares more in Lot No. 4, 2nd Div., originally granted to Nicholas Bale who conveyed the same to said Donnell, of whom Benaiah purchased the same; witnesses George Reddich, Joseph Billing [York Deed 31:63]. The second deed was an even exchange written up on the same dates: the Moulton brothers as Co-grantors conveyed to

Benaiah five shares in Lot No. 5, 2nd Div., of the Common Lands; witnessed by Jonathan Bean, Samuel Willard [York Deed 31:80].

Benaiah's last land deed was signed 1 Jun 1764, rec'd 31 Oct 1765, by which he sold for 6-13-4 lawful money, ten shares in Lot No. 5, 2nd Div., of the Commons, five shares of which he bought from John MacIntire, the other five from Jeremiah and Daniel Moulton, Esq. [see above]; witnesses Joseph Simpson, Daniel Moulton [York Deed 40:64]. The five shares which he bought from MacIntire [see above] was by deed signed and rec'd 4 Jun 1751; witnesses Jonathan Sayward, Daniel Moulton [York Deed 29:69].

Benaiah, being aged and infirm, drew up his will 27 Jan 1779, which was probated that year on 7th April. This provided the first indication that his spouse Ruth had passed on and that he had remarried. He devised to wife Dorcas, "1 cow and 6 sheep + the provision I leave + the household furniture she brought me at marriage + use of 1/3 of my real estate for life, in lieu of her dower." The remainder of his estate was to be sold by his executor, the proceeds to be divided among his living children, with "the children of a deceased child inheriting collectively a parent's share." However, Benaiah's will did not name his children; luckily his land deeds helped to identify some of his children. Son-in-law Daniel Grant was named Exec.; witnesses David Sewall, Alexander Carlisle, Elizabeth Moulton [York Probate #20918].

Inventory of Benaiah's estate dated 11 Feb 1779, attested to 8 Apr 1779, included about 25 acres land with the buildings thereon which were appraised at 562-10-0, by Johnson Moulton, Joseph Parsons and Capt. Abel Moulton. Total value of the estate came to 772-13-6 [York Probate 13:264]. On 12 Jul 1779, the three appraisers divided Benaiah's real estate so that widow Dorcas could receive her "Thirds" - eight acres touching the river, as well as the east end of the dwelling with the cellar under it, and the western end of the barn [York Probate 13:289].

Shortly thereafter, Exec. Grant sold for 85 pounds, 8 shillings silver money, "at 6 shillings 8 pence an ounce," to Abel Moulton, Esq. and Joshua Grant, Gent., in equal halves, all the right in Benaiah's homestead of 27 acres in York, beginning by the York River at the S.E. corner of Jonathan Haines' land, by Carlisle's land, saving only the widow the use and improvement of her "Thirds" mentioned above, already set off to her for her use during her lifetime only, by deed signed 20 Apr 1781, rec'd 20 Sep 1781; witnesses Daniel Moulton, Abigail Randell [York Deed 46:170].

Known ch. b York: Elizabeth+ (Young) Sayward Grant, b 25 Feb 1715; Ruth, b 2 Sep 1720, d.y.; Johnson+, b 7 Jan 1722; Benaiah+, Jr., b 9 Feb 1724; Mercy+ (Young) Booker, b 15 Jul 1728; Mary, b 18 Jan 1730; Hannah+ (Young) Booker, b 25 Dec 1733; Abigail aka Ruth, b 2 Sep 1732. (ME I.G.I.; Noyes et

al, pp383, 776-777; Bragdon & Frost's York V.R., p35; Ridlon's
Saco, p1218)

BENAIAH Jr., b 9 Feb 1724, York, mariner, 2nd s/o Benaiah
and Ruth (Johnson) Young, d pre Jul 1770, native town; filed
(Ints.) 18 Jun 1748, m 13 Jul 1748, York, Sarah Adams [b ca
1730, York]. Benaiah Jr. received a deed of gift from his
father of one acre land in York where the youth had lately
erected a house at his own cost, being part of Benaiah Sr.'s
homestead at the eastern corner of his land and by the
southern corner of Mehitable Haine's land, by deed signed and
rec'd 7 Jan 1752.

Benaiah Jr. died intestate, his own acre of land and
dwelling house in York which were conveyed to him by his
father Benaiah held for costs to pay off creditor Joseph Holt
Jr. of York who had recovered judgment in court on the 3rd
Tuesday of July 1770, during settlement of Benaiah's estate.
The estate was appraised by Joseph Simpson, Caleb Preble and
Timothy Frost at 15 pounds, the pay-off to creditor Holt set
at 22-16-8, by deed signed 14 Aug 1770, rec'd 18 Jan 1771
[York Deed 42:49]. (ME I.G.I.; Noyes et al, pp776-777;
Bragdon & Frost's York V.R., p133)

BENAIAH, b 1763, Old York, filed (Ints.) 13 Nov 1784,
m 25 Mar 1785 at First Parish Church, York, Esther Beedle aka
Beattle [b ca 1765, of same town]. Benaiah enlisted under
Capt. Sayer's Co. in the Revolutionary War according to Mass.
Pension Applic. # (S17216). By 1832 he resided in Wiscasset.
(Bragdon & Frost's York V.R., pp166, 363; Mass. Soldiers &
Sailors)

BENJAMIN, b 19 Nov 1810, Sanford, s/o Richard and Rebecca
(   ) Young, mason, alive 1855, Danvers, MA; filed (Ints.)
8 Apr 1837, Sanford, m 30 Apr 1837, Alfred, Fanny aka Jenny C.
Hobbs [b 10 Jun 1819, d/o William and Mary (Chadbourne) Hobbs,
d 1876, Danvers, MA]. For census listings on this family from
1840-1855 for Danvers, MA, and main entries on four of the
children listed below, please see Youngs of Essex County, MA,
Vol. II.

Ch. b Sanford: William A., b 3 Jan 1838. Ch. b Danvers,
MA: Mary F. (Young) Nelson, b 30 Sep 1839; Ellen Jane (Young)
Shatswell, b 31 May 1841; Charles Henry+, twin, b 26 Jul 1843;
Benjamin F., twin, b 26 Jul 1843; Louisa Augusta (Young)
Kelly, b 7 Apr 1847. (ME and MA I.G.I.; Danvers VR, Marr,
p330, Births, p423; F. R. Boyle's Sanford, p160)

BENJAMIN F., b ca 1855, of Biddeford, m 8 Nov 1878,
Biddeford, Alice A. Milgate [b ca 1860, of same town].
(Mormon/ME V.R., Wright-Zitkov)

BENJAMIN F., Jul 1855, of Biddeford, alive 1900, same
town; spouse was Olive A. (   ) [b Feb 1863, of Biddeford,
alive 1900, same town]. In 1900 Olive A., age 37, was listed
head of household in Biddeford with husband Benjamin at home,
at age 44. Family members were daughter Althea and son
Benjamin F. Benjamin F. Sr. and Olive were buried at St.
Martin's in the Field, n.d. Ch. b Biddeford, not traced

further: Althea F., b Dec 1887; Benjamin F. Jr., b Jan 1890. (Hale's Cems., n.p.; 1900 ME Soundex; Picton's ME Cem. Inscrips., V1, p228)

BETHIAH, b 5 Sep 1709, York, d/o Lt. Joseph and Abigail (Donnell) Young, d 28 Jun 1785, native town, age 76; filed (Ints.) 16 Oct 1731, m 30 Nov 1731, York, John Stackpole [b 1708, York, s/o John and Elizabeth (Brown) Stackpole, d 2 Dec 1798, native town]. Bethiah Stackpole was named married daughter and heir-at-law of Joseph of York, by his will drawn 1 May 1734, probated 4 Jun 1734.

Stackpole ch. b York: James Stackpole, b 14 Nov 1732; Phoebe Stackpole, b 13 Dec 1734; Hannah Stackpole, b 6 Mar 1736; John Stackpole, b 28 Sep 1739; Sarah Stackpole, b 16 Feb 1741; Andrew Stackpole, b 28 Mar 1745; Joseph Young Stackpole, b 28 Aug 1747; Elizabeth Stackpole, b 17 Dec 1749. (ME I.G.I.; Noyes et al, p776; Bragdon & Frost's York V.R., p120; Gray's ME Families, 1790, V1, p261; Biddeford V.R.)

BETHIAH, b 9 Feb 1717/8, York, d/o Joseph and Sarah (King) Young; filed (Ints.) 17 Jan 1735/6, m same date, York, Henry Ingraham [b ca 1710, of York]. Ingraham ch. b York: Aaron Ingraham, b 15 Sep 1737; Abraham Ingraham, b 15 Oct 1739. (ME I.G.I.; Bragdon & Frost's York V.R., pp56, 123)

BETHULAH, b 25 Feb 1707/8, York, d/o Lt. Joseph and Abigail (Donnell) Young, alive May 1734, native town; m 19 Nov 1726, Nicholas Bale aka Beale [b ca 1705, of York]. Bethulah Bale was named married daughter and heir-at-law of Joseph Young of York at age 27 when his will was drawn 1 May 1734, proved 4 Jun 1734. Bale ch. b York: Mercy Bale, b 10 Jun 1728. (ME I.G.I.; Noyes et al, p776; Bragdon & Frost's York V.R., pp42, 117)

BETSEY ( ) , b ca 1785, of Hollis, widow of ____ Young, listed as resident in the 1830 and 1840 census for Hollis. In 1830 her age was 40-50, household containing two males, one each 10-15 and 15-20, and one other female age 15-20. In 1840, her age was then 50-60; at home were two females both aged 20-30. (Census York Co., 1830, p170; 1840, Reel B, p323)

BETSEY H. ( ), b 1801, of Newfield, widow of ____ Young, listed as head of household in Newfield per the 1860 census, with real estate valued at $1,500. At home were Benjamin Durgin, farmer [b 1836], Sally Durgin [b 1827], ____ (female) J. Durgin [b 1843], William and Lucy A. Palmer [b 1835 and 1840 respectively] and their children Alfred Palmer [b 1859] and Sarah E. Palmer [b May 1860]. (Census York Co., 1860, Reel C, p660)

BETSEY, b ca 1790, of York, filed (Ints.) 6 July 1810, John Sedgeley [b ca 1785, of same town]. (Bragdon & Frost's York V.R., p196)

CALEB, b ca 1710, of York, filed (Ints.) 18 Oct 1735, Juliann Rairden [b ca 1715], of same town]. The banns were never published, being forbidden by Rairden. (Bragdon & Frost's York V.R., p123)

CALEB, b ca 1712, of York, bricklayer, conveyed to Jonathan Sayward, Gent. and David Moulton, scrivener, both of York for one pound money, his full two shares of the Common Lands in York that were granted to him 25 Sep 1732--one full share to each--by deed signed and rec'd 7 Jan 1737; witnesses John Sewall, William Dyer [York Deed 20:79].

As bricklayer, Caleb worked for Capt. Thomas Smith at the garrison and truck house on Saco River: on November 1736, Caleb was paid 2-10-0 "for working about the chimneys, hearths and ovens, pointing & Co., 5 days at 10/per day"; also, "at my table 18 meals and drink between meals," 1-7-0. (G. T. Ridlon, Saco V.R., p36)

CALEB HAMMOND, b ca 1710, of York, filed (Ints.) 20 Mar 1735/6, m 6 Apr 1736, York, Catherine Wilson [b ca 1715, of same town]. Ch. b York: Mary, b 6 Sep 1737. (ME I.G.I.; Bragdon & Frost's York V.R., pp56, 123)

CARMELA, see PAMELA

CAROLINE, b ca 1820, of Kittery, m 17 Aug 1839, Kittery, William Jackson [b ca 1815, of same town]. (Kittery V.R., p380)

CAROLINE, b 16 Jan 1838, Lebanon. (ME I.G.I.)

CAROLINE, b 1849, Kittery, d/o Edward C. and ____ (Daley) Young, gr.d/o Sarah Daley of Boston, MA. Caroline's natural mother had predeceased her father Edward. Upon his death pre 3 Nov 1856, Sarah Daley, maternal grandmother, was awarded guardianship of Caroline and her three siblings on the above date [York Probate #20923]. See her father's entry for full details.

CAROLINE ELIZABETH, b 24 Nov 1821, Lebanon, d/o Joseph and Patience (Wentworth) Young, d 24 Sep 1856, native town; filed (Ints.) 8 Dec 1838, m 16 Dec 1838, Lebanon, Benjamin Ayres Fernald Jr. [b ca 1815, of same town], by Elder Edward Blaisdell. Widower Benjamin Fernald m2 post 1856, Salome Bridges [b ca 1825, of Portland, d 27 Dec 1867]. For further background information please see Youngs of Strafford County, N.H., Vol. I.

Fernald ch. b Lebanon: John Franklin Fernald, b 6 Dec 1839; Benjamin Chandler Fernald, b 25 Feb 1842, d 10 Apr 1846; Sedelia Adeline Fernald, b 25 Jan 1845; Benjamin Marvin Fernald, b 14 Feb 1847; James Alvah Fernald, b 25 Nov 1852; and Caroline Elizabeth Fernald, b 2 Dec 1855. (Lebanon Marr, p224; ME I.G.I.; Wentworth Gen., V1, pp456-457)

CAROLINE M., b 1852, York, d/o Moses C. and Elizabeth (Trafton) Young, filed (Ints.) 18 Dec 1877, m 24 Dec 1877, York, George A. Todd [b 1848, York, s/o Andrew W. and Phebe K. (Littlefield) Todd]. (Bragdon & Frost's York V.R., p344; ME I.G.I.)

CHARLES, b 1795, Canada, resident of Saco in the 1860 census report; his spouse was Margaret ( ) [b 1803, Canada]. Their household contained seven children all born in Canada: John, b 1828; Francis, b 1832; Amelia, b 1819; Sophia, b 1836, twin; Frances, b 1836, twin; Harriet, b 1843; and Philamon, b 1847. (Census York Co., 1860, Reel C, p744)

CHARLES, b Jun 1812, resident of York in 1900 at age 88, single. (1900 ME Soundex)

CHARLES, b 1818, lived in York in 1850, single, at the home of Sally Preble [b 1793, age 57], her estate then assessed at $3,000. Mrs. Preble's children b ME: Elizabeth Preble [b 1830], James Preble [b 1833], Sally Preble [b 1835], and George Preble [b 1849]. (Census York Co., 1850, Reel A, p212)

CHARLES, b 1821, of York, tanner; m 1 Nov 1855, York, widow Eliza Ann (   ) Holman [b 1829, of York, alive 1860, York, age 31, married]. The 1860 census listed Charles as head of household in York; at home was wife Eliza A. and infant son William H. Cummings Young.
Ch. b York: William H. Cummings+, b Jul 1859. (ME I.G.I.; Bragdon & Frost's York V.R., p283; Census York Co., 1860, Reel C, p948; 1900 ME Soundex)

CHARLES, b Sept 1838, of Alfred, head of household in Alfred as of 1900, age 61; members of family included spouse Thursey (Pike) Young [b Jul 1838], mother-in-law Eunice Pike [b Dec 1815], and son-in-law Leonard S. Phinney [b Jan 1870]. In 1860, he had lived in Alfred at the home of Daniel and Mary Bennett [b 1802 and 1794, respectively]; his age then was 22, single, his occupation, day laborer. (Census York Co., 1860, Reel B, p753; 1900 ME Soundex)

CHARLES, b 1839, Nova Scotia, sailor, single, resident of Waterboro. On 30 Sep 1864, Charles enlisted as Pvt. in the 29th Infantry, was mustered in on 30 Sep 1864 from Portland, for a term of three years under the quota of Waterboro. His personal profile revealed that his complexion was dark, eyes were blue, and hair, black; he stood 5' 8-1/2" tall. (Civil War res. by T. E. Brooks of Maine)

CHARLES, b ca 1860, of Shapleigh, m 19 Jul 1885, Shapleigh, Narsis Albra Wright [b ca 1865, of same town]. (ME I.G.I.)

CHARLES F., b 1800, of York, tanner, head of household, widower at age 60, per 1860 census for York, with real estate valued at $6,500. His family then contained married daughter Hannah W. Beal, age 31, son-in-law George G. Beal, mariner [b 1823], age 37, and grandchildren Anna Beal and George Beal, Jr. Ch. b ME: Hannah W.+ (Young) Beal, b 1829. (York Census 1860, Reel C, p959)

CHARLES F., b 18 Apr 1819, York, farmer, s/o Noah and Lydia (Frost) Young, d 29 Mar 1897, native town, age 78, single. In the 1850 census for York, Charles was listed as head of household at age 31, farmer, bachelor, his estate valued at $2,500. Parents Noah and Lydia lived with him, having by then undoubtedly conveyed to Charles the deed of trust on the homestead. (Census York Co., 1850, Reel A, p216)

CHARLES H., b 1846, Lebanon, shoemaker. Charles H. was of Lebanon when he enlisted 23 Feb 1864 as Pvt. in the 32nd

14

Infantry, Co. F, for three years and was mustered in 5 Apr 1864 in Augusta. He was then transferred to Co. F, 31st ME, 12 Dec 1664, and was mustered out 15 Jul 1865. Charles was also listed in the 1890 ME Vets, Census Index of Civil War Vets or Their Widows, for District SD#1, Enum.#218. His personal profile stated that Charles H.'s complexion and hair were light, his eyes were blue, and his height, 5' 4" tall. (Civil War res. by T. E. Brooks of Maine)

CHARLES H., b Feb 1854, York, s/o Timothy and Mary Ann (Simpson) Young, d 1927, native town, age 73; m ca 1875, York, Mariette (   ) [b 1857, York, d 1931, native town, age 74, widow]. In 1900 Charles H. was listed as head of household in York, age 46, family containing spouse Mariette, age 43, their seven children, and boarder Daniel B. Harris [b Sep 1830]. Charles H., Mariette and child Bessie M., age 9, were buried at the Young family plot that belonged to his parents at York Cemetery, York.

Ch. b York, not traced further: Bessie M., b 1876, d 1885; John, b Sep 1881; David W., b Jan 1883; Silva H., b Feb 1886; Ellen, b Dec 1888; Mildred, b Nov 1891; Clifford H., b Oct 1894; and Elmer R., b Aug 1897. (Frost's York Cem., pp614-615; Hale's Cems., n.p.; 1900 ME Soundex; Picton's ME Cem. Inscrips., V3, p2367)

CHARLES HENRY, b 26 Jul 1843, of Alfred, s/o Benjamin and Jenny C. (Hobbs) Young of Danvers, MA, alive 1878, widower; m 20 Aug 1871, Alfred, Laura A. Rhodes [b 27 Oct 1847, Alfred, d 11 Nov 1878, native town, age 31-0-15, married]. Charles, Laura and son Lonnie were buried at the Young family plot on the S.W. side of Alfred Gore Road, Alfred. A fact to be noted is that the name of Ebenezer Bennett was also etched on the family headstone. Ch. b Alfred: Lonnie E., b 31 Oct 1875, d 13 Dec 1876, native town. (ME I.G.I.; Hale's Cems., n.p.; Lebanon Deaths, p149; MH&G Rec., V4, p268; Picton's ME Cem. Inscrips., V1, p79)

CHARLES M. H., b 1856, Dover, N.H., adopted s/o Masterson and Susan K. (Plaisted) Young, filed (Ints.) 1 Jul 1876, m1 9 Jul 1876, York, Alice P. Leach [b 1855, of York, d/o Andrew Leach, d 2 Aug 1880, York, age 25-5-0, married]. Charles, widower, filed (Ints.) 15 Dec 1881, m2 25 Dec 1881, York, Lydia A. Plaisted [b 1864, of York, d/o John H. and Ann J. (Fuller) Plaisted]. Charles' first wife Alice P. was buried at York Cemetery. (Bragdon & Frost's York V.R., pp320, 336, 349; Frost's York Cem., p527; Picton's ME Cem. Inscrips., V3, p2257)

CHARLES P., b ca 1805, of Newmarket, N.H., m 23 Nov 1831, So. Berwick, Cyrena Thinnell [b 1810, of So. Berwick]. (Mormon/ME V.R., Wright-Zitkov)

CHARLOTTE, b 1801, of York, d Feb 1850, York, of consumption, age 49. (ME 1850 Mort. Sched., p23)

CHARLOTTE, b ca 1825, York, believed to be d/o Jonathan Young, Esq. of York [b 1774], filed (Ints.) 2 May 1846, m 7 Jun 1846, Daniel Shorey [b ca 1820, of South Berwick].

Jonathan Young's will signed 14 Dec 1840, proved 5 May 1856, named single daughter Charlotte as heir-at-law who was to receive ten dollars upon her marriage. (ME I.G.I.; Bragdon & Frost's York V.R., p265)

CLAIBORNE A., b ca 1855, of Alfred. His spouse was Lucy Conant [b 9 Apr 1862, d 1 Mar 1901, Alfred, bur. at Congregational Church Cemetery]. Ch. b Alfred: Garth Galbraith, b 1892, d 1896, native town. (Hale's Cems., n.p.; Picton's ME Cem. Inscrips., V1, p92)

CLARA E., b ca 1850, York, m 7 Mar 1869, York, Jonathan Avander Bourne [b ca 1845, of Wells]. (ME I.G.I.; Bragdon & Frost's York V.R., p326)

CLARENCE L., b May 1856, Saco, s/o Elijah and Caroline (Smith) Young, alive 1900, native town, age 44; m 24 Jun 1878, Biddeford, Ida E. Wallett [b Jul 1856, of Biddeford, alive 1900, age 43]. The 1860 census showed that he and parents lived in Saco, Clarence then a child of four. In 1900 Clarence was listed as head of his own household on Hill Street, Saco. Spouse Ida and their three daughters Lewie F., Millie E. and Esther P. lived at home. Ch. b Saco, not traced further: Lewis F., b Feb 1882; Millie E., b Aug 1885; and Esther P., b Oct 1893. (Mormon/ME V.R., Wright-Zitkov; 1900 ME Soundex)

CYNTHIA DELANA, b ca 1823, of Lebanon, m 10 Jan 1843, Lebanon, Nathaniel Wentworth [b ca 1820, of same town]. (ME I.G.I.)

DANIEL, b ca 1725, of Biddeford, m ca 1748, Dorcas (   ) [b ca 1728, of same town]. Ch. bp Biddeford: Mary, bp 22 Jan 1748, at First Congregational Church. (MH&G Rec., V6, p340)

DANIEL, b 1747, of Sanford, s/o Daniel Young of York, gr.s/o Joseph and Sarah (King) Young [see main entry below], d 10 Jan 1826, Sanford, age 79, pauper; filed (Ints.) 20 Oct 1770, m 22 Nov 1770, at First Parish Church, York, Anne aka Anna Johnson [b ca 1750, Sanford, d/o Jonathan and first wife Sarah (Babb) Johnson]. This town was originally known as Littlefalls Plantation, evolving to present-day Sanford; see Topography for historical background.

Anna Young, wife of Daniel, was named married daughter of Jonathan Johnson, innholder of Sanford, in the probate of his estate dated 13 Apr 1784, attested 1 May 1784, each heir's share to be 3-6-8 [York Probate #10379]. Frederick R. Boyle's **Sanford Families,** pp173, 330-332, believed that there was enough evidence to indicate Daniel was an heir-at-law of Joseph and Sarah King Young of York, and "the father of, at least, Daniel Jr., Aaron and Joseph Young."

The Daniel Young family was found listed in the 1790 census for Littlefalls, and then in the 1810 census for Sanford. In 1790 his household contained one other male over 16, three males under 16, and three females. In the 1810 census, Daniel's age was age 45 plus, his large household containing a spousal figure age 45 plus, and another male whose age was 26-45, a female at age 16-26, and four daughters, their ages under 10.

The earliest land deed found for Daniel Jr., by date of 19 Jan 1793, rec'd 2 May 1793, indicated he was then of Littlefalls. He sold to Samuel Berry of Ossipee [Plantation], for 8 shillings his portion of land in Ossipee. Kinsmen John and Hezekiah Young were witnesses [York Deed 56:123]. Still of Littlefalls he bought from Joseph Dyer of the same town for 65-14-3 lawful money, 55 acres and 95 sq. rods of land adjacent to Smith's Landing by the Saw River and land of David Sewell's, by deed signed 9 Sep 1793, rec'd 20 Mar 1795; witnesses Daniel and Polly Granger [York Deed 57:147].

As husbandman, he next bought land in Littlefalls by deed signed 13 Nov 1794, rec'd 20 Mar 1795, from the Commonwealth of Massachusetts, for 9 pounds lawful money, lands that were of the estate of Sir William Pepperell, lately of London, being one-fourth part of Lot No. 4, 4th Range in the Div. of "Cooks Right," as surveyed by Samuel Titcomb--502 acres, and the one-fourth part of the same to be conveyed was found in the N.W. corner adjoining Lot No. 2, 3rd Range, northern division of the same Cook's Right, witnesses _____ Jordan, Benjamin Haley [York Deed 58:20].

The next two deeds were a double transaction, both signed 4 Mar 1796, and witnessed by Joseph and Polly Chadbourne: Daniel of Littlefalls sold to Joseph Dyer Jr. of the same town for 60 pounds, one-fourth part of Lot No. 4, 4th Range, "in the Division of Books Right, so called," 502 acres and "the 4th part of the same hereby intended to be conveyed lies in the N.W. corner adjacent to Lot No. 2, 3rd Range, North Division, a parallelogram 211-1/2 rods long by 95 rods wide" [York Deed 75:199]. The other deed signed on same date, but rec'd 16 Apr 1811, showed that Daniel bought from the same Joseph Dyer Jr. for 40 pounds, 30-1/4 acres in Littlefalls, beginning at the Saco River by lands owned by Daniel Young who purchased them from Dyer's father Joseph Dyer, near the Saco River; witnesses the same Chadbournes [York Deed 84:127].

The next deed signed 17 Oct 1797, rec'd 25 Nov 1809, revealed that Daniel was then buying land in Sanford: for $50.00, from Hunken Dennet of Portersfield, one-half of a lot of land in Sanford, N.E. in the Middle Range, beginning at Daniel's corner bounded by lands of Daniel W. Nowell which Dennet bought from Joshua Taylor on 3 Mar 1785; witnesses Joseph Howard, Reuben Dennet [York Deed 81:148]. Another purchase of this nature was signed 5 Sep 1799, rec'd 1 May 1804 when Daniel bought from Benjamin Estes of Sanford for $50.00, 100 acres (more or less) in the Middle Range of lots in Sanford, Lot No. 5; witnesses Henry Hamilton, Caleb Emery [York Deed 71:138]. Daniel's last deed before 1810 disposed of this last property and another piece of land to Joseph Young [son] of Sanford by deed signed 28 Jan 1805, rec'd 20 Feb 1805: for $25.00, one-half of Lot No. 5, in the Middle Range, Sanford, of 50 acres as well as 100 acres "being the same I purchased of Benjamin Estes of Sanford, beginning at the S.W. and N.W. sides of said lot and holding its width by the road leading to Wells," witness ____ Morrell, William Nason [York Deed 72:206].

Ch. b Sanford: Joseph+, b 1770s; Daniel+ Jr., b ca 1780; and Aaron+, b early 1780s. (Census York Co., 1790, p66; 1810, p1012)

DANIEL, b ca 1750, of Pepperellborough, known as Saco by 1805. He was listed as head of household in the 1800 census, age 45 plus with a spousal figure, age 26-45, two males, one under 10, the other 10-16, and three females, each under 10 years. (Census York Co., 1800, p926)

DANIEL, b 7 Sep 1753, Gloucester, trader, Essex Co., Massachusetts Bay Colony, s/o William and Susanna (Davis) Young, d 21 May 1790, native town, age 38. For full background information on Daniel and his family, see Youngs of Essex County, MA, Vol. II. As resident of Gloucester, Daniel bought for 160 pounds lawful money, 10 acres land with dwelling house and barn, fences, wharfs, trees and improvements in Arundel, York County, Middle Division, from Elisha and Mildred Byles of Arundel, York County, signed 18 Aug 1777, rec'd 7 Jan 1798; witnesses William Booden, John Scarlet [York Deed 44:111]. The land was "bounded with flats on the west side and by Dorman's land so-called on the south and by Capt. Perkin's land on the east, and the highway on the north."

This same property Daniel sold at a profit for 200 pounds lawful money to Francis Burnam, 3rd, fisherman of Ipswich, Essex County, by deed signed 13 Apr 1778, rec'd 12 Jan 1779; witnesses Anna and Polly Baker [York Deed 45:169].

DANIEL, b ca 1760, of Lyman, m 29 Feb 1784, Lyman or Littlefalls, 2nd Baptist Church, Dorcas Crocet [b ca 1765, of same town]. (ME I.G.I.; Marr., Lyman, 1784-1831 by Rev. Lock)

DANIEL, b 2 Nov 1765, Biddeford, s/o Thomas and Eunice (   ) Young, resident of Lyman, d 19 Jan 1848, Dayton, age 82, widower, buried Limerick; m 26 Nov 1789, Littlefalls Plantation, Lyman, by Rev. Simon Lock, 2nd Baptist Church, Abigail Dyer [b 1767, of same town, d 19 Jun 1827, Hollis, age 60, married, buried at Limerick]. Daniel of Dayton m2 23 Apr 1829, Lyman, Widow Miriam (   ) Dow [b Dec 1772, d 9 Feb 1861, Dayton, age 88-2-0, widow].

As widower with a large family by his first wife Abigail, Daniel remarried in 1829. All of this became self-evident by his will drawn up 8 Jan 1848 ten or eleven days before his death when he made provisions for his grown children and second wife Miriam. Probate papers were filed 6 Mar 1848 by son Elijah of Granville, sole Exec. and residuary legatee; witnesses John S. March, James R. Haley, and John Seavey [York Probate #20921]. Daniel bequeathed to 2nd wife Miriam all the personal property he had by her when they married. Elijah was devised the homestead farm in Hollis "on which I now live" except for one-half acre "around the grave of my first wife which I reserve for a family burying ground," as well as 20 acres bounded by lands of John Meserve, the county road, and lands of Daniel Smith, the 4th, and Elisha Cleaves.

Daniel's heirs-at-law were to receive these bequests: son Thomas, $5.00; the children of daughter-in-law Betsey Young, widow of his son Daniel Jr. [that is, grandson William Young, and granddaughters Harriet Haley and Abigail Waterhouse], $1.00 each; sons of deceased daughter Sally Sinnot, [that is, grandsons John Sinnot, Joseph Sinnot Jr., and Thomas Sinnot], $1.00 each; the children of his deceased daughter Abigail Kimball [that is, grandsons Daniel Kimball and Martha Chadbourn Kimball], $1.00 each; his married daughters Eunice Dow and Phebe Dow were to receive all his household furniture; son Joseph, $5.00; son Hiram, one bed and set of bedding. Son Elijah was to receive all the rest of the property with the object in mind that "he shall expend the bulk of said property, if need be, to support my son Hiram (he being non compos mentis) whom I leave to his care."

Appraisers of Daniel's estate were appointed 6 Mar 1848: James R. Haley, Joshua M. Goodwin and Mark Dennett of Hollis [York Probate 61:504]. Inventory was rendered 4 Sep 1848 by this committee of three and attested to that day by Elijah. Daniel's homestead farm valued at $576.69, was bounded on the N.E. by Saco River, S.E. by land belonging to Mrs. Mary Edgecomb, S.W. by the point road, so called, on the N.W. by the Daniel Haley farm. A woodlot in Hollis bounded N.W. by the country road leading past Samuel C. Hight's to Union Falls, N.E. by land of Daniel Smith, S.E. by land of Elisha Cleaves, and S.W. by land of John Meserve was appraised at $225.00. Considerable personal property was set at $1,206.35; total estate, both real and personal, came to $2,011.04.

Daniel and Abigail were buried at the Young Cemetery on Route 5, Limerick. Ch. b poss. Dayton: Elijah, b ca 1790; Daniel, b 1790s; Sally (Young) Sinnot, b 1790s, w/o Joseph Sinnot; Thomas+, b 1794; Abigail+ (Young) Kimball, b ca 1795; Eunice (Young) Dow, b 1800s; Joseph, b 1800s; Hiram, b 1800s; and Phoebe+ (Young) Dow, b 1802. (Mormon/ME V.R., Wright-Zitkov; ME I.G.I.; Hale's Cems., n.p.; Picton's ME Cem. Inscrips., V2, p1274; Thompson's Recs. of York Co., TMs, p416; Marr. 1784-1831, by Rev. Simon Lock)

DANIEL aka 2nd, b ca 1765, of Hollis when it was known as Littlefalls. He was named head of household in the 1790 census for Littlefalls, with another male under 16 and one female living at home. He then was listed in the census reports for Hollis from 1820-1840. In the 1820 census, his age was 45 plus, with a maternal figure of same age group and a growing family of four males, two age 10-16, one 16-18, and one 16-26, and one other female age 16-26. In 1830 his age was 60-70, as were two other males, one each 15-20 and 20-30, and two females, one a maternal figure age 60-70, and the other age 20-30. In 1840 his age was 70-80, his household containing a spousal figure of like years, and one other male age 40-50.   (Census York Co., 1790, p64; 1820, p378; 1830, p169; 1840, p321)

DANIEL Jr., b ca 1780, Sanford, laborer, s/o Daniel and Anna (Johnson) Young, m 11 Jun 1805, Sanford, Sarah Witham [b ca 1780, of Sanford, d/o Jeremiah Witham].   It is believed that in 1810, Daniel Jr., spouse Sarah [both age 26-45], and their four young daughters under the age of 10 lived with his parents Daniel and Anna in Sanford per census records taken that year.   See parents' entry for full enumeration.

Daniel and spouse left Sanford ca 23 Dec 1815, for perhaps Union, ME, after selling property which Sarah bought from her father.   (F. R. Boyle's **Sanford**, p330; ME I.G.I.; Mormon/ME V.R., Wright-Zitkov; MH&G **Rec.**, V2, p109)

DANIEL Jr., b ca 1785, lived in Hollis per 1820 census report, age 26-45, poss. s/o David Young of Hollis.   His household contained a spousal figure of the same age group, and one male and two females each under 10.   (Census York Co., 1820, p389)

DANIEL aka Jr., b ca 1790, Hollis, m 18 May 1814, Hollis, Betsey Townson [b ca 1795, of same town].   (V.R. of Hollis, Town Clerk, n.p.)

DANIEL, b ca 1795, of Acton, listed as resident in the 1830 census for Acton, age 30-40, with household containing a spousal figure of same age group and six children--four males each under the age of 15 and two females under the age of 10. (Census York Co., 1830, p66)

DANIEL, b 14 Jan 1800, Limington, s/o David and Elizabeth (Smith) Young, d 21 Jan 1873, Sebego; m (Ints) 14 Feb 1824/ 1825, Ann Babb [b ca 1805, of Baldwin].   He was listed as head of family in the 1830 census for Limington, age 20-30, with household containing a spousal figure of his own age bracket and four females each under the age of 10.   Circa 1832 he and family relocated in Sebego.

Ch. b Limington: Mary D., b 29 Sep 1824; Hannah, b 20 Apr 1826; Eunice D., b 6 Apr 1828; Eliza B., b 23 Jan 1830; Almon, b 10 Dec 1831.   Ch. b Sebego: Peter B., b 18 Oct 1833: James M., b 19 Feb 1836; Charles H., b 10 Mar 1838; Sarah A., b 23 Mar 1840; Amelia A., b 3 Sep 1842; Annette, b 19 Apr 1846; Bertha A., b 25 May 1848.   (Taylor's Limington, p87; Census York Co., 1830, p157)

DANIEL, b ca 1810, of Newfield, m ca 1835, Eunice Wagner [b ca 1815, of same town].   Ch. b Newfield: Hannah Jane+ (Young) Tuttle, b 1836.   (ME I.G.I.)

DANIEL, b 3 Feb 1814, Waterboro, later of Shapleigh, s/o John and Nancy (Horn) Young, d 5 Jan 1901, Waterboro, age 88-11-3; filed (Ints) 14 Sep 1835, Waterboro, Eunice Whitten [b Jul 1817, Waterboro, alive 1900, Shapleigh].   In 1840, Daniel was listed as resident of Waterboro, age 20-30; at home were a spousal figure and two young males under the age of five. In both the 1850 and 1860 census reports for Waterboro, he, spouse Eunice and their five children were listed as residents.   In 1850, Eunice was age 35; children at home were

20

Charles, Stephen, Rhoda, Frances and George A. In 1860 Eunice was age 45; members of family included children Rhoda, Francis and Freeth.

By 1900 Daniel and family had made the move to Shapleigh according to the census report that year, his age 88; he was head of a large household which represented four generations. At home were wife Eunice, age 82, widowed daughter Rhoda Beale [age 56], Rhoda's son Ansel Beale [Jun 1871], his wife Alfreda F. ( ) Beale [Dec 1873], and their two infant sons Roscoe E. [b Jun 1898] and Sidney R. Beale [b Jan 1900].

Daniel was buried at Pine Grove Cemetery, Waterboro, opposite the high school. Ch. b prob. Waterboro: Charles, b 1838; Stephen, b 1839; Frances, b 1841; Rhoda+ (Young) Beale, b Aug 1843; George A., b 1847; Hiram+, b May 1854; Freeth [female], b 1856. (Hale's Cems., n.p.; ME I.G.I.; Census York Co., 1840, Reel B, p194; 1850, Reel C, p207; 1860, Reel B, p964; 1900 ME Soundex; **Reg.** 90:335, 1936)

DANIEL L., b Mar 1828, Saco, of Sanford, s/o Joseph and Edna M. (Huston) Young, d 1905, Rochester, N.H., age 72; filed (Ints.) 9 Mar 1854, m1 9 Nov 1854, Alfred, Olive Ann Tripp [b 15 Oct 1832, Sanford, d/o Theodore and Mary G. (Clark) Tripp, d 1884, Saco, age 52]. Daniel m2 10 Oct 1886, Lebanon, by Rev. George N. Musgrove, Mrs. Myra S. (Prescott) Shapleigh [b 11 Oct 1846, Acton, widow of Oliver Waldron Shapleigh, d/o William Prescott of Lebanon, d 10 Mar 1911, Lebanon]. Please see Youngs of Strafford County, N.H., Vol. I for additional background material on Daniel and Myra.

The 1860 census for Saco listed Daniel L. as head of household with real estate valued at $1,800. At home was first spouse Olive A., age 27 and son Theodore, age 5. Both Daniel and Olive Ann were buried at Laurel Hill Cemetery, Beach Street, Saco; burial date of second spouse Myra Young was not given. Ch. b ME: Theodore T.+, b Oct 1854. (ME I.G.I.; F. R. Boyle's **Sanford**, pp301, 330-331; MH&G **Rec.**, V4, p268; Hale's Cems., n.p.; Lebanon Marr, p224; Census York Co., 1860, Reel C, p819; 1900 N.H. & ME Soundex; Picton's ME Cem. Inscrips., V2, p1503; Frost's Lebanon, TMs, p3.

DAVID, b ca 1695, of York, resident of Pepperrellborough [today known as Saco]; m ca 1720, Biddeford, Mary Edgecomb [b ca 1700, Saco, d/o Robert and Rachel ( ) Edgecomb, descendant of James Gibbons, planter, deceased as of 21 Jul 1730, of Scarborough, Cumberland County [adjacent to Saco]. David's name was found on the list of "the more prominent early townsmen who were settled [in Saco] before the beginning of the present century," (pre 1800), as was kinsman Thomas Young [Ridlon's Saco, p119]. As for the Young progenitor of the town of Biddeford, it would have to be David Young who was the senior of Thomas Young [b ca 1725].

David and Mary received a share of the Gibbons estate in 1730, a small tract of land in Saco. On 21 Jul 1730, David of Scarborough as husband and principal, and Thomas Edgecomb and Robert Edgecomb, kinsmen, both of Biddeford, paid bond of 200 pounds to act as guardian to David's daughter Mary, a minor; witnesses John Frost, Noah Emery [York Probate #20964].

David of Scarborough bought from Samuel Smith Sr. of Biddeford, forty acres land in Biddeford which had been granted to Smith by the town of Biddeford 21 Mar 1721; deed signed 27 Apr 1731, rec'd 11 May 1732; witnesses John Gordon, John Gray, Humphrey Scammon [York Deed 15:34-35].

Resident of Saco thereafter, David sold properties in Saco for 31-9-4 to James McClellen of the same town by deed signed 16 Nov 1762, rec'd 20 Jun 1763: two lots of upland and three lots of marsh in Saco on the east side of the Saco River; the first lot was bounded by lands of Capt. John Sharp and Robert Patterson, the 2nd lot, by lands of Widow Townsend and said McClellen; and three lots of marsh joining on Saco River which "were laid out to my daughter Mary Young," witnesses Robert and Martha McClellen [York Deed 37:227].

Another deed signed 16 Mar 1769 and rec'd 18 Jan 1772 dealt with David's sale of 640 acres land to Benjamin Nason of Biddeford for sixty pounds lawful money. The land formerly belonged to the right of Rachel Edgecomb, late of Biddeford, beginning at the N.W. corner of lands of Hannah Mase and running 160 rods N.W., then two miles S.W. to the Middle Line, then 160 poles S.E., and two miles N.E. to the first marker. The deed deposed that after Rachel Edgecomb's death, the land would fall to Mary, d/o Rachel and the wife of said David. After Mary's death, it would then go to Mary, David and Mary's daughter; witnesses Thomas Young, Jeremiah Hill [York Deed 42:50].

Ch. b Biddeford/Saco: Mary, b 27 Aug 1721, bp 6 Nov 1721, d 20 Oct 1738, age 17-11-14, of same town, bur. at Edgecomb Cemetery, Ferry Road, Saco; Sarah, b 22 Mar 1723, of whom nothing was further heard, and presumably, David Jr., b ca 1735. (ME I.G.I.; Folsom's Saco & Biddeford, p113; Hale's Cems., n.p.; Ridlon's Saco, p652)

DAVID, b ca 1735, of Pepperellborough [Saco], also of Biddeford, presumed to be s/o David given above, m 15 Aug 1761, Biddeford, Elizabeth (   ) Goodwin [b ca 1740, of Biddeford, formerly widow of Joseph Goodwin, d 14 May 1796, Limington]. David was listed as resident of Pepperellborough in the 1800 census, age 45 plus, with a spousal figure of the same age group. His name, or that of his father's, was found on Ridlon's list of "the more prominent early townsmen who were settled in Saco before the beginning of the present century," [pre 1800] as was kinsman Thomas Young. Two schools of thought could apply to David's parentage: that this David was either the s/o Thomas Young of Saco, or s/o David and Mary Edgecomb Young. It is to be remembered, though, that Mary died in 1730.

Willis' "Old Eliot, Maine" indicated that after the death of their father David, the children returned to Berwick. Ch. b Saco: David Jr., b 23 Oct 1763; Daniel, b 26 Aug 1764; Elizabeth, b 5 Oct 1766. Ch. b Biddeford: Sarah, bp 21 Sep

1773; Ada, bp 21 Sep 1773. (ME I.G.I.; Ridlon's Saco, p119; Census York Co., 1800, p926; MH&G Rec., V7, p182; Picton's ME Cem. Inscrips., V2, p1413; John L. M. Willis' Old Eliot, ME, V1, pp132-133)

DAVID, b ca 1760, of Little Ossipee, known as Limington today; filed (Ints.) 1 Jan 1788, m 2 May 1788, Betty Small [b ca 1765, of same town]. (Buxton V.R., Town Clerk, p350)

DAVID Jr., ba 23 Oct 1763, Saco, later of Limington, d 14 Apr 1843, age ca 80 years, same town; m 3 Apr 1785, Buxton, Elizabeth Smith [b 1764, of Limington, alive 1850, same town, widow, age 86]. As Robert L. Taylor's History of Limington, Maine narrated: "David came with his father and later settled near the Johnson cemetery on Lot 4, Range B." The identify of his father did not come to light, so it can be said that David was the known progenitor of the Youngs stemming from Limington.

David was listed as head of household in Limington from 1800-1830 inclusive. In 1800 his age was 26-45, with a family containing spousal figure of the same age and three males and three females from age 16 down to 5 and under. There would be ten children in all. In 1810, he was 45 plus, as were two females in a large household of eight children: four males, three under ten and one age 10-16; four females, one under 10, one age 10-16, and two 16-16. In 1820 he and spousal figure were 45 plus, with four males, two age 10-16, two age 16-26, and two other females, age 16-26.

In 1830 David had reached the age of 80-90 and from the number of members in household it would appear a married son and his family lived with him: there were seven family members, four males, one age 70-80, two age 5-10, and one age 30-40, as well as three females, one age 20-30 and two under 5. In 1850 Elizabeth was widowed and lived with son James, age 64, and his family in Limington.

Ch. b Limington: James+, b 19 May 1786; Francis+, b 14 Jul 1788; Betsey, b 12 Nov 1790, d 1 Jan 1844, age 54; Mary+ (Young) Duran, b 17 May 1793; Sally+ (Young) Moody, b 17 Dec 1795; David+ Jr., b 24 Jun 1798; Daniel+, b 14 Jan 1800; Hannah, b 6 Jun 1803, d 1822, native town, age 19; Joseph, b 1806, alive 1850, Standish; and John, b 1810s. (Hale's Cems., n.p.; Census York Co., 1800, p867, 1810, p699; 1820, p525; 1830, p157; 1850, Reel C, p294; Taylor's Liming-ton, TMs, p60)

DAVID, b pre 1775, resident of Hollis in 1820 census, age 45 plus; in household was a maternal figure of same age bracket. See main entry on Hezekiah+, b 1789, of Hollis, possibly a kinsman. (Census York Co., 1820, p378)

DAVID Jr., b 24 Jun 1798, Limington, s/o David and Elizabeth (Smith) Young, d 14 Jun 1872, native town, age 74; filed (Ints.) 29 Nov 1823, m 8 Jan 1824, Limington, Sally Small [b ca 1805, of Limington]. They raised a large family of twelve children. Ch. b Bradford: William J., b 1 Aug 1824; Joseph, b 16 Jun 1826; Nancy, b 23 Mar 1828; Sarah, b

13 Apr 1830; David Jr., b 7 May 1832; Elizabeth, b 13 May 1834; Enos, b 8 Feb 1837; Martha, b 1 Mar 1839; Daniel, b 15 Jun 1842; John L., b 9 Oct 1841; Sophronia, b 11 Jan 1847; Hannah, b 7 Jul 1850. (Taylor's Limington, TMs, p86, 136)

DAVID, b 1809, of Biddeford, d 15 Jun 1864, same town, buried in Young family plot, Biddeford. (Mormon/ME V.R., Wright-Zitkov)

DAVID, b 1810, of Saco, laborer; spouse was Sarah ( ) [b 1815, of same town]. In 1860 David, Sarah and son John, age 21, were listed as residents of Saco. Ch. b ME: John, b 1839. (Census York Co., 1860, Reel 3, p724)

DAVID, b 1822, listed as resident of Lebanon in the 1850 census, age 28, farmer; spouse was Mary A. ( ) [b 1827]. There was one other member of family, son Charles A., b 1849. (Census York Co., 1850, Reel B, p30)

DORCAS, b ca 1770, of York, filed (Ints.) 21 Oct 1791, m 11 Nov 1791, York, Benjamin McLucas [b ca 1765, of same town]. (ME I.G.I.; Bragdon & Frost's York V.R., p174)

DORCAS, b 21 Apr 1771, York, d/o Jonathan and Marcy (Nowell) Young, alive Nov 1798, native town, married; filed (Ints.) 8 Sep 1792, York/Kittery, Samuel Tucker [b ca 1765, of Kittery]. Dorcas Tucker was named married daughter of Jonathan Young of York by his will drawn 10 Nov 1798, probated __ Apr 1808; she was to receive ten dollars in addition to what had already been done for her which "shall be in full of her portion." (Bragdon & Frost's York V.R., p175; ME I.G.I.; Kittery V.R., p249)

DORCAS, b 26 Jun 1833, Parsonsfield, d/o George and Jane (Keazer) Young, filed (Ints.) 2 Oct 1853, Parsonsfield, Jacob D. Mudgett [b ca 1828, of same town]. (Parsonsfield V.R., Town Clerk, pp166, 207)

DORCAS, b Apr 1852, resident of Lebanon in 1900, age 48, single; she lived at the home of John McLaughlin, n.d. (1900 ME Soundex)

EBENEZER, b 5 Apr 1701, York, fisherman, s/o Matthews and Eleanor (Haynes) Young, alive 14 May 1765, native town, per last known deed; filed (Ints.) 11 Aug 1724, York, Sarah Batten aka Battin [b ca 1705, of same town, d/o Abraham Batten]. Ebenezer was named son and sole Exec. of Matthews' will drawn 20 Nov 1750, proved 1 Apr 1751, the residuary legatee of the estate.

Between 1752-1757, Ebenezer had drawn up three deeds of sale as grantor. The first of these was signed 5 Jun 1752, rec'd 8 Dec 1752 in which he sold to Jeremiah Moulton Jr. and Daniel Moulton, for 41 shillings, 4 pence, four shares in Lot No. 6, 2nd Div., in the York Common Lands; witnesses Jeremiah Moulton, Elizabeth Webber [York Deed 29:255]. The second deed was signed and rec'd 8 Jun 1752, with regard to the sale to Joseph Junkins Jr. of York for three pounds, 4 shillings, of his four shares in Lot No. 8, 1st Div., Commons, granted to him by the Proprietors; witnesses Thomas Bragdon, Daniel

Moulton [York Deed 29:211]. And the third deed, signed 21 Mar 1757, rec'd 25 May 1757, conveyed to Benjamin Holt of York for 2-4-8, all thirty-two shares in the Commons which were granted to Ebenezer's sibling Mathias Young who died intestate, "which became the estate of my honored father Matthews Young, now deceased who gave the same to me by his will," witnesses Daniel and Hannah Moulton [York Deed 33:55].

In the next decade, Ebenezer by deed signed 24 Dec 1761, rec'd 13 Jan 1762, conveyed to Samuel Bragdon of York for eight pounds legal money, ten acres land in York abutting N.W. by lands of Joseph Main; witnesses Job Lyman, David Sewall [York Deed 37:35]. On same date of signing, rec'd 16 Mar 1764, Ebenezer sold fifteen acres land in York to neighbor Joseph Main of York, situated at the S.W. corner of a small tract of land by Samuel Bragdon's in right of his wife, to said Joseph Main's land, for 2-13-4; witnesses Samuel Bragdon, Samuel Sewell [York Deed 38:188].

Yet another deed, apparently his last, signed 14 May 1765, rec'd 15 May 1765, concerned the sale of eighteen acres land in York where he then dwelt for 53-6-8, to Jonathan Sayward, Esq. of York, wife Sarah Young relinquishing Dower Rights; witnesses Jonathan Donnell, John Pile [York Deed 34:245]. This acreage abutting the property formerly belonged to the late Jonathan Young of York, which by then was in the possession of Samuel Bragdon, situated fairly close to York River.

Ch. b York: Susannah, b 5 Dec 1724, d 11 Jul 1729; Mary, b 24 Apr 1726; Hannah, b 24 Sep 1717; Ebenezer+, b 24 Aug 1729; Elizabeth, b 14 May 1731. (ME I.G.I.; Noyes et al, p776; Bragdon & Frost's York V.R., pp7, 46, 392)

EBENEZER, b 24 Aug 1729, York, mariner, s/o Ebenezer and Sarah (Battin) Young, alive 1761, native town; filed (Ints.) 10 Nov 1759, York, Abigail Grover [b ca 1740, of York, alive Mar 1761, d/o Matthews Grover Jr., gr.d/o of Dr. Andrew Grover]. Ebenezer, wife Abigail, and Abigail's maiden sister Sarah Grover, all of York, sold to Jonathan Sayward of York for ten pounds lawful money a two-sevenths part of real estate belonging to their grandfather Andrew Grover, or fifteen acres granted to their father Matthews Grover Jr. as described in the distribution of the estate per deed signed 3 Mar 1761, rec'd 6 Sep 1762; witnesses William Ball and Roger Mitchell for Ebenezer and Abigail Young, Daniel Moulton and Ezra Thompson for Sarah Grover [York Deed 37:52]. (Bragdon & Frost's York V.R., p143; ME I.G.I.)

EBENEZER, b ca 1740, of York, filed (Ints.) 5 Oct 1765, m 1765, Dorcas Babb [b ca 1745, of same town]. (Bragdon & Frost's York V.R., p148)

EBENEZER, b ca 1745, resident of Old York. Ebenezer was listed as one of the men mustered by Nathaniel Wells, Muster Master for York Co. on 1 Feb 1777, Wells, in Capt. Daniel Wheelwright's Regt. He enlisted for three years, his residence listed as Old York; he also served in Capt. Daniel Wheelwright's Co., Col. Ebenezer Francis' Regt. Continental Army pay accounts listed service from 25 Jan 1777 through 31 Dec 1779. (Mass. Soldiers & Sailors, p1017)

EDGAR J. aka Jacob E., b 26 Nov 1856, Freedom, N.H., s/o Daniel and Eleanor J. (Allard) Young [no main entry]; m 30 May 1881, Parsonsfield, Etta M. Alley [b Apr 1860, Cornish, res. of Parsonsfield]. For full family background, please see Youngs of Strafford County, N.H., Vol. I. Ch. b Freedom, N.H.: Eva M., b 1 Mar 1891. (Mormon/ME V.R., Wright-Zitkov)

EDMUND J., b ca 1838 or 1855, of Acton, either gr.s/o Jonathan and Mehitable (Moody) Young or s/o same who married later in life; filed (Ints.) 4 Mar 1881, m 21 Apr 1881, Portland, Sarah McGowan [b ca 1860, of Portland]. Jonathan's son Edmund J. was his "fourth son" and heir-at-law per his will written 8 Oct 1838, proved 7 Jan 1839. (Mormon/ME V.R., Wright-Zitkov)

EDWARD, b 1797, York, d 22 Nov 1858, native town, age 61, oldest s/o Samuel and Dorcas (Lowe) Young. Upon his demise and that of his brother Oliver who died the following year, kinsman Samuel P. Young made two separate petitions to the court to allow him to probate their estates. The first petition with regard to Oliver's estate in York was dated 18 Nov 1858 [York Probate #20977], and the 2nd petition regarding Edward's estate in York was dated the following month, 7 Dec 1858 [York Probate #20922].

Samuel P. stressed that each brother died "without father, mother, brother, sister, wife or issue," and that he, Samuel "was interested in their estates." Although kinship between Samuel P. and the two brothers posed a moot question as to their relationship, it was established that Samuel P. was kinsman when Letters of Admin. were granted him 4 Jan 1859 with regard to both petitions. (Bragdon & Frost's York V.R., pp180, 437, 621; ME I.G.I.; Hale's Cems., n.p.)

EDWARD C., b ca 1818, of Kittery, d pre 3 Nov 1856, Kittery, Sgt. of Marines; those who survived him were four minor children under the age of fourteen. The maternal grandmother Sarah Daley of Boston petitioned for custody since they were the children of her deceased daughter, and Sarah was the children's only known living relative. The court awarded custody of the four children to Sarah Daley, upon payment of a $60.00 bond [York Probate #20923]. Deposition was given as to the names and ages of the children: Edward C. Jr., b 1843; George, b 1844; Caroline+, b 1849; and Catherine, b 1850.

EDWARD D., b Apr 1855, York, s/o Jonathan and Olive (Moulton) Young, farmer, alive 1900, age 45, buried native town, n.d.; filed (Ints.) 5 Apr 1880, m 24 Apr 1880, South Berwick, Maria F. Johnson [b Nov 1857, York, d/o Theodore and Amanda (Fernald) Johnson, d 1932, age 75, native town]. In 1860 Edward D. lived in York with his widowed father Jonathan. In 1900 Edward D. was listed as head of his own household in York, married. Members of family included his spouse Maria, age 42, and three children George, Olive A., and Edna F.

Edward, spouse Maria F., and son were buried in the Young plot where his folks were buried, on the west side of Rte. 91 near York River, opposite 131 Cider Hill Road. Ch. b York, not traced further: Dwight G., b 1881, d 13 Oct 1893, age 12-1-0; George Johnson, b 17 Jun 1883; Olive A., b Mar 1888; and Edna F., b Sep 1896. (Bragdon & Frost's York V.R., pp347; Frost's York Cem., pp620-621; Hale's Cems., n.p.; Mormon/ME V.R., Wright-Zitkov; 1900 ME Soundex)

EDWARD E., b 5 Apr 1852, York, s/o Peter and Mary E. (Crosby) Young, d 20 Oct 1944, native town, age 92, single; listed as head of household in 1900 per census that year, age 48. Living with him was sibling Rowland [b 19 Jan 1850, d 5 Oct 1928, native town, age 78]. (1900 ME Soundex; Bragdon & Frost's York V.R., pp270, 489)

ELEANOR, b 6 Jan 1717/8, York, d/o Matthews and Eleanor (Haynes) Young; filed (Ints.) 9 Dec 1738, m 18 Jan 1739, York, Joseph Allen [b ca 1712, of same town]. Allen ch. b York: Mercy Allen, b 27 Mar 1740; Joseph Allen Jr., b 12 Feb 1742; Anne Allen, b 17 May 1744; Joel Allen, b 13 Feb 1746/7; Amos Allen, b 6 Mar 1749; Eleanor Allen, b 8 Jul 1751; Rhoda Allen, b 13 Nov 1753; Susanna Allen, b 26 Mar 1757; and Lydia Allen, b 22 Aug 1759. (Bragdon & Frost's York V.R., p66, 126; ME I.G.I.)

ELEAZER, bp. 25 Apr 1742, York, relative of Brigham Young. (ME I.G.I.)

ELIJAH, b 14 Feb 1830, of Biddeford/Saco, foundry worker, d 22 Mar 1899, Saco, age 60, married; m 31 Oct 1854, Biddeford, Caroline Smith [b 1 Jan 1836, of Dayton, d 10 Sep 1905, Saco, age 69, widow]. The 1860 census for Saco showed that Elijah, spouse Caroline and two children Clarence L. and Frederick were residents. The 1900 census indicated that Caroline was then widow at age 64 and that two grown children Elmer E., not hitherto disclosed, and Cora E. lived at home. Elijah and Caroline were buried at Laurel Hill Cemetery, Beach St., Saco.

Ch. b Saco: Elmer E., b 3 Jan 1853, d 25 Oct 1903, age 50; Clarence L.+, b May 1856; Frederick, b 1858; Cora E., b Nov 1879. (ME I.G.I.; Hale's Cems., n.p.; Census York Co., 1860, Reel 3, p773; 1900 ME Soundex; Picton's ME Inscrips., V2, pp1490-1491)

ELIPHALET, b ca 1760, of Lebanon, alive 1820, same town, married; m 9 Apr 1784, Lebanon, by Rev. Isaac Hasey, Susannah Wallingford [b ca 1765, of Lebanon, alive 1820, same town]. Eliphalet was the elder at least, if not the progenitor of the Youngs stemming from Lebanon. He was listed in four census reports there for a span of thirty years: in 1790, his household included one male under 16 and two females; in 1800, his age group was 26-45 with family containing a maternal figure of same age and three children all under 10 years, one male and two females; in 1810 his age was 45 plus, as was his spouse, with another female at home, age 16-26; and in 1820, he and spouse were 45 plus, with only one male at home, under ten years.

It is believed that Eliphalet and Susannah had one son at least who was christened Jonathan+, b ca 1790. (Census York Co., 1790, p63; 1800, p838; 1810, p930; 1820, p531; Lebanon Marr, p224)

ELIZA (   ), b 1810, of Berwick, widow of ___ Young and head of household in the 1860 census for Berwick, age 50. Members of her family were son Nathaniel+ [b 1828, N.H.], his wife Hannah (   ) [b 1831, N.H.] and their three young children John F. [b 1851], Ann J. [b 1854], and Lizzie [b 1857]. (Census York Co., 1860, Reel B, p880)

ELIZA (   ), b 1821, of Biddeford, widow of ___ Young per 1860 census for Biddeford, age 39, operative. Children at home included Charles F., machinist, William and Mary E. At home with them was Rachael Holt, age 73 [b 1787]. Ch. b ME: Charles F., b 1843; William, b 1846, and Mary E., b 1857. (Census York Co., 1860, Reel A, p312)

ELIZA, b 1813, of Dayton, d 9 May 1860, same town, age 47, single, buried at Young plot on River Road, Dayton. (Mormon/ME V.R., Wright-Zitkov; ME 1860 Mort. Sched., p29)

ELIZA, b 1836, of Biddeford per the 1860 census, age 24, single, operative. She lived at a boarding home. (Census York Co., 1860, Reel A, p259)

ELIZA, b 1842, of Saco, operative, lived at the home of Andrew J. and Susanna Leavitt [b 1829 and 1832, respectively] per 1860 census for Saco. (Census York Co., 1860, Reel C, p806)

ELIZA JANE (LITTLEFIELD), b 14 Feb 1836, York, w/o _____ Young, d/o Joseph and Eliza U. Littlefield, d 14 Jul 1891, native town, age 55-5-0, buried at York Cemetery, grave site headed by Jonathan Young and wives Joanna and Olive. (Hale's Cems., n.p.; Bragdon & Frost's York V.R., p621)

ELIZA JANE, b 1829, North Kennebunk, d/o Stephen and Abigail (Ricker) Young, resident of Newburyport, MA; m 27 Nov 1854, Newburyport, Ambrose Pike [b 1829, N.S., mariner, s/o William and Susan (   ) Pike]. (Mass. V.R., Marr, 78:219)

ELIZABETH, b 1679, also 1684, York, d/o Deacon Rowland and Susanna (Matthews) Young, alive Mar 1753/54, native town; m1 ca 1704, York, Samuel Webber Jr., millwright [b ca 1675, York, s/o Samuel Webber, d pre 29 May 1735, native town]. Elizabeth Webber was designated as married daughter in her father's will signed 14 Sep 1719, proved 2 Jan 1721/2.

Samuel Webber's will was drawn 25 Mar 1735, proved 29 May 1735, naming wife Elizabeth Young Webber as Exec. Twelve children were cited, see below. Widow Elizabeth (Young) Webber m2 filed (Ints.) 29 Aug 1741, York, widower George Stover [b ca 1670, of Gloucester, MA, and Cape Neddick, widower, formerly married to Abigail Elwell]. He named wife Elizabeth in his will which was signed 23 Mar 1747, proved 2 Apr 1753.

Widow Elizabeth Stover m3 18 Mar 1753/4, York, widower
Hon. Samuel Came, millwright [b ca 1675, York, s/o Arthur and
Violet Came]. Samuel Came's first wife was Patience Bragdon;
one of their daughters was Abigail Came [b 18 Sep 1700], who
married Jonathan Young, see his main entry. Samuel Came's
will was dated 28 Jun 1764, proved 2 Jan 1769.

Webber ch., b York: Elizabeth Webber, b 12 Oct 1705,
d 1721; Sarah Webber, b 31 Jan 1719/20; Nathaniel Webber,
b 9 Sep 1722; Joseph Webber, b 24 Jul 1727; and Paul Webber,
b 7 Oct 1729. (ME I.G.I.; Noyes et al, pp666, 729-730;
Bragdon & Frost's York V.R., p28)

ELIZABETH, b ca 1690, York, d/o Samuel and Elizabeth
(Masterson) Young; filed (Ints.) 18 Feb 1709, Ipswich, MA,
Joseph Greeley [b ca 1685, of Kingston, NH]. (Noyes et al,
p777; MA I.G.I.)

ELIZABETH, b 23 Apr 1710, York, d/o Jonathan and Margaret
(Stackpole) Young; filed (Ints.) 28 Sep 1734, m 5 Nov 1734,
York, Samuel Adams [b ca 1705, York]. (ME I.G.I.; Noyes et
al, pp776-777; Bragdon & Frost's York V.R., p122)

ELIZABETH, b 25 Feb 1715, York, d/o Benaiah and Ruth
(Johnson) Young; filed (Ints.) 27 Oct 1744, York, Joseph
Saywood [b ca 1720, of York, d pre 1755, same town]. Eliza-
beth Young Saywood m2 ca 1755, Daniel Grant [b ca 1710, of
York]. Daniel Grant, Esq. was named Exec. of Benaiah Young's
will signed 27 Jan 1779, probated that year on 7th April.
Grant ch., b York: Lydia Grant, b 8 Jun 1756; Philomalea
Grant, b 30 Mar 1759. (ME I.G.I.; Bragdon & Frost's York
V.R., pp69, 130)

ELIZABETH, b 10 May 1721, York, d/o Jonathan and Abigail
(Came) Young; filed (Ints.) 14 Oct 1775, m 9 Nov 1775, York,
Samuel Curtis [b ca 1750, of Wells]. By deed dated 3 Jul
1797, rec'd 4 Oct 1799, Elizabeth Curtis of York was identified by Eunice Junkins of York as her married sister who held
shares in their mother's Thirds. The deed conveyed to their
brother Jonathan Young Jr. of York for $50.00, all Eunice's
right, title and share that she had in their mother Abigail
Young's Thirds in the estate of their father Jonathan Young,
late of York. (ME I.G.I.; Bragdon & Frost's York V.R., p158)

ELIZABETH, b ca 1740, of York, filed (Ints.) 13 Aug 1762,
York, Jacob Redlon [b ca 1735, of same town]. (Bragdon &
Frost's York V.R., p145)

ELIZABETH, b 14 May 1741, Saco, relative of Mary Caroline
Turnbow. (ME I.G.I.)

ELIZABETH, b ca 1760, York, d/o Masterson and Susan aka
Sarah (Curtis) Young; filed (Ints.) 7 Dec 1783, m __ Jan 1784
at First Parish Church, York, Joseph Sedgeley [b ca 1755, of
same town]. Elizabeth Sedgely was named married daughter of
Masterson Young by his will written 6 Jun 1795, proved 17 Aug
1795. She was also acknowledged daughter by widow Sarah
Curtis Young in her will dated 16 Feb 1814, probated Nov 1819,
wherein she stated merely that Elizabeth had already received

"the full proportion of the estate" that was her due. (Bragdon & Frost's York V.R., pp165, 362)

ELIZABETH, b 1828, resident of Biddeford in 1850. She lived at the home of William and Mary Cummings, n.d. (Census York Co., 1850, Reel A, p36)

ELIZABETH C., b Dec 1824, resident of South Berwick in 1900, single, age 75, member of her sister Nancy S. Plumer's household on Main Street. Records did not indicate whether Elizabeth was widow or maiden lady. (1900 ME Soundex)

ELIZABETH S., b 1806, Acton, d/o Jonathan and Mehitable (Moody) Young, d 1889, native town, married, w/o Charles Standish Thompson [b 1801, d 1891, Acton, widower]. Elizabeth S. Thompson was named married daughter of Jonathan Young of Acton by his will signed 8 Oct 1838, probated 7 Jan 1839. She and husband Charles were buried at the Young family cemetery on Young's Ridge Road, Acton. (Hale's Cems., n.p.)

ELLEN F., b ca 1850, Buxton, m 29 Jul 1870, Buxton, Gilbert Johnson [b ca 1845, of same town]. (ME I.G.I.)

ELLEN F., b 21 Apr 1861, York, d/o Moses C. and Lydia E. (Trafton) Young; filed (Ints.) 25 Dec 1883, York, m 5 Jan 1884, South Berwick, William L. Trafton [b 1849, Alfred, s/o Ebenezer and Phebe P. (Osgood) Trafton, his 2nd marriage]. (ME I.G.I.; Bragdon & Frost's York V.R., p350)

EMMA, b Jun 1859, Sanford, d/o George W. and Abigail (Small) Young, d 5 May 1878, age 19; filed (Ints.) 6 Oct 1875, Sanford, James Mills Perkins [b 10 Sep 1842, Sanford, s/o Abner F. and Mary H. (Allen) Perkins, d 28 Dec 1892, age 50, native town]. (F. R. Boyle's Sanford, pp330-332)

ESTHER, b ca 1705, of Saco, filed (Ints.) 17 Sep 1724, Saco, Stephen Larrabee [b ca 1700, of Saco]. (Ridlon's Saco, Boston Recs., p871)

ESTHER, b ca 1765, York, d/o Masterson and Sarah (Curtis) Young, alive 16 Feb 1814, native town; filed (Ints.) 18 Mar 1785, m 14 Apr 1785 at First Parish Church, York, Joel Jellison [b ca 1760, of same town]. On date of marriage this cryptic message was written down by the Town Clerk in his Register: "The snow so deep could not ride all the way." Esther Jellison was named the married daughter of Masterson Young by his will drawn up 6 Jun 1795, probated 17 Aug 1795, and she was the acknowledged daughter of widow Sarah Curtis Young in her will dated 16 Feb 1814, probated Nov 1819. Sarah said merely that Esther had already received "the full proportion of the estate" that was her due. (Bragdon & Frost's York V.R., pp166, 363)

ETTA, b 22 Nov 1856, of Shapleigh, d 18 Jun 1894, same town, age 38; m ca 1880, Joseph Beal [b 13 Jun 1843, d 10 Oct 1899, of same town, age 56, widower]. They and their daughter Minnie were buried at the Beal family lot in Shapleigh, located one-half mile north of Ross Corner on the left side of the road. Beal ch. b Shapleigh: Minnie Beal, b 1884, d 28 Sep 1887. (Hale's Cems., n.p.; Picton's ME Cem. Inscrips., V3, p1977)

30

ETTA M., b ca 1869, of Shapleigh, m 6 Dec 1889, Shapleigh, Willie M. Temple [b ca 1865, of same town]. (ME I.G.I.)

EUNICE, b ca 1734, York, d/o Jonathan Jr. and Abigail (Came) Young, alive Jul 1797, York, widow; filed (Ints.) 18 Jan 1755, John Junkins [b 19 Jul 1733, York, s/o Alexander Junkins, mariner, d intestate pre 7 Jul 1783, native town]. It is to be noted that John Junkins' father Alexander forbade the banns. Probate on John Junkins' estate was filed 7 Jul 1783 by widow Eunice Junkins and son John Junkins, Jr., both of York, who gave bond for 400 pounds, with sureties Johnson Moulton, Esq. and Samuel Young, prob. Eunice's brother [York Probate #10669].

Eunice Junkins and her married sisters Abigail Grow and Patience Stover, with spouses co-signing, sold their shares in their father's estate in York to brother Samuel Young of York for 80 pounds lawful money; the only exclusion in the sale was that part of the real estate belonging to their mother Abigail Young as her Thirds, by deed signed 9 Jul 1766, rec'd 24 Oct 1772. See sister Abigail Grow for full documentation.

On 3 Jul 1797 Eunice sold to her brother Jonathan Young Jr. of York for $50.00, "all my right, title and share I have in and to my mother Abigail Young's Thirds in the estate of my honored father Jonathan Young, late of York," her right being one-tenth part of the above-mentioned Thirds, both real and personal, with her sister Elizabeth Curtis; witnesses John Kingsbury, Elihu Bragdon; rec'd 4 Oct 1799 [York Deed 64:121].

Junkins ch. b York: Susanna Junkins, b 24 Jun 1757; John Junkins Jr., b 15 Sep 1759, alive Jul 1783; Abigail Junkins, b 6 Aug 1761; Elijah Junkins, b 30 Aug 1763; Eunice Junkins, b 27 Feb 1766; and Hannah Junkins, b 1769, who m 1 Aug 1790, York, Joshua Grant, s/o David Grant. (ME I.G.I.; Bragdon & Frost's York V.R., p90)

EUNICE, b ca 1780, of York, m 13 Dec 1801, Lyman, 2nd Baptist Church, John Maston [b ca 1775, of same town]. (ME I.G.I.; Rev. S. Lock's Marr., Lyman, 1784-1831)

EUNICE, b ca 1800, of Hollis, filed (Ints.) 5 Sep 1819, Hollis, m ___ Dec 1819, Hollis, Jeremiah Moulton [b ca 1795, of Hampton]. (V.R. of Hollis, Town Clerk, n.p.)

EUNICE, b ca 1805, of Hollis, m 30 Sep 1827, Hollis, by Rev. Mr. Roberts, Thomas Huff [b ca 1800, of Saco]. (Thompson's Recs. of York Co., TMs, p417)

EUNICE, b 1836, resident of Biddeford in 1860, operative at mill, per census that year, age 24. Living with Eunice were her sister Emily [b 1838] and Margaret Durning [b 1841], both operatives. (Census York Co., 1860, Reel A, p198)

FANNIE A., n.d., widow of ____ Young of Kittery per 1890 ME Vets, Census Index of Civil War Vets or Their Widows, York County, District SD#1, Enum.#217.

FRANCIS, b ca 1650, of Ipswich and Buxton, d pre 8 Oct 1718, Ipswich. For extensive entry on Francis, please see Youngs of Essex County, MA, Vol. II. Francis' son-in-law John

Brown Jr., spouse of Francis' daughter Mary, received much of the property in Ipswich at the time of his death. However, as late as 1735, Francis' estate still held proprietory rights in Narraganset Township, No. 1, later to be known as Buxton. For example, it was voted on 24 Nov 1735 at a proprietors' meeting in Buxton that John Brown Jr. of Ipswich "shall draw on the right of Francis Young." (Goodwin's Proprietors' Recs. of Buxton, p95)

FRANCIS, b 14 Jul 1788, Buxton, mason, of Standish, s/o David and Elizabeth (Smith) Young, alive 1850, native town, age 61, m 20 Mar 1827, Fanny Bacon [b 1793, of Gorham, alive 1850, Buxton, age 57]. Francis was listed as head of household in the 1850 census for Buxton, age 61, his estate valued at $900.00; members of family were spouse Fanny ( ) [b 1793], son Francis Jr. and three daughters Delphina, Sally and Mary.

It would seem that Francis was the namesake of one of the original proprietors of Buxton by date of 24 Nov 1735. Ch. b poss. Buxton: Francis Jr., b 1831, laborer; Delphina, b 1833; Sally, b 1835; and Mary, b 1836. (Census York Co., 1850, p69; Taylor's Limington, TMs, p60)

FREDERIC L., b ca 1840, of Biddeford, m 13 Jun 1868, Biddeford, Rosanna Land [b ca 1845, of Saco]. (Mormon/ME V.R., Wright-Zitkov)

FURBER, b 19 Jan 1827, Farmington, N.H., s/o Benjamin F. and 2nd wife Deborah (Furber) Young [no main entry], d 8 Feb 1900, age 73-0-20, Alton, N.H., shoemaker; m 25 Sep 1845, Lebanon, by Elder Edward Blaisdell, Rhoda E. aka Elizabeth Goodall [b 1823, Farmington, d pre 1872, native town]. Upon the death of his father in 1840, Furber became the ward of Charles Dennett of Rochester. For full details on Furber's parents, his extended residence in Farmington and Alton, and marriages of siblings Fannie J. Hayes and Ella A. Foss, please see Youngs of Strafford County, N.H., Vol. I.

Ch. b Farmington, N.H.: Clara A., b 31 Jul 1846; Frances, b 11 Mar 1850, d.y.; Fannie J. (Young) Hayes, b 11 Mar 1856; Ella A. (Young) Foss, b 1858; and dau. b 26 Jun 1864. (ME I.G.I.; Lebanon Marr, p224)

GEORGE, b ca 1755, of Berwick, yeoman, s/o Abner Young of Somersworth, N.H. Three land deeds were found for George when he was resident of Berwick. It should be noted that the original purchase of the land described below was made by Abner Young of Somersworth, N.H. on 10 Oct 1780, but only put on record as of 24 May 1785, after George's first known deed of record; witnesses Susanna and Joanna Wentworth [York Deed 48:179].

George bought from Mary Wallingford, widow of Ebenezer Wallingford, for 33 pounds lawful money, 97 acres land in Berwick which had originally been sold by her to Abner Young, "but not being on record is now by consent of Abner, sold to his son George," acreage that was near Stair Falls, Lot No. 1, 1st Range in the division of Berwick proprietors' Common Lands above Little River that was set off to Ebenezer Wallingford as part of the estate of Thomas Wallingford, Esq., deceased; by deed signed 15 Dec 1784, rec'd 16 Dec 1784; witnesses Abner Young, Sally Carr [York Deed 48:101].

A dual deed was found for George of Berwick when he sold properties in Berwick to John Wallingford of Lebanon. The first of these, signed 26 Sep 1785, rec'd 23 Apr 1806, conveyed 51 acres of Lot No. 1, 1st Range in the Common Lands, situated between Berwick and Lebanon, for 29 pounds lawful money; witnesses Isaac Hasey, Samuel Jones [York Deed 77:255-256]. The second deed signed 10 Jan 1788, but rec'd on same date as in the first deed, conveyed 33 acres of Lot No. 1, 1st Range, Common Lands, for 27 pounds lawful money; witnesses Joseph Farnum, Samuel Hines [York Deed 77:255]

GEORGE, b ca 1766, of Shapleigh, filed (Ints.) 1 Jan 1791, m 24 Jan 1791, Shapleigh, Ransey Row [b ca 1770, of same town]. (Mormon/ME V.R., Wright-Zitkov)

GEORGE, b ca 1780, resident of Shapleigh per 1820 census, age 26-45, with household of a spousal figure of same age bracket, and two males and two females under the age of 10. (Census York Co., 1820, p577)

GEORGE, b 11 Jun 1786, N.H., of South Acton, shoemaker, d 11 Apr 1874, same town, age 87-10-0, widower. Spouse was Abra (   ) [b 7 Jan 1789, d 27 Apr 1869, South Acton, age 80-3-20]. The 1830-1860 census reports, inclusive, reflected that George and Abra lived in Acton with a growing family. In 1830 his age was 40-50, as was the spousal figure; at home were eight children all under the age of 15, two males and six females. In 1840 his age and that of the spousal figure was 50-60, with six offspring at home, one male age 20-30 and five females, one 5-10, two 10-15, and two 15-20. Then in 1850, he and spouse's age were 64 and 60 respectively; at home were daughters Lucinda and Olive. In 1860 George was age 74, and Abra, age 70; at home was a young lad of eight by the name of Frank Mason [b 1852].

George, spouse and daughters Sarah and Harriet were buried at Maple Grove Cem., Acton. Ch. b So. Acton: Sarah, b 1 May 1814, 10 Jan 1835, age 21-5-0; Lucinda, b 1825; Harriet M., b 11 Jan 1830, d 5 Nov 1835, age 5-4-0; Olive S., b 1839. (Hale's Cems., n.p.; Census York Co., 1830, p66; 1840, Reel B, p298; 1850, Reel B, p9; 1860, Reel B, p638)

GEORGE, b 1802, York, farmer/tanner, believed to be s/o Jonathan Young, Esq., d 21 Jul 1886, native town, age 84, widower; filed (Ints.) 30 Oct 1830, m 2 Dec 1830, York, Eliza Roberts [b 1807, of York, d 9 Nov 1862, York, age 55-4-0, married]. It is believed that this George was the one who was named heir-at-law of Jonathan, Esq. of York [b 1774] by Jonathan's will signed 14 Dec 1840, probated 5 May 1856.

George was listed as head of household in York per census reports from 1840-1860 inclusive. In 1840 his age was 30-40, as was a female parental figure, household containing one male age 5-10 and three females, one under 5 and two 5-10. In 1850 his spouse was named Eliza, age 43; their children were Amos, Julia A., Nancy, Lydia, and Mary, the estate worth $600. In 1860 George's estate was valued at $1,500; both spouse Eliza, age 52, and daughter Margit lived at home.

George and family were buried at the Young lot on the west side of Bog Road, next to the road, 0.7 miles north of the intersection of Bog Road and Rte. 91, York. Ch. b York: Amos+, b 1831; Julia A., b 1833; Nancy, b 1835; Lydia, b 1838, d 9 Jun 1856, age 18-3-0; Mary aka Margit, b 1847. (ME I.G.I.; Bragdon & Frost's York V.R., p235; Frost's York Cem., p632; Plaisted Private Recs.; Hale's Cems., n.p.; Census York Co., 1840, Reel B, p259; 1850, Reel A, pp217-218; 1860, Reel C, p956)

GEORGE, b ca 1805, resident of Sanford in the 1830 census, age 20-30. He lived alone. (Census York Co., 1830, p344)

GEORGE, b 11 Feb 1808, Berwick, s/o Richard and Rebecca (   ) Young, d 11 Aug 1849, native town, age 41-6-0, married; m ca 1835, Susan (   ) [b Jul 1807, of Berwick, d 30 Jul 1856, of same town, age 49-7-0, widow]. George, Susan and their four children were buried at the Richard and Rebecca Young plot at Evergreen Cemetery, Berwick. Ch. b Berwick: Eliza-beth, b 1834, d 22 Sep 1851, age 17; Benjamin F., b 9 Jun 1838, d 11 Mar 1842, age 3-9-2; George H., b 30 Jun 1841, d 22 May 1846; and Rebecca, b 31 May 1845, d 26 Aug 1846, age 1-2-26. (Mormon/ME V.R., Wright-Zitkov; Hale's Cems., n.p.)

GEORGE A., b 1839, Hollis/Dayton, s/o Thomas and Abigail (Cousens) Young, m 24 Dec 1864, Hollis Center, Lydia Jane B. Cleaves, dressmaker [b 2 May 1846, of Dayton, d/o Cyrus and Elizabeth Cleaves of Hollis, d 4 Nov 1918, Biddeford]. Both the 1850 and 1860 census reports listed George as member of his father household in Hollis and Dayton, respectively. (ME I.G.I.; Mormon/ME V.R., Wright-Zitkov; Picton's ME Cem. Inscrips., V1, p152)

GEORGE A., b Jan 1840, resident of Biddeford in 1900, address South Street, age 60. Member of household was daughter Inez M. [b 1870]. (1900 ME Soundex)

GEORGE A., b ca 1850, Berwick, poss. s/o George H. and Susan (   ) Young, cited below; m ca 1873, Amy (   ) [b ca 1855, of Berwick]. Family members were buried at Evergreen Cemetery, Berwick, at the family grave site headed by Richard and Rebecca Young. Ch. b Berwick: Almon G., twin, b 9 Jun 1874, d 19 Mar 1877, age 2-9-10; Harry M. E., twin, b 9 Jun 1874, d same age as twin, 19 Mar 1877; Nettie, 1870s; and Harry M., b 5 Apr 1881, d 5 Feb 1885. (Hale's Cems., n.p.)

GEORGE H., b May 1861, York, s/o Timothy and Mary Ann (Simpson) Young, d 1944, age 83, native town; filed (Ints.) 19 Jan 1885, m 25 Jan 1885, York, Mary A. Plaisted [b 1866, York, d/o Joseph and Hannah (Moulton) Plaisted, d 1955, age 89, native town]. In 1900 George H., spouse Mary A. and their children Arthur S., age 14, and Louella, age 12, lived at George's mother's home in York. George H. and Mary A. were buried at the Young family lot, Lot #25, York Cemetery, York, grave sites headed by parents Timothy and Mary A. Ch. b York, not traced further: Arthur Stuart, b 13 Aug 1885, d 1953; Louella, b Jan 1888, alive 1900. (Bragdon & Frost's York V.R., pp352, 486; Frost's York Cem., pp614-615; Hale's Cems., n.p.; 1900 ME Soundex)

GEORGE R., b 3 Dec 1799, of Parsonsfield, s/o John R. and Rebecca (Hutchins) Young, farmer, d 25 Jan 1871, same town; (Ints.) 24 Sep 1829, m 18 Oct 1829, Parsonsfield, Jane Keazer aka Kezer, [b 5 Oct 1805, d 1 Jul 1886, native town, age 80-8-27]. Per the 1850 census, George and spouse Jane lived in Parsonsfield, their estate valued at $2,000. Four children were at home: Dorcas, John, George, and Winfield Scott. A workman by the name of Daniel Mighel [b 1790] was a member of the household.

George, Jane K. and son George and spouse Mabel were buried at the family grave site in Parsonsfield headed by George's parents John R. and Rebecca. Ch. b prob. Parsonsfield: Sarah Jane, b 1 Feb 1831; Dorcas+ (Young) Mudgett, b 26 Jun 1833; John R.+, b 5 Dec 1836; George R.+, b 7 Apr 1843; and Winfield Scott+, b 15 Sep 1848. (Census York Co., 1850, p374; ME Cems., V2, p1355; Parsonsfield V.R., Town Clerk, pp101, 111, 207, 241; Hobb's Cem. Recs. of Parsonsfield, p107)

GEORGE R., b 7 Apr 1843, No. Parsonsfield, s/o George and Jane (Keazer) Young, d 15 Nov 1920, native town, age 77, widower; m1 22 Jul 1862, Parsonsfield, Mary Adler [b ca 1845, of same town, d pre 1900]; m2 Mabel L. Shedd [b 25 Feb 1861, MA, alive 1900, Parsonsfield, age 39]. In 1900 George R. and Mabel were members of Thomas S. Churchill's household [n.d.], Parsonsfield. George, first wife Mabel and son Eddie, age one, were buried at George's parents' burial site in No. Parsonsfield Cemetery. (Mormon/ME V.R., Wright-Zitkov; Hale's Cems., n.p.; 1900 ME Soundex; ME Cem. Inscripts., V2, p1355; Hobb's Cem. Recs. of Parsonsfield, pp107-108)

GEORGE W., b 7 Jul 1821, Sanford, farmer, s/o Joseph and Edna M. (Huston) Young, prob. gr.s/o Daniel and Anna (Johnson) Young, d 24 Mar 1901, age 79-5-17, native town, widower; m pre 1849, poss. Deerfield, N.H., Abigail Small [b 18 Feb 1824, Deerfield, N.H., d/o Samuel and Abigail (Fernald) Small, d 29 Sep 1896, Sanford, age 72-7-11, married]. George, wife Abigail and infant son Joseph lived in Sanford per the 1850 census. In 1860 George, age 38, and Abigail, age 37, were listed as residents of Sanford with two youngsters at home, Joseph and Emma.

What must be stressed here is that the dates of birth of George W. and his family as given in the 1900 Soundex are at variance with York burial records given above and below. The Maine Soundex gave George W.'s d-o-b as Oct 1826 and indicated he already was widower in the summer of 1900. George, Abigail and children were buried at the Young Cemetery on Old Mast Road, Sanford, Rte 109.

Ch. b Sanford: Joseph+, b 18 Jan 1849; Orrin, b 6 Jun 1851, d 29 Dec 1858, native town, age 7-6-23; Emma+ (Young) Perkins, b Jun 1859; Abby, b 10 May 1861, d 18 Oct 1864, native town, age 3-5-8. (Hale's Cems., n.p.; F. R. Boyle's **Sanford**, pp330-331; Census York Co., 1850, Reel C, p141; 1860, Reel A, p433; Picton's ME Cem. Inscrips., V3, pp1713-1714)

GEORGE W., b ca 1840, of Berwick, alive 1890, same town. George W. was listed in the 1890 ME Vets, Census Index of Civil War Vets for Berwick. (1890 ME Veterans, District SD#1, Enum. #200)

GEORGE W., b 1866, of Eliot, d 1943, same town, age 77; spouse was Isabel F. (   ) [b 1877, d 1943, Eliot, age 66]. Both were buried at Mt. Pleasant Cemetery on Bolt Hill Road, Eliot. (Hale's Cems., n.p.; Picton's ME Cem. Inscrips., V1, p649)

HANNAH (   ), b ca 1755, of York, widow of ____ Young, alive 1840, same town. Hannah was listed as head of household in York in census reports from 1820-1840. Per the 1820 census for York, her age was 45 plus, her family unit containing three other females, one age 26-45 and two under 10 years.

In the 1840 census for York, Hannah was age 80-90, her status clearly that of widow. The data showed she was either a parent or grandparent figure to four other females living in the household, rather than a sibling to any of them. Two females were ages 20-30, another was 40-50 and the fourth one, 50-60. (Census York Co., 1820, p595; Census York Co., 1840, Reel B, p259)

HANNAH (   ), b ca 1760, of York, d 12 Sep 1845, York, ca 85 years plus, no known antecedent; filed (Ints.) 4 Oct 1815, m2 7 Dec 1815, York, Oliver McLucas aka Lucas [b ca 1760, of York, alive 1848, same town, aged and infirm, same town]. Clearly this was Hannah's 2nd marriage, but the moot question is whether she was a Young by birth, or had married into the family. It is somehow assumed she married into the Young clan.

Petition dated 5 Jun 1848 for the recovery of $200.00 from Hannah Young's estate in York, deceased, was made by Oliver K. Lucas of York. Lucas was too infirm to handle the Admin. of her estate and prayed that Nathaniel G. Marshall, Esq. of York, be appointed Admin.; request granted same date. Sworn in on 12 Jun 1848 were the appraisers Charles Moody, Joseph Junkins and Luther Junkins [York Probate #20932]. (ME I.G.I.; Bragdon & Frost's York V.R., p202)

HANNAH, b 5 Jan 1698, York, d/o Matthews aka Mathias and Eleanor (Haynes) Young, alive 20 Nov 1750, native town; m 4 Dec 1724, York, John Preble [b 26 Nov 1699, York, s/o Benjamin and Mary (Baston) Preble]. Hannah Preble was named married daughter and heir-at-law of Matthews Young by will dated 20 Nov 1750, proved 1 Apr 1751.

Preble ch. b York: Tabitha Preble, b 7 Nov 1725; Jedediah Preble, b 11 Dec 1727; Abigail Preble, b 7 Nov 1729; Lydia Preble, b 20 Dec 1731; Benjamin Preble, b 14 Nov 1733;

Mercy Preble, b 22 Apr 1736; and Hannah Preble, b 17 Feb 1741. (Noyes et al, pp566, 776; ME I.G.I.; Bragdon & Frost's York V.R., pp7, 37, 115)

HANNAH, b 25 Dec 1733, York, d/o Benaiah and Ruth (Johnson) Young; filed (Ints.) 21 Sep 1753, York, m 3 Oct 1753, York, Nicholas Booker [b ca 1730, of York]. (ME I.G.I.; Bragdon & Frost's York V.R., p138)

HANNAH, b ca 1734, York, d/o Rowland and Hannah (   ) Young, alive Aug 1771, native town; filed (Ints.) 9 Jan 1754, m 24 Dec 1754, York, John Johnson [b ca 1730, of same town]. Hannah Johnson was named married daughter and heir-at-law of Rowland by his will signed 27 Aug 1771, probated 8 Apr 1782, her full portion from the estate, 5 pounds lawful money. Johnson ch. b York: John Johnson Jr., b 29 Dec 1754, Elizabeth Johnson, b 23 Feb 1757; Samuel Johnson, b 8 Aug 1759; Hannah Johnson, b 20 Mar 1761; Humility Johnson, b 5 Dec 1762; and Nathaniel Johnson, b 12 May 1764. (ME I.G.I.; Bragdon & Frost's York V.R., pp76, 82, 139)

HANNAH, b 8 Feb 1745, York, d/o Rowland aka Roland and Abigail (Dixon) Young, single, gr.d/o Rowland Young. By deed signed and rec'd 23 Mar 1767, Hannah, single, sold one full 8th share of her father Rowland's estate for 6-12-0 to John Cooley of York; her share represented one acre of land and a portion of the dwelling house, barn and orchard fronting N.W. by the country road leading to Cape Neddick "and all other ways by my grandfather Roland Young's land being the same whereon my late father Roland Young Jr. lived; witnesses Daniel Moulton, Patience Young [York Deed 39:149]. It should be noted that John Cooley was Hannah's brother-in-law; he was the spouse of her sister Abigail. (ME I.G.I.; Bragdon & Frost's York V.R., p56)

HANNAH, b ca 1750, of Berwick, m 23 Jul 1773, Berwick, Stephen Libby [b ca 1745, of same town]. (ME I.G.I.)

HANNAH, b ca 1775, of York, d/o Masterson and Sarah (Curtis) Young, alive early 1814, York; filed (Ints.) 4 Jan 1794, m 30 Jan 1794, York, Thomas Bragdon Jr. [b ca 1770, of same town]. Hannah Bragdon was named married daughter of Masterson Young by his will signed 6 Jun 1795, probated 17 Aug 1795. She was also acknowledged married daughter by her mother, the widow Sarah Curtis Young in will dated 16 Feb 1814, probated Nov 1819, wherein she merely stated that Hannah had already received "the full proportion of the estate" that was her due. (ME I.G.I.; Bragdon & Frost's York V.R., p178)

HANNAH, b ca 1805, Waterboro, m 5 Mar 1824, Waterboro, Joseph Henderson [b ca 1800, of same town]. (ME I.G.I.)

HANNAH, b ca 1815, York, d/o Samuel Young [no main entry]; filed (Ints.) 11 Dec 1833, m 1 Apr 1834, York, Daniel Bragdon Donnell [b ca 1810, of same town]. (ME I.G.I.; Bragdon & Frost's York V.R., p242)

HANNAH, b 1829, resident of Buxton in 1850, lived alone at age 19. (Census York Co., 1850, Reel B, p55)

HANNAH, b 1830, N.H., lived at age 20 with Kezia Day [b 1801] and family in Waterboro per 1850 census. (York Census Co., 1850, Reel C, p219)

HANNAH, b 1836, Ireland, resident of Biddeford per the 1860 census, operative, single. She lived at the home of James and Mary Murphy [b 1827 and 1830, Ireland, respectively]. (Census York Co., 1860, Reel A, p301)

HANNAH JANE,b 1836, Newfield, d/o Daniel and Eunice (Wagner) Young, m 1852, Newfield, John Henry Tuttle [b ca 1830, of Newfield]. (ME I.G.I.)

HANNAH W., b 1829, York, d/o Charles F. Young, filed (Ints.) 14 Sep 1850, m 22 Nov 1850, York, George G. Beal, mariner [b 1823, of York]. In 1860 Hannah, husband George G. and their two young children Anna and George lived at the home of her father Charles F., widower, in York, per the census that year. Beal ch. b York: Anna aka Ariana (Beal) Todd, b 1850, w/o George A. Todd of York; George Beal, Jr., b 1855. (ME I.G.I.; Bragdon & Frost's York V.R., pp272, 345)

HARRIET E., b ca 1820, Buxton, m 15 Dec 1842, Buxton, Joshua Moulton [b ca 1815, of same town]. (ME I.G.I.)

HENRY, b ca 1735, of Biddeford, Cmdr. of the ship "Three Brothers," laying at Biddeford. Henry sold by deed signed 19 Jun 1767, rec'd 7 Dec 1767, to George Buck of Biddeford, one-fourth of a certain parcel of land and saw mill built on the same along Saco River, beginning at Davis Brook four miles up the River Saco and extending four miles into the country. Also, on 7 Dec 1767, Henry conveyed full Power of Attorney to William Parker of Portsmouth, N.J. and David Sewall of York, Esq.; witnesses W. Buck, mayor of Biddeford, John Lloyd, Thomas May, James Chappel [York Deed 39:203]

HENRY J., b 1837, Lyman, s/o Thomas and Abigail (Cousens) Young of Hollis, m 7 Jan 1865, Lyman, Sarah E. Jellison [b 1846, Hollis, d/o Leland and Betsy (   ) Jellison, d 28 Mar 1867, Dayton, bur. at the family plot]. Henry J. was listed as member of his parents' household in Hollis per the 1850 census at age 13. Ch. b Dayton: Emma E., b 7 Mar 1865. (Mormon/ME V.R., Wright-Zitkov; V.R. of Lyman, Town Clerk, n.p.)

HERBERTA, b 1842, resident of Biddeford per the 1860 census, operative, single, living at a boarding home. (Census York Co., 1860, Reel A, p259)

HESTER ANN, b ca 1820, Wolfeboro, N.H., filed (Ints.), 18 Oct 1840, m 8 May 1841, Wolfeboro, N.H., James R. Frost [b ca 1815, of same town]. (Thompson's Recs. of York Co., TMs, p417; NHVR-Brides)

HEZEKIAH, bp 24 Jun 1753, Biddeford/Saco, s/o Thomas and Eunice (   ) Young of Saco, d 27 Jun 1845, Dayton, age 92, married; m 25 Sep 1788, Lyman, Mary Young [b 1769, of Lyman, d 11 Mar 1847, Dayton, age 78, widow]. In 1800 Hezekiah was listed as head of family in Pepperellborough (Saco, as of 1805), age 45 plus, with household containing a female figure of same age group and six children: three males and two females all 10 years or under, and one female age 10-16.

Revolutionary War records cited below also served to establish that Hezekiah of Pepperellboro was sibling of John Young of the same town. Hezekiah served in the Revolutionary War, having enlisted from Pepperellboro as Pvt., serving in Capt. John Elden's Co., Col. Lemuel Robinson's Regt. Travel allowance was made for him 26 Feb 1776, for 120 miles, also on 1 Apr 1776, dated Dorchester, MA. See also sibling John Young+, b 11 May 1755, for further war records.

Upon returning home from the war, Hezekiah relocated in a town that was originally known as Littlefalls, but in time became incorporated as Hollis in 1811, with the town of Dayton fragmenting therefrom [please see Topography for more details]. If census reports are any indication of population size, Hezekiah was undoubtedly the progenitor of the Youngs from this town and area. He was listed as head of household in census reports from 1790-1840 for Littlefalls. In the 1790 census for Littlefalls, his household contained one male under 16 and three females. From 1820-1840 he lived in Hollis: in 1820 his age was 45 plus, his family a large one containing three males, one each age 10-16, 16-26, and 26-45, and four females, two each under 10 and 10-16.

In 1830, with six Young heads of household then listed for Hollis, Hezekiah was the most senior member, age 70-80. His family then contained two other males, one each 20-30 and 30-40, and four females, the most senior member at age 60-70 (spouse), then one age 20-30, and two 15-20. In 1840 his age was 80-90, household containing a female figure age 60-70, poss. spouse, two other males ages 20-30 and 50-60, and one other female age 20-30.

The earliest deed found for Hezekiah of Littlefalls [later to become Dayton] described his sale of 92 acres land for 25 pounds lawful money, acreage by the river that had been sold for taxes by Joseph Dyer, Collector of Taxes, to Robert Nason by deed signed 24 Oct 1792, rec'd 21 Apr 1796; witnesses John Young [sibling], Joseph Patterson [York Deed 59:154]. On the following day, 25 Oct 1792, he sold to Joseph Nason of Littlefalls for 8 pounds lawful money, 71 acres land in Littlefalls, beginning at the Saco River; witnesses Joseph Patterson, John Young [York Deed 65:174].

Hezekiah's relationship to Thomas Young was given as son in land deed signed 23 Jul 1809, rec'd 31 Jul 1809, when John Young of Parsonsfield sold acreage with buildings thereon in Phillipsburg. John described the boundaries of the real estate in this fashion: "beginning at the N.E. corner of land of Hezekiah Young on the N.W. line, which land he bought from his father Thomas Young," to land once owned by Joseph Dyer, then S.W. to land of Dominicus Smith, etc. [York Deed 81:92].

He and wife Mary were buried at a private cemetery lot on Young Rivers Road, Dayton. Ch. b Biddeford: Hezekiah+, b 1789. **Dear reader, please note**: This main entry required a difficult judgment call to make: to decide whether there was one Hezekiah, not two, stemming from two different geographical areas and backgrounds. Putting aside geographics for a moment, it was decided there were enough deeds and vital records--baptism, marriage and burial record, to build a strong enough case that there was one only one Hezekiah in question. (Census York Co., 1800, p926; Mass. Soldiers & Sailors, p1020; Hale's Cems., n.p.; ME I.G.I.; Census York Co., 1790, p64; 1800, p926; 1820, p378; 1830, p170; 1840, Reel B, p321; ME Old Cem. Assoc., p781, No. 3686; Marr., Lyman, 1784-1831, by Rev. Simon Lock)

HEZEKIAH Jr., b 1789, Biddeford, s/o Hezekiah and Mary (Young) Young, resident of that part of Hollis that became Dayton in 1854, d 4 Jul 1875, Dayton, age 86, farmer, single. Hezekiah was listed head of household in Hollis in 1850; his spouse was Sally S. aka Sarah ( ) [1803]. Other family members included David [b 1808, poss. son, alive 1850-1860] and Eliza [b 1814]. In 1860 Hezekiah was head of household in Dayton per the census that year, farmer, with real estate valued at $2,000. Family members included spouse Sarah S., David mentioned above, and John Hood, age 14 [b 1846]. (Census York Co., 1850, Reel B, p107; 1860, Reel C, p980)

HIRAM, b 1852, of Shapleigh, lived at orphanage at age 8; matron was Roxanna Abbott [b 1802]. (Census York Co., 1860, Reel B, p657)

HIRAM, b May 1854, Waterboro, s/o Daniel and Eunice (Whitten) Young, d 1930, Sanford; m 21 Oct 1871, Wakefield, N.H., Mary M. Ham [b 1854, Newfield, d/o Charles and Mary (Shaw) Ham, d 1930, Sanford]. (Excerpt from Youngs of Strafford Co., N.H., Vol. I, p108; Picton's ME Cem. Inscrips., V3, p1941; NHVR-Marr)

HONORA ( ), n.d., widow of _____ Young of Biddeford per the 1890 ME Vets, Census Index of Civil War Vets or Their Widows, York Co. District SD#1, Enum.#208.

HULDAH, b ca 1750, York, filed (Ints.) 17 Mar 1770, m 1 Apr 1770, at First Parish Church, York, Samuel Shaw [b ca 1745, of same town]. (ME I.G.I.; Bragdon & Frost's York V.R., pp152, 357)

ICHABOD, b 1687, York, s/o Samuel and Elizabeth (Masterson) Young, blacksmith, drowned at sea Oct 1723, age 36; m (includes Ints.) 19 Apr 1716, Gloucester, MA, Abigail Elwell [b ca 1695, of Gloucester, alive 1824, same town]. Widow Abigail m2 (Ints.) 9 Dec 1724, Gloucester, John King [b ca 1700, of same town].

One land deed relating to Ichabod personally before his move from York to Gloucester, Essex County, MA was dated 28 Nov 1712, rec'd 7 Jul 1720: Ichabod and eldest brother Jonathan sold to their uncle Job Young of York, with the consent of their widowed mother Elizabeth Masterson Young for a certain sum of money, ten acres land in York where their father Samuel [then deceased] built a house and dwelt, "being a part of a grant of land given unto Rowland Young, the father of the said Samuel Young in the year 1667 by the town of York, and by said Rowland Young to...Samuel Young by deed of gift 18 Apr 1682." Please see sibling Jonathan Jr. of York for full citation.

Heirs-at-law Elizabeth Greeley [Ichabod's sister] and spouse Joseph Greeley of Kingston, N.H. sold to "our brother Jonathan Young" for twenty pounds old Tenor, all the right they held in the estate of our father and mother Samuel and Elizabeth Young of York by deed signed 9 Jul 1751, rec'd 6 Jun 1754; witnesses Jeremy Webster, Tristram Sanborn [York Deed 31:237-238]. And Ichabod's married daughter Abigail Newman and her husband Thomas Newman of Kingston sold to Abigail's uncle Jonathan Young, Gent. of York, for twenty pounds old Tenor, all their right in the estate of "our father Ichabod, and also of our grandfather Samuel Young and grandmother Elizabeth Young"; by deed signed 9 Jul 1751, rec'd 6 Jun 1754; witnesses Samuel Lock, Jeremy Webster [York Deed 31:237].

Ichabod, as full-time resident of Gloucester, earned the distinction of becoming one of the two Young progenitors of the town; for full details on his background and the marriages of his sister Elizabeth, daughter Abigail and son Ichabod Jr., please see Youngs of Essex County, MA., Vol. II.

Ch. b Gloucester, MA: Samuel, b 29 May 1717, d.y.; Abigail (Young) Newman, b 24 Oct 1718, w/o Thomas Newman; Samuel, b 16 Mar 1719, d 1738, age 19, native town; and Ichabod Jr., b 4 Aug 1722. (Noyes et al, p777; MA I.G.I.; Bank's Hist. of York, ME, VI, p229)

ICHABOD, b 15 Mar 1728, believed to be s/o Job and Patience (King) Young; filed (Ints.) 9 Apr 1753, York, Dorcas Young [b ca 1730, of same town]. (Bragdon & Frost's York V.R., p138; ME I.G.I)

ICHABOD, b ca 1730, of York, filed (Ints.) 28 Feb 1756, Hannah Dill [b ca 1735, of same town]. (Bragdon & Frost's York V.R., p141)

ISAAC J., b May 1853, Prince Edward Islands, alive 1900, Sanford, age 47; m pre 1886, ME, Florence S. (   ) [b Nov 1864, of ME, alive 1900, Sanford]. In 1900 Isaac J. was head of household in Sanford in 1900; family members at home were spouse Florence S. (   ), age 35 and their four sons. Ch. b ME, not traced further: Lawrence J., b Mar 1886; Jesse S., b Aug 1890; Andrew G., b Dec 1893; and Montague, b May 1896. (1900 ME Soundex)

ISRAEL, b ca 1680, of Eastham, Barnstable Co., MA, m 3 Jan 1708, Eastham, Katherine Frost [b ca 1685, heir-at-law of Nicholas Frost of Eastham, Barnstable Co.]. Israel and wife Katherine sold to Thomas Cole of Eastham for sixteen pounds, the one-sixth part or moiety of the upland meadow or marsh that Nicholas Frost [then deceased], used to own, situated in Newichawanock, York lands [Maine], deed signed 16 May 1715, rec'd 29 Jun 1715; witnesses Nathaniel Freeman, Mary Freeman [York Deed 8:123-124]. (MA I.G.I.)

ITHAMER, see THOMAS, b 1824

JABEZ, b 1772, York, alive 1820, same town, s/o Jonathan and Mercy (Wheeler) Young; m1 ca 1800, York, _____ [b ca 1780, d 15 Apr 1804, York]; filed (Ints.), m2 14 Dec 1811, York, Sarah aka Sally Grow [b 1789, of York, d 22 Dec 1820, York, age 32, of consumption].

The 1800-1820 census readings for York reported Jabez as head of household, age 26-45, with a spousal figure of the same age group in 1800. In 1810, he was widower with household containing two other males, one age under 10, the other age 16-26, and one female age 16-26. By 1820 the census revealed a spousal figure in his household, aged 26-45, and one young male under the age of 10.

One land deed was found for Jabez, a mortgage signed and rec'd 11 Jul 1803: Ephraim Littlefield, Theodore Webber, Gent. and Jabez, trader (both guardians of Ephraim), mortgaged to Edward Emerson Jr., Esq., 40 acres land in York including dwelling house, barn and blacksmith shop, for $218.00, bounded partly on Cape Neddick river and partly on Henry Talpey's land, and by lands of Daniel Simpson and David Webber, for the sum of $218.00 payable within one year, plus interest, to mortgagee Emerson; witnesses Daniel Sewall, Josiah Clark [York Deed 69:225)

Ch. b York, son, b pre 1820. (Bragdon & Frost's York V.R., pp198, 405, 417, 427, 601; Census York Co., 1800, p1021; 1810, p821; 1820, p582; ME I.G.I.)

JABEZ, b 1778, York, s/o Jonathan and Mercy (Nowell) Young, trader, Gent., d 27 Feb 1834, native town, age 56, of consumption; filed (Ints.) 12 Sep 1799, m 28 Nov 1799, at First Parish Church, York, Joanna Grant [b 1778, of York, d 4 May 1860, York, age 82, of dropsy, widow]. Jabez was named son and heir-at-law of Jonathan of York by will written 10 Nov 1798, probated __ Apr 1808, his inheritance to be one hundred dollars within four years' time after his father's death.

Vital records thus found have indicated there were two individuals by the name of Jabez whose backgrounds were somewhat similar, but land deeds helped to sort them out. The earliest land deed found for Jabez, s/o Jonathan of York, was signed and rec'd on 4 Dec 1799 when he bought for $240.00, two acres land in York with dwelling house from Matthew Perkins of York, his spouse Mary Perkins, the late widow of Richard Avery, ceding dower rights. Acreage was situated by the highway leading from Wells to York, which Nathaniel Freeman originally conveyed to Richard Avery, and by land of John Weare; witnesses Daniel Sewall, John Maxill [York Deed 65:3].

In Jabez's next deed dated 7 Oct 1800, rec'd same day, he held the mortgage of Ephraim Littlefield of York on five acres land in York, bounded easterly by Cape Neddick river; the acreage was mortgaged for $20.00, and was paid in full by Littlefield on 11 Jul 1802; witnesses Daniel Sewall, Joshua Bridges [York Deed 6:140]. His third known deed was signed 3 Nov 1800, rec'd three days later, when he bought from

William Stover of York for $30.00, a store and barn on land situated on the western side of the highway leading from York to Wells near Cape Neddick River in York; Anna Stover conveyed dower rights; witnesses Daniel and Abigail Sewall [York Deed 65:189].

The very same property Jabez bought from William Stover, exclusive of the barn mentioned in York Deed 65:189, was sold to Joseph Hutchings, mariner, for $200.00, with spouse Joanna Young relinquishing dower rights; deed signed 14 Oct 1801, rec'd the day after, witnesses William and Jacob Frost [York Deed 67:120].

Jabez sought mortgages from his father [pre 1807] on many of his properties in York, but in time overextended himself by so doing, most likely in anticipation of his father's bequests to him within four years of Jonathan's death. The first mortgage was for $800.00 based on speculation of property at Cape Neddick in York that was partly built up, and when finished, would contain 100 acres of land containing timber and other appurtenances; Jonathan of York complied, deed signed and rec'd 25 May 1801; witnesses Daniel and Abigail Sewall [York Deed 67:38]. The second mortgage Jabez sought from his father was on the heels of the first--$400.00 for two acres land in York with dwelling house that Jabez bought from Matthew and Mary Perkins of York late in 1799 [see above]--both signed and rec'd 3 Sep 1801, the proviso here being that Jabez make payment of the $400.00 within two months, plus interest; witnesses William Frost, Jacob Frost [York Deed 68:6].

Things began to get out of hand when Jabez was served with a Sheriff's Writ signed 5 Jan 1802, rec'd 13 Apr 1802: this was a demand that $177.35 be paid by Jonathan Young, 3rd of York, by virtue of an Execution issued upon a judgment of the Court of Common Pleas held at Boston, in favor of Bera. Tucker of Boston, merchant, against Jabez of York, trader: to sell to Jonathan Young a two-story house standing by the highway leading through Cape Neddick in York with land, dwelling house, and barn, "both being the property of Jabez Young, and being under the incumbrance of a mortgage from Jabez to Jonathan Young, due now $275.00," witnesses Daniel and Olive Sewell [York Deed 71:55].

Jabez had no other recourse to the Writ than to seek yet another mortgage from Jonathan, yeoman [parent or sibling?] for $250.00 on his "now" dwelling house with land in York at Cape Neddick, being the same piece of land he bought from William Stover on 3 Nov 1800, on condition that Jabez shall truly pay within six months from this date the sum of $250.00, plus interest; when paid, the deed would be void; witnesses William Frost, Jacob Frost [York Deed 68:160].

Following up on the Writ of Execution from the Court of Common Pleas cited above, the Sheriff declared that "recovered judgment" against Jabez Young of York, was $410.06 for damages, plus $9.15, cost of suit. "Execution remained to be done." The court ordered the property under the incumbrance of a mortgage to Jonathan Young be sold at public auction on 30 Mar 1804 at 2 p.m. and from the sale, the full damages and cost of suit would be paid in full to Bera. Tucker of Boston, merchant; deed signed 21 Feb 1804, rec'd 11 Apr 1804 [York Deed 70:272].

Interestingly enough, there appears to be a gap in the York Register of Deeds for Jabez from 1804 - 29 Sep 1810: on that date a dual recording of deeds was found. The first transaction signed on 12 Feb 1810, concerned Jabez's purchase at public auction, land held by widow Mary Hutchins, Admin. of the estate of her husband Joseph Hutchins of York: for $147.25, two-thirds part of the homestead containing 1-1/2 acres in York, N.E. by land of John Weare and N.W. by land set off to Mary Hutchins; this included the eastern end of the dwelling house and barn; witnesses David Sewall, James Hart [York Deed 83:113].

The other half of the dual recording was signed 9 Sep 1810: this involved Jabez mortgaging the very same property bought at public auction from Mary Hutchins of York as cited above, to Jonathan Young Jr. [sibling, b 1773, his father then deceased], Joseph Young [possibly sibling] and Nathaniel Parsons, all of York, for $200.00. The deed stipulated that the three grantees cited above were bound with Jabez by bond dated 7 Nov 1808; if Jabez indemnified (compensated) them, then the deed would become void; witnesses Daniel Sewall, James Hart [York Deed 83:113].

In the following year, another land deed was recorded wherein Jabez and Jonathan Young Jr. [sibling], both of York, were co-grantors, signed 28 Sep 1811, rec'd 1 Oct 1811: they sold to Peter Weare of York, mariner, for $600.00, a two-story house and stable standing by the highway leading through Cape Neddick in York, conveyed to Jabez by William Stover on 3 Nov 1800. Nancy Young, wife of Jonathan, conveyed dower rights; witnesses William Frost, James Hart [York Deed 84:236].

Ch. b York: Joanna, b Jan 1815, d 28 Feb 1816, 13 mos., native town. (ME I.G.I.; Bragdon & Frost's York V.R., pp183, 365, 412, 439; 1860 Mort. Sched., York Co.)

JAMES, b 19 May 1786, Limington, farmer, s/o David and Elizabeth (Smith) Young, d 24 Dec 1852, So. Limington, age 66, widower. Taylor's **Limington, ME** indicated that James married three times: m1 12 Oct 1816, Limington, Sarah Davis [b ca 1795]; m2 4 Mar 1821, Polly (Small) Coffin [b ca 1800]; and m3 17 Mar 1844, Alice Boulter Thomas aka Elsie Thombs [b 1803, of Standish, alive 1850, Limington, married].

The 1820, 1830 and 1850 census reports for Limington showed James as resident. In 1820 at age of 26-45 he was single and lived alone; in 1830 at age 40-50, there was no spousal figure, but rather, he was a recent widower inasmuch as there were three young children in the household, two males, ages 5-10 and 10-15, and one female under 5. In 1850 at age 64, James lived with third spouse Alice, age 47, and his widowed mother Elizabeth, age 86. There were four children at home: Martha J., Albert, Mary J. and Edmund. It is believed that son Albert, age 28, was then married, his spouse Martha included in the census taking of the household, age 25 [b 1825]. James was buried at the cemetery on Davis Boothby Road, South Limington.

It was not readily clear as to which spouse was buried with James. Hale's **Cems.** indicated that "Mary, b 23 Sep 1787, d 23 Feb 1841," was buried with James. However, Taylor's **Limington** did not list a marriage between James and Mary, but rather, three other marriages were on record.

Ch. b Limington: Albert+, b 1822; Martha Jane, b 1830; Mary J., b 1846; and Edmund, b 1849. (Hale's Cems., n.p.; Census York Co., 1820, p525; 1830, p157; 1850, Reel C, p294; Taylor's **Limington**, TMs, pp79, 83, 111, 152)

JAMES, b 1800, Wakefield, N.H., s/o James and Mary (Kimball) Young [no main entry], resident of West Parsonsfield, d 10 Apr 1868, same town, age 68, widower; (Ints.) 10 Dec, 1825, m 5 Jan 1826, Parsonsfield, Aurelia Marston [b 1803, ME, d 3 Sep 1866, West Parsonsfield, age 63, married]. For full details on James' parents and heritage, please see Youngs of Strafford Co., N.H., Vol. I. The married couple were buried at the Dodge-Marston-Doe Cemetery in Parsonsfield. (Picton's ME Cem. Inscrips., V2, p1359; Hale's Cems., n.p.; Parsonsfield V.R., Town Clerk, pp92, 104; Hobb's Cem. Recs., Parsonsfield, p4)

JAMES, b 1837, Wales, resident of Limerick, cigar maker. James enlisted 26 Sep 1864 for a three-year term, mustered in two days later, from Augusta, in the 19th Infantry. His complexion was light, eyes were blue, and hair was brown; he stood 5' 8" tall. (Civil War records res. by T. E. Brooks of Maine)

JAMES, b ca 1845, St. Johns, N.B., m 2 Feb 1870, South Berwick, Georgianna Summ [b ca 1850, Philadelphia, PA]. (Mormon/ME V.R., Wright-Zitkov]

JAMES MADISON, b 4 Jun 1849, South Berwick, s/o James Morrill and Susan (Henderson) Young of Lebanon, d 21 May 1936, native town, age 87, widower; m ca 1874, Mary S. Ryan [b 24 Jun 1852, Ireland, d 28 Jul 1925, South Berwick, married]. James M. was listed as member of his parents' household in South Berwick in the 1860 census at age 11. In 1900 he was head of household in his native town at age 50, his home address on Vine Street. Family members included spouse Mary S. and daughters Nellie F. and Ella M. James M., Mary and their four daughters were buried at South Berwick. Ch. b South Berwick, not traced further: Mary S., b 1 Apr 1875, d pre 1900; Jennie K., b 25 Nov 1866, d 2 Dec 1876; Dora M., b 28 Dec 1878, d 27 Mar 1879; and Susie Mabel, b 7 Apr 1879, d 20 Oct 1880. (1900 ME Soundex; Picton's ME Cem. Inscrips., V3, p2059)

JAMES MORRILL, b 6 May 1813, Lebanon, manufacturer, s/o Joseph and Patience (Wentworth) Young, d 22 Apr 1888, South

Berwick, age 73; m 9 Mar 1836, prob. Rollingsford, N.H., Susan P. Henderson [b 7 Dec 1814, N.H., d 22 Jul 1894, South Berwick]. By 1840 James and family settled in South Berwick per census that year which listed him as head of family, age 20-30. Family contained a spousal figure of the same age bracket and one young male age under five. By 1850 James, spouse and family had relocated in Middleton, N.H., but only for a short while. For this phase of their lives, please see Youngs of Strafford Co., N.H., Vol. I.

The 1860 census established that James and family had returned to Maine to live in South Berwick, his wife's age then 48, their real estate valued at $1,000. At home were grown sons Lysander and James M. Jr., and Lysander's wife Martha Winn Young [b 1840]. James M. and spouse Susan P., son Lysander B. and his wife Martha J. and their two sons were buried at South Berwick.

Ch. b ME: Lysander Bascom+, b 19 Jun 1836; Sarah Semantha+ (Young) Luke, b 12 Nov 1840; and James Madison+ aka Jr., b 4 Jun 1849. Ch. b prob. Middleton, NH: Melissa, b Sep 1849. (Wentworth Gen., V1, pp456-457; ME & N.H. I.G.I.; Census York Co., 1840, Reel B, p214; 1860, Reel B, p803; Picton's ME Cem. Inscrips., V3, pp2050-2051)

JAMES W., please see John W.+, b 30 May 1851.

JAMES W., b Feb 1856, South Berwick, s/o John M. and Mary A. ( ) Young, alive 1900, native town, age 44. His wife was Lizzie L. ( ) [b 2 Feb 1867, d 25 Aug 1896, South Berwick, age 29.] He was a young lad of four in his parents' household per the 1860 census for South Berwick. By 1900, he was widower and head of his own household at age 44, in his native town, with six children at home. His spouse Lizzie L. apparently was related to the Warren family inasmuch as she was buried in the Warren plot, on the N.W. side of Tatnic Road, to the rear of the residence of Joseph W. Turbull in South Berwick.

Ch. b South Berwick, not traced further: Ida M., b Sep 1873; Edwin R., b Feb 1886; Fred R., b May 1887; Ethel M., b Dec 1888; Rowland W., b Apr 1892; and Daisy E., b Jul 1894. (1900 ME Soundex; Picton's ME Cem. Inscrips., V3, p2094; see also p1995 which holds slight variations.)

JAMES W., b 1870, of Kennebunk, d 1915, same town, married. James, spouse Louella S. ( ) [b 1868, d 1949, of Kennebunk, widow], and baby [b 1893] were buried at a Kennebunk cemetery. (Picton's ME Cem. Inscrips., V2, p833)

JANE ( ), b Feb 1821, England, widow of ____ Young per the 1900 Soundex for Sanford, age 79, married before 1848. Two daughters lived at home. Ch. b England: Nellie, b Dec 1848; Tibbie, b Dec 1855. (1900 ME Soundex)

JANE (WENTWORTH), b Dec 1820, N.H., widow of ____ Young, resident of Berwick in 1900, age 79. Living with her was her mother Abbie Wentworth, n.d. (1900 ME Soundex)

JASPER S., b Sep 1847, resident of Old Orchard Town in 1900, age 52. He lived with spouse Eliza A. ( ) [b Apr

1847], and four children. Ch. b ME, not traced further: Mary B., b Apr 1880; Florence, b Nov 1886; Prescott J., b Sep 1889; and Amy S., b Mar 1893. (1900 ME Soundex)

JERUSHA, b 15 Mar 1711, York, d/o Jonathan and Margaret (Stackpole) Young; filed (Ints.) 2 Jun 1739, m 12 Jul 1739, York, Joseph Hatch, widower [b 8 May 1709, of Wells, s/o Samuel and Mary (Littlefield) Hatch]. Joseph Hatch's first wife was Hannah Sawyer [b ca 1710, York, d pre 1739, native town]. (ME I.G.I.; Bragdon & Frost's York V.R., p126)

JERUSHA, b 1802, York, m 16 May 1821, Bangor, Penobscot Co., Moses Hodsdon [b ca 1797, Berwick]. (ME I.G.I.)

JESSE, b 1780s, York, s/o Joel and Mary (Allen) Young, alive 1830, native town; filed (Ints.) 13 Jun 1819, m 24 Oct 1819, York, Hannah Sayward [b ca 1795, of York, alive 1830, same town]. Jesse, apparently eldest son, and sibling Joel were named Co-Execs. and residuary legatees of their father's estate in York by will signed 5 Aug 1820, probated 2 Dec 1828. His inheritance included part of the homestead farm and woodland in York.

The 1820-1830 census reports for York listed Jesse as resident: in 1820, when they had just married, his age was 26-45, and a spousal figure's age was 16-26; in 1830 he was 40-50, and she was 30-40, with a growing family containing two males, one each under 5 and 5-10, and three females, two under 5 and one age 5-10. (Bragdon & Frost's York V.R., p210; Census York Co., 1820, p604)

JOAN, b 10 Mar 1731/2, York, d/o Job and Patience (King) Young, m ca 1750, York, Michael McDonald [b ca 1725, of York]. McDonald ch. b York: Betty McDonald, b 1 Aug 1754; Daniel Mcdonald, b 23 Feb 1757; and James McDonald, b 25 Apr 1759. (Bragdon & Frost's York V.R., p82)

JOANNA, b ca 1800, of Parsonsfield; (Ints.) 6 Dec 1818, m 10 Jan, 1819, Parsonsfield, John Allen [b ca 1795, of same town]. (Parsonsfield V.R., Town Clerk, pp82, 87)

JOB, b 1664, York, s/o Rowland and Joan (Knight) Young, fisherman, prob. alive Jan 1732, age 68, native town, widower; m post Oct 1691, York, Sarah (Austin) Preble [b ca 1667, York, d/o Matthew Austin, weaver, widow of Joseph Preble, d 24 May 1720, native town, married]. Job served on the Grand Jury in 1694 and 1696. An early court record was found for Job dated 2 Oct 1716, at which time he was named as member of the Jury of Trials at the Inferior Court of Common Pleas [Court of Gen. Sessions, V5, p75]. The other occasion Job served on this panel was dated 29 Jan 1716/17 [Court of Gen. Sessions, V5, p84].

Numerous land deeds were found for Job, from 1701 up through the 1720s. They were drawn up with exactitude and fairness inasmuch as he was distributing his entire estate through deeds of gift to sons Rowland and Job Jr., while other land transactions dealt with nephews Jonathan and Ichabod. The first deed showed he was co-grantor with Lewis Bane of York, Bane's wife Mary ceding dower rights, in the sale of land in York formerly granted to Nicholas Davis 14 Jul 1701: Job sold his moiety, naming wife Sarah Austin Young who conveyed dower rights [York Deeds 7:31, 242]. In 1709, Job and brother-in-law Thomas Haynes conveyed four acres marsh land in Kittery formerly belonging to Rowland Young, "father of said Job and Thomas Haynes' wife," Lydia Young Haynes, to Alexander and Joseph Junkins of York by deed dated 3 Jan 1709, rec'd 1 Jan 1716/7; witnesses Daniel Black and Abraham Preble Jr. [York Deed 8:192].

In the next deed signed 28 Nov 1712, rec'd 7 Jul 1720, Job bought from his nephews Jonathan Jr. and Ichabod, the eldest and second sons of his brother Samuel, with the consent of their widowed mother Elizabeth Masterson Young, for a certain sum of money, ten acres land in York where Samuel Young had built a house and dwelt, "being a part of a grant of land given to Rowland Young, father of said Samuel Young in 1667 by the town of York, and by said Rowland Young to...Samuel Young by deed of gift 18 Apr 1682." See nephews Jonathan and Ichabod for documentation of deed.

On 6 Jan 1712/3, Job petitioned the court for confirmation of allowance for bringing up the children of Joseph Preble, lately deceased, and Sarah Austin Preble, their mother, until they reached the age of seven: the oldest, Nahemiah Preble, age 3-1/4 years, to the youngest, Joseph Preble, then age 5 to 7 months. The sum of 71-15-0 was allowed 6 Jan 1712 [York Probate #15461].

By deed dated the following day, Job and Sarah conveyed to William Bracey of York for a certain sum of money, 25 acres situated on the N.W. side of the fall mill brook, being one half of a 50 acre lot belonging to Job and Lewis Bean, which was formerly granted to Nicholas Davis by the town of York and given by said Davis to his son-in-law Matthew Austin, the father of Job's wife Sarah; witnesses John Burrell, Joseph Preble, rec'd 9 Jan 1712/3 [York Deed 7:243].

Two deeds of gift were made by Job and Sarah when they conveyed land held in fee simple (i.e., inherited) to eldest son Rowland: (1) deed signed 12 Feb 1714, rec'd 7 Jul 1720 for conveying twenty acres land in York situated on the S.E. side of the highway that leads from the meeting house to Cape Neddick and Wells, and by lands of George Norton to Job's fence; witnesses Johnson Harmon, Richard Milberry [York Deed 10:47]; (2) deed signed 26 Nov 1723, rec'd 10 Dec 1723 which conveyed an additional ten acres land situated upon the S.E. side of the highway leading from York Meeting House towards Cape Neddick, adjacent to Rowland's house and bounded on the S.E. side by lands of the late Joseph Ware; witnesses John Preble, John Burrell, Lewis Bane [York Deed 11:115-116].

Yet another deed of sale was made by Job for the sum of 28 pounds current money when he sold to John Woodbridge of York by deed signed 6 Dec 1723, rec'd 9 Dec 1723, a certain piece of swamp or meadow ground in York located on the N.E. side of the highway leading from the lower end of the town to the meeting house, being a part of Job's homestead which held about five acres, N.W. adjacent to Woodbridge's own land upon the N.E. end by Rowland Young's land, and by the land now in possession of the widow Hannah Ware aka Weare on the S.E. side; witnesses Joseph Moulton, Jeremiah Moulton [York Deed 11:115].

Another deed of gift was made by Job, widower, to sons Rowland and Job Jr., signed 21 Mar 1724, rec'd 6 Nov 1724: "all the land tenements where I now dwell" in York bounded on the S.W. end of a creek commonly known by the name of the Meeting House Creek, bounded on said road on the N.E., on the N.W. by land of John Woodbridge, and on the S.E. side by land of the Widow Black; witnesses John Woodbridge, Jeremiah Moulton [York Deed 11:169]. Included in this deed were "Articles of Agreement" drawn up for the benefit of Job's sons Rowland and Job Jr. which spelled out exactly how their father's estate and debts would be handled between them: (1) Rowland to receive two-thirds of their father's home lot, but was to pay two-thirds of their father's debts (which was forty pounds on the whole), and (2) Job Jr. to have one-third of their father's house lot, while he was to pay only one-third of their father's lawful debts, terms of which both sons accepted.

From the following deed it was learned that Job's occupation was fisherman: he sold for 25 pounds current money to Joseph Swett of York, yeoman, 30 acres land held in fee simple, located in York near Josiah's River which empties into Wells, deed of sale signed 25 Feb 1726/7, rec'd 17 Mar 1726/7 [York Deed 12:107].

Inasmuch as Job Sr.'s date of death was not firmly established, this next deed signed 2 Jan 1732, rec'd 7 Feb 1732, was provisionally entered here under Job Sr., rather than son Job Jr.: Job sold his "eight shares or common rights in the Common or undivided lands" in York, held in fee simple, to Caleb Preble of York for eight pounds current money; witnesses Edward Carpenter, John Higgins, Samuel Hamill [York Deed 15:179].

Ch. b York: Rowland+, b ca 1695; poss. Jonathan+, b ca 1696; Job+ Jr., b ca 1697; Joseph, b ca 1690s; Lydia+ (Young) Weare Wells, b ca 1700; Sarah+ (Young) Favour, b ca 1702. (Noyes et al, pp567, 775-776; ME I.G.I.; Bragdon & Frost's York V.R., p41)

JOB, b ca 1670, resident of York, ma pre 1719, York, Hannah ( ) [b ca 1675, of York]. By deed signed 26 Oct 1719, rec'd 10 Jun 1720, Job sold 30 acres land in York, located N.W. of the marsh called Barberry Marsh and Joseph Preble's house lot where he then lived (land that was granted to Job at a York town meeting 22 Mar 1697, and laid out to him 27 Nov 1702), to Benjamin Stone and Abiel Goodwin, both of York for fifteen pounds money; Hannah, his wife relinquished Dower Rights; witnesses Samuel Black, Abraham Preble, Diamond Sargent [York Deed 10:42].

JOB Jr., b ca 1697, York, laborer, s/o Job and Sarah (Austin) Preble Young, filed (Ints.) 11 Nov 1727, m 17 Nov 1727, Kittery, 7 Dec 1727, York, Patience King [b ca 1700, Kittery]. Job's name appeared on York Town's list regarding the final divisions of land in York, dated 20 Jun 1732, according to which he was granted eight shares. Five of these shares were sold to Nathaniel Donnell of York for seven pounds, 10 shillings by deed signed 3 Apr 1738, rec'd 11 Nov 1741; witnesses ___ Perkins, Allen Norwood [York Deed 22:235].

"Articles of Agreement" were arrived at between siblings Job Jr. and Rowland, by instrument signed 21 Mar 1724, rec'd 6 Nov 1724, as to how their father's estate and debts were to be handled upon his death, it being formally agreed upon that Job Jr. was to receive one-third of his father's house, but only paying one-third of their father's debts, while Rowland, as eldest son, accepted the remaining two-thirds inheritance with its responsibilities, in the interest of protecting their inheritances.

On same date as above agreement, Job Jr. and sibling Rowland sold to Jacob Curtis of York for 180 pounds money, the piece of land which their father settled upon and built his dwelling house, bounded by lands of John Woodbridge on the N.W. side and the Widow Sarah Black's on the S.E. side, running from said Meeting House Creek N.E. on two straight lines 40 rods in breadth to the country road; please see entry on Rowland for full documentation of these last two deeds.

Ch. b York: Ichabod+, b 15 Mar 1728; Sarah, b 18 Feb 1730, d 26 Mar 1731, age 1 mo., 8 days; Joan+ (Young) McDonald, b 10 Mar 1731/2; Sarah, b 23 Jul 1734; Robert+, b 20 Mar 1736/7; Job+ Jr., b 21 Apr 1739; Samuel, b 21 May 1740; Susannah, b 26 Feb 1741, d.y.; Susannah, b 21 Feb 1742; Phebe+ (Young) Young, b 8 May 1744; Patience, b 5 Dec 1745; Timothy, b 25 Dec 1747; and Dorcas, b 9 Oct 1750. (Noyes et al, pp31, 775; ME I.G.I.; Bragdon & Frost's York V.R., pp44, 82, 118, 392; Kittery V.R., p94)

JOB Jr., b 21 Apr 1739, York, s/o Job and Patience (King) Young of York, filed (Ints.) 26 Dec 1760, m 22 Jan 1761, York, Hannah Dill [b ca 1740, of same town]. (ME I.G.I.; Bragdon & Frost's York V.R., p144)

JOB, b 1788, York, s/o John and Naomi (   ) Young; filed (Ints.) 24 Jul 1806, York, Joanna Banks [b 1789, d 13 Jan 1817, York, age 28]. Job was named residuary legatee of his father's estate in York, and Co-Exec. with his mother Naomi, by will written 30 May 1801, probated 21 Feb 1803. He and mother, widow Naomi, sold by deed signed 28 Apr 1803, rec'd 11 Jan 1806, part of their homestead in York where they then lived, to Josiah Gilman, physician, extending the right to him to build upon or enlarge the house. A codicil to the land deed was attached on 24 Oct 1809, rec'd 22 Jun 1815, in which Job, "now being of age," attested that this deed was his free act and acknowledged that he had reached majority; witnesses

Stephen Preble, Joseph Young; please see full documentation of deeds under his father's entry.

Job was listed resident of York in the 1810 census, age 26-45. Family contained a maternal figure age 45 plus, and two other females, one under 10 and the other age 16-26. (Bragdon & Frost's York V.R., pp191, 413; Census York Co., 1810, p821)

JOEL, b ca 1758, York, eldest s/o Masterson and Sarah (Curtis) Young, d 5 May 1828, suddenly, native town, age ca 70, married; filed (Ints.) 2 Nov 1782, m 12 Dec 1782 at First Parish Church, York, Mary Allen [b ca 1760, of York, widowed in 1828, York]. Joel was listed as resident of York in four census reports from 1790-1820: in 1790 two other males were at home, both under 16 years of age, and one female; by 1800 Joel's age and that of the spousal figure advanced to the 26-45 bracket, household containing three males, one age under 10, one 10-16, and one 16-26.

In 1810 both he and a spousal figure were age 45 plus, with household of three other males, one age 10-16, one 16-26, and one 26-45; the distaff side held one other female under the age of 10. Lastly, in 1820 both Joel's and spousal figure's ages were 45 plus, with one other male in the household, age 16-26. It would be safe to assume that in 1830, Joel's widow Mary, age 70-80, lived in son Joel Jr.'s household in York per the census that year.

The first known property bought by Joel was a certain share in the York Common Lands, by deed signed and rec'd 10 Mar 1791: for 9 pounds lawful money, 14 shares in Lot No. 4, 1st Div., or 15 acres in all, from Elihu Bragdon of York, being the same land Bragdon bought from his father Arthur Bragdon by York Deed 49:64, in common and undivided with his uncle Capt. Thomas Bragdon; witnesses William Frost, Reuben Darby [York Deed 53:152]. The following year Joel bought at public auction from John Swett of York, Exec. of the estate of the late John Swett, Esq., for 40-19-0, 19-1/2 acres land in York beginning at the highway leading to Berwick by lands of Masterson Young and the widow Sarah Swett, leading to Bass Cove Creek and the highway, by deed signed and rec'd 26 Mar 1792; witnesses William Frost, Nathaniel Frost [York Deed 54:200].

Near the end of 1792, by deed signed 14 Dec 1792, rec'd the next day, Joel bought from widow Sarah Swett of York for 38-15-0 lawful money, 11 acres, 62 rods of mowing land in York, the widow stating it was "the same land that was my father's Joseph Plaisted, late of York, Esq," witnesses William Frost, John Moulton [York Deed 56:26]. On same date of recording, Joel stipulated in writing that he granted Widow Swett free liberty "to pass and repass through his field in the way that is usually passed," in order to haul up her hay [same witnesses, York Deed 56:27].

By will signed 6 Jun 1795 by their father Masterson, proved 17 Aug 1795, Joel and brother Jonathan were named joint

Execs. and residuary legatees of Masterson's estate, Joel to have the house where he then dwelt, and Jonathan the house where Masterson then dwelt, but the barn was to be shared equally as well as the funeral cost and legacies. On same date the will was signed, Joel sold to sibling Jonathan Jr. for 39-14-0, the one-half part of a certain tract of land in York, 19-1/2 acres which Joel bought from John Swett and 11 acres, 65 rods that he bought from widow Sarah Swett, deed rec'd 4 Jul 1795; witnesses Daniel Sewall, John Swett [York Deed 57:230].

Several land deeds were found to be signed jointly by brothers Joel and Jonathan, yeomen. The first of these was dated 1 Jun 1796, rec'd 14 Jun 1796: their maiden aunts Sarah and Dorcas Young sold to them for $267.00, all their right and title to the real estate of their late father Jonathan Young, each nephew to receive equal shares; for full documentation on deed, please see main entry under Jonathan and Abigail Came Young. Their second joint deed was signed and rec'd 14 Oct 1802, wherein the brothers bought from Theodore Grant of York, yeoman, for $11.00, the one-quarter part of a mill privilege in York called Fall Mill Brook, which Grant bought from James Gray and Tamsen, his wife; witnesses Daniel and Abigail Sewall [York Deed 69:20].

Yet a third known deed between the brothers turned up, dated 5 Apr 1803, rec'd 9 Apr 1803: for $12.00, they bought from John and Daniel Moulton of York four acres land situated by lands of Samuel Young and brothers Joel and Jonathan, acreage that the Moulton brothers owned at the S.W. end of the lot, fenced in; Persis, wife of John Moulton and Abigail, w/o Daniel Moulton released their dower rights; witnesses William Frost, Lydia Lowe, John Lambly, Josiah Moulton [York Deed 68:267].

Joel was also named an heir-at-law in his mother's will of 16 Feb 1814, probated Nov 1819, but the terms of the will clearly reminded him he had already received his "full proportion of the estate." His own will signed 5 Aug 1820 and probated 2 Dec 1828, named sons Jesse and Joel as joint Execs. and co-residuary legatees of his estate; witnesses Alexander McIntire, Joseph Gilman, Samuel Sayward [York Probate #20938]. His wife Mary was to receive her thirds of the real estate, one half of the cattle and one half the furniture, son Masterson to receive $5.00, and married daughter Mary Simpson, w/o Ivory Simpson, one hundred dollars in neat stock.

However, a codicil written 2 May 1828 updated the terms of Joel's bequest to son Masterson: instead of the original $5.00, Masterson (2nd) was to receive "all the right Joel had in the property which Masterson purchased of Timothy Simpson and which was deeded from Masterson to Joel, excepting the N.W. field reserved for sons Joel and Jesse." It was stressed that the terms of the codicil could not be contested, or Masterson would forfeit the bequest. Daughter Mary Simpson's inheritance was then revised downward to $50.00.

Ch. b York: Jesse+, b 1780s; Masterson+, Esq., b 1783; Joel S.+ Jr., b 1790; Mary+ (Young) Simpson, b ca 1800. (Census York Co., 1790, p72, 1800, p1034, 1810, p822; Bragdon & Frost's York V.R., pp164, 362, 423)

JOEL S. Jr., b 1790, York, farmer, s/o Joel and Mary (Allen) Young, d pre 6 Apr 1869, York, married, testate; filed (Ints.) 5 Feb 1825, m 10 Apr 1825, Alfred, Susan Sayward [b 1805, of Alfred, d 1876, York, age 71, widow].   Joel and sibling Jesse were named Co-Execs. and residuary legatees of their father Joel's estate by will signed 5 Aug 1820, proved 2 Dec 1828.

The census reports for York listed Joel as head of household for 1830-1860 inclusive: in 1830 his age was 30-40, with family containing an elderly female figure age 70-80 [his widowed mother, no doubt], a spousal figure age 20-30, and one male and one female both under the age of 5; in 1840 Joel's age was 40-50, with a family of two males both under 15, a female figure age 30-40 and three other young females, one each age 15-20, 10-15 and 5-10. The 1850 census found Joel's age to be 55, his spouse Susan's age 45, the family containing five children Albert, Julia, Mary, Joseph, and Samuel.   In 1860 Joel's real estate was appraised at $3,000; at home were spouse Susan, age 55, and three sons Albert, Joel Jr. and Samuel.

Joel's own will written 27 Jun 1855, proved 6 Apr 1869, established that oldest son Albert was named sole Exec. and residuary legatee of his estate; witnesses Mark Dennett, Oren W. Dennett, Julia A. Clough [York Probate #20939].   The bequest to wife Susan comprised the household furniture and one-half of the neat stock during her natural life.   Other heirs-at-law received these bequests: daughter Julie, $50.00 and the right of a home while she remained single; son Joel S., $275; and son Samuel P. to receive $275 when he arrived at age 21.

Family members were buried at York Cemetery, York, Lot #42. A woman by the name of Hannah Phillips [b 1800, d 1872, York, age 72] was also buried at this family plot, kinship unknown. Ch. b York: Albert+, b Apr 1826; Julia M.+ (Young) Mitchell, b Sep 1829; Mary, b 1832, d 23 Dec 1852, age 20, of consumption, native town; Joseph, b 1836; Joel S. Jr., b 1837, at home 1860, teacher; and Samuel P., b 1846, at home in 1860. (Bragdon & Frost's York V.R., pp221, 433; Frost's York Cem., p621; ME I.G.I.; Hale's Cems., n.p.; Census York Co., 1830, p249; 1840, Reel B, p259; 1850, Reel A, p216; 1860, Reel C, p959; Picton's ME Cem. Inscrips., V3, p2373; MH&G **Rec.**, V4, p268)

JOHN, b 2 Nov 1649, Exeter, NH, s/o John and Sarah (   ) Young of Saco and Wells [no main entry], slain by Indians 10 Jun 1697, native town; filed (Ints.) Feb 1671, Exeter, Sarah Wadleigh [b 1655, prob. Wells, d/o Robert and Sarah (Smith) Wadleigh of England, alive 1733, age 78, Exeter].

Please see Youngs of Essex County, MA, Vol. II for extensive entry on John and family stemming from Exeter which included vital records, land deeds, probate and early civic court records, etc.

Additional land deeds of John and Sarah Young of Exeter that were on record in York County were included here. By deed of gift dated 1 Sep 1675, Sarah received her marriage portion from her father Robert Wadleigh of Lamprell River in the County of Norfolk [Old Norfolk], a one-third share of his farm which he had received from his father John Wadleigh, situated on the S.W. side next to the Town lot, both upland, meadow, and salt marsh, beginning at Webbhannet River and so extends backward into the country; also one third part of the falls upon that brook which runs past his dwelling house for the building of a mill, deed rec'd 18 Nov 1685; witnesses John Barber, John Wadleigh [York Deed 4:47].

This very same parcel of land representing Sarah's marriage portion was sold by John and Sarah "in full satis-faction" to William Sawyer of Wells by deed dated 7 Aug 1685, rec'd 23 Nov 1685; witnesses James Daniel, Henry Wadleigh [York Deed 4:47-48]. It should be noted that main entries on each of their sons listed below will be found in the Youngs of Essex County, MA, Vol. II.

Ch. b Exeter: John, b ca 1672; Robert, b ca 1674; Joseph, b ca 1675, Israel, b ca 1677; Daniel, b ca 1680; and James, b 1685. (Noyes et al, pp13, 707, 775-776; NH Gen. Recs. 3:84; LDS Computer Search)

JOHN, b ca 1690, of Boston, Suffolk Co., joiner, d pre Jan 1772, Salem; m1 21 May 1713, Boston, Elizabeth LeBreton [b ca 1695, Boston, d/o Philip and Elizabeth (   ) LeBreton, alive 1736, d pre 1743, Salem]. (Please see John's main entry in Youngs of Essex County, MA, Vol. II.)

Early York County deeds did indeed yield one land record for John and spouse Elizabeth of Boston: on 15 Feb 1715, rec'd 15 May 1718, Elizabeth's parents conveyed to her and her husband John Young, sixty acres land lying at Falmouth in the County of Maine bounded on the S.W. side upon the Casco river, west upon the land of Thadeus Clark, and east upon the land of James Frieze by a town grant, per records of Falmouth, thirty acres of which were sold to Phillip LeBreton by Dennis Marrough, and the other thirty acres being granted to LeBreton by the town of Falmouth with all salt and fresh meadows; witnesses Thomas Bedell, Robert Forrester [York Deed 9:46-47].

JOHN, b ca 1700, of St. George's River. John signed an indenture dated 26 Jan 1733, rec'd 3 May 1744, in favor of Samuel Waldo of Boston, Esq., Suffolk Co., for five shillings sterling, in consideration of the rent especially paid of one peppercorn per annum that would be paid yearly by Young on every 29th day of September forever; now in his actual possession by virtue of a grant made to sundry of the inhabit-ants on the upper part of St. George's River and by the force of the statute made in Great Britain, all that parcel of

54

upland ground and swamp in St. George's River on the eastern side, the western branch containing 100 acres, by land of Alexander Campbell, known as Lot No. 11; witnesses William Lithgow, Pat James [York Deed 24:170].

The following year, it was agreed by deed signed 9 Oct 1734, rec'd 3 May 1744, that John would pay said Waldo five shillings yearly on every 25th June on the 100-acre Lot No. 11; witnesses Arthur Savage, Robert McIntire [York Deed 24:156].

JOHN, b 1720, York, mariner, s/o Rowland and Hannah (   ) Young, d 11 Jan 1803, York, age 83; m ca 1745, Sarah Dixon [b ca 1725, of same town]. Two deeds were found with John as grantee, father Rowland as grantor, within a nine-year period between 1746-1755. The first of these was signed and rec'd 15 May 1746, when Rowland sold John three acres land in York which fronted north on the road leading to Long Sands, and east by land of Col. Nathaniel Donnell, S.W. by lands of the late Samuel Black and N.W. by Peter Weare's land, enclosed within a fence. The other document was a deed of gift from Rowland to son John, signed and rec'd 14 Feb 1755, which agreed that John would receive one acre of land from Rowland's homestead "as part of John's portion of the estate where Rowland then dwelt," situated north of Rowland's now dwelling house by the country road, with the liberty to build on the land or enlarge the same dwelling house; see John's father's entry for full documentation.

John and daughter Eleanor [in lieu of Eleanor's deceased sibling John] were the residuary legatees cited in Rowland's will signed 27 Aug 1771, codicil written 6 Jun 1781, and probated 8 Apr 1782. The homestead itself was comprised of a few acres land in York. Included in the family estate were six shares in Lot No. 5 , 1st Div. of the Common Lands which were bequeathed to John, three of which he sold to Jonathan Young of York [specific kinship not known], yeoman for three pounds, 12 shillings, by deed signed and rec'd 4 Apr 1791; witnesses William Frost, Reuben Darby [York Deed 53:181].

Ch. b York: John Jr., b ca 1745, died as a youth; Sarah, b 19 Feb 1749, d 12 Apr 1750, native town; Eleanor, b 12 Jan 1750, was age 21-31 when she died, between date of will and date of codicil. (ME I.G.I.; Bragdon & Frost's York V.R., pp70, 405)

JOHN, b ca 1725, of York. John made deed of gift to grandson William Norton [b ca 1771, of York], dated 22 Dec 1794, rec'd 6 Feb 1795, for the sum of 5 shillings: one-third part of an acre in York, where Norton built a house, property lines beginning by the highway by land of the widow Olive Grow, as her dower in the estate of Edward Grow, and by land of Thomas Lowe; witnesses Samuel Bragdon, Joseph Tucker [York Deed 57:131]. For similarities of property lines, please see main entry on John and Hannah (Banks) Young.

JOHN, b 1726, of Lebanon, d 3 Sep 1785, same town, age 59, Lebanon; m1 Susannah Gatchell [b ca 1730, of same town];

m2 Theodora (Wheelock) Phelps [b ca 1735, of same town. (ME Old Cem. Assoc., p781, No. 6114)

JOHN, b ca 1735, of York, filed (Ints.) 23 Oct 1756, m 21 Nov 1756, York, Elizabeth Hill [b ca 1740, of same town, d/o James Hill]. Ch. b York: John+ Jr., b 15 Sep 1757; Elizabeth, b 8 Feb 1759; Sarah, b 20 Oct 1760; Pamela+ aka Parmela (Young) Hill, b 1 Feb 1763. (ME I.G.I.; Bragdon & Frost's York V.R., pp70, 141, 362)

JOHN, b ca 1750, of Kittery. John enlisted for the town of Kittery in Capt. Robert Oliver's Co., Col. John Greaton's 2d Regt., return [year not given]. He was reported deserted. (Mass. Soldiers & Sailors, p1023)

JOHN, b ca 1750, of York. John enlisted as Pvt. in Capt. Samuel Darby's Co., Col. James Scamman's 30th Regt.; muster roll dated 1 Aug 1775, enlisted 3 May 1775, service 3 mos., 6 days. Also company return, prob. Oct 1775, including abstract of pay to last of July 1775, as well as order for bounty coat dated Cambridge, 28 Oct 1775. (Mass. Soldiers & Sailors, p1023)

JOHN, b ca 1750, of York, listed in the 1790 census for York, his household containing one male under 16 and three females. (Census York Co., 1790, p71)

JOHN, b pre 1755, of York, listed as head of household in the 1800 census for York, age 45 plus, with family containing a spousal figure of the same age group and one other male age 16-26. (Census York Co., 1800, p1017)

JOHN Jr., aka Jonathan, b ca 1755, of York, mariner, d 1798, York, intestate, buried at York; filed (Ints.) 25 May 1781, m 14 Jun 1781 at First Parish Church, York, Hannah Banks [b 1758, of York, d 22 Oct 1848, York, age 90-10-0, widow]. Letters of Admin. on the estate of Lydia Preble of York, kinswoman of John's wife Hannah, were granted to John 16 Dec 1793, who gave bond of 40 pounds [York Probate #15466]. From the division of Lydia Preble's estate, it was learned that John's wife Hannah was an heir of Peter Preble, deceased, and his widow Abigail Preble. The probate court determined 21 Dec 1795 that since the premises would not suitably accommodate all the heirs, John Young Jr. and his wife Hannah would pay the following sums of money to the heirs of Peter Preble: Patience Preble, $18.67; Benjamin McLucas, $18.67, and Pelatiah Banks and Phebe Banks, each $6.22 [York Probate 16:411].

The first of two land deeds for John and Hannah was signed 15 Nov 1796, rec'd 13 May 1801: they sold to Joshua Lunt of York, trader, for $20.00, two acres, 23 rods land being part of the real estate lately belonging to Lydia Preble, late of York, single woman, which was settled on John and Hannah by a decree of the Judge of Probate 18 April last, together with one acre, 114 rods land, which Lunt purchased out of the estate; witnesses Daniel and Lucy Sewall, Samuel Derby (or Dooley?) [York Deed 67:32].

John's name was listed in Charles J. House's "Names of Soldiers of the American Revolution," p50, as was his wife Hannah. His residence and date of death were given as York, 1798. Letters of Admin. on John's estate were filed 23 Jun 1800 by widow Hannah of York who gave bond for $200, with sureties Samuel Derby and Simon Fernald [York Probate #20940]. Inventory of John's estate dated 17 Oct 1800, taken by Daniel Sewall, Samuel Derby and Simon Fernald, amounted to $98.62. This included 3-1/2 acres of undivided land in York in common with Joshua Lunt [York Probate 18:324].

Widow Hannah made petition 21 Apr 1801 to the Court of Common Pleas to be licensed to sell enough of John's estate strictly for the payment of debts and incidental charges; approved 30 Mar 1803, and deed rec'd 1 Apr 1803, bringing about their 2nd land deed: Jotham Young, mariner, bought for $71.75, 4 acres pasture land in York, by lands of Edward Emerson Jr., Esq. and by lands of the heirs of John Young Sr., deceased and by heirs of Rowland Young deceased, as well as two additional acres found N.W. by the highway, N.E. by John Tenny's land, and S.W. by lands set off to widow Olive Grow as "her Thirds" in the estate of William Grow; witnesses Daniel Sewall, Simon Fernald [York Deed 68:260].

Ch. b York: Jotham+, b ca 1782; Perthenia+, b 1788, single; Sally+ (Young) Sherman, b 1790. (Bragdon & Frost's York V.R., pp163, 361, 510; ME Old Cem. Assoc., p781, No. 5671)

JOHN, bp 11 May 1755, of Biddeford/Saco, s/o Thomas and Eunice (   ) Young, d 1798, Dayton, m ca 1780, prob. Dayton, Martha Miller [b ca 1760, of Dayton]. At one time he resided in Windham and served in the Revolutionary War in Col. Phinney's Regt. In 1800 John, age 45 plus, was named head of family in Pepperellboro [Biddeford], with a large household containing a spousal figure and another adult male both age 45 plus, three children under 10, two males and one female, and three daughters, two age 10-16 and one under 10.

John and sibling Hezekiah, both of Saco, had seen service in the Revolutionary War. They joined a company that was being raised February 1776, commanded by Capt. John Elden of Buxton, from the towns of Buxton, Arundel, Biddeford and Saco, for a short term of service in the Continental Army. The company belonged to the regiment of militia which was assigned the task of fortifying Dorchester Heights on the night of March 4th, under Col. Lemuel Robinson's command.

"Maine Revolutionary Soldiers' Graves" indicated that John's grave was located in Biddeford, as was his brother Hezekiah, both listed on the rolls of Rebecca Emery Chapter, D.A.R., p10. However, V.R.'s indicated John was buried at the Young-Hood Cemetery, Hollis Road in Dayton. See also entry on sibling Hezekiah+ Young, bp 24 Jun 1753. (Census York Co., 1800, p926; Mass. Soldiers & Sailors, pp1020, 1023; Folsom's Saco, p286; ME I.G.I.; ME Old Cem. Assoc., p781, No. 3192; Revol. Soldiers & Sailors)

JOHN, b ca 1755, of Parsonsfield, alive same town, 1830, age 70-80, widower. John was listed as head of household in Parsonsfield according to the 1820-1830 census reports. In 1820 his age was 45 plus, as was the spousal figure, one male age 16-18, three males age 16-26, three females, one each under 10, 16-26 and 26-45. In 1830 John's age was 70-80, a widower. Family contained four other males, two 10-15, and one each 20-30 and 30-40, as well as four females, one each 15-20, 20-30, 30-40 and 40-50. (Census York Co., 1820, p490; 1830, p277)

JOHN Jr., b 15 Sep 1757, York, s/o John and Elizabeth (Hill) Young, most likely the John Jr. who was listed in the 1790 Census for York with family containing two males under 16 years and two females. (ME I.G.I.; Census York Co., 1790, p71)

JOHN, b ca 1760, of Hollis [aka Littlefalls]. He was listed as head of household in Littlefalls per the 1790 census, with family of one male under sixteen and four females. The next listing for him was found in the 1830 census for Hollis when his age was 50-60, apparently a widower: at home were four other family members, two males under 5 and two females, one age 20-30, and one under 5. The profile on this household suggested that a married daughter, a widow with three small children to take care of, had returned to live at her father's home in Hollis. (Census York Co., 1790, p64; 1830, p169)

JOHN, b ca 1760, of York, d pre 21 Feb 1803, York, testate, m ca 1785, Naomi (   ) [b 1760s, alive 1803, York, widow]. Naomi was designated as spouse in John's will signed 30 May 1801, proved 21 Feb 1803, with this bequest: she was to receive John's personal property and enjoy the use of the dwelling house during the term of her natural life. Naomi and son Job were named joint Execs. of his estate, Job designated as residuary legatee, in order "to settle my small estate." John did not elaborate about those family members who survived him, but rather advised that "the representatives of my son John, deceased" were to receive one dollar each, his other children, twenty cents each. A $600.00 Admin. bond was posted by Naomi, Josiah Gilman and Jim Lyman; witnesses Elizabeth Sewall, Eliza Langdon, David Sewall [York Probate #20941].

Widow Naomi and son Job sold by deed signed 28 Apr 1803, rec'd 11 Jan 1806, part of their homestead in York where they then lived--part of the house, land and cellar--to Josiah Gilman, physician, extending the right to him to build upon or enlarge the house; witnesses William Frost, James H. Sargent [York Deed 74:88]. A codicil to the land deed was attached on 24 Oct 1809, rec'd 22 Jun 1815, in which Job Young, "now being of age," attested that this deed was his free act and acknowledged that he was of age; witnesses Stephen Preble, Joseph Young. Known ch. b York: Job+, b 1788.

JOHN, b ca 1761, Dover, N.H., s/o Capt. Thomas Young of Dover, resident of Berwick, d 1 Aug 1813, Ossipee, N.H., see main entry in Youngs of Strafford Co., N.H., Vol. I; m 7 Sep 1783, Berwick, Sarah Nason [b ca 1760, of Berwick, alive 1791, married]. John and brothers Joseph and Moses were originally from Dover, sons and heirs-at-law of Thomas Young of Dover as given by will signed 7 Apr 1791, proved 25 Apr 1795, John receiving a moiety of land in Lebanon.

Additional information found on John and Sarah showed that they settled in Berwick for a while. He was listed as head of household there in the 1790 Census, with family containing one male under 16 and three females. Yet he moved on to Ossipee, N.H., making that their legal address at least by early 1806, where his brothers still lived.

Sarah Nason came from a large family, having eight brothers and one sister. In a Letter of Attorney authorized 27 Dec 1791, rec'd 21 Apr 1796, her brother Mark Nason devised her the sum of five shillings; witnesses William Frost, Perrin Hay, Abner Rumrill, Jacob Nash [York Deed 59:106]. The other Nason siblings, all of Berwick, were John, Nathaniel, Daniel, Molly, wife of Ichabod Marse, Ham, Caleb, David, and Batholomew.

One of two land deeds found for John of York County indicated he and Sarah then lived in Berwick. John purchased on 13 Apr 1793 from John Plaisted of Berwick for 20-12-0, 4 acres, 20 rods land in Berwick, beginning at the highway adjoining Capt. Caleb Lord's land where he dwelt; rec'd 18 May 1805; witnesses John Hill, Moses Emery [York Deed 72:232].

This very same property was sold after their relocation to Ossipee, Strafford County early in 1806. Sarah's sibling John Nason of Berwick bought from John Young of Ossipee, Strafford County, by deed signed 22 Feb 1806, rec'd 21 Apr 1806, for $150.00, the very same 4 acres, 20 rods land "with house and barn in Berwick, situated by Richard Hodsdon's land where he now dwells, and late the property of Capt. Caleb Lord, which is the same I bought from John Plaisted," spouse Sally Young relinquishing dower rights; witnesses Nathaniel Nason, Thomas Abbott [York Deed 74:136].

Please see John's main entry in Youngs of Strafford Co., N.H., Vol. I, which detailed an account of his children and Letters of Admin. filed by his widow Sarah on John's estate on 10 Sep 1813. Ch. b Berwick: Daniel, b 1785. Known ch. b Ossipee, NH: Nathaniel, b ca 1806; John Jr., b 26 Jul 1807; and Rhoda, b ca 1810. (NH & ME I.G.I.; Mormon/ME V.R., Wright-Zitkov; Census York Co., 1790, p56)

JOHN, b 25 Oct 1767 aka 3rd, York, cordwainer, s/o Rowland and Mary (Norton) Young, m 2 Nov 1791, Kittery, Ruth Wilson [b ca 1770, of Kittery]. It is quite probable that the following two land deeds pertained to this John 3rd, s/o Rowland and Mary Young of York: (1) For 47 pounds lawful money, John 3rd bought from William King of Scarborough, Cumberland County, three acres land including house and barn, situated on the south side of the highway leading from the meeting house to the house that Deacon Coward then lived in;

witnesses John Harman, William Milberry, Rowland Young, by deed signed 9 Feb 1792, rec'd 8 Jul 1793 [York Deed 56:167]. (2) John 3rd then sold this property in York to Rowland Young of York, yeoman, presumably his father, for 47 pounds lawful money, "that I bought from William King on 9 Feb instant," witnesses William Frost, John Sewall [York Deed 60:273]. (Kittery V.R., p181)

JOHN Jr., b ca 1777/8, Berwick/Old York, relative of Willard Young. (ME I.G.I.)

JOHN, b ca 1785, of Saco, m 29 Apr 1812, Saco, Miriam Haley [b ca 1790, of Saco Valley]. (Ridlon's Saco, p710)

JOHN, b 1787, of Waterboro, alive 1850, same town; m 23 Jan 1813, Waterboro, Nancy Horn [b 1795, of Shapleigh, alive 1850, same town]. The 1820, 1840 and 1850 census reports for Waterboro listed John as resident. In 1820 his age was 26-45, as was the spousal figure, with one male child at home, age ten. In 1840, he and spousal figure were age 50-60. Other members of household were an elderly female figure age 70-80, one male age 15-20 and two females age under 5. The 1850 census revealed his age as 63; members of household were spouse Nancy, age 55, and children Hannah and William. It is believed that John could be considered the Young progenitor of Waterboro.

Ch. b Waterboro: Daniel, b 2 Feb 1812, d.y.; Daniel+, b 3 Feb 1814; John, b 9 Feb 1824; Hannah, b 25 Mar 1829, d.y.; Hannah, b 1836; William, b 1843. (ME I.G.I.; Census York Co., 1820, p673; 1830, p88; 1840, Reel B, p194; 1850, Reel C, p207; Reg. 90:243, 254, 1936)

JOHN, b 1788, of North Berwick, alive 1860, same town, age 79; m2 28 Sep 1817, Berwick, Esther Hall [b 10 May 1790, d 10 Oct 1873, North Berwick, age 83-5-0]. Per the 1810 census, John lived in Berwick, age 26-45, with family containing a spousal figure of same age group and one female under 10 years. It is believed that this was John's second marriage. His name appeared again in the census reports for Berwick and North Berwick from 1830-1860. In 1830 his age was 40-50, with a spousal figure age 30-40, family containing a young male under 5 and seven females, two under 5, and one each 5-10, 10-15, 15-20, and 20-30. In 1840 John was age 50-60, a spousal figure age 40-50; at home were one male age 10-15 and three females, two 10-15 and one 15-20. In both 1850 and 1860 Esther was named his spouse. In 1850 his estate was valued at $1,500; other members of household were daughter Olive E., age 21, and James Hellins, bachelor [b 1815]. In 1860 Esther was 70 years old; member of household was James M. Estes [b 1848].

Esther and daughter Margaret were buried at the Young plot on Turkey Street, North Berwick. Ch. b No. Berwick: Margaret, b 16 Apr 1821, d 20 May 1849, age 28-1-4; Olive Esther+ (Young) Lord, b 29 Mar 1829. (Hale's Cems., n.p.; Census York Co., 1810, p962; 1830, p350; 1840, Reel A, p49; 1850, Reel C, p340; 1860, Reel B, p909)

JOHN, b 1794, farmer, of Lyman and Dayton/Hollis, believed to be descendant of Thomas Young of Littlefalls, alive 1860, age 66, Dayton; m 19 Mar 1826, Lyman, 2nd Baptist Church, Olive Haley [b 1798, of Lyman, alive 1860, Dayton]. In 1850 John and Olive were listed on the census reports for Hollis, the estate valued at $1,600; living with them were children John, Francis and Mary. Per the 1860 census for Dayton he and spouse Olive lived with Levi and Bridget Cousens from Ireland [b 1821 and 1830, respectively]. Their sons John and Francis and married daughter Mary E. Adams were buried at the family burial plot on Young River Road, Dayton, no dates given on John and Olive Young.

Ch. b Hollis: John Jr., b 21 Sep 1826, d 21 Jul 1853, age 26-10-0, native town, age 29; Francis H., b 1827, d 29 Sep 1856, age 29; Mary E. (Young) Adams, b 1830, d 3 Aug 1854, w/o A. A. Adams. (Census York Co., 1850, Reel B, p107; 1860, Reel C, p979; ME I.G.I.; Hale's Cems., n.p.; Picton's ME Cem. Inscrips., V2, p1277; Lyman Marr., 1784-1831, by Rev. Lock)

JOHN, b ca 1800, head of household in Hollis per 1840 census, age 30-40. At home was a spousal figure of the same age group, and two males and one female each at age 10-15. (Census York Co., 1840, p321)

JOHN, b 1815, Texas, hired hand at age 15, living in Saco at the home of William and Irene Fogg [b 1828 and 1827, ME respectively]. (Census York Co., 1860, Reel C, p807)

JOHN, b 1815, York, tanner, s/o Jonathan Young, Esq. [b 1774], d 8 Aug 1891, York, age 76, married; filed (Ints.) 12 Jan 1844, York, m1 4 Feb 1844, York, Mary Abigail Junkins [b 1815, of same town, d 7 Aug 1869, bur. 11 Aug 1869, York, of consumption, age 54, married]. John filed (Ints.) 12 Sep 1871, m2 1 Oct 1871, York, Adeline P. Spinney [b 11 Oct 1834, of Kittery, d 11 Dec 1897, York, age 63-2-0, widow]. By his father's will signed 14 Dec 1840, proved 5 May 1856, John was designated as son and Exec. of his estate as well as the sole residuary legatee of his estate, both real and personal. His will served to establish the identities of siblings: George Young, Asenith Twombly, Nancy Bacheldor, Mercy Moulton, and Charlotte Shorey.

In 1850 he, wife Mary and sons John and Joseph lived at home in York, the estate valued at $3,000. The 1860 census declared that John was head of household in York, age 45, with an estate valued at $4,000; at home were spouse Mary A., age 45, and children John M., age 14, and Mary L., age 4. John, his two wives and family were buried in the Young Lot adjacent to burial sites of his paternal grandparents Jonathan and Mercy, located at the N.E. side of Scituate Pond Road, near the cellar hole.

Ch. b York: John M., b 1845; Joseph M., b 1848, d 29 Aug 1852, age 4; George M., b 1853, d 29 Jul 1858, age 5; Jonathan, n.d., d 21 Feb 1856; Mary L., b 1856. (ME I.G.I.; Bragdon & Frost's York V.R., pp259, 316; Frost's York Cem., p633; Hale's Cems., n.p.; Census York Co., 1850, Reel A, p217; 1860, Reel C, p958; 1870 Mortality Sched., York Co., p64)

JOHN, b 1823, of Newfield, stone polisher. In 1860 John was head of household which contained spouse Mary ( ) [b 1819], and children Irene, Rose Etta, Anna Bell, and John M., as well as Arena Libby, age 13 [b 1847]. See following main entry for similarities to this one: Mary may have been John's 2nd wife. Ch. b prob. Newfield: Irene, b 1849; Rose Etta, b 1852, Anna Bell, b 1854; and John M., b 1856. (Census York Co., 1860, Reel C, p668)

JOHN, b 1824, of Newfield, laborer. John and spouse Sally ( ) [b 1822] were listed as residents of Newfield in the 1850 census, living at the home of John Daniels [b 1786, MA]. At home was infant daughter Irena, eleven months old, b May 1850. (Census York Co., 1850, Reel C, p274)

JOHN Jr., b ca 1825, of Waterboro, m 26 Oct 1849, Sarah Runnels [b ca 1830, of Newfield]. (**Reg.** 91:126, 1937)

JOHN, b ca 1835, of Biddeford, m 2 Dec 1860, Biddeford, Louisa Baker [b ca 1840, of same town]. (ME I.G.I.; Mormon/ME V.R., Wright-Zitkov)

JOHN, b 1840, of York, d 15 Mar 1873, York, age 33, buried at the Young Lot, on the N.E. side of Scituate Pond Road, York, apparently single. The family lot was headed by John Young [b 1815] and his two wives Mary A. and Adeline P. Young. No further identification was made. (Hale's Cems., n.p.; Frost's York Cem., p633)

JOHN A., b 1842, Canada, resident of Waterboro, laborer; enlisted in the Civil War at age 22 as Pvt. on 21 Oct 1864, from Waterboro, mustered in same date at Portland for three years, in the 20th Infantry, I Co.; mustered out 16 Jul 1865, honorably discharged, at Washington, D.C. Personal profile showed that John A.'s complexion and hair were dark; eyes were hazel; he stood 5' 4-1/4". (Civil War res. by T. E. Brooks of Maine)

JOHN HENRY, b 10 May 1841, Farmington, N.H., resident of South Berwick, s/o Hiram H. and Margaret (Hall) Young of Farmington [no main entry], alive 1890, South Berwick, buried n.d. at Pleasant Hill Cem., Lot 94A, South Berwick. For details of parents' background, please see Youngs of Strafford County, N.H., Vol. I. According to the 1890 ME Vets, Census Index of Civil War Vets, John H. was listed for South Berwick, District SD#1, Enum.#231. He had joined Co. H., 6th N.H. Volunteers. In 1900, he and companion Jane A. Goodwin [b 4 Jan 1842, d/o Nathaniel and Betsey (Bennett) Goodwin, d 27 Aug 1919] lived together on Brattle Street, South Berwick. (1900 ME Soundex; Picton's ME Cem. Inscrips., V3, p2062; Civil War res. by T. E. Brooks, Maine)

JOHN R. aka 3rd, b 1760s, York, of Kittery, yeoman, alive 1809, Parsonsfield; filed (Ints.) 9 Mar 1791, York, m 12 Mar 1791, Kittery, Rebecca Hutchins [b 1757, of Kittery, d 7 Oct 1848, Parsonsfield, age 91]. It can be said that John R. was one of the earliest Youngs to settle in Parsonsfield; see also main entry on John Young, b ca 1755.

The following two deeds seemed to go hand-in-hand with John Young of Parsonsfield, rather than with John Young of Phillipsburg [now Hollis]. The first land deed found for John of Phillipsburg was signed 15 Sep 1806, rec'd 10 Sep 1807. He and John Marsten bought from Andrew M. Chapman of Parsonsfield for $800.00, Lot No. 10, otherwise known as "45 in the 10th Range of lots," the same which Andrew Chapman bought from Samuel Chapman of New Market, Rockingham Co., N.H.; Elinor Chapman ceded dower rights; witnesses John Greenlow, Henry Boothly [York Deed 77:118].

The second deed signed 23 Jul 1809, rec'd 31 Jul 1809, dealt with John of Parsonsfield: he sold acreage with buildings thereon in Phillipsburg for $2,000 to James Wakefield, Gent. of Phillipsburg, land beginning at the N.E. corner of land of Hezekiah Young on the N.W. line, which land he bought from his father Thomas Young, to land once owned by Joseph Dyer, then S.W. to land of Dominicus Smith; wife Rebecca ceded dower rights; witnesses Andrew M. C. Chapman and James Bradbury for John Young; James Bradbury and John Marston for Rebecca Young [York Deed 81:92].

John, Rebecca and kinswoman Betsey Young [b 1756, d 22 Feb 1817, age 61] were buried at North Parsonsfield Cemetery, along with their son George and his wife Jane K. Ch. b York: Joanna Billings, b 11 Aug 1792; Rowland, b 23 Sep 1794; George+, b 3 Dec 1799. (ME I.G.I.; Hale's Cems., n.p.; Kittery V.R., pp181, 247; Bragdon & Frost's York V.R., pp100, 173; Picton's ME Cem. Inscrips., V2, p1355)

JOHN R., b 5 Dec 1836, Parsonsfield, s/o George and Jane (Keazer) Young, d 1908, native town, age 63; filed (Ints.) 12 Nov 1859, m 24 Nov 1859, Parsonsfield, Mary E. aka Eveline Dearborn [b Oct 1841, Parsonsfield, d 1907, native town]. According to the 1900 census John lived with spouse Mary E. and their adopted son Freddie E., b May 1891, N.H. John R. and spouse were buried in Parsonsfield. The family plot included son Willis E., b 1871, d 1895. (Picton's ME Cem. Inscrips., V2, p1386; 1900 ME Soundex; Parsonsfield V.R., Town Clerk, pp176, 241; Hobb's Cem. Recs. of Parsonsfield, p38)

JOHN S., b 1868, of York, d 1955, York, widower, age 87; spouse Mary K. (   ) was b 1865, of York, d 1929, York, age 64, married. They were buried at the family plot in York Cemetery. (Bragdon & Frost's York V.R., p507)

JOHN W., b 21 Jun 1820, of South Berwick, farmer, d 23 May 1897, South Berwick, age 77, married; m ca 1845, same town, Mary A. (   ) [b 8 Jan 1822, d 3 Jul 1904, South Berwick, age 82, widow]. In 1860 John W. was listed as head of household in South Berwick, age 39, his real estate valued at $1,800. Family then included spouse Mary A. (   ) and five children. Mary A. was widowed by 1900 in South Berwick; at that time she lived with son James W. and his children. John W. and Mary were buried in the Warren Plot on the N.W. side of

Tatnic Road, to the rear of the residence of Joseph W. Turnbull, South Berwick.
Ch. b prob. South Berwick: Clara, b 1848; Rachael, b 1851; Olive A., 1853; James W.+, b Feb 1856; and Emma A., b 1858. (Census York Co., 1860, Reel B, p816; 1900 ME Soundex; Picton's ME Cem. Inscrips., V3, p2094)

JOHN W., b 27 May 1840, South Berwick, s/o William A. and Dorcas N. ( ) Young, d 9 Apr 1883, South Berwick, died relatively young, age 43; m 1860s, Mary A. Warren [b ca 1845, of same town]. In the 1850 census for South Berwick, John W. was a child of ten in his parents' household; he was buried at his parents' grave site in South Berwick. Ch. b So. Berwick: Warren Pike, b 3 Nov 1865. (Mormon/ME V.R., Wright-Zitkov; Picton's ME Cem. Inscrips., p3, p2047)

JOHN W. aka James W., b 30 May 1851, Canada, resident of Kennebunk, d 7 Jul 1921, same town, age 70, widower; m 1871-72, Kennebunk, Caroline A. ( ) [b 15 Mar 1852, N.H., d 9 Jan 1920, Kennebunk]. John W. was listed as resident of Kennebunk in 1900, age 49; members of family included spouse Caroline A., surviving daughter Addie W. and boarder Lucinda M. Young [b Aug 1826].

John, Caroline and three children were buried at Kennebunk. Ch. b Kennebunk, not traced further: Lizzie E., b 23 Dec 1872, d 10 Mar 1893, age 21; George A., b 23 Jun 1875, d 21 Jan 1894; Wilson C., b 18 Mar 1880, d 18 Aug 1880; and Addie W., b Jan 1882, alive 1900. (Hale's Cem., Series I; Picton's ME Cem. Inscrips., V2, p852; 1900 ME Soundex)

JOHN W., b Jan 1870, N.H., head of household in Kennebunk as of 1900, age 30, with family containing spouse Luella S. ( ) Young [b Dec 1868] and their two young children. Ch. b ME, not traced further: Elsie M., b Jun 1895; and Lizzie F., Feb 1898. (1900 ME Soundex)

JOHN WESLEY, b 12 Jul 1838, of Eliot, d 22 Jun 1866, age 27-11-10, same town; m 21 Jul 1861, Kittery, Rebecca Emery [b 11 Aug 1838, d 22 Jun 1866, Eliot, age 27-11-10]. Both husband and wife died the same day, presumably from a severe illness or accidentally. The family were buried at the Nason plot on Hanscom Road, Eliot. Ch. b Eliot: Charles W., b 28 Jul 1865, d 14 Feb 1867, age 1-6-17. (Hale's Cems., n.p.; Kittery V.R., p364; Picton's ME Cem. Inscrips., V1, p689; Frost's **Eliotiana**, Deaths, pD102)

JOHNSON aka JOSEPH, b 7 Jan 1722, York, mariner, s/o Benaiah and Ruth (Johnson) Young, d pre Dec 1761, native town, married; filed (Ints.) 31 Dec 1748; m 19 Jan 1749, York, Betty aka Elizabeth Card [b ca 1725, York, alive Dec 1761, widow, d/o William Card, native town].

Betty Card Young of York sold to Jeremiah Moulton Jr. for 1-6-0 legal money, 10 acres land laid out originally to John Card, her great grandfather on 27 Feb 1678, and since then on 27 Nov 1750, laid out to his heirs William Card, eldest son of Thomas Card, and Thomas, son of John Card, as by York Town Record, Libre 2, p133; witnesses Daniel Moulton, Martha Banks

[York Deed 42:187]. Another deed was found for Johnson Young, grantor, deed signed 14 Nov 1754, rec'd 20 Nov 1754: he and wife Elizabeth and Joseph and Hepsibah Card of York [the heirs of William Card] sold to Samuel McIntire of York for 2-13-4, four shares in Lot No. 7, 1st Div. in the Common Lands, York; witnesses Daniel and Jeremiah Moulton [York Deed 32:61]. (ME I.G.I.; Bragdon & Frost's York V.R., p134)

JONATHAN, b 1674, York, s/o Rowland and Susanna (Matthews) Young, alive May 1768 at age 94, native town; m 7 Jan 1707/8, Kittery, Margaret Stackpole aka Stagpole [b ca 1685, alive 1730s]. Jonathan was named son and heir in his father's will drawn 14 Sep 1719, proved 2 Jan 1721/2, his inheritance a one-half share in two acres salt marsh in the western cove, sibling Benaiah to receive the other half share.

An early court record was found for Jonathan [Jr.] dated 3 Apr 1716 in the Inferior Court of Common Pleas when Jonathan and colleagues Bragdon, Hoult, Kingberry, Harmon, Stagpole, Stone and Bane put in a plea of trespass and ejectment against Thomas Baker, defendant. Baker pled that he held the land in light of a lease from Charles Frost, Esq. Since Frost was one of the justices, and there being but two besides him at present in Commission, it was decided to postpone the hearing until the next session of the Inferior Court on the first Tuesday, April next [Court of Gen. Sessions, V5, p66].

The earliest land deed for Jonathan, signed 6 May 1717, rec'd following day, pertained to the very same combine of men cited above, that is, Jonathan Young, J. Harmon, B. Stone, J. Kingsbury, J. Bane, S. Bragdon, J. Holt and J. Stagpole, all from York. They sold for 220 pounds to William Moody, Gent. of Newbury, Essex Co., MA, land that was situated between Thomas Adams' land and the land that was formerly Thomas Beson's according to two grants given by the Town, the first dated 8 Mar 1714/5, and the other, 13 Mar 1715; witnesses Lewis Bane, Nathaniel Freeman [York Deed 8:207].

Jonathan bought from his younger brother Benaiah of York, by deed signed 8 Jan 1731, rec'd 1 Apr 1736, a certain parcel of marsh lying in the S.W. branch of York River, "being a point of marsh that was the estate of our honored father Roland Young of said York deceased," abutting the lands of Daniel Pall and Robert Cutts.

One major deed of Jonathan's was signed and rec'd 8 Jan 1754, when he turned over to his son Joshua the following property in York. As he expressed it: Joshua, having been, and is still dutiful, helpful and very serviceable to me in my advanced age in managing my affairs and assisting in the support of me and my wife and for the love and affection, and forty pounds lawful money paid by Joshua, conveyed to him the homestead land in York on the S.W. side of York River "where I now dwell," containing 24 acres bound north by the river, and by lands of Ebenezer Young, Samuel Bragdon and Josiah Main; witnesses Daniel Moulton, Nathaniel Milberry [York Deed 31:162].

Jonathan's spouse Margaret and son Joshua's spouse Mary ceded Dower Rights in the sale of these two acres of salt marsh: Jonathan and Joshua sold by deed signed 29 Apr 1762, rec'd 30 Apr 1762, to John McIntire Jr. of York for 10-13-4, all their part and parcel of the salt marsh located on the western side of the S.W. branch of York River, "beginning at the salt marsh of the late Matthews Young until it comes to the marsh of the late Daniel Junkins," containing about two acres; see son Joshua for full citation.

Jonathan bought additional shares in the York Common Lands by deed signed and rec'd 26 Jun 1762: two shares in Lot No. 4, 1st Div. from Jonathan Sayward of York for two pounds, originally granted to James Hill who sold them to Thomas Donnell, "of whom I purchased them," witnesses Daniel Moulton, Robert Mills [York Deed 37:169]. It was shown by deed signed 5 May 1768, rec'd 16 May 1768 that Jonathan also made deed of gift to son Rowland of Wells of four shares out of the eight in Lot No. 3, 3rd Range, 4th Div. of the Outer Commons granted him by the Town Proprietors; witness Alexander MacIntire [York Deed 41:51].

Ch. b York: Miriam+ (Young) Chapman, b 31 Jan 1707; Elizabeth+ (Young) Adams, b 23 Apr 1710; Jerusha+ (Young) Hatch, b 15 Mar 1711; Rowland+, b 4 Feb 1713; Abijah+, b 10 Aug 1720; John, b 11 Dec 1723; Jonathan, n.d., d 1 Feb 1729; Joshua+, b ca 1730. (ME I.G.I.; Noyes et al, pp776-777; Bragdon & Frost's York V.R., pp7, 392; Kittery V.R., p36)

JONATHAN Jr., b 1680s, York, weaver, s/o Samuel and Elizabeth (Masterson) Young, gr.s/o Rowland Jr. and Susanna (Matthews) Young, d pre 2 Apr 1764, native town, intestate; m ca 1720, York, Abigail Came [b 18 Sep 1700, York, d/o Capt. Samuel and Patience (Bragdon) Came, alive 1764, native town].

The earliest deed found for Jonathan Jr. and sibling Ichabod involved the sale of ten acres land in York where Samuel Young built a house and dwelt, to their uncle Job Young of York for a certain sum of money, having obtained the free consent of their widowed mother Elizabeth. This land had been "a part of a grant of land given unto Rowland Young, father of the said Samuel Young in the year 1667 by the town of York, and thence by said Rowland Young to...Samuel Young by deed of gift 18 Apr 1682," signed 28 Nov 1712, rec'd 7 Jul 1720; witnesses Henry Scott, Sampson Underhill [York Deed 10:45-46].

Inherited lands aside for the moment, Jonathan Jr. bought many properties in York, first deed dated 24 Nov 1724, rec'd 10 Mar 1747: for eleven pounds money, one-1/4th acre of salt marsh and thatch ground in York from Benjamin Stone of York, shipwright, land situated on the S.W. side of the N.W. branch of York River, bounded S.W. by lands of Capt. Samuel Came; witnesses Joseph Bragdon, Joseph Plaisted, John Battin [York Deed 26:286]. Another purchase of land was dated 23 Apr 1719, rec'd 30 Mar 1730/31: from grantor, father-in-law Samuel Came, Esq., paid sixty pounds for a piece of land at a place called Birch Hill which Came bought from John Hinkel on 13 Apr

1716, bounded partly by Jonathan's land, partly by lands of Joseph Junkins, deceased, and by Came's; witnesses Noah Emery, Timothy Leighton, James Carr [York Deed 19:376].

Yet another piece of land at Birch Hill by land of John McIntire was bought from Jonathan's father-in-law Samuel Came for six pounds money by deed signed 8 Apr 1743, rec'd 14 Apr 1743; witnesses Elihu Gunnison, Joseph Sayer [York Deed 23:231]. It should be noted here that the appraisal of Jonathan's estate identified thirty acres land located at Birch Hill.

Jonathan Jr., with wife Abigail ceding Dower Rights, sold to Joseph Preble of York for sixty pounds current money, one full moiety or half part of a certain parcel of land in York adjoining the Barberry Marsh containing forty acres, "it being the same tract of land which was granted and laid out to my honorable father Samuel Young and Samuel Johnson deceased" per York Town Records 1:56; by deed signed 26 Nov 1728, rec'd 27 Nov 1728; witnesses Samuel Sewald, Joseph Moody [York Deed 12:343].

The last piece of land Jonathan bought from father-in-law Came was dated 7 Jul 1747, deed rec'd 10 Mar 1747/8: for forty pounds bills of credit old Tenor, three acres of salt marsh and thatch bed at the S.E. side of Bass Cove; spouse Patience Came ceded Dower Rights; witnesses Norton Woodbridge, Elias Weare [York Deed 26:286-287].

Having turned his full attention to shares in York's Common Lands and subsequent "trade-offs," Jonathan bought four shares out of thirty in Lot No. 3, 12th Range for five pounds, by deed signed 6 Jul 1736, rec'd 6 Feb 1748, from Philip Welch of York who had originally received these shares from the town 25 Sep 1732; witnesses Sarah Came, Mary Brown [York Deed 27:108]. He next bought three shares in Lot No. 4, 1st Div., Common Lands from Samuel Moulton of York for 3-12-0, by deed signed and rec'd 19 Jun 1754; these shares Moulton had bought from Jonathan Sayward of York, two of which were originally granted to Caleb Young and the one other to John Wells from whom Sayward bought them; witnesses Daniel Moulton, William Dunning [York Deed 31:238].

Upon the death of Jonathan's sibling Ichabod of Gloucester, heirs-at-law Elizabeth Greeley [sibling] and spouse Joseph Greeley of Kingston, N.H. sold to "our brother Jonathan Young" for twenty pounds old Tenor, all the right they held in the estate of their father and mother, Samuel and Elizabeth Young of York, by deed signed 9 Jul 1751, rec'd 6 Jun 1754. In addition, niece Abigail Newman of Kingston, d/o Ichabod and Abigail Young of Gloucester, and husband Thomas Newman sold to her uncle Jonathan Young, Gent. of York, for twenty pounds old Tenor, all their right in the estate of "our father Ichabod, and also of our grandfather Samuel Young and grandmother Elizabeth Young," by deed signed 9 Jul 1751, rec'd 6 Jun 1754.

Letters of Admin. on Jonathan's estate were granted 2 Apr 1764 to sons and heirs-at-law Masterson and Samuel, both of

York, yeomen, with instructions that an inventory be taken on or before 2 July next, and a true and complete account submitted by 2 Oct 1764 [York Probate #20945]. The estate was sizeable, containing over 130 acres in the York area, attested to 11 Jul 1764 by appraisers Abel Moulton, Joseph Simpson Jr. and Joseph Parsons, appraised at 494-18-8. Inventory included homestead of 24 acres land and marsh with the house and barn, about 22-1/2 acres land called the Rocky Pasture, 30 acres land at Birch Hill, 1 acre salt marsh at same, about 23 acres land where he lived, about 7 acres land at the head of Scituate Millpond, 8 acres land in No. 8, 2nd Div. of the Inner Commons, about 16 acres fresh meadow near Groundnut Hill, and a pew in the Meeting House Gallery [York Probate 11:250].

Soon thereafter, by will signed 28 Jun 1764, probated 2 Jan 1769, Samuel Came of York devised to widowed daughter Abigail Young, twenty-five acres land in York which Samuel Came bought from Capt. Bane, in addition to what he had already given her [York Probate #2477]. These same twenty-five acres widow Abigail conveyed to her son Masterson who had helped her out tremendously, for the price of six shillings, deed signed and rec'd 23 Mar 1774. There was one stipulation: Masterson's unmarried sisters Sarah and Dorcas would be able to live there in their remaining years and/or use the pastures for their gain; witnesses Daniel Moulton, Ebenezer Sayward [York Deed 43:83].

Jonathan and Abigail's three married daughters Abigail Grow, Eunice Junkins, and Patience Stover, sold their shares in their father's estate to their brother Samuel by deed signed 9 Jul 1766, rec'd 24 Oct 1772; see daughter Abigail Grow for documentation of deed. However, Samuel and his three sisters mentioned above quitclaimed their shares and interests in this estate to sibling Jonathan 3rd, the sale to exclude their mother Abigail's Thirds; deed signed and rec'd 25 Nov 1778; see Samuel's entry for documentation.

Married daughter Eunice Junkins of York helped to identify another sister, Elizabeth Curtis of York, who held shares in their mother's "Thirds," by deed dated 3 Jul 1797, rec'd 4 Oct 1799: the deed conveyed to brother Jonathan Young Jr. of York for $50.00, "all my right, title and share I have in and to my mother Abigail Young's Thirds in the estate of my honored father Jonathan Young, late of York," her right being one-tenth part of the above-mentioned Thirds, both real and personal; see sister Eunice for documentation of deed.

Ch. b York: Elizabeth+ (Young) Curtis, b 10 May 1721; Masterson+, b 24 Dec 1722; Sarah, b 20 Dec 1724, alive 1 Jun 1796, single; Samuel+, b 27 Feb 1727; Abigail+ (Young) Grow, b 11 Jul 1729, twin; Jonathan+, b 11 Jul 1729, twin; Dorcas, b 1733, York, d 12 Feb 1819, native town, age 86, single; Eunice+ (Young) Junkins, b ca 1734; Patience+ (Young) Stover, b ca 1741. (Noyes et al, pp125, 775-777; ME I.G.I.; Bragdon & Frost's York V.R., pp25, 415)

68

JONATHAN, b ca 1696, York, weaver, poss. s/o Job and Sarah (Austin) Preble Young. Belief is held that the following two purchases of land by Jonathan of York, weaver, pertained to the son of Job and Sarah Young of York. In the first instance, with deed signed 23 Oct 1721, rec'd 8 Dec 1721, the land in question belonged to Thomas Haines and Samuel Black, both neighbors of Job and Sarah Young. Samuel Black of York sold to Jonathan, weaver, for ten pounds, ten acres of fresh meadow and swamp land in York, lying about a half mile to the N.E. of the great pond of fresh water commonly called Cape Neddick, adjoining a parcel of marsh or meadow land laid out the same day to Thomas Haines of York, for ten pounds money; Sarah Black ceded her dower rights; witnesses John Burrell, Jonathan Bane [York Deed 10:229].

In the second case, with deed both signed and rec'd 4 Nov 1723, Jonathan, weaver, bought from Arthur Bragdon Jr. of York for 15 pounds current money, eight acres land in York that was formerly granted to the late John Twisden of York on 10 Dec 1659, and laid out to said Bragdon, the Exec. of Twisden's estate, situated by lands of Capt. Samuel Came, Joseph Junkens, late of York, and Capt. Peter Nowell; witnesses Benjamin Stone, Jeremiah Moulton [York Deed 11:124-125].

JONATHAN, b ca 1710, of Biddeford or Saco, d pre 6 Oct 1753, Biddeford, intestate. Thomas Young of Biddeford, kinsman of Jonathan, filed Admin. Papers on Jonathan's estate on the above date. He was to render an inventory of the estate on or before 6 Jan next, submitting a true account by 6 Oct 1754 [York Probate #20944]. Inventory on Jonathan's estate was taken by Martin Jameson, Tristam Jordan and Amos Chase which they assessed at 10-10-4, and was verified by Thomas Young [York Probate 9:52].

JONATHAN 3rd, b 11 Jul 1729, twin, York, younger s/o Jonathan and Abigail (Came) Young, d 2 Nov 1807, native town, age 78, married, testate; filed (Ints.) 22 Oct 1762, m1 18 Nov 1762, York, Mercy aka Marcy Nowell [b 1736, York, d/o Peter and Katherine Nowell, d 29 Jun 1800, native town, age 64]. Widower Jonathan 3rd m2 (Ints.) 13 Mar 1801, York, Nancy McIntire [b ca 1776, of Brixham, d/o Daniel and Susanna (Simpson) McIntire, d 20 Feb 1814, York, age 68, widow].

Peter Nowell's will, dated 30 Mar 1775, probated 8 Jun 1775, devised to married daughter Mercy Nowell Young, spouse of Jonathan, 20 pounds to be paid by her brothers in lumber or quick stock; witnesses Dan Moulton, Abraham Nowell, Samuel Kingsbury [York Probate #14250].

Although Jonathan 3rd's father Jonathan Jr. left no will, he and siblings were heirs-at-law to a sizeable estate of over 130 acres in York. They also held shares in their mother Abigail's Thirds, which his six sisters and brother Samuel quitclaimed to Jonathan [see below quitclaim signed and rec'd 25 Nov 1778] and the main entry on Samuel. In time Jonathan became landowner of considerable acreage in York.

As husbandman, Jonathan 3rd bought and sold quite a number of shares of York Common Lands. In the first instance, he bought from William Dunning of York, cordwainer, for 53-6-8, forty-three shares in Lot No. 4, 1st Div., in the Commons which were set off to Dunning, containing 36 shares, beginning at Folly Brook at the road at the east corner of Young, the father of said grantee, whose pasture was in Lot No. 4 by lands of James Grant, by deed signed and rec'd 14 Apr 1760; witnesses Abel and Daniel Moulton [York Deed 34:61].

Jonathan sold, with spouse Mercy ceding Dower Rights, to Elijah Blaisdell for 26-13-4, fourteen shares out of thirty in Lot No. 5, 1st Range, the Outer Commons, eight of which were originally granted to his late father Jonathan; by deed dated 3 Dec 1762, rec'd 29 Oct 1765, witnesses Daniel Moulton, Ezra Thompson [York Deed 38:223-224]. Curiously enough, for the same sum of money 26-13-4 paid by Jonathan 3rd thirteen years later, he bought through a quitclaim signed and rec'd 25 Nov 1778, by his siblings Samuel Young, Abigail Grow, Eunice Junkins and Patience Stover and their spouses, all of their shares and interest in the estate, both real and personal, belonging to their parents Jonathan Jr. and Abigail Came Young, excepting the land that was their mother's Thirds. See brother Samuel for full documentation.

He bought another piece of land in York by deed signed and recorded 12 Feb 1779: from Joseph and Daniel Bragdon, both of York, for seven pounds legal money, seven of the 23 shares in 24-1/4 acres abutting lands of Ebenezer Sayward, his own lands, the home of Masterson Young [sibling], and Lot No. 4, 1st Div.; witnesses Daniel Moulton, Paul Preble [York Deed 45:186].

There were six more known land deals Jonathan made with reference to York Common Lands, shares of which added up considerably. (It was interesting to learn that townspeople then could hold shares "in common" in any one lot.) With reference to Lot No. 4, 1st Div., only, Jonathan bought from Matthew Austin of York, two shares or "four full ninth parts," and with regard to Lot No. 5, 1st Div., five shares; by deed signed 15 Nov 1770, rec'd 21 Nov 1770 [York Deed 41:265].

Concerning Lot No. 5, 1st Div. only: Jonathan (1) bought for eight pounds lawful money, eight shares from Jeremiah, Ebenezer and Joseph Bragdon of New Bristol, Lincoln Co., their father being Joseph Bragdon, Sr., by deed signed and rec'd 4 Nov 1768 [York Deed 41:176]; (2) bought from Jonathan Sayward seven shares in this lot for seven pounds by deed dated 19 Mar 1770, rec'd 10 May 1770 [York Deed 41:213]; (3) bought for 6 pounds lawful money, six shares in the lot originally granted to Hezekiah Adams, from Daniel Moulton of York, by deed signed 1 Dec 1778, rec'd 18 Dec 1778 [York Deed 45:150].

The next deed of purchase referred only to York Common and Undivided lands, signed 4 Feb 1774, rec'd the next day: Jonathan bought from Joseph and Mary Parsons of York, [Mary being "one of the children and heirs of John Higgins, late of York], for 1-10-0, all Mary's rights in the two shares which were granted to her father John Higgins [York Deed 44:136]. Then by deed signed 3 Jan 1807, rec'd 20 Jul 1807, Jonathan bought from Samuel Sayward of York, Gent., of 6-1/4 acres wood land in Lot No. 6, Inner Div. of York Commons for $64.34 [York Deed 77:96].

Sons and heirs-at-law Jonathan and Joel were named joint Execs. and residuary legatees of their father Jonathan's estate by will signed 6 Jun 1795, proved 17 Aug 1795: Joel was to have the house where he then dwelt and Jonathan, the house where Jonathan [Sr.] dwelt, the barn to be shared equally between them, as would be their father's funeral cost and legacies to be paid out. On the very same date of 6 Jun 1795 when their father's will was signed, Jonathan Jr. bought from sibling Joel for 39-14-0, the one-half part of a certain tract of land in York, 19-1/2 acres which Joel bought from John Swett and 11 acres, 65 rods that Joel bought from widow Sarah Swett; see brother Joel for documentation.

Numerous land deeds were found for Jonathan dated between 1789-1796, indicating he wanted to settle accounts and dispose of his property. The first of these was his deed signed 9 Jan 1789, rec'd 17 Mar 1789 petitioning the court to have his part of Lot No. 5, 1st Div., Inner Commons, set off to him. Those others who shared this lot in common were Jonathan Sargent, Thomas Boston, Jonathan Hutchins, each of whom owned two-fifths part of 32 shares. In response, on 18 Mar 1789, a plot of land was set off to him, 7-1/2 rods by 175 rods bounding on Lot No. 4, 36 rods by Folly Brook and 7-1/2 rods by Lot No. 6 [York Deed 53:137].

The 1790-1800 census reports for York listed Jonathan as resident: in 1790 his family contained two other males over 16, one male under 16, and three females; in 1800 his age was 45 plus, as was a maternal figure, with one male and one female at the somewhat mature age of 16-26.

The next property Jonathan bought and sold within a short time was by deed signed 8 Jun 1790, rec'd 2 Nov 1790: from Samuel Milberry and his wife Lucy, one of the heirs of John Higgins of York, for 1-10-0, all of Lucy Milberry's right in the two shares of Lot No. 4, 10th Range, Outer Commons, which were granted to her father John Higgins in York; witnesses William and Joseph Milberry [York Deed 53:81]. This same property Jonathan sold to Joseph Preble Jr. of York for 1-13-0 by deed signed and rec'd 14 Feb 1791; witnesses William and Elizabeth Frost [York Deed 53:139].

The following year by deed signed 27 Nov 1792, rec'd 14 Jan 1793, Jonathan bought from the Moody brothers, Thomas, Samuel and Joseph, sons of Joseph Moody, for 16 pounds, 16 shillings, 16 of the 23 shares in Lot No. 4, 1st Div., Common Lands, that is, 24-1/4 acres, which were originally granted to the Reverends Samuel and Joseph Moody now deceased; witnesses William Frost, Reuben Darby [York Deed 56:60].

Jonathan made deed of gift to his eldest son Joseph on date of 4 Apr 1796, rec'd same date, of a plot of land approx. 36 rods by 175 rods between Lots 4 and 5, and adjacent to Folly Marsh and lands of Samuel Sayward, with a reserve of a road through said land at the most convenient place; witness William Frost [York Deed 59:96].

That same year maiden aunts Sarah and Dorcas Young of Jonathan and Joel, sons of Masterson Young, sold all their right and title to the real estate of their late father Jonathan Young, to said nephews Jonathan and Joel, for $267.00 by deed signed 1 Jun 1796, rec'd 14 Jun 1796. See full documentation under main entry of Sarah's and Dorcas' parents Jonathan and Abigail Came Young.

One deed, as late as 3 Jul 1797, rec'd 4 Oct 1799, revealed that Jonathan Jr. of York bought for $50.00, all of sister Eunice Junkins right, title and share in their mother Abigail Young's Thirds of the estate of their honored father Jonathan Young, late of York," Eunice's right actually being one-tenth part of the above-mentioned Thirds, both real and personal. The last deed of Jonathan's up through 1810 was signed 3 Jan 1807, rec'd 20 Jul 1807, when he bought from Samuel Sayward of York for $64.34, 6-1/4 acres woodland in Lot No. 6, Inner Div. of York Commons; witnesses Alexander McIntire, Elihu Hernden [York Deed 77:96].

About a year and a half before his first wife Marcy passed on, Jonathan had his will drawn up 10 Nov 1798, proved in Apr 1808, in which he devised one third of the estate, both real and personal, to wife Marcy in right of "her Thirds." It was not apparent that he updated his will by codicil in favor of 2nd wife Nancy. He chose his namesake Jonathan 3rd, one of four sons, as sole Exec. and residuary legatee of the estate which included uplands and marsh in York; witnesses Isaac Briggs, Benjamin Kingsbury, John Paul [York Probate #20946].

The bequests Jonathan made to sons were: Joseph, one-fourth part of a sawmill privilege, not to be disposed of, unless to one of his brothers; Timothy, the barn standing on the land Jonathan deeded to him; and Jabez, one hundred dollars to be paid out four years thereafter. To his single daughter Lydia, he devised a feather bed and suitable bedding, one cow, and the improvement of the room in the front of the dwelling house, to be provided for as long as she remained single, and a gift of fifty dollars when she married. Married daughters Marcy Hodsdon and Dorcas Tucker were devised small bequests in money, plus "that with what I have already done...shall be [considered] in full of her [their] portion." Otherwise the three sisters were to share equally in all his household goods after their mother's decease."

As will be seen under the main entry of son Jabez, in anticipation of his inheritance from his father, Jabez incurred much debt in speculation over real estate in York during the late 1790s and early 1800s. This amounted to having his father assume mortgages on these properties.

Please see entry on Jabez for further details and how the situation was resolved before his father's death.

Jonathan and wife Mercy were buried at York Cemetery, York. Ch. b York by Mercy: Lydia, b 27 Aug 1763, alive 10 Nov 1798; Joseph+, b 8 Feb 1766; Mercy+ (Young) Hodsdon, b 19 Dec 1768; Dorcas+ (Young) Tucker, b 21 Apr 1771; Jonathan+, 3rd, b 12 Dec 1773; Timothy, b ca 1775; and Jabez+, b 1778. (ME I.G.I.; Census York Co., 1790, p72; Bragdon & Frost's York V.R., pp25, 89, 145, 427; Frost's York Cem., p633; Hale's Cems., n.p.; Gray's ME Families, 1790, V1, p201)

JONATHAN, b ca 1735, of York, alive 1776, same town; m 1760, York, Mercy Wheeler [b ca 1840, of same town]. Ch. b York: Lydia, b 1762; Joseph, b 1764; Mercy, b 1766; Jabez+, b 1772; and Timothy, b 13 Apr 1776. (ME I.G.I.)

JONATHAN, b 1763, York, younger s/o Masterson and Sarah (Curtis) Young, d 14 Nov 1827, age 64, native town, married, intestate; filed (Ints.) 18 Oct 1810, York, Joanna Nowell [b 1774, of York, d 2 May 1860, York, of dropsy, age 86, widow]. Since Jonathan married at age 47, it is a good possibility that this was his second marriage. Jonathan was the younger son mentioned in Masterson's will; he was named Co-Exec. and joint residuary legatee with elder brother Joel, by will signed 6 Jun 1795, probated 17 Aug 1795. Masterson devised to Jonathan the "house where I dwell," and an equal share of the barn after taking care of debts, funeral costs and legacies.

Per the 1810 census, Jonathan lived in York, his age and that of a spousal figure, 45 plus; at home were two other females, one 45 plus and one age 26-45. He was acknowledged the son of widow Sarah Curtis Young by her will dated 16 Feb 1814, probated Nov 1819, which said merely that he had already received "the full proportion of the estate" that was his due.

Three land deeds were found to be jointly signed by Jonathan and elder brother Joel: (1) dated 1 Jun 1796, rec'd 14 Jun 1796, as grantees, maiden aunts Sarah and Dorcas Young sold to them for $267.00, all their right and title to the real estate of their late father Jonathan, each nephew to have the same in equal shares; for full documentation on deed, please see main entry under Jonathan and Abigail Came Young. (2) as grantees, dated and rec'd 14 Oct 1802, bought from Theodore Grant of York, yeoman, for $11.00, one-quarter part of a mill privilege in York called Fall Mill Brook, which Grant bought from James Gray and Tamsen, his wife; see Joel for full citations. (3) as grantees, joint deed dated 5 Apr 1803, rec'd 9 Apr 1803, bought for $12.00 from John and Daniel Moulton of York, four acres land situated by lands of Samuel Young and brothers Joel and Jonathan, acreage that the Moulton brothers had owned on the S.W. end of the lot, fenced in. For complete documentation on the first and third joint deeds, please see Joel+ [b ca 1758].

A dual land deed of Jonathan Jr.'s was signed 23 Jun 1810, rec'd 28 Jun 1810. In the first case he sold to Masterson Young of York [not his father] for $161.25, 13 acres, 20 rods land at the eastern corner of the mill pasture so called, adjacent to lands of Joel and Jonathan Young, Thomas Moulton, and Samuel Sayward; spouse Joanna relinquished dower rights, witnesses Jeremiah Paul, Samuel Sayward [York Deed 83:49,50]. In the second case Jonathan Jr. sold to Jeremiah Paul, Gent. of York for $450.00, 12 acres of mowing land in Birch Hill, so called, adjacent to lands of Joel and Jonathan Young, Thomas Moulton and Samuel Sayward by the S.W. corner of Capt. Samuel Young's land; Anna aka Joanna Young ceded dower rights; witnesses Samuel Sayward, Jonathan Young [York Deed 83:50-51].

Letters of Admin. on Jonathan's estate in York were filed 15 Apr 1828 by widow Joanna; inventory on the estate was returned 2 Dec 1828 by appraisers Alexander McIntire, David Moulton, and Elihu Bragdon; attested to same date by widow Joanna. The homestead farm with buildings in York, as well as tillage, mowing, orchard, woodland and salt marsh contained 27 acres, estimated value, $1,400.00. Another 56 acres of pasture or woodland in York was set at $560.00. Odds and ends of a 1/8th share of an old saw mill called Fall Mile was set at $20.00, and part of a pew in the York Meeting House valued at $1.00; sum total of real estate holdings, $1,981.00 [York Probate #20947].

Probate papers filed 6 Dec 1830 made deposition that George Grant of York was awarded guardianship of Jonathan's three sons over the age of fourteen: Jonathan Jr., Timothy, and Masterson Jr., as well as son Mark R., under the age of fourteen [York Probate #20948]. Jonathan and family were buried at York Cemetery, York.

Ch. b York: Jonathan+ Jr., b 16 Jan 1809; Timothy+, b 25 May 1813; Masterson+ Jr., b 1816; and Mark R., b 1821, alive 1830. (Bragdon & Frost's York V.R., pp197, 423, 621; Hale's Cems., n.p.; Census York Co., 1810, p822; Thompson's Recs. of York Co., TMs, p416; J. E. Frost's York Co. Mort. Scheds., 1850-1870, p44)

JONATHAN Lt., aka Gent., b ca 1765, originally a resident of Wells, and then of Shapleigh. He represented the earliest Young living in Shapleigh per census reports from 1810-1820, and can be considered the progenitor of the Youngs from the town of Shapleigh. In 1810 his age was 26-45, with household containing a female person of same age group, four males--two under 10, one age 10-16, and one age 16-26 and one female under 10 years of age. In 1820 his age was 45 plus, and possible spousal figure was age 26-45 with a large household of nine individuals: three males, one age 16-18, two 16-26, and six females, four under 10 years and two age 16-26.

While still of Wells, he and co-grantee Benjamin Deighton, mariner, bought from James and Elizabeth Kimball, by deed signed 10 Apr 1799, rec'd 15 Apr 1799, for $150.00, a piece of land in Wells, 36 sq. rods, which adjoined the post road; Mrs. Kimball ceded dower rights; witnesses Samuel Emerson of York, Polly Bond of Wells [York Deed 62:254]. Then by deed signed

30 May 1800, rec'd 3 Feb 1801, Jonathan sold his moiety of the
land and dwelling house in Wells to Benjamin Deighton for
$650.00, on land located nearly opposite the meeting house in
Wells; witnesses James Kimball, Phineas Hemingway [York Deed
65:223]. (Census York Co., 1810, p988; 1820, p572)

JONATHAN, b ca 1760, resident of York in the 1820 census,
age 45 plus, most likely widower, with a much larger family
than the Jonathan just listed above, containing three males,
one under 10 and two age 10-16, and four females, one under
10, two 10-16, and one age 26-45. (Census York Co., 1820,
p590)

JONATHAN, b ca 1765, lived in York per the 1820 census,
age 45 plus. His household contained three males under 10,
and two females, one age 26-45 and one age 10-16. (Census
York Co., 1820, p603)

JONATHAN, b ca 1770, of York, resident of York per the
1800 census, age 26-45, with only a spousal figure of the same
age bracket at home. (Census York Co., 1800, p1034)

JONATHAN, Jr., b ca 1770, of York, yeoman, s/o Jonathan
Young, no known antecedents. By deed signed 19 Jul 1804,
rec'd 8 Sep 1804, Jonathan sold to John Kingsbury Jr. and
Benjamin Kingsbury of York, for $100.00, 7 acres land in York,
"being the same which was set off by a committee to my late
father Jonathan Young, deceased, 14 Jun 1753, Book 32:22;
beginning at the western corner of land that used to belong to
James Junkins, and now owned by Jonathan Junkins, turning
north 80 rods by lands of Samuel Shaw, then 14 x 80 rods;
witness Jeremiah Linscott [York Deed 72:23].

JONATHAN 3rd, aka Esq., b 12 Dec 1773, York, s/o Jonathan
and Mercy (Nowell) Young, d 19 Oct 1838, Acton, age 65,
married; m ca 1799, Mehitable Moody [b 4 Dec 1775, of Saco,
d/o William Pepperell Moody and Elizabeth Scannan Moody,
d 4 Dec 1848, Acton, age 73, widow]. Jonathan 3rd became a
graduate of Harvard, class of 1798, and was considered the
earliest Young to relocate in Acton, circa 1830, making him
the progenitor of this branch of Youngs in Acton. He was
named sole Exec. and residuary legatee of his father's estate
by will drawn 10 Nov 1798, probated Apr 1808, and was to
receive all his father's real estate of upland and marsh
including the buildings, livestock and farming utensils, with
the exception of one-fourth part of the sawmill privilege.

After probate of his father's estate in Apr 1808,
Jonathan 3rd raised the amount of $500.00 by mortgaging "all
my homestead farm in York with buildings, given to me by my
honored father's last will," with the proviso that if Jonathan
made payment of $410.00 plus interest to grantees Elihu
Bragdon, Esq., Jonathan Young, yeoman and John Junkins,
yeoman, all of York, on a certain note jointly signed 2 Apr
1803, the homestead would revert to his estate; witnesses
Alexander MacIntire, Jacob Frost [York Deed 81:238].

On 9 Sep 1810 Jonathan Jr. of York became grantee in a
mortgage Jabez Young signed as grantor; this involved Jabez

mortgaging a property in York which he had bought at public auction from Mary Hutchins of York, giving title to Jonathan Jr., Joseph Young [believed to be sibling] and Nathaniel Parsons, all of York, for $200.00. The deed stipulated that the three grantees cited above were bound with Jabez by bond dated 7 Nov 1808; if Jabez made payment in full, then the deed became void.

Another land deed wherein Jonathan Jr. and Jabez Young were co-grantors was signed 28 Sep 1811, rec'd 1 Oct 1811: they sold for $600.00, a two-story house and stable standing by the highway leading through Cape Neddick in York, conveyed to Jabez by William Stover on 3 Nov 1800. Wife Nancy conveyed dower rights. See Jabez for further details on both land deeds.

Jonathan 3rd and Mehitable relocated in Acton at least by 1830. Here their children were born and raised. The 1830 census for Acton listed Jonathan, Esq. as resident, age 50-60, and revealed a large household containing ten other persons: a spousal figure of same age bracket, five males one each 5-10, 10-15, 20-30, 30-40, 40-50, and four other females, two each 10-15, and 15-20.

Jonathan's own will was drawn up 8 Oct 1838, probated 7 Jan 1839, in which he named sons William M. and Peter as Co-Execs. of his will, devising to wife Mehitable her one-Thirds of all his real and personal property; witnesses Timothy Shaw, Paul S. Adams, Nicholas E. Paine [York Probate Co. #20949]. Bequests were made to six daughters and four sons in this particular sequence: 3rd son Joshua M., $50; 4th son Edmund J., $100; eldest daughter Sarah H., $50; 2nd daughter Elizabeth S. Thompson, w/o Charles Thompson, $50; 3rd daughter Mary H., $50; 4th daughter Mehitable H. Gorman, w/o Hugh J. Gorman, $50; 5th daughter Martha C., $50; 6th and last daughter Pamelia A., $50. Daughters were to receive equal shares of his personal estate.

His 9th and 10th bequests devised to oldest sons William M. and Peter all his real estate, subject to the life estate of one-third part that his wife would hold during her life. However, Jonathan stipulated that "my dwelling house...shall be equally owned by my son William and such of my daughters as shall be unmarried."

John Hubbard, Moses Garvin and Jonathan Sanborn were appraisers of Jonathan's estate; on 4 Mar 1839 the Co-Execs. were advised to file their inventory within three months, and a true account within one year. Family members were buried at the Peter Young lot on Young's Ridge Road, Acton.

Ch. b Acton: Peter+, b 14 Jan 1800; Sarah H.+ (Young) Green, b 1802; William M.+, b 19 Apr 1804; Elizabeth S.+ (Young) Thompson, b 1806; Joshua Moody+ aka Josue Maria Young, b 29 Oct 1808; Mary H., b ca 1810; Mehitable H.+ (Young) Gorman, b 1810s; Martha C., b 1820s; Pamelia A.+ (Young) Hicks, b ca 1830; Edmund J.+, b ca 1838. (ME I.G.I.; Hale's Cems., n.p.; Family Recs., courtesy of Forest G. Hicks,

Oxnard, CA; Census York Co., 1830, p66; Thompson's Recs. of York Co., TMs, p416)

JONATHAN, Esq., b 1774, of York, alive 1850, York, age 76, widower, spouse unknown. On 14 Dec 1840, Jonathan had his will drawn up, naming son John his Exec. and sole residuary legatee of the estate, real and personal; probated 5 May 1856, witnesses Charles O. Emerson, Edward G. Brooks, George Dannel (or Daniel?) [York Probate #20950]. He made the following bequests: son George, five dollars; married daughter Asenith Twombly, ten dollars; married daughter Nancy Bacheldor, ten dollars, the above three legacies to be paid within one year after his decease; single daughters Mercy and Charlotte, each "a home at my house" and a "comfortable support" to be furnished by his son and Exec. John; and if they should marry, each would receive ten dollars; lastly son John, "all his estate not herein before disposed of, real, personal, and mixed." One of the public places where John posted notices to make known his appointment as Exec. was at the Congregational Meeting House in York.

In 1850 Jonathan was head of household in York, age 76, estate assessed at $3,000 per census that year. Family members included son John, daughter-in-law Mary and their young sons John and Joseph. Ch. b at York: prob. George+, b 1802; Asenith (Young) Twombly, b 1810s; Nancy+ (Young) Bacheldor, b 8 Jul 1810; John+, b 1815; prob. Mercy+ aka Mary (Young) Moulton, b 7 Sep 1818; and prob. Charlotte+ (Young) Shorey, b ca 1825. (Census York Co., 1850, Reel A, p217; Frost's York Cem., p620)

JONATHAN, b ca 1775, of Pepperellborough, aka Saco, listed as head of family in the 1800 census, age 16-26, with a spousal figure of the same age group and one male under the age of 10 at home. (Census York Co., 1800, p939)

JONATHAN Jr., b ca 1775, of York, listed in their 1810 census, age 26-45, with a young household containing a maternal figure [b ca 1780] and four children--two males and two females each under the age of 10. (Census York Co., 1810, p822)

JONATHAN, b ca 1775, resident of York. Jonathan was listed in the 1830-1840 census reports for York. In the 1830 census, his age was 50-60, as was the spousal figure: his household contained two males, one each 15-20 and 20-30, and four other females, one each 5-10, 10-15, 15-20 and 20-30. In the 1840 census, Jonathan's age was reported as 60-70, as was a senior female figure. His household contained one other male and two other females, each age 20-30. (Census York Co., 1830, p238; 1840, Reel B, p259)

JONATHAN, b ca 1790, of Lebanon, poss. s/o Eliphalet and Susannah (Wallingford) Young; m 2 Jun 1816, Lebanon, by Elder David Blaisdell, Lydia Downs [b ca 1795, of same town]. It is most likely this Jonathan was listed in the 1820 census for Lebanon, age 26-45, as head of household, with spousal figure in same age bracket and two young females under the age of 10 at home. (Lebanon Marr, p224; Census York Co., 1820, p531)

JONATHAN Jr., b 16 Jan 1809, York, s/o Jonathan and Joanna (Nowell) Young, d 16 Jul 1885, native town, age 74-6-0, married. Jonathan filed (Ints.) 28 Nov 1850, m1 5 Jan 1851, York, Olive Moulton [b 3 Jun 1820, York, d 3 Aug 1858, native town, of cancer, age 38-2-0, married, a Baptist]. The 1860 census showed that Jonathan was widower, age 50; his household contained sons J. Bradford and Edward D., and laborer James Austin, n.d.

Jonathan filed (Ints.) 27 Feb 1863, m2 5 Mar 1863, York, Alice P. Littlefield [b 27 Mar 1821, of Wells, d 27 May 1899, age 78-2-0, widow]. Records did not surface indicating that Jonathan had children by second wife Alice.

As for his teen years, Jonathan Jr.'s father died 14 Nov 1827 when the son was merely 18 years old. He and his three brothers were made wards of George Grant of York on date of 6 Dec 1830, indicating Jonathan had by that time reached the age of majority. While still young and not yet married Jonathan was given a lot of adult responsibility; he was listed as head of a large household in York in both the 1840 and 1850 census reports. In 1840, his age was 20-30 as were two other males; a fourth male was age 15-20; on the distaff side, there was a maternal figure age 60-70, one female age 40-50, and another female age 10-15. These figures on the distaff side suggested his widowed mother and sisters. In the summer of 1850, the census showed he was still single, his age 41. The family estate was valued at $2,500; at home were his widowed mother Joanna, age 73, his younger brother Mark, Alexander Perkins [b 1835] and Dorcas C. Nowell [b 1794].

Four generations of this family were represented in this entry: (1) Jonathan and Joanna Nowell Young via their (2) son Jonathan Jr. and spouses Olive Moulton Young and Alice P. Young, down to their (3) son Edward D., and his son (4) Dwight G. They were buried at York Cemetery in the Young Lot on the west side of Rte. 91 near York River, opposite 131 Cider Hill Road.

Ch. b York by first wife Olive: J. Bradford, b 1851; Edward D.+, b Apr 1855. (ME I.G.I.; Bragdon & Frost's York V.R., pp273, 297-298; Frost's York Cem., pp620-621; Hale's Cems., n.p.; Census York Co., 1840, Reel B, p259; 1850, Reel A, p215; 1860, Reel C, p961; Picton's ME Cem. Inscrips., V3, p2372)

JONATHAN, b 1821, farmer and resident of Lebanon in 1850. He lived alone at age 29. (Census York Co., 1850, Reel B, p34)

JOSEPH, n.d., d Jun 1809, Kennebunk. (Thompson's Recs. of York Co., TMs, p416)

JOSEPH, Lt., b 1671, York, Gent., eldest s/o Rowland and Susanna (Matthews) Young, gr.s/o Rowland and Joan (Knight) Young, d 6 May 1734, York, age 63, married, testate; m ca 1695, York, Abigail Donnell [b ca 1675, of York, d 17 Oct

1746, same town, widow]. The earliest land deed found for Joseph Jr. of York was dated 21 Aug 1707, rec'd 1 Jan 1716/7: he sold to Alexander Junkins of York, two acres salt marsh and thatch ground which he inherited from his father, located on the N.W. branch of the York River and bounded by marshes of Arthur Bragdon, Sr.; witnesses Joseph Sayward, Micom MacIntire [York Deed 8:194].

The earliest court entry found for Joseph of York in the Court Records of Maine was dated 6 Jan 1712/13, at the Inferior Court of Common Pleas, his name listed on the Jury of Trials [Court of Gen. Sessions, V5, p8]; his name was likewise listed on the Jury of Trials for 5 Jan 1713/14; 3 Apr 1716; 29 Jan 1716/17; 24 Feb 1717/18; and 7 Oct 1718 [Court of Gen. Sessions, V5, pp12, 67, 84, 96, 210]. Then Joseph's name and that of younger brother Matthews, both of York, were included in a warrant issued 28 December 1719 to the Sheriff of the county [Court of Gen. Sessions, V6, p33]: the brothers were named to a committee of twelve townsmen to view and lay out a way, according to their best skill and judgment with the most "conveniency" to the public and least prejudice or damage to any particular person, a passageway through the lands of Jacob Remick Jr. of Kittery, who had complained in the warrant "that he is greatly Damnified by the highway running through his land and that the said way may be altered without prejudice to the public."

Siblings Joseph and Benaiah and neighbor Henry Donnell were witnesses to Rowland Young's exchange of land between neighbor John Pickering of Portsmouth, N.H. and himself on __ Nov 1718, rec'd 15 May 1719, it being their preference to swap acreage: Rowland had 24 acres and Pickering had the same quantity of land adjoining him, granted to each one by the town of York.

Joseph, as oldest son, was named his father's sole Exec. in will drawn 14 Sep 1719, proved 2 Jan 1721/2; he was devised the homestead where they then dwelt as well as one-half of the little pasture adjoining it, including housing, orchard and about one acre of salt marsh next to Kittery. The following year Joseph conveyed to his youngest brother Benaiah of York for seven pounds current money, one-1/2 acres of fresh marsh or meadow ground in York, located on the north side of York River by Benaiah's land and upon the S.W. side of Joseph's land lately given him by his father Roland of York, by deed signed 18 Feb 1722, rec'd 3 Jan 1723/4; witnesses Henry Simpson, Abraham Preble [York Deed 11:121].

At the age of 25 [as of 16 Oct 1696], Joseph was granted 30 acres land by the town of York, only to sell 15 acres from this plot by deed signed 8 Dec 1721, rec'd same date, for a certain sum of money, to Elihu Parsons of York; witnesses John Woodbridge, John Cheesebrough [York Deed 10:236]. To his brother Jonathan of York he sold a certain parcel of marsh lying in the S.W. branch of York River, by deed rec'd 8 Jan 1731, rec'd 1 Apr 1736, "being a point of marsh that was the estate of our honored father Roland Young of said York deceased," which Joseph had inherited, abutting the lands of Daniel Pall and Robert Cutts; witnesses John Carlisle, Benaiah Young [York Deed 18:284].

Before Joseph's will was drawn up in 1734, he executed two deeds of gifts, the first of these to his only son Samuel, signed 30 Apr 1729, rec'd 5 Feb 1730, with wife Abigail relinquishing Dower Rights: he conveyed the tract of land in York "it being the same land whereon my honored father Rowland Young deceased lived and which my honored grandfather Rowland Young deceased gave to my said father," by deed dated 25 Aug 1685; witnesses Edward Preble, Edmund Black, John Higgins [York Deed 14:76]. This deed of gift reserved to himself "a certain two acres of land on the N.E. side thereof to be laid out...as I shall think fit."

The second deed of gift was to his married daughter Abigail Bradbury, wife of John Bradbury, signed 13 Apr 1734, rec'd 20 May 1734: for ten pounds current money, Joseph sold two acres land in York, that is, his father's homestead, beginning at the S.W. corner of the land John Bradbury bought of Joseph Jr. and by land of Alexander Junkins bought of Joseph, which Joseph's honored father devised to him in his last will; witnesses John Carlisle, Benaiah Young [York Deed 17:185].

Joseph became Admin. of his son Samuel's estate upon his death in Dec 1730, at the age of 26. His first accounting of costs and disbursements was attested to and allowed 10 May 1732; total expenses came to 171-18-3, which included sundries allowed the widow in bringing up two small children. Another accounting by Joseph, allowed 17 Jul 1733, gave additional costs and distributions in the amount of 20-5-6. As Admin., he obtained license to sell some of Samuel's estate in May 1732, in order to pay off debts. Please see main entry on Samuel regarding the myriad details of business transactions amidst the insolvency of Samuel's estate.

In his will drawn 1 May 1734, probated 4 Jun 1734, Joseph left all his estate both real and personal to his wife Abigail for the term of her natural life, and named her and son-in-law John Bradbury as Co-Execs; witnesses Jeremiah Moulton, Sarah Favour [d/o of Job and Sarah Preble Young], Daniel Moulton [Maine Wills, pp351-352]. It was Joseph's intent that upon Abigail's death, the estate would revert to grandson Joseph Young, viz. only son of Samuel, deceased. In the event his grandson should die before coming of age, Joseph's estate would thus be equally divided among Joseph's and Abigail's grown surviving daughters: Mary, Abigail, Bethulah and Bethiah [Phebe Bradbury then deceased]. Should grandson Joseph come of age, he was to pay three pounds apiece to Joseph Sr.'s four daughters mentioned above, as well as Joseph Sr.'s granddaughter Abigail Young.

Letters Test. on Joseph's estate were granted 4 Jun 1734, at Wells, to John Bradbury [son-in-law] and widow Abigail, Co-

Execs. of Joseph's will, the inventory and accounting due before 10 Jan next [York Probate #20952]. Inventory on Joseph's estate in York was taken by Daniel Stimpson, Samuel Sewall and Samuel Milberry at [zero total], attested at Wells 29 Jan 1734/5. This included the homestead of about six acres, dwelling house and barn, wharf, warehouse and orchard, valued at 236 pounds, plus one common right, one-third of a coasting sloop and books [York Probate 5:77].

Petition for Widow's allowance for Abigail's necessaries was made 27 Jun 1738, totalling 23-10-0; additional inventory, exhibited 28 Jun 1738, came to 54-11-2. The accounting by Abigail and said Bradbury as Co-Execs. was attested to on same date, with disbursements totalling 185-1-5 and 74-4-0. Included in this were the expenses of maintaining Joseph Young, minor son of Samuel Young [York Probate 5:128].

Inasmuch as Joseph's estate fell short 63 pounds to pay off debts, petition to sell real estate was filed by Exec. Bradbury on the 3rd Wed. of June 1739, rec'd 18 Feb 1741. The court empowered Bradbury to sell, and two and one-half acres of Joseph's land at the upper end of the homestead and eight shares of Common Rights granted to Joseph 19 Jun 1732, were sold at auction for eight pounds per common right to Amos Gowdy of York [York Deed 23:11].

Ch. b York: Mary, b 2 Jan 1697, alive 1 May 1734, age 37; Abigail+ (Young) Bradbury, b 22 Aug 1699; Phebe+ (Young) Bradbury, b 25 Jan 1702; Samuel+, b 21 Jul 1704; Bethulah+ (Young) Beale aka Bale, b 25 Feb 1707/8; Bethiah+ (Young) Stackpole, b 5 Sep 1709. (ME I.G.I.; Noyes et al, p776; Bragdon & Frost's York V.R., pp392-393)

JOSEPH Jr., b ca 1680, York, s/o Robert and Mary (Say-ward) Young, gr.s/o Henry and Mary (Peasley) Sayward, alive Mar 1734/5, ca age 54, native town; m1 Jan 1700/1, York, Mary Hutchins [b ca 1680, d pre 1708, York]; m2 1708, York, Sarah King [b 17 May 1687, of Kittery, d/o Ens. Richard and Mary (Lydston) King, alive 6 Mar 1734, York, age ca 47]. Sarah's father Richard King, shipwright, received a grant of 90 acres land from the town of Kittery in 1663; she was the eldest of seven children.

Frederick R. Boyle's Sanford indicated his strong belief that Joseph Young, husband of (1) Mary Hutchins and (2) Sarah (King) Young, and off-shoot from the York Youngs headed by Robert and Mary Sayward Young, was the progenitor of the Youngs from the Sanford area. The earliest deed found for Joseph Jr. was signed 10 Jun 1717, rec'd 15 May 1718, in which he sold to John Sayward of York for 31 pounds money, 21 acres land, 15 of which were given to Charles Martin by the town of York 18 May 1667, and was bounded on the upper side of a lot of land formerly laid out to Dodavah Hull [male], late of York; the other six acres of upland were granted to Robert Young, late of York, father of said Joseph, by the town of York 17 Jun 1685; witnesses Jotham Odiorne, Johnson Harmon, Nathaniel Freeman [York Deed 9:34].

The first reference to Joseph Jr. found in Court Records of Maine was dated 1 Apr 1718, when he was named to serve on the Grand Inquest [grand jury] for the following year. In the following quarter this jury service was renewed 1 Jul 1718 for another year [Court of Gen. Sessions, V5, pp206-207].

Joseph Jr. sold to Jonathan Preble of York, millwright, for six pounds the lands and marsh known as Cousin's Lands and Marsh in North Yarmouth, which were formerly given by John Cousins to Mrs. Mary Sayward, late of York, Joseph's maternal grandmother, by deed signed 3 Nov 1718, rec'd 30 May 1721; witnesses Mary Preble, Edward Preble [York Deed 10:175].

And by deed dated 18 Apr 1720, rec'd 1 Aug 1720, Joseph bought from Abraham Battin of York [brother-in-law, husband of Joseph's sister Mary] for twenty-one pounds, land that had been in the possession or improvement of "my deceased father Robert Young late of York...which now doth of right belong unto the said Joseph Young," Mary Battin ceded dower rights; witnesses Abraham Preble, Nathaniel Freeman [York Deed 10:70].

A sale of 30 acres of inherited land in York was made by Joseph to the same John Sayward of York cited above, "for a valuable consideration," on 9 Feb 1721/2, deed rec'd 12 Feb 1721; witnesses Isaac Provender, Edward Preble [York Deed 10:252]. Joseph's next deed signed 4 Apr 1721, recorded the day after, revealed that his 2nd wife Sarah ceded her dower rights in the mortgage of some of his property to William Pepperell for 38 pounds lawful money, due and payable with interest twelve months hence: one certain parcel of land in York containing 30 acres and Joseph's dwelling house where he then lived, bounded on the S.W. by Rowland Young, on the S.E. by Joseph Young, Sr., and N.W. and N.E. by Capt. Pickerin's land; witnesses Thomas Mannering, John More, Thomas Huff [York Deed 10:123-124]. Joseph redeemed this mortgage by payment of 38 pounds Province bills to William Pepperell on 21 Dec 1724, rec'd 6 Jan 1724/5; witnesses William Pepperrell Jr., John Bradbury [York Deed 11:184].

Joseph Jr., with spouse Sarah ceding dower rights, sold to John Bradbury of York for the consideration of four score pounds current money, a tract of land in York lying on the north side of York River containing twelve to thirteen acres and the "house that had formerly been inhabited by Deacon Rowland Young and now by said Bradbury," by deed signed 27 Jan 1724/5, rec'd 24 Feb 1724/5; witnesses Abraham Battin, John Bean [York Deed 11:189-190].

As mentioned earlier, Joseph's maternal grandparents were Henry and Mary (Peasley) Sayward of York. The following deed which was rec'd 19 Feb 1724, listed the eight surviving heirs-at-law of Henry Sayward as of 9 Feb 1724: Edward Preble, Joseph Sweat and Hannah his wife, John Sayward, Joseph Sayward, Abraham Battin and Mary his wife, and Joseph of this entry. The heirs-at-law sold their shares in a tract of land of 370 acres in York, 20 acres of which were swamp lands, located on the S.W. side of York River, to William Moody of

82

York; witnesses Samuel Came, Daniel Farnam [York Deed 11:187-188].

A deed of sale followed which did not include the signature of spouse, signed 1 Mar 1726/7, rec'd 3 Mar 1726/7: to Abraham Martin Jr. of York, "a certain dwelling house of one story high standing on the lot of land which the said Abraham Martin lately purchased of Joseph Sayward, "it being the same house wherein I have dwelt for several years last past," witnesses A. Baker, Joseph Moody [York Deed 12:103].

The next four deeds of sale will show second spouse Sarah King Young ceding dower rights: (1) by deed dated 26 Jul 1727, rec'd 15 Feb 1728, to John Racklefe of York, for six pounds money, a tract of land in York formerly granted to Joseph's father Robert Young at a Town Meeting 17 Jun 1685; situated between the lots of Charles Martin and Thomas Moulton on the S.E. side of the mill Creek and a lot of land granted to Lewis Bane and laid out to Mr. Brisson; witnesses Abraham Martin, Daniel Martin [York Deed 13:2].

(2) to John Carlisle of York, signed 13 Jun 1728, rec'd 26 Jul 1728, for 124 pounds current money, a tract of thirteen acres, beginning at the corner bounds as the fence now lies between Benaiah Young [sibling] and Joseph on the S.E. side of the road leading from Trafton's ferry to the York Meeting House, and running along on the S.W. side of the road joining to said road as the said Young's fence now lies, till it comes to the corner bounds between Joseph Young and John Bradbury, "it being a small tract of land that John Bradbury purchased of Joseph, joining along by said Bradbury's bounds till it comes to the old fence formerly made between said Joseph Young's father Robert Young and Rowland Young," thence W.N.W. on a straight line by Benaiah Young's fence; witnesses Jonathan Young, Hannah Shaw [York Deed 12:308].

(3) by deed signed 2 Feb 1732, rec/d 16 Jun 1735, Joseph Jr., husbandman, sold to Caleb Preble of York for eight pounds current money, all his eight shares in the Common and undivided lands in York which were granted to Joseph at a town meeting begun and held in York 19 Jun 1732 and continued by adjournment to the 25th of Sep following; witnesses Jeremiah Moulton, Hannah Moulton [York Deed 17:105-106].

And (4) with Sarah signing as one of the daughters and co-heirs of Richard King late of Kittery and sibling to Daniel King, deceased. Joseph and Sarah sold outright to Thomas Knight of Kittery, cordwainer, any remaining interest or share in either her father's or brother's estate, for 27 pounds current money by deed signed 6 Mar 1734, rec'd 16 Apr 1735; witnesses Jeremiah Moulton, Daniel Moulton [York Deed 17:78].

Ch. b York by 2nd wife Sarah: Mary, b 22 Apr 1709; Robert, b 15 Jul 1711; Rowland, b 11 Oct 1713; Joseph+, b 1 Dec 1715; Bethiah+ (Young) Ingraham, b 9 Feb 1717/8; Susanna, b 6 Aug 1720; Joanna, b 20 Apr 1723; Daniel, b 14 Dec 1725; Abraham, b 10 Oct 1728, twin, d 2 Apr 1729; and Nathaniel, b 10 Oct 1728, twin. (Noyes et al, pp336, 401, 776; ME I.G.I.; Bragdon & Frost's York V.R., p49; MH&G **Rec.**, V1, p6)

JOSEPH, b ca 1700, of Falmouth, Cumberland County, laborer, landowner and potential resident of York County. Joseph bought from John and Martha Elden of Scarborough for 75 pounds lawful money, **two** parcels of land holding 70 acres of meadows and upland, including dwelling house and outbuildings, the first part of which was located in that part of the town that is called Dunstown, and the other lying upon that part of the town called Bluepoint Tide; by deed signed 15 Jan 1731, rec'd 14 Mar 1744; witnesses Solomon Lombard, Thomas Starboard [York Deed 25:38]. Strangely enough, the deed held the proviso that if Joseph and family were "molested" by predators, satisfaction from the grantors in the amount of 37 pounds-10 shillings would be upon demand.

Another deed of that era, signed 1742, rec'd 24 May 1743, could conceivably have referred to this same Joseph. Joseph, the grantor, was of Wiscassett, and sold to Abraham Tyler, Gent. of Scarborough for eighteen pounds, fifteen shillings, 43 acres land of upland and meadow, beginning at the turn of Dunstown River just below Pine Bridge on the southern side of the river; witnesses Samuel Milliken, Robert Jameson [York Deed 23:245].

JOSEPH, b ca 1715, of York, one of the soldiers under William Pepperrell, in Capt. John Harmon's Company, took part in the expedition to and reduction of Cape Briton, sold to John Whitney of York, physician for 20 pounds bills of credit, old Tenor, "any premises that he may receive as bounty for his service at Cape Briton"; witnesses Daniel Moulton, Thomas Curtis [York Deed 26:270].

JOSEPH Jr., b 1 Dec 1715, York, s/o Joseph Jr. and Sarah (King) Young; filed (Ints.) 27 Dec 1740, York, Susanna Johnson [b ca 1720, Andover, MA]. Ch. b York: Abraham+, b 8 Jan 1742; Joseph+ Jr., b 31 Oct 1744. (ME I.G.I.; Bragdon & Frost's York V.R., p127)

JOSEPH, b ca 1725, York, filed (Ints.) 11 May 1751, m 17 Jun 1751, York, Dorcas Babb [b ca 1730, of same town]. (ME I.G.I.; Bragdon & Frost's York V.R., p136; F. R. Boyle's **Sanford**, p330)

JOSEPH, b ca 1730, York, filed (Ints.) 21 Apr 1753, m 8 May 1754, York, Elizabeth Carpenter [b ca 1735, of same town]. (ME I.G.I.; Bragdon & Frost's York V.R., p138)

JOSEPH, b ca 1740, of York, most likely b 31 Oct 1744, York as s/o Joseph Jr. and Susanna (Johnson) Young; filed (Ints.) 26 Nov 1766, York, Mary Johnson [b ca 1745, of Phillipstown]. (Bragdon & Frost's York V.R., pp127, 149)

JOSEPH, b ca 1745, of York, prob. the Joseph listed immediately above; head of household in the 1790 Census for York, with family containing two males under 16 and two females. (Census York Co., 1790, p72)

JOSEPH, b 1758, Wells (also given as Sanford), d 1808, Wells, **age** 50; m ca 1782, Wells, Martha aka Patty (   ) [b ca

1762 of Kennebunk]. During the American Revolution, Joseph of
Wells mustered in for a three-year term by Nathaniel Wells,
Muster Master for York Co., dated 6 Mar 1777, in Capt. Daniel
Wheelwright's Co., Col. Ebenezer Francis' Regt. He received
State and Continental bounties. Continental Army pay accounts
cited service from 28 Mar 1777 to 31 Dec 1779. Subsistence
was allowed from date of enlistment, 28 Feb 1777 to date of
marching, 22 Mar 1777. A contradictory statement said that
Joseph resided in Sanford and was engaged for two years's
service for this town. A change of residence may have arisen
perhaps in the time between mustering out and re-enlisting by
January 1781, see below.

A descriptive list was dated 10 Jan 1780: Joseph served
in Capt. Nehemiah Emerson's Co., 10th Mass. Regt., with rank
of Corp., age 19, stature, 5 ft., 7 in., complexion dark,
hair, brown, residence, Wells; re-enlisted during war, served
as Corp. in Col. Benjamin Tupper's 10th Regt., service from
1 Jan 1781, 24 months. Joseph's name was also found in
Charles J. House's "Names of Soldiers of the American Revolution," p50, under the listing of those who applied for State
Bounty.

Joseph was listed as resident of Wells in the 1800
census, age 26-45, with spousal figure of the same age and one
young son under 10 at home. ((Mass. Soldiers & Sailors,
p1028; Census York Co., 1800, p991)

JOSEPH, b pre 1765, the earliest and sole resident by the
name of Young in the 1810 census for Buxton; his age was then
45 plus, with a spousal figure of the same age group. They
lived alone. (Census York Co., 1810, p735)

JOSEPH, b 8 Feb 1766, York, joiner, eldest s/o Jonathan
and Mercy (Nowell) Young, bur. 6 Jul 1820, native town, age
54, of consumption, intestate; filed (Ints.) 13 Sep 1786,
m 5 Oct 1786 at First Parish Church, York, Mary Carlisle [b ca
1765, of York, alive Nov 1820, same town, widow]. Joseph was
named heir-at-law of Jonathan by will signed 10 Nov 1798,
proved Apr 1808, his bequest, a one-fourth part of a sawmill
privilege with stipulation attached that he could not sell
this outside of the family.

Joseph's father Jonathan previously made deed of gift to
·him on 4 Apr 1796, rec'd same date, of a plot of land approx.
36 rods by 175 rods between Lots 4 and 5, and adjacent to
Folly Marsh and lands of Samuel Sayward, with a reserve of a
road through said land at the most convenient place.

The 1800-1810 census reports for York listed Joseph as
head of family. In 1800 his age was 26-45, family containing
spousal figure in same age bracket and five children--one male
and one female both under 10, and one male and two females
ages 10-16. By 1810 Joseph's family had grown to five males,
two under 10 and three age 16-26, and six females, one
maternal figure at age 26-45, one under 10, and two each age
10-16 and 16-26.

Admin. Papers on Joseph's estate were filed by widow Mary, and accepted 14 Aug 1820, Mary having given bond that date [York Probate #20955]. On 27 Nov 1820, Miles Wilson deposed that he had caused to have posters hung in public places in York and Eliot advertising that Mary Young was to be appointed Admin. The Widow's allowance for "necessaries for upholding life" of $96.83 was granted on same date. Surviving children were not mentioned, nor identified. (Bragdon & Frost's York V.R., pp168, 363, 417; ME I.G.I.; Census York Co., 1800, p1012; 1810, p821)

JOSEPH, b 1770, Sanford, believed to be s/o Daniel and Anne (Johnson) Young, d 18 Oct 1841, native town, age 71, prob. widower, buried on Old Mast Road, native town; filed (Ints.) 30 Oct 1797, m1 19 Jan 1798, York, Ruth Ramsdell [b ca 1780, of same town, d 17 Jun 1810, Sanford, married, age ca 30]. Joseph m2 (Ints.) 19 Sep 1814, Hannah Morrill [b ca 1790, d 18 Mar 1815, Sanford, age ca 25]. He m3 29 Oct 1820, Rhoda ( ) Thompson [b ca 1785, poss. widow of Reuben Thompson, with a boy under 10, alive 1830]. Joseph and family lived on the Old Mast Road where the Young family cemetery was located.

For $25.00, Joseph bought from Daniel Young of Sanford one-half of Lot No. 5, in the Middle Range, Sanford, 50 acres more or less of the 100 acres Daniel bought from Benjamin Estes of Sanford, beginning at the S.W. and N.W. sides of the lot and holding its width by the road leading to Wells, all right and claim in said half lot No. 5; see Daniel's entry for full documentation.

The census reports for Sanford from 1810-1830 listed Joseph as head of family. In 1810 his age was 26-45, apparently a widower with family of two females under the age of 10 and one female age 10-16. In 1820, he and spousal figure were age 45 plus; at home were one male and one female both age 16-26, and two females age 10-16. In 1830, his age was 60-70, with a spousal figure of the same age bracket; they lived alone. It is believed that by the 1840 census Joseph was widower; he lived with married son Joseph Jr. in Sanford.

Known ch. b Sanford or York by first wife Ruth: Joseph+, b 11 Apr 1800; Naomi, b 1805, d May 1825, age 20. Ch. b Sanford by 2nd wife Hannah: child, d 27 Mar 1815. (ME I.G.I.; Bragdon & Frost's York V.R., p182; F. R. Boyle's Sanford, pp330-331; Mormon/ME V.R., Wright-Zitkov; Census York Co., 1810, p1014; 1820, p550; 1830, p344; MH&G Rec., V2, p112; Picton's ME Cem. Inscrips., V3, p1713)

JOSEPH, b ca 1780, of Wolfeboro, m 2 Dec 1813, Parsonsfield, Olive Folsom [b ca 1785, of Parsonsfield]. (Parsonsfield V.R., Town Clerk, p117)

JOSEPH, b ca 1785, resident of York according to the 1830 census, age 40-50, as was a maternal figure. The family contained three males, one each under 5, 5-10, and 15-20, as well as two other females, one each 10-15 and 20-30. See entry immediately below for a probable connection. (Census York Co., 1830, p249)

JOSEPH, b 1786, of York, d 2 Aug 1835, York, age 49, of typhus fever. (Bragdon & Frost's York V.R., p427)

JOSEPH, b 7 Aug 1788, Lebanon, farmer, poss. s/o Eliphal-et Young, d 14 Apr 1871, Somersworth or Rollingsford, N.H., age 83, married; m1 4 Mar 1812, Lebanon, Patience Wentworth [b 9 Aug 1790, Lebanon, d/o Samuel and Rosanna (Hill) Wentworth, gr.d/o Samuel and Patience (Downs) Wentworth, d Sep 1845, Milton, N.H.]. At time of marriage, Joseph lived in Dover, N.H., Patience in Somersworth. Joseph m2 14 Sep 1845, Lebanon, Sarah Ricker [b 1802, East Lebanon, d 10 Nov 1888, native town, age 86, widow, at the home of Willis Ricker, bur. on Gowell place].

Joseph and family relocated in Somersworth, N.H. in the 1840s after their children were born. Please see Youngs of Strafford County, N.H., Vol. I for full bibliography and entries on grown children who moved from Maine to New Hampshire.

Joseph was listed as head of household for Lebanon in census reports from 1820-1860, with the exception of the 1840 report. In 1820 Joseph's age and that of spouse were listed as 26-45; they had a young family of one male and two females, each under the age of under 10. In 1830 his age was 40-50, family containing a spousal figure of same age bracket, three males and three females all under 20 years of age. In 1850 Census, second wife Sarah was named as spouse, age 48; three children then lived at home, Augusta, Sophia and Charles. In 1860 Joseph was age 71, wife Sarah, 59; the two youngest children Sophia and Charles were at home.

Ch. b Lebanon by first wife Patience: James Morrill+, b 6 May 1813; Sarah Ann+ (Young) Clements, b 14 Sep 1815; Sophia, b 28 Jul 1818; Caroline Elizabeth+ (Young) Fernald, b 24 Nov 1821; Joseph Charles Wentworth, b 9 Oct 1824, d Jul 1846; Shadrach Hill, b 15 Jul 1827, d 27 Apr 1832; Shadrach H., b 29 Apr 1832; Harriet Augusta, b 7 Apr 1835, at home in 1850, single in 1900, resident of Rollingsford, N.H., living with nephew Nicholas A. Abbott and family; Patience Adeline, b 30 May 1831, d Apr 1843, age 12.

Ch. by second wife Sarah: Sophia, b 1846; Charles, b 1848. (1900 NH Soundex; NHVR-Marr; Wentworth Gen., V1, pp456-458; Lebanon Marr, p224, Births, pp159, 168, Deaths, p149; ME I.G.I.; Census York Co., 1820, p537; 1830, p263; 1850, Reel B, p41; 1860, Reel A, p82)

JOSEPH, b 1791, York, believed to be youngest s/o Samuel and second wife Mary (   ) Young of York, d 25 Jul 1837, native town, age 46; filed (Ints.) 16 Mar 1822, 17 Apr 1822, York, m 24 Apr 1822, Kittery, Susannah aka Susan Preble [b 1784, York, d/o Samuel Preble, alive 1860, native town]. Joseph was youngest s/o Samuel Sr. and a minor when his father Samuel made out deed of gift to elder sons Samuel Jr. and Noah of York on 10 May 1811, rec'd 11 May 1811. Inasmuch as his brothers were destined to receive most of Samuel Sr.'s estate in York, they were instructed to provide support and care not only to their parents, but also to younger sibling Joseph. The sum of $800.00 was specified by the father that was to be settled upon Joseph for his own farm, within four years' time after the father's death. One good reason for that delay was that Joseph was yet a minor.

In 1860 at the age of 76, widow Susan lived at the home of son Samuel in York per census that year. Ch. b York: Samuel Preble+, b 22 Apr 1823; Joseph Gilman, b 1820s, bur. 8 Sep 1832, York. (Bragdon & Frost's York V.R., pp215, 426, 526; Lebanon Marr, p224)

JOSEPH, b ca 1795, of Berwick, filed (Ints.) 2 Jun 1821, Berwick, m 29 Jul 1821, Durham, N.H., Mary Tebbetts aka Tibbetts [b ca 1800, of Durham, N.H.]. The married couple lived in Durham from at least 1842 up through 1854 when Joseph served as Selectman in Durham. (ME & N.H. I.G.I.; Stackpole's Durham, V1, pp366, 384)

JOSEPH Jr., b 11 Apr 1800, of Sanford, farmer, s/o Joseph and Ruth (Ramsdell) Young, d 23 Oct 1872, Sanford, age 72-6-12, married; m ca 1825, prob. Sanford, Edna M. Huston [b 7 Jun 1801, Sanford, d/o Abraham and Sarah (Littlefield) Huston, d 5 Oct 1882, Sanford, age 81-3-28, widow]. Joseph Jr. was listed as head of family in census reports for Sanford from 1830-1860 inclusive. In 1830 his age was 20-30, as was the spousal figure; at home were four males and one female all under 5 years. The 1840 census indicated Joseph's father, age 70-80 and widower, lived with Joseph Jr., then age 40-50; the family contained a spousal figure age 40-50, and eight children from ages 5-20.

In the 1850 census for Sanford, Edna was named his wife; value of the estate was set at $1,600. Family members included children Thomas, Irene, Edna, Hannah, Mary and Sally A. Ten years later, Joseph and Edna lived alone, their estate valued at $2,500. Joseph and family were buried at the Young Cemetery on Old Mast Road, south of Route 109, Sanford.

Ch. b Sanford: George W.+, b 7 Jul 1821; Thomas+ aka Ithamer, b 1824; poss. Marcia+ (Young) Taylor+, b ca 1826; Daniel L.+, b Mar 1828; Irene, b 20 May 1830, d 19 Sep 1905, age 75, presumed to be single; Edna, b 19 Mar 1832, d 13 Jun 1850, native town, age 18-2-25; Hannah F., b 11 Jul 1834, d 23 Mar 1851, native town, age 16-8-12; Mary Jane+ (Young) Perkins, b 17 Dec 1836; Sally A.+ (Young) Cram, b 6 Feb 1840. (Hale's Cems., n.p.; F. R. Boyle's **Sanford**, pp330-331; Census York Co., 1830, p344; 1840, Reel A, p153; 1850, Reel C, p126; 1860, Reel A, p433; Picton's ME Cem. Inscrips., V3, p1713)

JOSEPH, b 1814, Kennebunk, farmer, alive 1850, native town, s/o ____ and Martha (   ) Young; m 27 Nov 1842, Kennebunk, Miriam Littlefield [b 1819, of Kennebunk, alive 1850, same town]. Joseph was listed resident of Kennebunk in the 1850 census, his estate rated at $2,000. Members of family were spouse Miriam, age 31, two young daughters Miriam and

Elizabeth, and Martha Young [b 1763], presumed to be Joseph's widowed mother. Ch. b Kennebunk: Miriam, b 1846; Elizabeth, b 1849. (ME I.G.I.; Census York Co., 1850, Reel A, p86)

JOSEPH 2nd, b Oct 1821, of Waterboro, very poss. s/o John F. and Sarah (Saunders) Young [no main entry], d 1910, age 89, Ossipee, widower; m 5 Dec 1844, Waterboro, Hannah Chick [b 28 Jul 1821, Waterboro, d/o Noah and Mary (Hanson) Chick, d 28 Jan 1895, Ossipee, N.H., age 73-6-0, married]. Joseph was listed resident of Ossipee from 1850-1870, with spouse Hannah at home. It would seem that Joseph's background was Ossipee, whereas Hannah Chick's was Waterboro. He and family members were buried at the Young Cemetery at Center and South Effingham Road from Granite on the east side of the road. For census reports during this time, main entries on married sons and daughters, and N.H. bibliography, please see Youngs of Strafford Co., N.H., Vol. I.

Ch. b Ossipee, N.H.: John F. aka Frank, b 1845; Willard A., b 1846; Arthur P., b 26 Feb 1849; Roswell Byron, b 1853; Sarah F. aka Florence S. (Young) Whiting, b 1855; Clarissa A. aka Clara, b 1857, d 1934, Ossipee; Alice C. aka Eliza C. (Young) Maybury, b 25 May 1860; and Walter H., b 19 May 1868. (N.H. and ME I.G.I.; 1900 Soundex)

JOSEPH, b 18 Jan 1849, Sanford, s/o George W. and Abigail (Small) Young, d 18 Jul 1900, native town, age 51-6-0; dual marriage 21 Aug 1871, Sanford and Alfred, Charlotte E. aka Lottie E. Flanders [b 1847, prob. Hopkinton, N.H., d 1889, Sanford, age 42, married]. Joseph m2 9 Sep 1890, Sanford, Alice C. Flanders [b Jul 1851, Hopkinton, alive 1900, Sanford, age 49, married]. In the early summer of 1900 Joseph and Alice were listed with their infant son Joseph H. as members of his father's household in Sanford. Joseph H.'s death occurred shortly thereafter. Joseph and wives were buried at the Young plot on Old Mast Road, south of Route 109, Sanford.

Ch. b Sanford by first wife Charlotte, not traced further: John Howard, b ca 1891, d pre 1900. Ch. b Sanford by second wife Alice: Charlotte Emma, b 17 Mar 1892, d 24 Mar 1892, age 7 days; Joseph H., b Jul 1898. (F. R. Boyle's **Sanford**, pp330-332; Hale's Cems., n.p.; MH&G **Rec.**, V4, p268; 1900 ME Soundex; Picton's ME Cem. Inscrips., V3, p1713)

JOSEPH A., b Oct 1846, ME, mill hand, most likely s/o Samuel and Mathilda ( ) Young of Canada, d 1920, same town, age 74, widower; m ca 1870, Rebecca Milliken [b Jan 1850, of Biddeford, d 1905, same town, age 55, married]. There is a strong possibility that Joseph, at age 4, was the youngest son of Samuel and Mathilda Young who were listed residents of Biddeford in the 1860 census, the family then living at a boarding house. In 1900 Joseph A. was listed as head of household in Biddeford, address Pool Street, age 46. Family members included spouse Rebecca, son Charles and daughter Winnefred M. Joseph, Rebecca and four children were buried in Biddeford: Franklin P., George W., Winfield H. and Frederic.

Ch. b Biddeford, not traced further: William Albert,

b 29 Dec 1871, d.y.; Franklin P., b 1883, d same year; George W., b 1885, d 1887; Winfield H., b 1882, d 1889; Charles, b Jan 1888; Frederic C., b 1889, d same year; and Winnefred M., b Jun 1892. (Mormon/ME V.R., Wright-Zitkov; 1900 ME Soundex; Picton's ME Cem. Inscrips., V1, p166)

JOSEPH TIMOTHY, b Feb 1847, York, s/o Timothy and Mary Ann (Simpson) Young, alive 1900, native town; filed (Ints.) 30 May 1874, m 3 Jun 1874, York, Mary Clark Smith [b Jun 1852, York, alive 1900, native town, age 48]. In 1900 Joseph T. was listed head of household in York, age 53, with family containing spouse Mary C., age 47, and son Horace, age 21. Other members of household included Clara J. Junkins, servant, age 13 [b Jun 1886] and boarder Ernest Porter, age 45 [b Jan 1855, MA].

Ch. b York Village, not traced further: Horace J., b 25 Aug 1878, alive 1900, age 21. This was a delayed recording of birth as reported by uncle George H. Young. (ME I.G.I.; Bragdon & Frost's York V.R., pp319, 334; Mormon/ME V.R., Wright-Zitkov; 1900 ME Soundex)

JOSEPHINE, b 10 Oct 1868, Acton, d/o Joshua M. and Georgianna (Ricker) Young, d 1951, native town, age 83, widow of Frank Topliff Grant [b 1870, d 1921, Acton, age 51, married], both buried at the Young family plot on Young's Ridge Road, Acton. (Picton's ME Cem. Inscrips., p30)

JOSHUA, b ca 1730, of York, Yeoman, laborer, s/o Jonathan and Margaret (Stackpole) Young of York, d 14 Oct 1803, York, testate, widower; filed (Ints.) 27 Dec 1755, York, m 15 Jan 1756, York, Mary Young [b ca 1735, of York, d pre 1790, same town].

Before Joshua married, he acquired two lots of land, buying his first acreage in Kittery, from Sir William Pepperrell of Kittery, Baronet, one acre at sixteen pounds lawful money, located at the line between York and Kittery at the N.W. corner of Samuel and Jeremiah Bragdon's lands by deed signed 23 Jan 1753, rec'd 24 Aug 1753; witnesses Edward Ingraham, Benjamin Greenleaf, Jonathan Young [York Deed 31:112]. The second property Joshua bought from his father Jonathan Young of York by deed signed and rec'd 8 Jan 1754: for being helpful to him and his wife in their old age, for his love and affection, and forty pounds lawful money paid by Joshua, Jonathan conveyed to him his homestead land in York on the S.W. side of the York River where he then dwelt, containing 24 acres bound north by the river, and by lands of Ebenezer Young, Samuel Bragdon and Josiah Main.

Another early deed found for Joshua, husbandman, was dated 14 Sep 1763, rec'd 27 Aug 1765; he sold for 1-10-0 lawful money to Jeremiah Paul of York, a certain piece of "thatch beads" lying at the head of York River adjoining said Paul's land beginning at Henry Simpson's marsh leading to a certain clay bank by the side of the river; witnesses Joseph Paul, Arthur Came [York Deed 39:32].

The next three deeds heighten the "probability factor" that they "belong" to this same Joshua of York and his father Jonathan Young: (1) Joshua, husbandman, sold to Daniel Moulton Esq. for 20 shillings, two acres plus of land in Lot No. 2, 8th Range, in the Outer Commons, "originally granted to my father Jonathan Young of York, of whom I purchased the land," deed signed 27 Apr 1762, rec'd 5 Apr 1773; witnesses Jeremiah Moulton, Daniel Bridges [York Deed 42:185].

(2) The next deed showed that Joshua and his father Jonathan sold by deed signed 29 Apr 1762, rec'd 30 Apr 1762, to John McIntire Jr. of York for 10-13-4, their part and parcel of the salt marsh located on the western side of the S.W. branch of York River, "beginning at the salt marsh of the late Matthews Young until it comes to the marsh of the late Daniel Junkins," containing about two acres. (3) A couple of months later, Joshua, husbandman, sold to Samuel Shaw of York for 42 shillings, 8 pence, four shares in Lot No. 8, 2nd Div., in the Common Lands, that were originally granted to Joshua's father Jonathan, "of whom I purchased the land," signed 15 Jul 1762, rec'd 25 Jan 1763; witnesses Daniel and Hannah Moulton [York Deed 37:185-186].

Another purchase of Common Lands by Joshua was by deed dated 26 Dec 1771, rec'd 16 Jan 1772, bought from Joseph Holt of York for 6-18-8, six shares in land called Lot No. 2, 5th Range, in the Outer Commons, being three-quarters of a lot containing 140 acres; witnesses Joseph Sewall, Joseph Bragdon Jr. [York Deed 42:49]. Yet another purchase in the Outer Commons was by deed signed 5 Jul 1773, rec'd 30 Jun 1777, when Joshua bought from the Littlefield brothers Josiah, John, Jeremiah and Elias for 2-13-4, two shares in Lot No. 4, 4th Range, originally granted to William Peirce, of whom their father John Littlefield purchased the same; the land now lies in common with the rest of the proprietors of said lot; witnesses Richard Travett, Richard Keating [York Deed 44:51].

Joshua's shares in both these last two properties in the Outer Commons, Lot No. 2, 5th Range, and Lot No. 4, 4th Range, were sold to Jonathan Sayward of York by deed signed and rec'd 30 Jul 1779, for 53-2-6; witness Daniel Moulton [York Deed 44:68].

As husbandman, he sold by deed signed and rec'd 10 Feb 1780, to Samuel Moulton Jr. of York for 2-13-4, one acre land in Kittery which Joshua previously bought from Sir William Pepperrell on 23 Jan 1753 [see above], situated at the line which runs between York and Kittery at the N.W. corner of the lands belonging to the late Samuel and Jeremiah Bragdon, and thence by the York line 8 rods, S.W. by 20 rods, S.E. by 8 rods to said Bragdons' land; witnesses Daniel Moulton, Sr. and Jr. [York Deed 46:44].

Joshua of York was listed in the 1790 census, with one other male under 16, and four females in the household, which most likely included his wife Mary. The 1800 York census revealed Joshua's age group was 45 plus, and that he was then widowed; three females were in the household, one age 10-16, and two age 16-26.

On 14 Nov 1797, widower Joshua had his will drawn up in which he devised to son Joshua Jr., a minor, of Pleasant River at Eastward, a piece of salt marsh of one acre at the head of York River in the upper parish of York and his personal effects, wearing apparel, firearm and cutlass, and nine dollars in money to be paid him in one year after his father's demise. His three unmarried daughters Persis, Mary and Martha were bequeathed the homestead, farm and buildings in equal shares; however, it was understood that they were to pay their brother Joshua three dollars each within one year after their father's decease. Lastly, Joshua appointed his three daughters the Execs. of his will, and requested his friend Elijah Blaisdell to advise and assist them in discharging the terms of his will; witnesses David Sewall, Thomas Low, John Low [York Probate #20957].

On 21 Nov 1803, Joshua's will was presented for probate by two of the witnesses, David Sewall, Esq. and Thomas Lowe, allowed same date. At time of probate Persis was known as Persis Moulton. As a postscript to Joshua's will, single daughters Mary and Martha Young bought by deed dated 5 Apr 1806, rec'd 8 Apr 1806, a dwelling house in York standing on the parsonage land which had of late been occupied by Abigail Kimball, now deceased, but was bequeathed to Margaret Kimball, now deceased, and Elizabeth Oliver, spouse of grantor Daniel Oliver of Boston, Suffolk Co., Mass. Bay Colony; witnesses David and Daniel Sewall [York Deed 74:125].

Ch. b prob. York: Persis (Young) Moulton, b ca 1758, alive 1803; Mary, b 1760s, alive 1806; Martha, 1760s, alive 1806; and Joshua Jr., b ca 1770. (ME I.G.I.; Census York Co., 1790, p72, 1800, p1030; Bragdon & Frost's York V.R., p405)

JOSHUA Jr. aka Rev., b ca 1760, of Beverly, MA, s/o Joshua Young, alive ca 1805, spouse of Elizabeth Wallace [b ca 1765, of Beverly]. Joshua Jr. became the first minister of the First Baptist Church of Beverly, organized 25 Mar 1801, by fourteen members formerly of the Danvers Baptist Church; however, Joshua was not actually "installed." [See Youngs of Essex Co., Mass, Vol. II for further details].

Interestingly enough, additional information was found for Joshua within York County: by deed signed 7 Nov 1804, rec'd 30 May 1805, Joshua sold to Benjamin Kingsbury of York for $40.00, one acre of salt marsh in York, bounded by the southern branch of York River, and on the other side by land owned by Jeremiah Paul of York; this acreage was bequeathed to Joshua by his late father Joshua Young; witnesses John and Samuel Kingsbury [York Deed 73:95]. (Mass. I.G.I.; Stone's **Hist. of Beverly**, pp286-287)

JOSHUA, b ca 1765, of Chester, m 3 Jan 1789, Kittery, Sally Emery of Kittery [b ca 1770, of Kittery]. (Kittery V.R., p245)

JOSHUA, b ca 1810, Lyman, m 24 Sep 1834, Lyman, Esther Kimball [b ca 1814, of same town]. (ME I.G.I.)

JOSHUA MOODY aka Josue Maria, b 29 Oct 1808, Acton, s/o Jonathan and Mehitable (Moody) Young, d 18 Sep 1866, Roman Catholic prelate. He was designated as 3rd son and heir-at-law of Jonathan Young by will signed 8 Oct 1838, proved 7 Jan 1839. Mehitable Moody was the d/o William Pepperrell Moody of Saco, ME, whose ancestors came from England. Joshua's background was written up in several Catholic reference sources. The following was derived from R. H. Clarke's **Lives of the Deceased Bishops of the Catholic Church in the U.S.**, Vol. II (1888): "Joshua was trained in a country school in Saco, where he lived with his uncle Sam Moody, a Congregationalist. In 1828 he became a member of the Catholic Church, into which eight brothers and sisters later followed him. At this time he changed his name to Josue Maria. Soon thereafter he went west for his health. Employed as a journeyman printer, he settled down in Cincinnati where he worked for the **Catholic Telegraph** and spent his spare time teaching Sunday School and involving himself in relief work among the poor. He eventually studied for the priesthood at Mount St. Mary's Seminary, Emmitsburg, MD, and was ordained in 1838. He accepted the see of Erie and was consecrated on 23 Apr 1854, at St. Peter's Cathedral, Cincinnati." This account barely scratches the surface as to the good works Father Josue Maria accomplished. (Family Recs., courtesy of Forest G. Hicks of Oxnard, CA)

JOSHUA MOODY, b 9 Apr 1836, Acton, twin, s/o Peter and Mary (Garvin) Young, d 15 Jun 1915, age 79, widower, native town; m 21 Nov 1861, Biddeford, Georgianna Ricker [b 16 Jan 1845, N.H., d/o John and Sarah (   ) Ricker of Biddeford, d 24 May 1915, age 70, Acton]. In 1900 Joshua was listed head of family in Acton, age 64; household included spouse Georgianna, sons Lewis J., Alphonsus B., and Edward, daughter Agnes M., and his older sister Betsey Young, age 66, single [b 3 Apr 1834].

Joshua, spouse and children were buried at the Young family cemetery on Young's Ridge Road, Acton. His parents Peter and Mary as well as Peter's 2nd wife Deborah M. Berry were also buried there. Ch. b Acton: Florence, b 1 Nov 1862, d 23 Mar 1884; John W., b 31 Oct 1864, d 19 Sep 1868; Mary G., b 13 Dec 1867, d 4 Sep 1868; Josephine+ (Young) Grant, b 10 Oct 1868; William P., b 8 Oct 1870, d 30 Aug 1873; Emma Elizabeth, b 26 Mar 1873, 7th child; William P., b 10 Apr 1875, d 24 Jan 1876; Lewis J., b Nov 1876, alive 1900; Alphonsus B., b Jun 1879, alive 1900; and Edward, b Feb 1884, alive 1900. (ME I.G.I.; Mormon/ME V.R., Wright-Zitkov; Wentworth Gen., V2, pp88-89; Hale's Cems., n.p.; 1900 ME Soundex; Picton's ME Cem. Inscrips., V1, p30.)

JOSIAH T., b 1831, of Buxton, resident as of the 1850 census, age 19, ostler. He lived with Josiah and Sally Berry [b 1801 and 1802, respectively]. (Census York Co., 1850, Reel B, p55)

JOTHAM, b pre 1775, of Kennebunk, listed as resident in the 1820 census, age 26-45; household contained two females, their ages 45 plus, and two males under 10. (Census York Co., 1820, p399)

JOTHAM, b ca 1782, York, mariner, prob. s/o John and Hannah (Banks) Young, filed (Ints.) 14 Mar 1807, York, Hannah Sherman [b ca 1785, of same town]. By deed signed 30 Mar 1803, rec'd 1 Apr 1803, Jotham bought at public auction, real estate in York belonging to the estate of the late John Young of York, from John's widow Hannah Young: for $71.75, 4 acres pasture land in York, by lands of Edward Emerson Jr., Esq. and by lands of the heirs of both John Young Sr., and of Rowland Young deceased, as well as two additional acres found N.W. by the highway, N.E. by John Tenny's land, and S.W. by lands set off to widow Olive Grow as "her Thirds" in the estate of William Grow. For full documentation, please see entry on John and Hannah Banks Young.

The 1810 census for York listed Jotham as resident, age 26-45; household contained a maternal figure of same age, as well as one 45 plus, and two young females, both under ten years of age. It was entirely possible that Jotham had a daughter by the name of Abigail, b ca 1800, who married a Goodwin; it was common practice for a maternal grandfather to have a namesake: York V.R. listed a Jotham Young Goodwin [b ca 1825, of York] who filed (Ints.) 20 Jun 1850, m 4 Jul 1850, Sarah Ann Robes [b ca 1830, of York]. (Bragdon & Frost's York V.R., p192, 272; Census York Co., 1810, p821)

JULIA A., b Mar 1823, listed as resident of Berwick in the 1900 census, age 71, single; she lived at the home of her nephew Herbert L. Whitehouse, n.d. She may have been the same Julia A. Young from North Berwick who was listed as widow of _____ Young in the 1890 ME Vets, Census Index of Civil War Vets or Their Widows, York County, for North Berwick, District SD#1, Enum.#223. (1900 ME Soundex)

JULIA A., b 1855, of Dover, N.H., d/o Joseph and Mary (   ) Young [no main entry]; m 30 Sep 1876, Lebanon, James W. Brock [b 1851, Strafford, N.H., of Rochester, N.H., s/o Elijah and Nancy H. (   ) Brock]. (NHVR-Brides; Rochester TR, Marr, n.p.; Lebanon Marr, p224)

JULIA M., b Sep 1829, York, d/o Joel S. and Susan (Sayward) Young, d 19 Jun 1917, Kittery Point, widow, age 88; filed (Ints.) 27 Nov 1856, Kittery, m 4 Dec 1856, York, Capt. Isaac Mitchell [b 1828, d 18 Nov 1860, Kittery Point, age 32-3-0]. Julia lived at home in York per the 1850 census, and while still single, was named heir-at-law in her father's will signed 27 Jun 1855, probated 6 Apr 1869. By 1900 Julie M. was widowed, then aged 70; she and son Alfred M., age 43, lived with her brother Albert and his family in York.

She and husband Capt. Isaac Mitchell had been residents of Kittery Point; there they were buried at First Baptist Cemetery on Haley Road. Mitchell ch. b York: Alfred M. Mitchell, aka Alfred M. Young, b Sep 1857. (Hales Cems.,

Series I; ME I.G.I.; Kittery V.R., p400; Picton's ME Cem. Inscrips., V2, 1012; 1900 Soundex)

JULIE ANN, b ca 1830, of York, filed (Ints.) 25 Jan 1851, m 8 Feb 1851, York, Benjamin Trafton [b ca 1825, of same town]. (Bragdon & Frost's York V.R., p273)

LAURA A. (   ), b 1861, of Biddeford, d 1924, age 63, w/o Perley B. Young [n.d.].; she was buried at Greenwood Cemetery, Biddeford. (Picton's ME Cem. Inscrips., V1, p328)

LAVINIA, see LOVINIA

LEON G., b Jan 1867, VT, resident of Kittery in 1900, age 33, household containing spouse Cora C. (   ) [b Feb 1868, VT], and three children. Ch. b VT, not traced further: Lillian C., b Aug 1887; Carl F., b Aug 1892; and Mabel C., b Apr 1896. (1900 ME Soundex)

LEWIS aka Capt., b 7 Jan 1773, Orleans, Barnstable Co., MA, mariner, s/o Edmund and Mary (   ) Young [no main entry], d 10 Apr 1817, Biddeford, age 43, intestate, leaving a wife and family. Lewis m1 4 Aug 1797, Orleans, Jerusha Higgins [b 1780, d 6 Feb 1806, Biddeford, age 26, by whom there was no issue, buried at Nason-Dean Cemetery, Biddeford]. Lewis m2 ca 1807/8, Biddeford, Susanna (   ) [b ca 1785, of Biddeford, alive 12 Jul 1824, same town, widow].

While Lewis and Jerusha still lived in Orleans, Lewis bought from Nathaniel Webster of Biddeford for $355.00, one-third of an acre of land in Biddeford, beginning at the road leading from Saco Falls to Winter Harbor in Biddeford adjoining Amos Gordon's land; Judith Webster relinquished dower rights; witnesses John Hartley, Sally Webster [York Deed 70:64]. Shortly thereafter, Lewis and family moved to Biddeford, as indicated by the 1810 census for Biddeford: Lewis was then head of household there, age 45 plus, spouse age 26-45, their family containing six children, three males, two under 10 years, one age 10-16, and three females, two under 10 and one age 10-16.

Two other deeds of purchase were found for Lewis of Biddeford up through 1810: (1) The first of these was signed 4 Dec 1806, rec'd 19 May 1807: for $270 Lewis bought 30 acres land in Biddeford from Aaron Porter of Biddeford, physician, acreage situated at the head of land formerly owned by Joshua Haley, running S.W. by the parsonage and by lands of Benjamin H. Coles, and William Smith; Porter's spouse Paulina relinquished dower rights; witnesses Mary Coffin, Rufus H. Porter [York Deed 76:234]. (2) The second deed was dated 26 Jun 1810, rec'd 12 Jul 1810: Lewis bought for $288.00, 7-1/4 acres in Biddeford from Edward Hogan of Newberry, Essex Co., Mass. Bay Colony. This was the same land Hogan bought of Andrew Smith on 23 Aug 1809, adjacent to lands of Benjamin Gordon and Nathaniel Webster; witnesses Jeremiah Hill, Tristam Morrill [York Deed 83:62].

Letters of Admin. on Lewis' estate in Biddeford were filed 19 May 1817, by widow Susanna, approved 16 Jun 1817 [York Probate #20961]. Seven years later on 12 Jul 1824, she petitioned not only for Widow's Dower in Lewis' real estate for herself, but also for the "necessaries for upholding life" from his personal estate; the court allowed the sum of $322.50 "on condition that she release all claims for the support of her minor children since the decease of her said husband to this time." It was also determined on that date that both the guardianship of Lewis' two daughters Mary and Jerusha Young, minors above the age of fourteen, as well as guardianship of Lewis' four children under the age of fourteen, Susan, Eleanor, Lawrence and Lewis Young, were to be awarded to Daniel Deshon of Biddeford [York Probate #20962].

Known ch. b Biddeford by 2nd wife Susanna: Mary, b 31 Dec 1807; Jerusha, b 19 Apr 1809; Susanna aka Susan, b 7 Dec 1810; Eleanor, b 1810s; Lawrence, b 1810s; and Lewis, b ca 1820. (ME & MA I.G.I.; Census York Co., 1810, p912; Picton's ME Cem. Inscrips., V1, p222; Thompson's Recs. of York Co., TMs, p416)

LOUISA, b 1803, of York, d 12 Sep 1848, York, single, age 45, of consumption. (Hale's Cems., n.p.; Bragdon & Frost's York V.R., p431)

LOUISA, b ca 1815, South Berwick, spouse of David Forbush [b ca 1810, of same town]; no further data. (ME I.G.I.)

LOVINIA aka Lavinia, b 1803, of Buxton, d 1900, South Buxton, age 97, widow; filed (Ints.) 25 Oct 1821, Waterboro, m 24 Nov 1821, either Hollis or Waterboro, Stephen Warren [b 12 Dec 1800, Hollis, s/o Benjamin and Eunice (Weymouth) Warren, d 25 Feb 1873, South Buxton, married]. Lovinia and Stephen Warren were buried at Tory Hill, South Buxton.

Warren ch. b Hollis: Eunice Warren, b 20 Aug 1822, d 7 Dec 1839; Dr. Francis G. Warren, b 4 Mar 1828. (Ridlon's Saco, pp1206-1207; Hale's Cems., n.p.; Picton's ME Cem. Inscrips., V1, p479; **Reg.** 90:316, 1936).

LUCINDA, b 1790, listed as resident of Lebanon in 1850 census; she lived alone, age 60. (Census York Co., 1850, Reel B, p36)

LUCY, b ca 1760, of York, filed (Ints.) 18 Sep 1779, m 14 Oct 1779 at First Parish Church, York, Warren Bragdon [b ca 1755, of same town]. (Bragdon & Frost's York V.R., pp161, 361)

LUCY, b 1842, of Saco, operative, resident of Saco per the 1860 census for Saco; she lived at the home of Asa and Dorothy Livingston [b 1819 and 1819, respectively]. (Census York Co., 1860, Reel C, p806)

LUCY E., b 1840, of Biddeford, operative in mill per 1860 census, single, living at boarding home; m 2 Mar 1861, Biddeford, Daniel T. Mitchell [b ca 1835, of same town]. (Census York Co., 1860, Reel A, p270; ME I.G.I.)

LURANA, b ca 1735, of Lebanon, spouse of William Tibbetts [b ca 1730]. (ME I.G.I.)

LYDIA (   ), b 1787, of York, d 1 Mar 1859, York, age 72, widow, of palsy and collapse. (Bragdon & Frost's York V.R., p438; 1860 Mort. Sched., York Co.)

LYDIA, b 1672, York, d/o Rowland and Joan (Knight) Young, alive Apr 1757, native town, age 85, widow; m pre 12 May 1698, York, Thomas Haines [b 27 May 1670, Salisbury, MA, d 3 Apr 1757, York, age 87, married]. The will of Lydia's mother Joan, widow of Rowland, signed 12 May 1698, probated 20 Jun 1698, devised to her married daughter Lydia Haines three acres of marsh land lying up in York River with all her neat cattle and two sheep, the clothing and bedding. On 10 May 1711, Lydia's elder brother Job and her husband Thomas Haines conveyed marsh land formerly belonging to her father Rowland Young, then deceased.

Husband Thomas Haines had his will drawn 20 Jun 1721, probated after Apr 1757, wherein he named spouse Lydia as sole legatee. Widow Lydia m2 post Apr 1757, York, Samuel Bragdon [b 1682, York]. (ME I.G.I.; Noyes et al, pp106, 296)

LYDIA, b ca 1700, York, d/o Job and Sarah (Austin) Preble Young, alive 1737, native town, widow; m Jan 1718, York, Hopewell Weare [b ca 1690, York, s/o Peter Weare and possibly first wife Ruth Gooch or 2nd wife Mary Purington, d 7 Jun 1721, native town, married]. Inventory of the late Peter Weare's estate showed that his property was assessed at 162-10-0.

Widow Lydia obtained the license to sell land from father-in-law Peter Weare's estate on 14 May 1724 in order to satisfy debts: sold eighteen acres to her sibling Rowland Young for 59-10-0, the land bounding on the country road between the meeting house and the sea side, and by lands of Stephen Preble, Joseph Weare and the Blacks, by deed signed 22 Jan 1724/5, rec'd 15 Feb 1724/5; witnesses Benjamin Stone, James Tyler [York Deed 11:188]. Weare ch. b York: Joseph Weare, b 25 Oct 1718; John Weare, b 9 Sep 1720.

Lydia Young Weare m2 3 Aug 1725, John Wells [b ca 1695, of York]. Wells ch. b York: Lydia Wells, b 22 Jan 1727/8; Job Wells, b 17 Jan 1729/30; Sarah Wells, b 25 Aug 1733; and Nehemiah, b 1737. (ME I.G.I.; Bragdon & Frost's York V.R., pp21, 41; MH&G **Rec.**, V7, pp90-99; Noyes et al, p727)

LYDIA, b 15 Oct 1711, York, d/o Matthews and Eleanor (Haines) Young, d pre 20 Nov 1750, native town, married; filed (Ints.) 29 Aug 1730, m 12 Nov 1730, York, Nathan Whitney [b ca 1705, Biddeford]. In 1730 Stephen Presbury sold a property in Saco to Nathan Whitney of York. Her father Matthews' will signed 20 Nov 1750, indicated that Lydia Whitney was then deceased; will proved 1 Apr 1751. (Noyes et al, pp568, 776; Bragdon & Frost's York V.R., p119; ME I.G.I.)

LYDIA, b ca 1790, of York, filed (Ints.) 21 Oct 1810, York, James Hart [b ca 1785, of same town]. (Bragdon & Frost's York V.R., p197)

LYMAN, W., b 1 Jan 1858, of Biddeford, d 25 Dec 1933, age 75, buried in Biddeford. (Picton's ME Cem. Inscrips., V1, p317)

LYSANDER BASCOM, b 19 Jun 1836, South Berwick, millsman, s/o James M. and Susan P. (Henderson) Young, d 3 Oct 1878, native town; m 28 Jun 1856, Martha Winn [b 1840, of Wells, d 11 Feb 1868, South Berwick]. In 1860 Lysander and wife Martha lived with his parents.

Lysander B.'s served in the Civil War; these are taken from his service records: married, he enlisted 10 Sep 1862 in Portland, mustered in 30 Sep 1862 at Portland, in Co. B., 27th ME Infantry, with the rank of 2nd Lt. He was commissioned 17 Oct 1862, resigned 15 Feb 1863 at Camp Casey, VA, but was officially discharged 17 Jul 1863. This personal profile on him was given in his records: complexion dark; eyes, dark; hair, brown; height, 5 ft., 7-1/2 in.

Lysander B. and wife Susan P., his parents James and Susan, and sons William H. and Frank E. were buried at cemetery on Portland St., Portland. Ch. b South Berwick: Susan Eva, b 14 May 1864. (ME I.G.I.; Wentworth Gen., V1, pp456-457; Civil War res. by T. E. Brooks of Maine; Picton's ME Cem. Inscrips., V3, p2051)

MARGARET ( ), b 1778, Scotland, d 6 Apr 1859, South Berwick, age 81 years, spouse of David Young, n.d. In 1850, she lived in South Berwick, age 72, at the home of Moses Hanson [b 1810, N.H.] and Mary A. Hanson [b 1810, N.H.]. (Census York Co., 1850, Reel C, p334; Picton's ME Cem. Inscrips., V3, p2079)

MARGARET, b ca 1808, of Parsonsfield, filed (Ints.) 29 Mar 1828, Parsonsfield, filed (Ints.) 4 May 1828, Limington; m 11 May 1828, Limington, Hiram Emery [b ca 1803, of same town]. (Parsonsfield V.R., Town Clerk, p108; Taylor's **Limington**, TMs, p140)

MARGARET, b Sep 1839, Scotland, lived in Saco at the age of 60, single, at the home of brother-in-law John Strickland, n.d., on Wakefield Street per 1900 census report,. (1900 ME Soundex)

MARIETTA, b ca 1855, of York, filed (Ints.) 18 Oct 1875, m 23 Oct 1875, York, Charles W. Plaised [b ca 1850, of same town]. (ME I.G.I.; Bragdon & Frost's York V.R., pp320, 334)

MARK A., b ca 1845, Cornish, m 17 Feb 1870, Anna L. Sawyer [b ca 1850, of same town]. (ME I.G.I.)

MARTHA, b ca 1790, of York, filed (Ints.) 10 Jul 1811, York, Timothy McIntire [b ca 1785, of same town]. (Bragdon & Frost's York V.R., p198)

MARTIN, b 1803, of York, drowned Eastward 26 Dec 1821, York. (Bragdon & Frost's York V.R., p418)

MARY ( ), n.d., w/o James Young of Limington [n.d.], d 23 Feb 1841, Limington, bur. Johnson Cem. (Mormon/ME V.R., Wright-Zitkov)

MARY ( ), b 1738, of York, bur. 13 Feb 1828, York, age 90/91 years, died of old age. (Bragdon & Frost's York V.R., p423)

MARY ( ), b 1741, of York, d 2 Feb 1823, York, age 82, of palsy, widow. (Bragdon & Frost's York V.R., p420)

MARY ( ), b ca 1765, of York, age 45 plus, widow and resident of York in the 1820 census; her household contained

another female of the same age bracket and one male age 10-16.
(Census York Co., 1820, p595)

MARY (   ), b ca 1765, resident of York who lived alone
in 1840, her age 60-70. (Census York Co., 1840, Reel B, p259)

MARY (   ), b ca 1767, of York, widow and head of
household in 1820 at age 45 plus. Others in the family were
three males, one each under 10, 16-18, and 16-26, and three
other females, one 45 plus, and two age 16-26. (Census York
Co., 1820, p599)

MARY (   ), b 1773, head of household in York in the 1850
census, age 77, widowed, with an estate valued at $4,000.
Members of family included Edward, b 1800; Oliver, b 1811; and
Olive, b 1819. (Census York Co., 1850, Reel A, pp215-216)

MARY (SADLER), b 17 Mar 1841, of Limerick, d 3 Jan 1899,
same town, age 58, buried at Highland Cemetery, Limerick,
spouse not known. (Hale's Cems., n.p.; Picton's ME Cem.
Inscrips., V2, p1505)

MARY, b 1653/4, York, d/o Rowland and Joan (Knight)
Young, d 3 Jun 1723, native town, age 69, married; m between
12 Aug 1673 - 24 Jun 1678, York, Jeremiah Moulton, Esq. [b ca
1650, York, d 26 Dec 1731, native town, widower]. Mary
Moulton attested 24 Jun 1678 that she witnessed a deed of sale
of her grandfather Robert Knight which conveyed four acres of
upland in York to her brother Rowland Young Jr., deed signed
12 Aug 1673. She was known by her married name of Moulton in
the will of her mother Joan Knight Young that had been signed
12 May 1698, probated 20 Jun 1698, wherein Mary was devised
six shillings.

Jeremiah Moulton m2 post 1723, Widow Alice (Chadbourne)
Donnell [b 1663, York, d 18 Jun 1744, native town, age 81].
His will, signed 9 May 1727, probated post Dec 1731, named his
2nd wife Alice, his son and daughter by first wife Mary, and
six grandchildren as heirs-at-law. Ch. b York by first wife
Mary: Joseph Moulton, b 18 Jan 1679/80; and Mary Moulton,
b 14 Jan 1681/2. (ME I.G.I.; Noyes et al, pp497-498, 776-777)

MARY, b 1676, York, d/o Rowland and Susanna (Matthews)
Young, m1 ca 1700, York, Dependence Stover, shipwright [b ca
1670, of same town, d 25 Sep 1723]. At age 43, daughter Mary
Stover was mentioned in her father's will signed 14 Sep 1719,
native town, proved 2 Jan 1721/22. Widow Mary m2 20 May 1725,
York, John Wells Jr. [b ca 1680, York].

Stover ch. b York by first husband Dependence: Mary
Stover, b 8 Jun 1702; Susanna Stover, b 5 Nov 1705; Joseph
Stover, b 29 Jan 1712/3, (Samuel Came became his guardian,
with Joseph receiving two-thirds of the homestead); Deborah
Stover, b 14 Apr 1717 (Richard Milbury having been named her
guardian). Daughter Abigail Stover d 30 Jun 1723. (Noyes et
al, pp666, 776-777; ME I.G.I.; Bragdon & Frost's York V.R.,
p27)

MARY, b 1681, York, d/o Robert and Mary (Sayward) Young,
d 30 Nov 1726, native town, age 45, married; m pre Jul 1702,
York, Abraham Batten aka Battin [b ca 1675, York, s/o John and

Sarah (Main) Batten, d Aug 1751, native town]. By deed dated
18 Apr 1720, rec'd 1 Aug 1720, Mary Batten ceded her dower
rights in the property which her husband Abraham of York sold
to her brother Joseph Young of York for twenty-one pounds,
land that at one time belonged to her deceased father Robert
Young of York.

    Batten ch. b York: Sarah Batten, b 11 Jun 1702; John
Batten, b 23 Dec 1704; Bethia Batten, b 20 Mar 1706/7; Rowland
Batten, b 22 Dec 1708; Abraham Batten, b 31 Jan 1713/14;
Joseph Batten, b 3 Jan 1716/17; Mary Batten, b 8 Mar 1718/19;
and Miriam Batten, b 13 Feb 1722/23. (Noyes et al, p83; ME
I.G.I.; York VR, p25)

    MARY, b ca 1690, Ipswich, Essex Co., MA, d/o Francis and
Rebecca (   ) Young, w/o John Brown [b ca 1685, of the same
town]. Mary Brown and husband John of Ipswich sold for 22
pounds bills of credit to Benjamin Woodman of Newbury, Essex
Co., one full share of Township No. 1 on the northern side of
Saco River, "which by right descended to us from our late
father Francis Young," by deed signed 26 Mar 1735, rec'd 4 May
1740; witnesses Daniel Moulton, Daniel Wells [York Deed
23:239]. For Mary's main entry and that of her father
Francis, please see Youngs of Essex County, MA, Vol. II.

    MARY, b ca 1698, of York, m ca 1718, Wells, Gershom
Maxwell [b ca 1696, Wenham, MA, father hailing from Scotland].
"Gershom Maxwell received baptism upon a profession of his
faith, 13 Mar 1720. He was received to full communion with
the church in Wells, and eight others, 10 Jan 1742, at a time
of great revival in Wells," according to family papers in the
possession of Capt. Daniel F. Maxwell of Wells.

    Maxwell ch. b Wells: Abigail Maxwell, b Mar 1720,
single; John Maxwell, b Mar 1722; David Maxwell, b Jun 1724;
Miriam Maxwell, b Mar 1729, w/o Abel Gatchell; Barak Maxwell,
b Jan 1732; Susanna Maxwell, b Mar 1734, w/o Roger Littlefield; Martha Maxwell, b Apr 1736, w/o Benjamin Brown; Gershom
Maxwell Jr., b Mar 1740. (MH&G Rec., V4, p263)

    MARY, b ca 1705, York, filed (Ints.) 21 Oct 1727,
m 14 Dec 1727, York, Samuel Rounds [b ca 1700, of same town].
(ME I.G.I.; Bragdon & Frost's York V.R., p118)

    MARY, b ca 1723, York, d/o Rowland and Hannah (   )
Young, alive Aug 1771, native town; filed (Ints.) 23 Jun 1743,
York, m 25 Jun 1743, Kittery, John Norton Jr. [b ca 1720, of
Kittery]. Mary Norton was named Rowland's married daughter in
his will signed 27 Aug 1771, probated 8 Apr 1782, her full
portion from the estate, 5 pounds lawful money. (Bragdon &
Frost's York V.R., p129; Kittery V.R., p215)

    MARY, b ca 1765, of York, listed as head of household in
York in the 1810 census, age 26-45, with one other female in
the household of the same age bracket. This same household of
two females, both age 45 plus, was listed in the 1820 census
for York. (Census York Co., 1810, p822; 1820, p599)

    MARY, b 1772, of York, d 13 Mar 1858, York, age 86, of
old age; resident of York per the 1850 census, age 78, living

alone. (Bragdon & Frost's York V.R., p436; Census York Co., 1850, Reel A, p201)

MARY, b ca 1775, of York, filed (Ints.) 19 Sep 1795, York, Daniel Sargent [b ca 1770, of same town]. The banns were forbidden. (Bragdon & Frost's York V.R., p179)

MARY, b ca 1776, of York, filed (Ints.) 21 Apr 1796, York, George Chapman [b ca 1770, of Sanford]. (Bragdon & Frost's York V.R., p180)

MARY, b 1793, N.H., resident of Lebanon in 1860, age 67, single, living at the home of Ruth Whitney [b 1804, N.H.]. Other members of household were Charles Stephens, shoemaker [b 1842] and Emma J. Kimball [b 1858]. (Census York Co., 1860, Reel A, p95)

MARY, b 17 May 1793, Limington, d/o David and Elizabeth (Smith) Young, m 20 Feb 1815, Nathaniel Duran of Durham, N.H. [b ca 1790, N.H.]. (Taylor's Limington, TMs, pp60, 131)

MARY, b ca 1800, York, d/o Joel and Mary (Allen) Young, alive 29 Dec 1880, native town, married; filed (Ints.) 7 Nov 1819, m 2 Dec 1819, York, Ivory Simpson [b 1794, York, d 5 Dec 1885, York, age 91, native town, widower]. Mary Simpson was named married daughter of Joel Young in his will signed 5 Aug 1820, probated 2 Dec 1828: she was to receive $100.00 in neat stock within one year of his decease. Joel's codicil signed 2 May 1828 revised this figure downward to $50.00. This married couple lived together for 66 years. Simpson ch. b York: Charles E. Simpson, b 1841, spouse of Ann L. Plaisted. (ME I.G.I.; Bragdon & Frost's York V.R., pp212, 349)

MARY, b ca 1805, of York, filed (Ints.) 23 Nov 1826, m 10 Dec 1826, York, Sherburne Sleeper [b ca 1800, of Dover, N.H.]. (Bragdon & Frost's York V.R., p225)

MARY, b ca 1808, of York, filed (Ints.) 4 Nov 1828, m 30 Nov 1828, York, Eastman Hutchins [b ca 1800, of same town]. (ME I.G.I.; Bragdon & Frost's York V.R., p230)

MARY, b 8 Feb 1819, York, spouse of Daniel Emery [b ca 1815, of same town]. (ME I.G.I.)

MARY A., b 1830, Wakefield, N.H., d/o Daniel and Betsey (Cook) Young [no main entry]. Mary A. Young and Moses Sweat of Parsonsfield [b ca 1825, Parsonsfield] had by mutual consent on 21 Dec 1861, given up their "intentions of marriage for the present." They were duly married 21 Mar 1863, Ossipee, N.H. For full entry on Daniel Young of Wakefield, please see Youngs of Strafford County, N.H., Vol. I. (NHVR-Brides; Parsonsfield V.R., Town Clerk, p180)

MARY ANN, b ca 1830, of Strafford, N.H., m 23 Oct 1853, Lebanon, by Elder Edward Blaisdell, George E. Mason [b ca 1825, of Franklin, N.H.]. Please see Youngs of Strafford County, N.H., Vol. I for main entry on their son Stephen, b 22 Oct 1854, Strafford, physician. His grandparents Stephen and Lydia (Main) Young of Strafford adopted him. (Lebanon Marr, p224)

MARY CAROLINE, see also CAROLINE, b ca 1820, of Kittery,
m 12 Sep 1839, Kittery, William Jackson [b ca 1815, of same
town]. (Thompson's Recs. of York Co., TMs, p417)
     MARY ELIZABETH, b ca 1813, of Litchfield, filed (Ints.)
3 Oct 1833, m 1 Jan 1834, York, Capt. Edward Simpson [b ca
1810, of York]. (Bragdon & Frost's York V.R., p242)
     MARY JANE, b 17 Dec 1836, Sanford, d/o Joseph and Edna M.
(Huston) Young, d 25 Feb 1919, same town, age 83; filed
(Ints.) 14 Aug 1858, Edmund Trafton Perkins [b 11 Jun 1836,
Sanford, s/o Abner F. and Mary H. (Allen) Perkins]. Mary Jane
was buried at cemetery on Old Mast Road, Sanford. (F. R.
Boyle's **Sanford**, pp330-332; Hale's Cems., n.p.; Picton's ME
Cem. Inscrips., V3, p1713)
     MARY K. (NUTTER), b 1808, Wolfeboro, N.H., w/o Moses C.
Young of Dover, N.H., d 14 Feb 1867, Eliot. Please see main
entry on Moses C. Young in Youngs of Strafford County, N.H.,
Vol. I. (Frost's **Eliotiana**, Marr., pD102)
     MASTERSON, b 24 Dec 1722, York, eldest s/o Jonathan and
Abigail (Came) Young, gr.s/o Samuel and Elizabeth (Masterson)
Young, d 16 Jun 1795, age 73, native town; filed (Ints.)
18 Jul 1752, m 11 Aug 1752, York, Sarah Curtis [b ca 1740,
alive 16 Feb 1814, ca 74 years, prob. d 29 Mar 1834, age 94,
native town, widow]. Masterson was listed head of household
in York in the 1790 census, household containing two other
males above the age of 16 and three females.
     Letters of Admin. on Masterson's father's estate were
granted 2 Apr 1764 to Masterson and sibling Samuel, both of
York, yeomen, with instructions that an inventory be taken on
or before 2 July next, and a true and complete account be
submitted by 2 Oct 1764 [York Probate #20945]. The estate was
sizeable, attested 11 Jul 1764 by the appraisers, over 130
acres all in all, plus a pew in the York Meeting House
Gallery; please see father's entry for the full inventory of
estate [York Probate 11:250].
     One of the earliest deeds found for Masterson, husband-
man, was signed 15 Jun 1769, rec'd 28 Dec 1769, when he bought
from Benjamin Holt of York, mariner, ten shares in a tract of
land called Lot No. 4 in the 1st Div. of the Common Lands,
five of which Holt purchased from Josiah Black Jr. on 8 Mar
1757; witnesses Daniel and Hannah Moulton [York Deed 41:170].
     By will signed 28 Jun 1764, probated 2 Jan 1769, Master-
son's maternal grandfather Samuel Came of York devised to
Masterson's mother Abigail, widow of Jonathan Young, twenty-
five acres land in York which Samuel Came bought from Capt.
Bane, besides what he had already given her. These same
twenty-five acres widow Abigail conveyed to Masterson who had
helped her out tremendously over the years; for the token sum
of six shillings she sold this land to him by deed signed and
rec'd 23 Mar 1774, with the stipulation that Masterson's
unmarried sisters Sarah and Dorcas would be able to live there
in their remaining years and/or use the pastures for their own

gain; witnesses Daniel Moulton, Ebenezer Sayward [York Deed 43:83].

As a postscript on Masterson's unmarried sisters Sarah and Dorcas Young, they sold out "all their right and title to the real estate of our late father Jonathan Young, each to have the same in equal shares," to their nephews Joel and Jonathan Young Jr. of York, sons of sibling Masterson Young, for $267.00 by deed signed 1 Jun 1796, rec'd 14 Jun 1796; witnesses Jeremiah McIntire, Daniel Sewall [York Deed 59:207].

At one point between 1755-1780, Masterson was a member of a consortium which included Ebenezer Sayward, John, Edmund and Daniel Bridges, Zebulon Williams, and Elizabeth Oliver, all of whom owned various shares of land in the Common Lands: Lots 4, 5, 6 in the 1st Div., and Lot No. 4 in the 2nd Div. By deed dated 21 Aug 1755, rec'd 16 Jun 1763, they petitioned at the Superior Court in Boston for a partition of their various 106 shares in the Common Lands inasmuch as the parties concerned were numerous, the group becoming unwieldy as they lived far from one another, some unknown, some off at sea, all of which in effect retarded the settlement of these lands.

After court-appointed agents had appraised these lots, the court decided that the consortium may all hold their respective shares "in severalty." By deed signed 18 Jun 1763, rec'd 8 Apr 1780, Masterson was awarded 18 shares, or 18-1/4 acres in Lot No. 4, 1st Div., beginning at the western corner of Thomas Bragdon's land, S.E. by Capt. Abel's land, then S.W. 18 rods by Moulton's land, past the brook, by lands abutting Jonathan Young's land [Jr.], north to the corner of his father Jonathan Young's land, up to the dividing line between Lots 4 and 5 [York Deed 46:56].

Masterson's last will and testament was written 6 Jun 1795, proved 17 Aug 1795, naming his two sons Joel and Jonathan as Co-Execs. and residuary legatees of his estate [York Probate #20467]. His wife Sarah was to receive her "Thirds" of his real estate, the cattle and household furniture to be at her disposal. Masterson devised the following legacies to married daughters: 3 shillings each to daughter Olive, w/o Stephen Grant, and Elizabeth, w/o Joseph Sedgley, "only because of what I have given them in the past," and 5 shillings each to married daughters Esther, w/o Joel Jellison and Hannah, w/o Thomas Bragdon Jr. Single daughter Sally aka Sarah was to have the use of a room in his dwelling house and of one cow winter and summer while she is unmarried, and equalized with her sisters upon marriage. Sons Joel and Jonathan were devised the remainder of the estate, "Joel to have the house where he now dwells and Jonathan the house where I dwell," sharing both the barn, the funeral costs and legacies; witnesses Daniel Sewall, Samuel McIntire, 3rd, John Swett.

Youngest daughter Sarah was designated the sole beneficiary of her mother Sarah's will signed 16 Feb 1814, probated Nov 1819, to receive all that "I shall die possessed of" [York

Probate #20988]. Mother Sarah's will recognized sons Joel and Jonathan, and daughters Esther Jellison, Elizabeth Sedgeley, Hannah Bragdon, and heirs of daughter Olive Grant, deceased, stating that they all had previously received their full proportion of the estate. Sarah, the daughter, died at the age of 65, and was buried at York Cemetery.

Masterson and wife Sarah were buried (n.d.) at York Cemetery, York. Ch. b York: Joel+, b ca 1758; Elizabeth+ (Young) Sedgeley, b ca 1760; Jonathan+, b 1763; Olive+ (Young) Grant, b ca 1764; Esther+ (Young) Jellison, b ca 1765; Sarah, b 1767, d 4 Mar 1832, age 65, single, native town, buried at family grave site; and Hannah+ (Young) Bragdon, b ca 1775. (ME I.G.I.; Noyes et al, p777; Census York Co., 1790, p72; Bragdon & Frost's York V.R., pp137, 405, 486, 621; Hale's Cems., n.p.)

MASTERSON, Esq., b 1783, York, farmer, teacher, s/o Joel and Mary (Allen) Young, alive 1860, native town, widower, age 77; filed (Ints.) 29 Nov 1817, m 30 Jan 1818, York, Mrs. Olive ( ) Curtis [b ca 1800, of same town, d pre 1840, York, married]. Masterson was named son and heir-at-law of Joel Young Sr. of York by will signed 5 Aug 1820, probated 2 Dec 1828, his bequest, five dollars. However, Joel's codicil written 2 May 1828 devised to son Masterson, "All the right I have in the property which Masterson purchased of Timothy Simpson and which was deeded from Masterson to me, excepting the N.W. field which I reserve for sons Joel and Jesse." The terms of the codicil could in no way be broken, or Masterson would forfeit the property.

By deed of purchase made on 23 Jun 1810, rec'd 28 Jun 1810, Masterson bought from Jonathan Young Jr.+ [b 1763] of York for $161.25, 13 acres, 20 rods land at the eastern corner of the mill pasture so called, adjacent to lands of Joel and Jonathan Young, Thomas Moulton, and Samuel Sayward; see Jonathan Jr. for full documentation.

The land deed on Masterson's original purchase of the property from Timothy Simpson, Gent. of Township #2, 4th Range, north of the Waldo Patent, Hancock County, was signed and rec'd 26 Oct 1811 [before Masterson's father's will of 1820]: Masterson paid $1,700.00 for orchard, tillage and pastures with the buildings thereon, being the former dwelling house, barn and land adjoining Timothy Simpson, containing 45 acres on the road leading from Portsmouth to York Court House, adjacent to David Bennett's land; spouse Humility Simpson relinquished dower rights; witnesses Mary McIntire, William and Nancy Frost [York Deed 84:249].

The 1820-1860 census reports for York listed Masterson as head of household. In 1820 his age was 26-45, with a spousal figure at home of the same age bracket; there was also another female age 45 plus and one young female under ten years. In 1830, his age and that of a maternal figure was 40-50; household contained one young male age 5-10 and one female age 10-15. From 1840 on Masterson was widower; in 1840, the

census gave his age as 50-60; the family contained one male
and one female both age 20-30; and in 1850 Masterson's age was
67, household including son Moses and his family.
    In 1860 it was apparent that he had by then deeded the
family homestead over to his son Moses C. as Moses was listed
as head of household; Masterson, whose occupation was listed
teacher, lived with his son and his family in York.
    Ch. b York: Moses C.+, b 1822. (ME I.G.I.; Bragdon &
Frost's York V.R., p207; Census York Co., 1820, p591; 1830,
p249; 1840, Reel B, p259; 1850, Reel A, p212)
    MASTERSON Jr., b 1816, York, house carpenter, s/o
Jonathan and Joanna (Nowell) Young, d 16 Nov 1881, native town
age 65-5-0; filed (Ints.) 10 Feb 1842, m 26 Feb 1842, York,
16 Mar 1842, Kittery, Susan K. Plaisted [b May 1815, York,
alive 1900, native town]. After his father's death in 1827,
Masterson Jr. and his three brothers, all minors, became the
wards of George Grant of York 6 Dec 1830; it should be noted
that Masterson's age was then fourteen plus, indicating he was
eligible to have some say on the choice of guardian.
    In 1860 Masterson was head of household in York, which
included wife Susan K., age 45, two adopted children Anna L.
and Charles M., and kinswoman Dorcas Nowell, age 75 [b 1785]
at home. In the 1900 census for York, Susan K., widow, was
listed as resident, age 85; she lived alone.
    Ch. b Dover, N.H.: Anna L., b 1846, adopted; Charles S.,
b Apr 1852, adopted, d 11 Oct 1854. Ch. b York: Charles P.,
b Apr 1855, adopted, d 3 Oct 1857; Charles M. H.+, b 1856,
adopted. (Bragdon & Frost's York V.R., pp256, 349, 519;
Census York Co., 1860, Reel C, p959; 1900 ME Soundex; Kittery
V.R., p304)
    MASTERSON, b ca 1825, of York, m 28 Jul 1849, Kittery,
Mrs. Nancy Cutts [b ca 1830, of same town]. (Kittery V.R.,
p389)
    MATHIAS, b 16 Nov 1708, York, cooper, s/o Matthews aka
Mathias and Eleanor (Haines) Young, d pre 21 Apr 1741, fairly
young, native town; filed (Ints.) 3 Nov 1733; m 9 Jan 1733/4,
York, Mercy Main [b ca 1710, York, d/o Josiah and Dorothy
(Trafton) Main of York]. Mathias received a deed of gift from
his father Matthews, signed 23 Jan 1733/4, rec'd 24 Jan
1733/4: six acres land in York which Matthews bought from
John Adams of Kittery, adjoining a tract of land belonging to
Josiah Main of York [Mathias' father-in-law]. It was understood from the terms of the deed that Matthias was not to take
full possession of this land until his father's decease.
    One of Mathias' last deeds was signed 12 Nov 1736, rec'd
8 Mar 1736/7, in which he bought from Daniel Farnum of York
for 322-10-0, 32-1/4 acres land on the S.W. side of York
River, beginning at the N.E. corner of the land he sold that
day to Joseph Main, and S.E. by lands of Jonathan Young, with
a sufficient way or entry to drive cattle from the road of the
Cove, formerly called Wilber Cove, to the town road; witnesses
Jeremiah Moulton, Christopher Bradbury [York Deed 19:46].

However, Mathias predeceased his father Matthews. Widow Mercy Young received a deed of gift dated 1 Jul 1741, rec'd 21 Jul 1741, from her father Josiah Main of York, a dwelling house on one-half of an acre in York with a convenient way to the river and another parcel of 30 acres bounded N.E. by York River, south and S.W. by a cove once called Watts Cove, then by lands of Ralph Farnam and Christopher Pottle, and N.W. by lands given by Matthews Young to his son Matthias, since deceased; witnesses Nicholas Shapleigh, Tobias Leighton [York Deed 22:209].

Upon Mathias' death, the thirty-two shares in the Commons granted to him by the Town Proprietors became part of the estate of his father Matthews Young; see Mathias' sibling Ebenezer of York for the disposal of these shares dated 21 Mar 1757. Letters of Admin. on his estate were granted 21 Apr 1741 to widow Mercy Young; inventory was due on or before 21 Jul next, and a true accounting by 21 Oct 1741 [York Probate #20970]. Inventory taken on Mathias' estate was appraised 13 Jul 1741 by Benjamin Stone, Henry Simpson Jr., and Tobias Leighton, at 393-10-0, attested to same date by widow and Admin. Mary Young. His estate included 32-1/4 acre of mowing and pasture land valued at 322-10-0 and a canoe at 20 shillings [York Probate 5:267A]. Another inventory was taken 20 Apr 1742, which amounted to 119-19-11, only to be appraised at 32-1-0 [York Probate 6:13].

Widow Mary, Admin., filed petition in Jun 1743, rec'd 29 Sep 1746, seeking to sell part of Mathias' estate since his personal estate was not large enough to pay the debts, falling short 93-10-3. At public auction widow Mary sold about two acres land in York by lands of Joseph Main and Jonathan Young, to John Main of York for 101-14-6 old Tenor, deed rec'd 29 Sep 1746; witnesses Tobias Leighton, Prudence Bracey [York Deed 26:35].

Accounting was made 18 Oct 1743: additional costs and distributions amounted to 12-17-6. By 17 Jan 1743, five townsmen were appointed to make a just division of what was left over after the accounting. On 13 Apr 1744, a division was made in favor of widow Mercy of 9-1/4 acres, 13 rods of land, with the remainder set off to Matthews Young, father of the deceased and nearest of kin [York Probate 6:123]. Unfortunately probate papers did not reveal the existence of children. For probable son, please see next entry. (Noyes et al, pp453, 776; Bragdon & Frost's York V.R., p121)

MATHIAS, b ca 1740, York, perhaps s/o Mathias and Mercy (Main) Young, alive 1800, native town; filed (Ints.) 17 Aug 1763, m 24 Oct 1765, York, Mary Card [b ca 1745, of same town, alive 1800, York]. This may have been the Mathias who was listed as resident in the 1790 census for York with two females in the household; in the 1800 census for York, his age was 45 plus, as was a spousal figure. They lived alone. (ME I.G.I.; Census York Co., 1790, p72; 1800, p1018; Bragdon & Frost's York V.R., p148)

MATHILDA, b ca 1800, of Waterboro, m 20 Dec 1823, Waterboro, William Boynton [b ca 1795, of same town]. (ME I.G.I.)

MATTHEWS aka MATHIAS, b ca 1675, York, fisherman, s/o Rowland and Susanna (Matthews) Young, d pre Apr 1751, native town; m 23 Apr 1696, Newbury, Essex County, MA, also York, York Co., Eleanor Haines aka Haynes [b ca 1675, of same town]. For further information on Matthews, his family, and sale of property in Amesbury, Essex County, Mass., by Eleanor Haynes Young and siblings in 1706 [Essex Co. Deed 19:137], please see Youngs of Essex County, MA, Vol. II.

The earliest court record found for Matthews was dated 4 Jan 1714/15 at a session of the Inferior Court of Common Pleas in York. He appeared that date and "owned a judgment for the sum of 25-5-7 due to Capt. Richard Wilbird," [Court of Gen. Sessions, V5, p43].

Matthews' inheritance from his father Rowland was a one-half share of two acres salt marsh near the western cove which was to be shared with younger brother Benaiah, according to the terms of his father's will signed 14 Sep 1719, proved 2 Jan 1721/2. An early entry in the Court of General Sessions, V6, p33, was found for Matthews and eldest sibling Joseph of York when they were invited to join a committee to survey a neighbor's property in response to a warrant issued 28 December 1719, to the Sheriff of the county by the complainant; please see entry on Joseph for full details.

The mortgage deed Matthias assigned to John Adams of Kittery, shipwright, was signed 6 Apr 1720, rec'd one day later, for the sum of 14-10-0, due and payable one year hence plus interest: 8-1/2 acres land, part of which Thomas Wise sold to Isaac Gutteridge by his deed dated 6 Dec 1685, lying on the south side of York River; witnesses Samuel Came, Joseph Moulton, Richard King of Kittery [York Deed 10:23-24].

It is worthy of note that at this early date these three witnesses, **Came, Moulton** and **King** became not only neighbors, but friends of the family, and soon represented heads of allied families of the Youngs in York in succeeding generations.

By deposition signed 4 Apr 1728, rec'd same date, Matthews testified his age was upward of fifty years, that he knew Timothy Yeales, late of York deceased, and that in 1686, Yeales had a house in York on the S.W. side of York River between Holts Cove and Whitneys Cove; witnesses William Pepperell, John Penhallow [York Deed 12:258].

Before he had his will drawn up in 1750, he made a deed of gift to son Matthias of six acres land in York which Matthews purchased of John Adams of Kittery and adjoining to a tract of land belonging to Josiah Main of York. It was understood by the terms of the deed that Matthias was not to take full possession of this land until after Matthews' decease; deed signed 23 Jan 1733/4, rec'd 24 Jan 1733/4; witnesses Amos Main, Elizabeth Main [York Deed 16:80].

Other deeds were made prior to his will. One was signed 31 Oct 1748, rec'd 4 Aug 1750, in which Matthews sold to Jeremiah Moulton, Gent. and Daniel Moulton, Esq. of York for 70 pounds old Tenor bills of credit, eight-1/2 acres land being part of a ten-acre grant of land by the town of York to Matthews on mortgage dated 23 Mar 1712, but "being upon other men's property which was before appropriated the same, remains to be laid out in the Commons," six acres more part of a grant of thirty acres to the said Matthews by mortgage held 23 Jun 1699, and yet remains to be laid out on the Commons; witnesses Joseph Trafton, Charles Trafton [York Deed 28:270].

To these same gentlemen Matthews sold for 7-6-8, another seven shares in the Common Lands granted to him in June 1762; witnesses Stephen Lovejoy, Ebenezer Young [York Deed 29:54].

Matthews' own will, signed 20 Nov 1750, proved 1 Apr 1751, named son Ebenezer as only surviving son and sole Exec. "who has kindly and diligently ministered to me hitherto," witnesses Jonathan Young, Benaiah Young [siblings], Aquila Haines, Joseph Farnam [**Maine Wills**, pp646-647]. His instructions indicated that of his six daughters, Lydia Whitney was then deceased; those five who survived were Susanna Redlan, Hannah Preble, Tabitha Murch, Mercy Webber, and Eleanor Allen, all residents of York.

Letters Test. were granted to son Ebenezer as sole Exec. of Matthew's will, with inventory and full accounting due by 1 Jul next [York Probate #20969]. Inventory of Matthew's estate was appraised 14 May 1751, by Ralph Farnam, John Bradbury and Samuel Sewall Jr. in the amount of 160-5-8, attested to 1 Jul 1751 by the appraisers. Real estate included the homestead [about sixteen acres land with one-half of the house], about 18 acres of pasture land, and two-3/4 acres of marsh [York Probate 8:177].

Ch. b York: Susanna+ (Young) Austin Redlon, b 3 Nov 1696; Hannah+ (Young) Preble, b 5 Jan 1698; Ebenezer, b 1699, d.y.; Ebenezer+, b 5 Apr 1701; Tabitha+ (Young) Murch, b 6 Oct 1705; Mathias+, b 16 Nov 1708; Lydia+ (Young) Whitney, b 15 Oct 1711; Mercy+ (Young) Webber, b 25 Jan 1714; Eleanor+ (Young) Allen, b 6 Jan 1717/8. (Mass. & ME I.G.I.; Noyes et al, pp776-777; Bragdon & Frost's York V.R., p7)

MEHITABLE H., b 1810s, Acton, d/o Jonathan and Mehitable (Moody) Young, m pre Oct 1838, Hugh J. Gorman [b ca 1810, of Acton]. Mehitable Gorman was named married daughter of Jonathan in his will written up 8 Oct 1838, proved 7 Jan 1839. (ME I.G.I.)

MELISSA O., b ca 1850, of York, filed (Ints.) 14 Dec 1871, m 19 Dec 1871, York, Augustus T. Littlefield [b ca 1845, of Wells]. (Bragdon & Frost's York V.R., p317)

MERCY, b 1685, York, d/o Rowland and Susanna (Matthews) Young; m ca 1715, York, Henry Simpson [b ca 1680 of York]. Simpson ch. b York: John Simpson, ca 1718, d.y.; Abigail Simpson, b 17 Jul 1722; Paul Simpson, b 1 Jan 1723; Abigail Simpson, b Dec 1723; John Simpson, b Nov 1724; Samuel Simpson, b 30 Nov 1726; Tabitha Simpson, b 22 Jul 1730; Henry Simpson Jr., 8 Jul 1732; Ebenezer Simpson, b 8 Jan 1736/7; Thomas Simpson, b 9 Oct 1738; Mercy Simpson, b 27 Feb 1741. (ME I.G.I.; Bragdon & Frost's York V.R., p28)

MERCY, b 25 Jan 1714, York, d/o Matthews and Eleanor (Haynes) Young, alive 20 Nov 1750, native town; filed (Ints.) 26 Jun 1736, m 14 Jul 1736, York, Gershom Webber [b ca 1710, of same town]. Mercy Webber was named daughter and heir-at-law of Matthews Young by will signed 20 Nov 1750, proved 1 Apr 1751. (Noyes et al, p776; ME I.G.I.; Bragdon & Frost's York V.R., p123)

MERCY, b ca 1718, York, d/o Robert Young. (ME I.G.I.)

MERCY, b ca 1725, York, filed (Ints.) 8 Oct 1746, m 11 Nov 1746, York, Samuel Bragdon [b ca 1720, of same town]. (ME I.G.I.; Bragdon & Frost's York V.R., p131)

MERCY, b 15 Jul 1728, York, d/o Benaiah and Ruth (Johnson) Young, filed (Ints.) 10 Oct 1747, York, m 11 Nov 1747, Harpswell, Cumberland Co., James Booker [b ca 1700, of Harpswell]. (ME I.G.I.; Bragdon & Frost's York V.R., p132)

MERCY aka Marcy, b 19 Dec 1768, York, eldest d/o Jonathan and Mercy (Nowell) Young, alive Nov 1798, married; filed (Ints.) 27 Oct 1788, m 10 Jan 1789, York, Moses Hodsdon Jr. [b ca 1765, of Berwick]. Marcy Hodsdon was named married daughter of Jonathan by his will written 10 Nov 1798, probated April 1808. Her father's bequest to her was one dollar, which was merely in addition to what he had previously given her. (Bragdon & Frost's York V.R., p171; ME I.G.I.)

MERCY, b ca 1795, of York, filed (Ints.) 6 Mar 1815, m 13 Apr 1815, Wentworth Tebbetts [b ca 1790, of same town]. (Bragdon & Frost's York V.R., p202)

MERCY aka MARY, b 7 Sep 1818, York, believed to be d/o Jonathan Young, Esq., d 17 Sep 1903, age 85, native town, widow; filed (Ints.) 27 Jun 1846, m 19 Jul 1846, York, Jonathan Moulton [b 19 Jul 1820, York, s/o George and Nancy ( ) Moulton, d 12 Sep 1881, native town, married]. Jonathan Young [b 1774] had his will drawn up 14 Dec 1840, probated 5 May 1856, in which he named single daughter Mercy as heir-at-law who was to receive ten dollars upon her marriage. The Moulton family were buried at the Moulton Lot located on the west side of Rte. 91, York, in the field between Gowen Lane and York River.

Moulton ch. b York: Nancy C. Moulton, b 1847, d 11 Aug 1852, age 5-5-0; George M. Moulton, b 1849, d 7 Aug 1852, age 3-4-0; Nancy A. Moulton, b 1853, d 19 Sep 1857, age 4-6-0; George C. Moulton, b 1855, d 26 Sep 1857, age 2-5-0; Herbert H. Moulton, b 1858, d 13 Sep 1876, age 18. (ME I.G.I.; Bragdon & Frost's York V.R., pp265, 270; Frost's York Cem., p620)

MERCY, b ca 1825, Freedom, N.H., d/o Daniel and Elizabeth (Nason) Young [no main entry], alive 1 Oct 1866; (Ints.) 25 Dec 1843, Parsonsfield, m 28 Jan 1844, Effingham, Samuel Allen [b ca 1820, of Parsonsfield]. Mercy Allen was named married daughter and heir-at-law of Daniel Young of Freedom by will drawn 1 Oct 1866, proved 31 Aug 1874. For extensive background information on Daniel Young of Freedom, please see Youngs of Strafford County, N.H., Vol. I. (Parsonsfield V.R., Town Clerk, p147; NHVR-Brides)

MILTON L., b 9 Feb 1869, of Biddeford, d 23 Apr 1955, age 86, same town, widower; his spouse was Mary E. Knox [b 11 Feb 1878, d 27 May 1950, age 72, of the same town]. (Picton's ME Cem. Inscrips., V1, p347)

MIRIAM, b 31 Jan 1707, York, d/o Jonathan and Margaret (Stackpole) Young; filed (Ints.) 2 Aug 1735, m 27 Nov 1735, York, Nathaniel Chapman Jr., expert builder [b 1703, Ipswich, Essex Co., MA, s/o Nathaniel and (1st wife) Ruth Davis Chapman, (2nd wife) Mary (Wilborne) Chapman. Chapman ch. b Nobleboro, Lincoln Co., ME: Miriam (Chapman) Glidden, b 1728, w/o Tobias Glidden; Nathaniel Chapman, 4th, b 1730, spouse Mary Hodgdon; Israel Chapman, b ca 1732, single; Mary Chapman, b ca 1733, single; John Chapman, b ca 1735, d 4 Feb 1818, spouse Priscilla Chapman; and Jonathan Chapman, b 1737, d 27 May 1825, spouse Mrs. Rachael (   ) Knowlton. (Noyes et al, pp137, 776-777; Bragdon & Frost's York V.R., pp122-123; Chapman Fam. Recs., courtesy of Joan Reed Miller of York, ME; Nobleboro V.R., to 1892; George F. Dow, Pres. Nobleboro Hist. Society)

MIRIAM, b 1773, of Lyman, d 9 Feb 1861, same town, age 88, single, buried at Goodwin's Mills, Rte. 35, Lyman. (Hale's Cems., n.p.)

MOLLY, b pre 1755, of York, listed as resident of York in the 1800 census, age 45 plus, single. (Census York Co., 1800, p1018)

MOSES, b ca 1725, of Falmouth [now under jurisdiction of Cumberland County], blacksmith, bought land by deed signed 14 Jul 1758, rec'd 9 Oct 1758, from Josiah Noyes of Falmouth for forty pounds lawful money, situated at the western corner of land by Jonathan Morse Jr.'s house lot on the N.E. side of King Street; Noyes' spouse Mary relinquished Dower Rights [York Deed 35:26].

MOSES, b 1766, Dover, N.H., s/o Capt. Thomas Young [no main entry], d 5 Dec 1836, Wakefield, N.H., age 70, married. His spouse was Mary aka Molly Chadwick [b 23 Nov 1769, Berwick, twin, d/o William and Elizabeth (Goodwin) Chadwick, alive 1850, Wakefield]. For full details on Moses and family contained in census reports from 1810-1840, allied family records of N.H., and main entries on children, please see Youngs of Strafford County, N.H., Vol. I. (Wentworth Gen., V1, pp169, 282, 501-502; Young Family Recs., courtesy of Alden N. Young of East Wakefield, N.H.)

MOSES, b 1778, Lebanon, of Alton and Rochester, N.H., d 13 May 1865, age 87, Alton, N.H.; m1 15 Dec 1808, Lebanon, by Elder John Blaisdell, Dorothy Peavey [b 1789, alive 1850, Alton, N.H., age 51]. Moses m2 11 Sep 1853, Alton, Alice (Peavey) Young, widow of Jonathan Young of Lebanon or Farmington, NH [b 8 Oct 1800, Alton, d/o Daniel and Mary (   ) Peavey, d 8 Apr 1874, Milton]. Moses was listed as head of household in the 1830-1860 census reports for Alton, N.H., which gave Maine as his place of birth. For full details on N.H. census readings and bibliography, please see Youngs of Strafford County, N.H., Vol. I.

While of Lebanon, Moses and co-grantee John Wallingford bought from Peter Guptil of Berwick for $60.00, 60 acres land in Lebanon along the county road, formerly owned by Benjamin Chadwick, Esq.; witnesses Moses Guptil, Elmer Chamberlain [York Deed 77:258]. By 1830 Moses and family had relocated to Alton, N.H. Widow Alice Young, age 62, m3 7 Oct 1865, Alton, Joseph Wiggins [b 1804, of Upper Gilmanton]. Alice spent her remaining years in Milton, N.H.

Known ch. b ME by Dorothy: Alvah, b 19 Jul 1818, twin, relocated to Alton, N.H.; Henry, b 19 Jul 1818, twin, d 11 May 1882, age 63-11-4, Alton with wife surviving; and Lavina J. (Young) Ellis, b 1828, relocated to Alton. N.H. (Lebanon Marr, pp168, 224)

MOSES C., b 1822, York, master mariner, s/o Masterson and Olive (   ) Curtis Young, alive 1860, native town; filed (Ints.) 23 Oct 1847, m 6 Nov 1847, York, Lydia Elizabeth Trafton [b 1827, York, alive 1860, native town, age 33]. In 1850 Moses, Lydia and their two daughters lived at the family homestead with his father Masterson who was then widower. In 1860 Moses C. was listed as head of household in York, his estate appraised at $1,500; at home were spouse Lydia E., five daughters Clara C., Olive M., Caroline M., Mary Etta and Susan A., and his father Masterson, then age 77. Moses and members of his family were buried at the Young lot on the east side of Hilltop Drive, to the rear of the Frederick J. Ricker residence in York.

Ch. b York: Clara C., b 1848; Olive M., b 1849; Caroline M.+ (Young) Todd, b 1852; Mary Etta, b 1856; Fannie J., b 1857, d 26 Aug 1858, age 0-9-12; Susan A.+ (Young) Scruton, b 1859; Ellen F.+ (Young) Trafton, b 21 Apr 1861; Julia E., b 1865, d 1 Feb 1877, age 11-1-0. (ME I.G.I.; Bragdon & Frost's York V.R., pp267, 344, 349-350; Frost's York Cem., p655; Hale's Cems., n.p.; Census York Co., 1860, Reel C, p918; Picton's ME Cem. Inscrips., V3, p2400)

MOSES M., b Oct 1823, N.H., head of household in the 1900 census for South Berwick, age 77. His spouse was Eleanora E., age 40 [b Nov 1859]. They lived alone. (1900 ME Soundex)

NANCY, b ca 1800, Waterboro, filed (Ints.) 24 Nov 1821; m 9 Dec 1821, Waterboro, Simeon Bragdon [b ca 1795, of same town]. (ME I.G.I.; Reg. 90:316, 1936)

NANCY, b 8 Jul 1810, York, d/o Jonathan Young, Esq. [b 1774], filed (Ints.) 4 Oct 1839, m 27 Oct 1839, at First Parish Church, York, Josiah Batchelder [b ca 1805, of Amesbury, MA]. Nancy Bachelder was named married daughter of Jonathan Young, widower, in his will signed 14 Dec 1840, probated 5 May 1856. (ME I.G.I.; Bragdon & Frost's York V.R., pp252, 366)

NANCY ELIZABETH, b 1836, York, filed (Ints.) 14 Mar 1859, m 20 Mar 1859, York, at age 23, Warren Harriman [b 1833, of Haverhill, MA, age 26]. (ME I.G.I.; Bragdon & Frost's York V.R., pp289, 291)

NANCY FROST, b 28 Mar 1828, York, most likely d/o Noah and Lydia (Frost) Young of York, d 8 Jan 1909, Alfred, age 81, widow; filed (Ints.) 5 May 1849/19 May 1849, York, m 23 May 1849, Kittery, George D. Moulton [b 29 Feb 1824, of York, d 10 Jan 1907, Alfred, age 83, married]. Both were buried at Evergreen Cemetery, Alfred, as were their two daughters Nettie, b 17 Sep 1856, d 18 Dec 1877 and Addie, b ca 1860. (Bragdon & Frost's York V.R., p271; Hale's Cems., n.p.; Kittery V.R., p316; Picton's ME Cem. Inscrips., V1, p62)

NATHANIEL, b ca 1725, of Boston, MA, filed (Ints.) 9 Dec 1752, m 14 Mar 1753, York, Anne Barton [b ca 1730, of same town]. (ME I.G.I.; Bragdon & Frost's York V.R., p138)

NATHANIEL, b ca 1750, resident of Old York, reported d 1 Apr 1778, Valley Forge, PA. Nathaniel enlisted from York 4 May 1775, muster roll dated 1 Aug 1775, and served in Capt. Jonathan Nowell's Co., Col. James Scammon's 30th Regt., service, 3 months, 5 days. He also served in Capt. Jedediah Goodwin's Co., Col. Edward Wiggelsworth's Regt. Pay abstract for travel allowance, etc. from Albany home, 280 miles travel allowed him. Company was discharged at Albany 30 Nov 1776. Continental Army pay accounts for service were from 7 Feb 1777 to 1 Apr 1778. Company return dated Valley Forge, 25 Jan 1778. (Mass. Soldiers & Sailors, p1030)

NATHANIEL, b ca 1805, resident of Newfield per 1830 census, age 20-30, as was the spousal figure; apparently they were recently married. (Census York Co., 1830, p310)

NATHANIEL, b 1828, N.H., of Berwick, s/o widow Eliza ( ) Young, m 25 Jun 1853, Berwick, Hannah Mathias [b 1831, N.H.]. In 1860 Nathaniel, spouse Hannah and their three young children lived with his widowed mother Eliza [b 1810] in Berwick after a brief stay in Vermont. It is believed that the family unit headed by Nathaniel moved on to Rochester, N.H., or perhaps returned there, as noted in the 1870 census for Rochester, and in the Youngs of Strafford County, N.H., Vol. I. Ch. b VT: John F., b 1851; Ann J., b 1854. Ch. b N.H.: Lizzie, b 1857. (Mormon/ME V.R., Wright-Zitkov; Census York Co., 1860, Reel B, p880)

NEWELL H., b ca 1850, of Berwick, widower; spouse was Sarah A. ( ) [b 1854, d 23 Mar 1877, Berwick, age 23-7-0, married, buried at Lord's Cemetery, Berwick]. (Mormon/ME V.R., Wright-Zitkov)

NOAH, b 11 Feb 1775, York, s/o Samuel Young of York, Gent., d 22 Jul 1858, native town, married, age 83; filed (Ints.) 9 Jan 1819, m 24 Jan 1819, Sunday p.m., York, Lydia Frost [b 31 Mar 1787, York, d/o William Frost, Esq., d 1 March 1860, native town, widow, age 73]. Noah lived in York per the

four census reports from 1820-1850. In the 1820 census, his age was 26-45, with household containing another male of the same age group, one male under 10, two females age 26-45, and one female 45 plus, revealing a parental figure and siblings, along with his bride and recent offspring. In 1830 his age was 50-60, the spousal figure age 40-50, and young people included one male age 10-15, and one female age 5-10. In 1840 Noah was age 60-70, a female parental figure was 50-60, and one male and one female both age 15-20. By 1850 Noah and spouse Lydia lived with their son Charles F. who had become head of household in York. The estate was valued at $2,500.
  Cemetery inscriptions indicated Noah and Samuel of York were siblings, but parentage was not altogether clear. They and their families were buried at the Young Lot on the east side of Route 91, next to the road and adjoining driveway at 204 Cider Hill Road, York. Ch. b York: Charles F.+, b 18 Apr 1819; Mary E., b 31 May 1822, d 15 Apr 1824, native town; most likely Nancy Frost+ (Young) Moulton, b 28 Mar 1828. (ME I.G.I.; Bragdon & Frost's York V.R., pp209, 436; Frost's York Cem., p621; Hale's Cems., n.p.; Census York Co., 1820, p604; 1830, p249; 1840, Reel B, p259; 1850, Reel A, p216; J. P. Thompson, Recs. of York Co., TMs, p417)
  OLIVE, b ca 1760, of York, filed (Ints.) 16 Oct 1773, m 24 Nov 1773 at First Parish Church, York, Samuel Tenny [b ca 1755, of same town]. (Bragdon & Frost's York V.R., pp156, 359)
  OLIVE, b ca 1764, York, d/o Masterson and Sarah (Curtis) Young, d pre 16 Feb 1814, native town; filed (Ints.) 29 May 1784, m 22 Jul 1784, at First Parish Church, York, Stephen Grant [b ca 1760, of same town]. Olive Grant was named married daughter of Masterson Young in his will signed 6 Jun 1795, probated 17 Aug 1795, York. She was also mentioned as heir-at-law, deceased however, in her mother Sarah's will drawn up 16 Feb 1814. (ME I.G.I.; Bragdon & Frost's York V.R., pp165, 362)
  OLIVE, b ca 1770, York; filed (Ints.) 29 Oct 1791, m 11 Nov 1791, York, William Norton [b ca 1765, of same town]. (ME I.G.I.; Bragdon & Frost's York V.R., p174)
  OLIVE, b 1780, of York, bur. 31 Mar 1834, York, age 54, of consumption. (Bragdon & Frost's York V.R., p427)
  OLIVE A., b ca 1855, of North Berwick, prob. d/o John M. and Mary A. (   ) Young of Berwick; m 1 Oct 1875, North Berwick, Albert F. Getchell [b ca 1850, of same town]. (ME I.G.I.)
  OLIVE ANN, b 19 Jan 1818, York, d/o Samuel and Grace (Hutchins) Young, alive 19 May 1885, native town; m 30 Sep 1842, York, John Hutchins [b ca 1815, of same town]. Olive Ann Hutchins, w/o John, was named sibling and heir-at-law of Samuel Young of York by will signed 19 May 1885, probated 6 Oct 1885, her legacy, five hundred dollars. (ME I.G.I.; Bragdon & Frost's York V.R., p257)

OLIVE B., b ca 1820, of York, filed (Ints.) 6 Mar 1841, m 20 Mar 1841, York, Grenville Perkins [b ca 1815, of same town]. Perkins ch. b York: Edward M. Perkins, b 1854, spouse of Sarah L. Kimball of York. (Bragdon & Frost's York V.R., pp254, 348)

OLIVE ESTHER, b 29 Mar 1829, North Berwick, d/o John and Esther (Hall) Young, resident of Lebanon. Olive Esther married late-summer 1850, John Calvin Lord [b ca 1825, of same town]. In early 1850 Olive E. lived with her parents at age 21. It is of note that Mormon/ME V.R., Wright-Zitkov gave her d-o-b as 20 Mar 1820, North Berwick "from George W. Chamberlain's book." (ME I.G.I.)

OLIVER, b 1802, d 19 Mar 1830, Berwick, age 28. (Mormon/ME V.R., Wright-Zitkov)

OLIVER, b 1804, prob. of Berwick, d testate 17 May 1830, age 26, Somersworth, N.H.; see main entry under Youngs of Strafford Co., N.H., Vol. I; m 30 Mar 1828, Somersworth, Hannah E. Gordon [b ca 1805, Berwick]. Not quite two years after their marriage, Oliver died, survived by wife and young son Oliver, member of the Freewill Baptist Church.

Oliver's will was drawn 22 Mar, proved 17 May 1830, and appointed Nathaniel Grant of Berwick as his sole Exec.; witnesses W. A. Marston, Richard Shapleigh, Artemas Pratt [Strafford Co. Probate 41:6]. Exec. Grant gave bond of $3,000.00 with sureties James Martin, Joseph Stackpole, Ezra Harthern and John T. Nute [Strafford Co. Probate 30:259]. Grant soon filed petition 5 Dec 1831 to have Oliver's will, originated in Somersworth, Strafford County, N.H., be filed in York County [York Probate #20976].

Exec. Grant was named guardian of Oliver's infant son Oliver Martin Young until the son reached the age of 14, at which time Oliver Jr. would be old enough to elect his guardian. His half-sister Joanna Young and his own father, if in need of assistance, were other legatees. For full details on the Admin. of his estate, inventory, and the claims against it, please see Oliver's main entry in Youngs of Strafford Co., N.H., Vol. I. On 20 Sep 1830, widow Hannah E. was granted an allowance of $300 from Oliver's estate [Strafford Co. Probate 43:13]. Ch. b Somersworth, N.H.: Oliver Martin, b ca 1830. (Morning Star, p376; NHVR-Marr)

PAMELA aka PARMELA, b 1 Feb 1763, York, d/o John and Elizabeth (Hill) Young, m 17 Mar 1784, at First Parish Church, York, Theodore Hill [b ca 1760, of York]. (ME I.G.I.; Bragdon & Frost's York V.R., p362)

PAMELIA A., b ca 1830, Acton, d/o Jonathan and Mehitable (Moody) Young, m 13 Oct 1852, Acton, Robert E. Hicks [b ca 1825, of same town, s/o Daniel and Sarah ( ) Hicks]. Pamelia was quite young when she was named daughter and heir-at-law in Jonathan's will signed 8 Oct 1838, probated 7 Jan 1839. (ME I.G.I.; Family Recs. courtesy of Forest G. Hicks, Oxnard, CA)

PATIENCE, b ca 1741, York, youngest d/o Jonathan Jr. and Abigail (Came) Young, filed (Ints.) 16 Jan 1762, m 4 Feb 1762, York, John Stover [b ca 1735, of same town]. Patience Stover and married sisters Abigail Grow and Eunice Junkins, with spouses co-signing, sold their shares in their father Jonathan's estate in York to sibling Samuel Young for 80 pounds lawful money. The only exception made to the disposal of the estate was that part belonging to their mother Abigail Young which came to her as her Thirds, by deed signed 9 Jul 1766, rec'd 24 Oct 1772. See sister Abigail Grow for documentation.

Stover ch. b York: John Stover, b 16 Oct 1762; Henry Stover, b 26 May; Mehitable Stover, b 3 Apr 1766; William Stover, b 25 Apr 1768; Patience Stover, b 5 Feb 1770; Hannah Stover, b 28 Nov 1771; Olive Stover, b 5 Nov 1773; Joseph Stover, b 23 Nov 1776. (ME I.G.I.; Bragdon & Frost's York V.R., pp82, 144)

PATIENCE, b ca 1752, Gorham, Cumberland Co., filed (Ints.) 13 May 1773, York, m 13 Dec 1773, York, Stephen Longfellow [b ca 1745, of York]. (ME I.G.I.)

PATIENCE, b ca 1770, York, filed (Ints.) 7 Aug 1792, m 14 Aug 1792, York, Richard Curtis [b ca 1765, of same town]. (ME I.G.I.; Bragdon & Frost's York V.R., p175)

PATIENCE, b ca 1790, of Lebanon, m 22 May 1815, Lebanon, by Elder David Blaisdell, Arthur Randell [b ca 1785, of same town]. (Lebanon Marr, p224)

PATTY, b ca 1805, of Kennebunk, listed as head of household in Kennebunk per 1840 census, age 30-40; at home was a female parental figure age 70-80. (Census York Co., 1840, Reel A, p6)

PERTHENIA, aka Parthena, b 1788, York, single, d/o John and Hannah (Banks) Young, d 14 Apr 1846, native town, age 58, testate. At age seventeen, Perthenia had her will drawn 15 Sep 1829, proved 3 May 1847. It should be noted that York V.R. gave her date of death in York as 17 Apr 1847. According to her will, her widowed mother Hannah was to have the use and improvement of her real estate in York, six acres of tillage and the pasture land. Her married sister Sally Sherman, w/o Ivory Sherman of York, was to receive the same real estate after her mother's demise plus Perthenia's personal property, and then after Sally's demise, Sally's daughters Perthenia Sherman and Sally Sherman [Jr.] were to receive it. Perthenia appointed her sister Sally as sole Exec.; witnesses Charles O. Emerson, Abigail Hutchins, Stephen Grant [York Probate #20978]. (Bragdon & Frost's York V.R., pp163, 361, 430, 510)

PETER, b ca 1730, York, filed (Ints.) 17 Apr 1756, m 9 May 1756, York, Naomi Hill [b ca 1735, York]. (Bragdon & Frost's York V.R., p141; ME I.G.I.)

PETER, b 1746, of York, d 1 Sep 1829, age 83. Peter was buried at the Young Cemetery on the north side of Young's Ridge Road, York, next to the grave sites of Joshua M. and Georgianna (Ricker) Young and their family. (ME Cemetery Inscrips., V1, p30)

PETER, b ca 1750, of Dover, N.H., extensive landowner in both Green Hill, Barrington, N.H. and Shapleigh, ME in the late 1790s (please see main entry in Youngs of Strafford Co., N.H., Vol. I). The question kept arising whether Peter of Barrington ever established a homestead of his own on any of the acreage he bought in Shapleigh [part of this town to become Acton in 1830]. Yet as late as 1800, no documentation to that effect was ever found. It is believed he and his wife, first cousin Sarah Hayes Young, chose to remain in Barrington where they enjoyed a substantial estate; it was shown that the properties he bought in Shapleigh were all for speculation, but one especially was sold to Jonathan Young of Acton, Maine; see deeds below.

Katherine Richmond's **Hayes Genealogy** [V1, pp75, 76], stated that Peter Young (b 14 Jan 1800, Acton, eldest s/o Jonathan and Mercy (Nowell) Young), "was a lineal descendant of Sarah Hayes Young," spouse of landowner Peter Young of Barrington [b ca 1750, of Dover, N.H.]. She added that a branch of the Hayes family settled in Acton, ME. Thus Peter's purchase of lands in Acton ca 1795-1800, all the while maintaining his residence in Barrington, served to establish that family link that had long been elusive between Peter Young of Barrington and Peter Young of Acton, s/o Jonathan cited just above.

As part of one deed signed 10 Sep 1795, rec'd 14 Nov 1795, Peter of Barrington bought in Acton [that area which had formerly been part of Shapleigh up to 1830] from Samuel Hall, Gent. of Wakefield, N.H. for 540 pounds: (1) 150 acres in Lot No. 13, 9th Range, in the 2nd Div., Shapleigh, York County, which had been conveyed to Hall by Gilman Leavitt; (2) a certain piece of land in Lot 12, 9th Range, Shapleigh, adjoining a cove; and (3) a small gore of land in Lot No. 11, 9th Range, 89 acres, 62 rods; witnesses Charles Pelham, Daniel French [York Deed 58:203].

There were two other deeds that indicated Peter was still a resident of Barrington up through 1800. The first of these was signed 26 April 1798, rec'd 25 Jul 1798: a Writ of Possession by the Court of Common Pleas was awarded to Peter against Jonathan Abbott of Shapleigh. This established Peter's claims of ownership of the 150-acre plot of land known as No. 13, 9th Range, 2nd Div., in Shapleigh [as cited above], and 60 acres of Lot No. 12, 9th Range, in the 2nd Div.; Peter was awarded damages in the amount of $8.54, said Abbott having been sent to jail for unjustly withholding possession of these lands from Peter; witness Richworth Jordan, Esq. [York Deed 62:148].

This very same Lot No. 13, in 9th Range, 2nd Div. of 150 acres was sold by Peter to [son] Jonathan Young of Shapleigh for $800.00, by deed signed 8 Mar 1800, rec'd 19 Sep 1803, two parcels of land in Shapleigh: 150 acres along with Lot No. 12, 9th Range, and 89 acres, 62 rods of land from a small gore of land in Lot No. 11 at the N.E. corner of the lot; witnesses Clement Ham, Betsey Tenney [York Deed 70:86].

PETER, b 29 Apr 1784, York, s/o Rowland and Mary (Norton) Young, d 1838, age 54, native town; m 18 Sep 1806, York, Mary Long [b ca 1786, of Bridgton]. Peter was eight years old when his father's will was written 20 Feb 1792, and seventeen when it was probated 9 Feb 1801. He was listed as resident and head of household in York per the 1810 and 1830 census reports: in 1810 his age was 26-45, with one female in the household, age 16-26; in 1830, his age and that of his spouse's was 40-50 years--at home were one male and one female both under the age of 15.

One deed only was found for Peter of York up through 1810, after the death of his father Rowland and after he had relocated in Alton, Strafford Co., N.H.: by deed dated 9 Sep 1806, rec'd 25 Mar 1809, he sold to William Hutchins of York for $90.00, a one-sixth part of real estate that had belonged to his father Rowland Young, late of York, cordwainer, remaining undivided, "and said Hutchins to come into posses-sion of the premises after the decease of my mother Mary Young and not before," witnesses Joseph Bragdon, Timothy Lyman [York Deed 80:142].

Upon being ordained as the first pastor of the York Christian Church at the age of twenty-four in 1808, the same year that Peter's leg had to be amputated above the knee, he became an itinerant Free-Will Baptist preacher. His early mentor was the elder Elias Smith, an itinerant Calvinistic Baptist preacher. His preaching entailed traveling through Maine, New Hampshire and parts of Massachusetts. Children, if any, were not identified. (Bragdon & Frost's York V.R., p85; Census York Co., 1810, p821; 1830, p247; Hist. of York, pp168-169, 406, 407)

PETER, b 14 Jan 1800, Acton, eldest s/o Jonathan and Mercy (Nowell) Young, farmer, d 21 Nov 1872, native town, age 72, married, testate; m1 ca 1830, Acton, Mary Garvin [b 31 May 1809, Wakefield, N.H., d/o Wentworth and Sarah (Wentworth) Garvin, d 27 Jun 1841, Acton, age 32]. Peter m2 1840s, Acton, Deborah M. Berry [b 4 Jan 1806, d 10 Aug 1876, Acton, age 70, widow]. Peter and sibling William were named Co-Execs. of their father's will drawn up 8 Oct 1838, probated 7 Jan 1839, and were to share all their father's real estate, "subject to the life estate of one-third part of his wife to hold the same equally." Yet in fact the dwelling house itself was intended only for William and their unmarried sisters.

Peter was listed as head of family in Acton in three census reports from 1840 to 1860. In 1840 his age was 40-50, the spousal figure age 30-40; at home were two males and one female under 5, and another female age 5-10. In 1850 his age 50, his family contained second spouse Deborah, age 41, and seven children: Betsey, Thomas, John, Mary Jordan, Edmund, Samuel and Mary. In 1860, Peter's real estate was assessed at

$2,500; at home were wife Deborah and five of their children Betsey, John M., Edmund J., Samuel P., and Mary J.

Peter's will was written 19 Dec 1870, proved two years later on 3 Dec 1872, in which he named sons Edmund J. and Samuel P. as joint Execs. and in effect, residuary legatees; witnesses Horace Bodwell, John B. Bodwell, Julia B. Bodwell [York Probate #20979]. Second wife Deborah M. was devised a one-third part of the real estate, and all household furniture excepting that which belonged to first wife Mary. Daughter Mary Ann by wife Mary was to receive the other part of the furniture belonging to her late mother. Single daughter Elizabeth G. was devised the chamber over the dining room, and single daughter Mary M., the N.E. front room that would be finished off by Edmund J. and Samuel P. Both single daughters were to avail themselves of "the wood standing upon any one piece of 20 acres in common on old Lot No. 13 in Acton over a twenty-year period." Joshua M. was devised twenty dollars and Sarah H., fifty dollars.

According to Katherine Richmond's **Hayes Genealogy** [V1, pp75-76, one can only surmise that Peter was a lineal descendant of Sarah (Hayes) Young, spouse of landowner Peter Young of Barrington [b ca 1750, of Dover, N.H.]. Mrs. Richmond added that a branch of the Hayes family settled in Acton, ME. For further background information on Peter and Sarah Young of Barrington, N.H., please see main entry on Peter in this volume as well as the original entry in the Youngs of Strafford County, N.H., Vol. I.

Peter and wives were buried at the Young Cemetery on Young's Ridge Road, Acton. Ch. b Acton by first wife Mary: Elizabeth aka Betsey Garvin, b 3 Apr 1834, alive in 1900 at the home of her younger brother Joshua M. in Acton; Joshua Moody+, b 9 Apr 1836, twin; Thomas, b 9 Apr 1836, twin; John William, b 7 May 1838, fought in the Revolutionary War, was taken prisoner and died at Andersonville, GA, 8 Sep 1864; Mary Jordan, b 1839; and Sarah Hayes, b 8 Jun 1840.

Ch. b Acton by second wife Deborah: Edmund, b 1844; Samuel P.+, b 1845; Mary M., b 1846; and Jonathan, b 1840s. (Hale's Cems., n.p.; Wentworth Gen., V1, pp89-90; ME I.G.I.; Census York Co., 1840, Reel B, p298; 1850, Reel B, pp7-8; Thompson's Recs. of York Co., TMs, p416)

PETER aka Capt., b 29 May 1815, York, master mariner, believed to be s/o Samuel and Grace (Hutchins) Young, d 17 Dec 1895, age 80, native town, married; filed (Ints.) 16 Dec 1848, m 10 Jan 1849, York, Mary Elizabeth Crosby [b 23 Jan 1813, of Portsmouth, N.H., d 17 Dec 1899, York, age 86, widow]. Peter was named brother and heir-at-law of Samuel Young of York, widower, by will drawn 19 May 1885, probated 6 Oct 1885, his inheritance, $500. In 1850 Peter held the rank of sailor in the census listing for York, age 35, with an estate valued at $1,500; in household was spouse Mary E. and infant Roland.

By 1860 he had graduated to rank of master mariner, his real estate valued at $2,500 with personal property set at

$5,000; members of household included spouse Mary C., age 47, and sons Rowland, Edward and Charles. Peter and family were buried at York Cemetery, York.

Ch. b York: Rowland, b 19 Jan 1850, d 5 Oct 1928, native town, age 78; Edward E.+, b 5 Apr 1852; Charles, b 25 Apr 1855, d 16 Dec 1934, age 79. (ME I.G.I.; Bragdon & Frost's York V.R., p270; Frost's York Cem., p489; Census York Co., 1850, Reel A, p199; 1860, Reel C, p955)

PETER, b 1823, GA, resident of Kittery in 1850, member of the U.S. Marine Corps, age 27. (Census York Co., 1850, Reel B, p281)

PHEBE, b 25 Jan 1702, York, d/o Lt. Joseph and Abigail (Donnell) Young, d 20 Apr 1731, native town, predeceased her father; filed (Ints.) 25 May 1728, m 20 Jun 1728, York, Wymond Bradbury Jr. of Brunswick [b 13 May 1669, Ipswich, s/o Wymond and Sarah (Pike) Bradbury]. Wymond remarried after 1731, York, Mary Donnell [b ca 1710, York].

Bradbury ch. b Buxton by first wife Phebe: Susanna Bradbury, b 26 Jan 1728/9; Samuel Bradbury, b 26 Mar 1731. Bradbury Ch. b Buxton by 2nd wife Mary, at Brunswick Fort: Mary Bradbury, b 30 Apr 1734; Jacob Bradbury, twin, b 8 May 1736; Thomas Bradbury, twin, b 8 May 1736; Elizabeth Bradbury, b 6 Jul 1738, d same month. (Noyes et al, pp104, 776; ME I.G.I.; Bragdon & Frost's York V.R., pp43, 118; Marshall's Buxton, ME, pp234-235)

PHILAMON, b 1837, Canada, operative, of Biddeford as of 1860 census. He lived at boarding home with Eliza Young [b 1844, Canada], who was either sibling or wife. (Census York Co., 1860, Reel A, p279)

PHILAMON, b 1838, Canada, of Saco, believed to be s/o Samuel and Mathilda (   ) Young of Canada, operative in mill, resident of Saco per 1860 census, single, living at the home of John and Sophia Shamber [b 1816 and 1820, respectively]. (Census York Co., 1860, Reel C, p743)

PHOEBE aka PHEBE, b 1802, York, d/o Daniel and Abigail (Dyer) Young of Hollis, alive 1848, native town; m 1828, York, Jeremiah Dow [b ca 1800, of same town]. Phebe Dow was named married daughter and heir-at-law of Daniel Young of York by his will signed 8 Jan 1848, probated 6 Mar 1848. (ME I.G.I.)

POLLY, b ca 1785, formerly of Ossipee, N.H., then of Parsonsfield; (Ints.) 3 Dec 1808, Parsonsfield, m 29 Dec 1808, Wolfeboro, Tobias Pray [b ca 1780, Parsonsfield, of Brookfield, N.H.]. (Parsonsfield V.R., Town Clerk, p77; NHVR-Brides)

POLLY, b ca 1790, of Waterboro, filed (Ints.) 12 Feb 1808; m 24 Apr 1808, Waterboro, Aaron Kimball [b ca 1785, of same town]. (ME I.G.I.; **Reg.** 90:230, 251, 1936)

POLLY, b 14 Apr 1800, of Waterboro. (ME I.G.I.)

PRESTON B., M.D., b 1858, Berwick, d 1900, native town, buried at the Richard and Rebecca Young family plot at Evergreen Cemetery, Berwick. (Hale's Cems., n.p.)

REBECCA ( ), b Aug 1813, Canada, d 1905, Saco, age 92. She had lived in Saco as of 1900, age 87, widow, at the home of son-in-law Charles Dean, Temple Street. (1900 ME Soundex; Picton's ME Cem. Inscrips., V2, p1518)

REBECCA O., b 31 Oct 1847, South Berwick, d/o William A. and Dorcas N. ( ) Young, lived alone, single, in her native town in 1900, age 52, d 2 Jul 1927, buried at the family plot in South Berwick. As a young child she was listed as a member of her parents' household in the 1850-1860 census reports. (1900 ME Soundex; Picton's ME Cem. Inscrips., V3, p2047)

REUBEN, b 1810, of Hollis, laborer, listed as head of household in the 1850 census for Hollis, married to Sarah ( ) [b 1814]. Four children at home were Olivia, Mary, Margaret, and Edwin. Ch. b prob. Hollis: Olivia, b 1834; Mary, b 1838; Margaret, b 1840; and Edwin, b 1846. (Census York Co., 1850, Reel B, p109)

RHODA, b Aug 1843, Waterboro, d/o Daniel and Eunice (Whitten) Young, alive 1900, Shapleigh, age 56, widow; m 7 Jul 1865, Waterboro, Levi Beale [b ca 1838, of Waterboro, d pre 1900]. In 1900 Rhoda Beale, widow, her married son Ansel Beale, his wife Alfreda F. Beale [b Dec 1873], and their two infant sons Roscoe E. Beale [b Jun 1898] and Sidney R. Beale [b Jan 1900] lived at her father Daniel's home in Shapleigh. Beale ch. b Waterboro: Ansel Beale, b Jun 1871. (ME I.G.I.)

RICHARD, b ca 1631, Cape Porpoise, s/o Rowland Young Sr., d pre May 1683; m ca 1656, Cape Porpoise, Margery (Batson) Kendall [b ca 1635, of Saco, widow of William Kendall of Cape Porpoise, d/o Stephen and Elizabeth ( ) Batson]. At an early age Margery Batson had been indentured to Capt. Bony-thon. Widow Margery Young m3 9 May 1683, Robert Elliot [b ca 1631, of Portsmouth, carpenter]. This was Elliot's 2nd marriage. (ME I.G.I., Noyes et al, pp82, 219; MH&G Rec., V3, p55)

RICHARD, b ca 1775, of Berwick, n.d.; spouse was Rebecca ( ), b 1790, of Berwick, d 26 Aug 1846, Berwick, age 56, Their two sons George and Benjamin and families relocated in Danvers, MA when young men. Richard, Rebecca and sons George H. and Benjamin were buried at Evergreen Cemetery, Berwick. Ch. b Berwick: George H.+, b 11 Feb 1808. Ch. b Sanford: Benjamin+, b 19 Nov 1810. (Mormon/ME V.R., Wright-Zitkov; Hale's Cems., n.p.; ME and MA I.G.I.; Danvers VR, Marr, p330, Births, p423; F. R. Boyle's **Sanford**, p160)

RICHARD P., b ca 1775, sole resident by the name of Young in the 1810 census for Alfred, age 26-45, with a female person of same age bracket and three young males under 10 years of age. This was also the sole reference bearing his name for either the town of Alfred or York County. (Census York Co., 1810, p1018)

RICHARD P., b ca 1815, of Parsonsfield, filed (Ints.) 26 Nov 1842, (Cert.) 21 Dec 1842, Parsonsfield, Mary Whittum [b ca 1820, of same town]. (Parsonsfield V.R., Town Clerk, p146)

ROBERT, b 1658, York, s/o Rowland Jr. and Joan (Knight) Young, d 22 Aug 1690, native town, age 32, predeceasing parents; m pre 4 Jul 1676, York, Mary Sayward [b ca 1660, York, d/o Henry and Mary (Peasley) Sayward, alive 1691, known then as Mary Young Bray]. Widow Mary Young m2 by Oct 1691, Richard Bray Jr. [b ca 1655, York, shoemaker, s/o Richard and Rebecca (   ) Bray, d 6 Jan 1717-18].

Robert was the first recipient of a series of deeds of gift from parents Rowland Sr. and Joan Young. His was dated 3 Jun 1680, rec'd 13 May 1688: ten acres land which were part of the tract of land formerly owned by Robert Knight where he used to live, bounded by a small brook, and near the house of Mary Sayward, widow; see father's entry for full documentation. The only other land deed found for Robert was a mortgage dated 14 Dec 1681, rec'd 18 Dec 1683, which he granted to Thomas Heath of Boston, in the amount of fifteen pounds current money of New England with Heath's promise to pay in full at or before 5 Nov next; witnesses John Penwell, John Hoy [York Deed 3:138].

Robert led an eventful life. On 21 Aug 1683 he escaped from a shipwreck when bound from York to Piscataqua, received a town grant in 1685, was voted selectman in 1686, and served on trial jury in 1689. But when traveling to Kittery on 22 Aug 1690 he was killed by Indians.

Ch. b York: Robert+, b ca 1678; Joseph+ Jr., b ca 1680; and Mary+ (Young) Battin aka Batten, b 1681. (Noyes et al, pp108, 366, 610, 776; ME I.G.I.; MH&G Rec., V4, p62)

ROBERT, b ca 1678, York, eldest s/o Robert and Mary (Sayward) Young; received a grant of 30 acres from the town of York on 23 Mar 1712/13. Robert sold this acreage for 30 shillings money to kinsman John Sayward of York by deed signed 19 Jun 1717, rec'd 9 Feb 1721; witnesses Samuel Bray, Jonathan Bane, Joseph Bragdon [York Deed 10:251].

ROBERT, b ca 1710, of St. George's River, cordwainer. He signed an indenture on behalf of Samuel Waldo, Esq. of Boston, Suffolk Co. in the amount of five shillings sterling in consideration of the rent of one pepper corn per annum to be paid yearly on the 29th day of September forever, for a certain tract of land on the western side of St. George's River below the block house, 100 acres which included swamp and uplands, woods, trees, river waters, fishing mines and mineral quarries by deed signed 5 Oct 1744, rec'd 4 Feb 1744/5; witnesses Thomas Proctor, William Lettigow [York Deed 25:15].

ROBERT, b ca 1720, of Boston, Suffolk County, laborer. He and co-grantors S. Drown, Thomas Garvin conveyed a short-term loan of 250 pounds old Tenor to Robert Sproul of Pemaquid upon Sproul's purchase of 80 acres land in Harrington on the eastern side of John's River, so-called, the sum payable within the space of thirty days; witnesses John North, Jonathan Rand Jr., Adam Richardson [York Deed 28:275].

Harrington is a seaport town, today under the jurisdiction of Washington County.

ROBERT, b 20 Mar 1736/7, York, s/o Job and Patience (King) Young; filed (Ints.) 5 Jan 1760, York, m 22 Jan 1761, York, Mary Dill [b ca 1740, of same town]. (ME I.G.I.; Bragdon & Frost's York V.R., p143)

ROWLAND Sr., b ca 1603, of York. (ME I.G.I.)

ROWLAND Sr., b ca 1620, England, fisherman, arrived in York ca 1636, d ca 1690, York, testate, married; m 1647/8, York, Joan Knight [b ca 1625, York, d/o Robert Knight, alive 1690, native town]. Rowland served on the York Jury in 1650, and took oath of allegiance, "Freeman's Oath," to the Mass. Government 22 Nov 1652. As explained by Lucius Paige's **List of Freemen of Massachusetts, 1630-1691**, (pp3, 9, 23): "Before a member of society could exercise the right of suffrage, or hold any public office, he must be made a freeman by the general or quarterly court. To become such he was required to produce evidence that he was a respectable member of some Congregational church." The records showed, moreover, that Rowland Sr. was the sole Young listed from this region to take this oath between 1630-1691. Then too, according to remarks made by Mr. Savage, taken from his edition of Winthrop's Journal: "These [Freemen] are probably ancestors of near three fourths of the present inhabitants of the six New England states, with almost half of New York and Ohio."

A grant of land was made to him by the town in 1653 on Bass Cove. Then on 12 Jun 1666, a case was made against him and Mr. Harbert for travelling between Kittery and York on the Lord's Day. In being called to answer his presentment, he used scurrilous language against the Grand Jury, for which he was fined 50 shillings, office's fees 5 shillings, Case 3:53, 12 Jun 1666. And on 9 Jul 1667, Rowland was tried as a defendant by John Growth for dismembering and curing the leg of Samuel Young [believed to be his son], to the value of 44 shillings; case 3:69 withdrawn.

By deed of gift signed 12 Aug 1673, rec'd 24 Jun 1678, Joan's father Robert Knight conveyed four acres upland and two small pieces of marsh in York to his grandson Rowland Young Jr., son of Rowland and Joan; witnesses John Twisden, mother Joan Young, sibling Mary Young Moulton [York Deed 3:25].

Richard Knight of Boston, brother-in-law of Rowland Sr., sold to him for 86-10-0, all the housing, marsh and uplands which "did belong unto my father Robert Knight, deceased, and according as his last will and testament makes mention, hath sold the same unto my brother Rowland Young," by deed signed 15 Feb 1677, rec'd 28 Feb 1678; witnesses Peter Weare, Sr., Job Alcock, John Twisden [York Deed 3:38]. Then by deed signed 25 Aug 1685, rec'd 18 Mar 1686, Knight's married daughter Joan Young conveyed a tract of land that had formerly been her father's homestead to her son Rowland Jr.; witnesses Samuel Matthews, Timothy Yealls [York Deed 4:53-54].

In Rowland Sr.'s last days, he and wife Joan began to dispose of their estate within York County by deeds of gift to three of their sons: (1) Son Robert was the first recipient by date of 3 Jun 1680, attested to 13 May 1688: ten acres land "which is a part of the....tract of land which was formerly Robert Knight's land where he formerly lived," bounded by a small brook, which is near the house of Mary Sayward, widow; witnesses Arthur Bragdon, Daniel Livingstone [York Deed 6:25-27]. (2) Son Samuel, the second recipient by deed dated 18 Apr 1682, rec'd 23 Nov 1685: ten acres land lying and being part of a tract of land granted to Rowland by the Town of York at a town meeting held on 15 Sep 1667, and laid out to Rowland on 9 Apr 1679; it was situated behind Rowland Sr.'s dwelling house; witnesses Arthur Bragdon, Daniel Livingstone [York Deed 4:48]. This same acreage was disposed of after Samuel's death by Samuel's sons Jonathan and Ichabod who sold it to Samuel's sibling Job Young of York.

(3) Son Rowland Jr. of the "Isles of Shoals the Northernmost," the third grantee of land from his parents's estate by deed dated 25 Aug 1685, rec'd 18 Mar 1686: one tract of land being on the north side of the River in York, part of which said tract of land was formerly the homesfall and in the possession of Rowland Jr.'s maternal grandfather Robert Knight, deceased, adjacent to the former above said land and lying to the N.W. of it, and "to carry as much breadth as our father Knight's old field until it meets with our son Robert's grant and also adjoining a parcel of land now in possession of our loving son Robert;" witnesses Samuel Matthews, Timothy Yealls [York Deed 4:53-54].

Rowland's will was in substance a deed of gift, n.d., but attested to 6 Nov 1685 by Jeremiah Moulton [son-in-law] and Timothy Yealls, probated 24 Nov 1685, wherein Rowland devised to his wife Joan, his sole Exec., "all my Estate that I have in this world, during the time of her natural life...," that included houses, lands and marshes [**Maine Wills**, pp85-86]. Abraham Preble and Arthur Bragdon were appointed appraisers of his estate 25 Sep 1685, inventory returned in the amount of 224-06-0 [York Deeds 5:38], a considerable amount at that point in time.

Widow Joan of York had her will drawn up 12 May 1698, proven 20 Jan 1698; witnesses Isaac Negus, Daniel Smith, Thomas Baker [**Maine Wills**, pp124-125]. She appointed her well-beloved son Rowland to be sole Exec. of her estate and her "trusty and well-beloved friends Abraham Preble Esq. and James Plaisted, both of York, to be her overseers." She devised to son Rowland, four acres of marsh up in York River, and 23 acres land lying on the south side of the river, adjacent to his dwelling house in York. Son Job was to receive, "all the housing and land where her old dwelling house now stands adjoining to George Norton, to be for his use and improvement while he lives, but not to be sold nor alienated by him...but to descend unto his son or male heirs," plus three acres of marsh land up the river and two sheep. Daughter Mary Moulton was to receive six shillings, and daughter Lydia Haines, three acres of marsh land lying up in York River with all the neat cattle, two sheep and the clothing and bedding.

Ch. b York: Rowland+ Jr., b 1649; Samuel, b 1650s; Richard, b 1653; Mary+ (Young) Moulton, b 1653/4; Robert+, b 1658; William+, b 1663; Job+, b 1664; Lydia+ (Young) Haines Bragdon, b 1672. (Pope's Pioneers, p244; Noyes et al, pp296, 404-405; ME I.G.I.; ME Prov. & Ct. Recs., 1:155, 266, 280)

ROWLAND Jr. aka Deacon, b 1649, York and the Isles of Shoals, fisherman, s/o Rowland and Joan (Knight) Young, d 28 Jun 1721, age 72, native town; m ca 1669, York, Susanna Matthews [b ca 1650, of same town, d/o Walter and Mary ( ) Matthews, alive 1683, York]. Rowland Jr. received lands in York from his maternal grandfather Robert Knight by deed of gift dated 12 Aug 1673, rec'd 24 Jun 1678; witnesses John Twisden, mother Joan, and sibling Mary Young Moulton [York Deed 3:25].

Rowland Jr. of the "Isles of Shoals the Northernmost," was the third recipient of land from his parents' estate by deed of gift dated 25 Aug 1685, rec'd 18 Mar 1686: land being on the north side of the River in York, part of which was formerly the homesfall of Rowland Jr.'s maternal grandfather Robert Knight, deceased, adjoining said land and lying to the N.W. of it, and "to carry as much breadth as our father Knight's old field 'til it meets with our son Robert's grant, and adjoining a parcel of land now in possession of our loving son Robert." For documentation on this deed, see parents' main entry.

On 16 Oct 1683, Rowland sold his property on Smuttynose Island to Edward Martin of the Islands for a valuable consideration, deed rec'd 19 Jul 1684, with wife Susanna's seal upon it; witnesses Phillip Odiorne, Samuel Matthews [York Deed 4:13].

As will be noted above, his mother's will, signed 12 May 1698, probated 20 Jun 1698, devised to Rowland Jr. four acres of marsh belonging to her up in York River and twenty-three acres lying on the south side of the river by his dwelling house in York. Sons Joseph and Benaiah Young and Henry Donnell were witnesses to Rowland's exchange of land between neighbor John Pickering of Portsmouth, N.H. and himself on Nov 1718, rec'd 15 May 1719, preferring to swap the acreage: Rowland had 24 acres granted him by the town of York and Pickering had the same quantity of land granted to him, adjoining Rowland's [York Deed 9:177].

By deed signed 1 Jul 1703, rec'd 30 Jul 1722, Rowland, Jr. deeded to Josiah Main of York, seven acres land located on the south side of the river upon the neck of land where said Main lived, bounded by lands of Matthews Young and said Rowland, "which is part of a grant of forty acres land formerly granted to my father Rowland Young late of York," for a certain sum of money; witnesses Mary Preble, Abraham Preble [York Deed 11:38].

Rowland Jr.'s own will, signed 14 Sep 1719, proved 2 Jan 1721/22, named his heirs-at-law: wife Susanna and their four sons and five daughters. First-born son Joseph was named sole Exec.; witnesses Samuel Moody, Hannah Moody, Mary Moody [**Maine Wills**, pp229-230]. Wife Susanna was devised her Dower Rights, the use of a third of all his lands and marsh during her natural life, the moveable estate, in essence, "wholly and forever."

Sons Joseph and Benaiah were in effect residuary legatees: Joseph was to receive the homesfall where they then lived and one half of the little pasture adjoining it, with the housing and orchard, as well as the point of salt marsh that lies next to Kittery, one acre more or less. Benaiah was devised the other half of the little pasture and all twenty-six acres of land which adjoined on York River upon which he then dwelt, plus one half of the two acres of salt marsh in the western cove.

Son Matthews's inheritance was 1-1/4 acres of salt marsh adjoining Widow Johnson's marsh. Son Jonathan was to share the other half of the two acres in the western cove. It was Rowland's wish that Joseph and Benaiah pay six pounds each to their sisters Mary, Susanna, Elizabeth, Sarah and Mercy.

Letters Test. were granted to Rowland's son Joseph, sole Exec., 2 Jan 1721/2, with instructions that an inventory and an accounting be made on or before 2 Apr next [York Probate #20980]. Inventory of Rowland's estate was returned same date by Benjamin Stone, Samuel Sewall and Joseph Holt; the listing included the home place of 20 acres and buildings at 150 pounds, 26 acres where "Benjah Young lives" at 100 pounds, and four acres of marsh at 30 pounds [York Probate 3:110].

G. T. Ridlon's Saco quoted the following stipulation from Rowland's will that reads almost like an epitaph: "In his will, made 1719, Rowland Jr. provided that his sons should not dispose of any of their lands 'outside of the Young family.'"

Ch. b York: Joseph+, b 1671; Benaiah+, b early 1670s; Jonathan+, b 1674; Matthews+, b ca 1675; Mary+ (Young) Stover Wells, b 1676; Susanna+ (Young) McIntire, b 1677; Elizabeth+ (Young) Webber Stover Came, b 1679; Sarah+ (Young) Brookin, b 1681; Mercy+ (Young) Simpson, b 1685. (ME I.G.I.; Noyes et al, pp776-777; Ridlon's Saco, p1218)

ROWLAND, b ca 1690, York, yeoman, m ca 1715, York, Hannah Preble [b 7 Feb 1694, Charlestown, MA, eldest d/o Benjamin and Mary (Baston) Preble of York]. The Court of General Sessions, V6, p223, showed that on 5 Apr 1726, Rowland Young and Nathaniel Freeman were bound over to this Court by Samuel Came, Esq., one of his Majesty's Justices of the Peace for the county on suspicion of taking away a horse from Benjamin Stone per the records of said Justice appears and they were directed by Capt. Edward Preble to take the horse for his Majesty's service. Inasmuch as they did not acquaint Stone with it, it was considered they should be acquitted, paying only the cost of court, two shillings, and stand committed.

Ch. b York: Nathaniel, b 1716, d 25 Sep 1742; Benjamin, b 21 Oct 1724, d 8 Aug 1728, native town, age 3-9-18. (Noyes et al, p566; Bragdon & Frost's York V.R., pp20, 392-393)

ROWLAND, b ca 1695, York, eldest s/o Job and Sarah (Austin) Preble Young, d testate pre 8 Apr 1782, native town, about 87 years old; m ca 1718, Hannah ( ) [b ca 1695, of York, d pre 6 Jun 1781, same town]. The probability is good that this main entry on Rowland and Hannah ( ) referred to Rowland and Hannah Preble Young cited in the entry just above.

Rowland's parents Job and Sarah conveyed to him two different properties by deeds of gift: (1) First deed dated 12 Feb 1714, rec'd 7 Jul 1720, twenty acres land in York situated on the S.E. side of the highway that led from the York meeting house to Cape Neddick and Wells, by lands of George Norton to Job's fence. (2) Second deed, signed 26 Nov 1723, rec'd 10 Dec 1723, whereby Job granted Rowland an additional ten acres land which were located on the S.E. side of the highway that led from the York meeting house towards Cape Neddick, adjacent to Rowland's own house and bounded on the S.E. side by lands of the late Joseph Weare. See parents Job and Sarah for full documentation.

Twenty acres in York were sold by Rowland to John Preble of York for 7-10-00 in Bills of Credit, by deed signed 27 May 1729, rec'd 29 Jul 1729: (1) the first ten acres came from one full moiety of a certain "peel of marsh" situated on the N.E. side of Cape Neddick Pond, which comes into where Joseph Weare and Nathaniel Donnell Jr. had a piece of fresh marsh joining to Joseph Bragdon's marsh--ten acres which were granted to Benjamin Preble by the town of York on 8 Mar 1714/15. (2) The other ten acres were granted to Rowland by the town of York on the same date given above, held in fee simple; witnesses Lucy Moody, Joseph Moody [York Deed 13:80-81].

Rowland's sister, the widow Lydia Weare obtained the license to sell land from her late husband Peter Weare's estate on 14 May 1724: she sold eighteen acres land to her sibling Rowland for 59-10-00, the land bounding on the country road between the meeting house and the sea side, and by lands of Stephen Preble, Joseph Weare and the Blacks; by deed signed 22 Jan 1724/5, rec'd 15 Feb 1724/5. In turn, Rowland sold fourteen of these acres to Nathaniel Donnell of York for 42 pounds lawful money, land situated at the N.E. corner of Samuel Black's homestead and up the N.W. side of said Donnell's land to Stephen Preble's land, by deed signed 26 Jan 1742/3, rec'd 1 Feb 1742; witnesses Daniel Bragdon, Alexander Bulman [York Deed 23:176].

Articles of Agreement were formally arrived at between Rowland and sibling Job Jr. as to how their father's estate and debts were to be handled upon Job Sr.'s death, by deed signed 21 Mar 1724, rec'd 6 Nov 1724: Job Jr. was to have one-third of their father's house lot, he paying but one-third of their father's lawful debts, while Rowland accepted the remaining two-thirds inheritance along with its debt responsibilities of two-thirds, for the sake of receiving their part of their father's inheritance. See Job Jr. for documentation.

On same dates of signing and recording the above agreement, Rowland and sibling Job Jr. sold to Jacob Curtis of York for 180 pounds money, the piece of land which their father settled upon and where his dwelling house then stood, bounded by lands of John Woodbridge on the N.W. side and the Widow Sarah Black's on the S.E. side, running from said Meeting House Creek N.E. on two straight lines 40 rods in breadth to the country road; see Job Jr. for documentation.

With Hannah releasing Dower Rights, Rowland conveyed two different properties to son John in a nine-year period. (1) By deed of gift signed and rec'd 15 May 1746, three acres land in York which fronted north on the road leading to Long Sands, and east by land of Col. Nathaniel Donnell, S.W. by lands of the late Samuel Black and N.W. by Peter Weare's land, enclosed within a fence; witnesses Edward Grow, Joseph Tappan [York Deed 25:237]. (2) By deed of gift signed and rec'd 14 Feb 1755, agreement was arrived at that son John would receive one acre of land from Rowland's homestead "as part of John's portion of the estate where Rowland then dwelt," situated north of Rowland's new dwelling house by the country road, with the liberty to build on the land or enlarge the same dwelling house; witnesses Daniel Moulton, Jacob Rhodes [York Deed 31:259].

Rowland and Hannah also made deed of gift to son Rowland Jr., with Hannah ceding Dower Rights, dated 13 Mar 1748, rec'd one day later, of "a part of his portion and inheritance of his father's estate, one acre land as part of the homestead on which he erected a dwelling house where he lives and planted a small orchard; witnesses Norton Woodbridge, John Young [York Deed 27:119].

Rowland disposed of his six shares in Lot No. 6, 2nd Range, of the York Outer Commons which the town granted to him, for 4-13-4, to Jonathan Sayward, by deed signed 23 May 1766, rec'd the day after; witnesses Joseph Bragdon, Daniel Moulton [York Deed 38:275].

Rowland's will, signed 27 Aug 1771, proved 8 Apr 1782, was very helpful in gaining some grasp on three generations of this family. He devised to Hannah the use and improvement of his estate real and personal in York for the duration of her life. Residuary legatees of his estate were his grandson Rowland, son of his eldest son Rowland, deceased, and grandson John, son of John. He stipulated that if he should die without issue, his share would go to John the elder's daughter Eleanor. Grandson Rowland was to pay five pounds lawful money to each of Rowland Sr.'s married daughters Mary Norton, wife of John Norton Jr., and Hannah, wife of John Johnson. Son John and grandson Rowland became in effect co-residuary legatees, the better to enable them to pay the legacies named; after his wife's life term was ended, both were to receive the remainder of his personal estate. The homestead, itself, comprised a couple of acres land in York; witnesses John Bradbury, Daniel Moulton, and Daniel Moulton, Jr. [York Probate #20983].

Upon the deaths of wife Hannah and granddaughter Eleanor in the previous decade [1771-1781], Rowland was faced with the necessity of writing a codicil to his original will on 6 Jun 1781; witnesses Edward Emerson, David Sewall, John Sewall, Jr., Mark Walton, the codicil probated 8 Apr 1782. The essential difference between Rowland's original will and the codicil was that he had changed the residuary legatees from son John and grandson Rowland (issue of another son of Rowland's), to the same son John but **grandson John**, issue of same. A subscript to these lengthy probate papers was the dire note appended to the document, which contended that Rowland Young, the testator, was in such a state of insanity as to be incapable of making a will, but [son] John Young denied this and the court upheld his opinion.

Eight children were born to Rowland and Hannah, born York 1716-1735, but the record books were too worn to be able to decipher most of the names. Ch. b York: Rowland, ca 1718, deceased at time of father's will in Aug 1771; John+, b 1720; Mary+ (Young) Norton, b ca 1723; Hannah+ (Young) Johnson, b ca 1734. (ME I.G.I.)

ROWLAND, b ca 1710, York, filed (Ints.) 16 Sep 1738, m 11 Oct 1738, York, Alice Ingraham [b ca 1715, of same town]. (ME I.G.I.; Bragdon & Frost's York V.R., p125)

ROWLAND Jr., aka Roland, b ca 1711, York, cordwainer, s/o Rowland Young Sr., of York, d pre 10 Jan 1761, York, intestate; filed (Ints.) 4 Nov 1735, York, m 16 Oct 1735, Kittery, Abigail Dixon [b ca 1715, d/o Peter and Elizabeth (   ) Dixon of Kittery, d pre 10 Apr 1780, York]. Abigail's father Peter Dixon devised six shillings apiece to the surviving heirs of his married daughter Abigail Dixon Young, by will signed 18 Feb 1779, probated 10 Apr 1780 [York Probate #4412].

Two land deeds were found for Rowland, cordwainer. The first was signed and rec'd 4 Apr 1739 when Rowland bought from Ichabod Austin of Biddeford for 40 pounds Bills of Credit, thirty acres land granted by the town of York to Austin's father Ichabod, late of York, on 25 Mar 1712/3, "being not as yet laid out," witnesses Jeremiah and Daniel Moulton [York Deed 19:251]. The second deed was signed and rec'd 18 Mar 1742, when Rowland Jr., sold to Jeremiah L. and John Littlefield of Wells for 70 pounds Bills of Credit, old Tenor, the self-same thirty acres land granted by the Town of York to Ichabod Austin on 23 Mar 1712/3, and conveyed to Rowland on 4 Apr 1739, situated at the east end of Nathaniel Chapman's land; witnesses Cotton Bradbury, Daniel Moulton [York Deed 23:65].

Admin. Papers on Roland Jr.'s estate were granted to Daniel Bragdon of York, merchant, 10 Jan 1761, with instructions that inventory was due on or before 10 Apr next, and an accounting no later than 10 Jul 1761 [York Probate #20981]. These probate papers were very helpful in establishing Rowland's and Abigail's children: Stephen, Abigail, Hannah, Sarah, Jane, and Roland Young [York Probate 11:5]. Their names came to light when Admin. Bragdon disclosed additional expenses and disbursements of the estate, n.d.

Another insight into the family structure was gained when Admin. Bragdon was appointed guardian to three minor children on 21 Oct 1761: Miriam, minor and granddaughter of Rowland Jr., and "Sarah Jane" and Stephen, minors and children of Rowland Jr. [York Probate #20971]. It would be pure speculation as to which of Roland's grown children was the deceased parent of Miriam--eldest son Peter whose name did not appear in Roland's will of 1761? Also, human error may have caused the names of daughters Sarah and Jane to be joined as in "Sarah Jane." There were two daughters, not one! On same date, 21 Oct 1761, the court appointed Bragdon as guardian to only Stephen and Hannah Young, minors above the age of fourteen and children of Rowland Young, who had chosen him for said trust [York Probate #20982].

Inventory of Rowland's estate was submitted before 6 Aug 1761 by Benjamin Stone, Richard Trevett and George Goodin at the appraised value of 94-16-6, attested to that date by Capt. Daniel Bragdon, Admin. The inventory included dwelling house, one acre of land and barn, appraised at 64 pounds, and a gold ring valued at one pound [York Probate 10:396]. See main entry on daughter Hannah Young for her sale of her "one full eighth's share."

Ch. b York: Peter, b 12 Dec 1737, not mentioned in probate of 1761, most likely predeceased his father; Abigail (Young) Cooley, w/o John Cooley of York, b 29 Jul 1739, see sibling Rowland for details on land deed; Nathaniel, b 21 Oct 1742, d 28 Oct 1742; Nathaniel, b 12 Oct 1743, predeceased his father; Hannah+, b 8 Feb 1745; Rowland+ Jr., b 11 Jan 1747/8; Sarah, b 20 Aug 1750, alive 5 Jul 1768, for details, see sibling Rowland Jr.; Jane, b 24 Nov 1752; and Stephen, b 10 May 1755. (ME I.G.I.; Bragdon & Frost's York V.R., pp56, 124, 393; Kittery V.R., pp100, 129)

ROWLAND, b 4 Feb 1713, of York and Wells, cordwainer, s/o Jonathan and Margaret (Stackpole) Young, alive 1768. It was shown by deed signed 5 May 1768, rec'd 16 May 1768 that Rowland was resident of Wells when he sold to Jonathan Sayward of York, Esq. for eight pounds lawful money, four shares out of eight, being one-half of the lot called No. 3, 3rd Range, in the 4th Div. of the Outer Commons in York that had originally been granted to his late father Jonathan Young, "of whom I purchased the same" on same date as given above; witnesses John Storer, Abraham Barrons [York Deed 39:261 and 41:51]. (ME I.G.I.)

ROWLAND aka Roland, b 11 Jan 1747/8, York, cordwainer, s/o Rowland and Abigail (Dixon) Young, d pre 9 Feb 1801, prob. 7 Dec 1800, native town, married, testate; m ca 1766, Mary Norton [b ca 1749, York, d/o John and Mary Norton of Kittery, alive 8 Oct 1800, native town, widowed by Feb 1801]. Rowland Jr. was named heir-at-law of his maternal grandfather Peter Dixon, by Dixon's will signed 18 Feb 1779, probated 10 Apr 1780. Mary Norton Young was named the daughter of John and Mary Norton in the deed of sale of the Dower Rights of Mary's mother in the estate of John Norton, to William Gunnison of York, for 13-10-0, by deed signed 30 Mar 1791, rec'd 14 Mar 1792; witnesses William Frost, Charles Beam [York Deed 54:190].

Census reports listed Rowland resident of York from 1790 to 1800. In 1790, his family contained one male over 16, three males under 16, and three females. The 1800 census gave his and his wife's ages as 45 plus, their household containing five somewhat mature children, one male age 10-16, and two males and two females within the 16-26 age bracket.

The earliest deed found for Rowland of York dealt with his purchase of a sibling's share in the estate of their father Rowland, signed 4 Aug 1767, rec'd 9 Oct 1767. He bought from his sister Abigail Cooley and her husband John Cooley of York their "right in our sister Hannah Young's share in their father's estate which they bought from her," Abigail Cooley ceding Dower Rights; witnesses Samuel Moulton, Elizabeth Welch [York Deed 41:24]. Rowland's next land deed was signed 5 Jul 1768, rec'd the day after, when he bought from his married sister Sarah Ide and her husband Ezra "of Attleboro, now of Mount Desert," all Sarah's share in the estate of their late father Rowland Young; Sarah Ides relinquished her Dower Rights; witnesses Daniel Moulton, Eleanor Young [York Deed 40:124].

Rowland Jr. and spouse Mary Norton Young sold to Mary's sibling John Norton of Kittery, yeoman, for nine shillings, six pence, all her right and interest in their father John Norton's estate or her grandfather John Norton Sr.'s estate, excepting Mary's reversion in her mother's Thirds which was not intended to be sold, by deed signed and rec'd 28 Oct 1773; witnesses Daniel and Dorcas Moulton [York Deed 42:250].

Another purchase of land in York was made by Rowland by deed signed 18 Mar 1777, rec'd 16 Feb 1778, for thirty-three pounds, twelve shillings, from John and Elizabeth Bradbury of York: an acre of land in York which Bradbury bought from Joshua Mitwin and the widow Hannah Banks, seven and three-fourths acres and a half-quarter of an acre that Bradbury bought from Joshua McLucas and the widow Hannah Banks, situated at the east end of the Gap that leads from the country road through the homestead farm of the later Peter Weare near Rowland's land, being a part of the homestead of Peter Weare's; witnesses David Sewall, Joseph Parsons [York Deed 44:126].

Rowland's next deed of purchase was signed 19 Jun 1780, rec'd 27 Dec 1780: for 30 pounds lawful money he bought from Jonathan Sayward of York, Esq., two tracts of land in York situated on the S.W. side of Cape Neddick River. The first tract contained 19-1/2 acres that had been laid out to Daniel Weare and Peter Preble as of 4 Jun 1764, and 6-1/4 acres land by lands of Samuel Preble. The second tract contained 14 acres which had been purchased of Daniel Weare by deed dated 27 Mar 1771, by lands lately owned by Samuel Milberry and by the heirs of Alexander Woods; witnesses Abraham Nowell, Jane Dunning [York Deed 46:141].

Rowland bought from son John 3rd, property in York for 47 pounds lawful money, which John bought from William King of Scarborough, Cumberland County: three acres including house and barn, situated on the south side of the highway leading from the meeting house to the house that Deacon Coward then lived in, by deed signed 9 Feb 1792, rec'd 8 Jul 1793; see son John 3rd for full documentation.

Within two weeks of that purchase of property, Rowland had his will drawn up 20 Feb 1792, probated 9 Feb 1801. He named wife Mary as sole Exec. and full residuary legatee of his estate during her natural life; thereafter the estate would be divided equally among their surviving children John, Mary, Stephen, Abigail, Peter and Samuel [some of whom were minors at the time Rowland's will was written]; witnesses William Frost, John Swett, Nathaniel Frost [York Probate #20984].

In late 1799, Rowland bought for $30.00, from Nicholas Sewall of York, Sewall's right in the pew bought from Jeremiah Moulton in the Gallery by deed signed 3 Dec 1799, rec'd 30 Dec 1799, witnesses William Frost, David Bennett [York Deed 65:12]. Shortly thereafter, Rowland and co-grantor William Hutchins of York sold for $350.00 to Daniel Sewall of York, Esq., 4-1/4 acres land beginning at the highway leading to the lower part of the town at the northern corner of land belonging to Timothy Grow, down to the creek, by deed signed 8 Oct 1800, rec'd 17 Nov 1800; Mary Young ceded dower rights; witnesses Lucy and Abigail Sewall [York Deed 65:197].

Ch. b York: John+, b 25 Oct 1767; Rowland, b 17 Nov 1769, d.y.; Mary, 30 Apr 1772; Abigail, b 4 Aug 1774, d.y.; Nathan, b 1 Feb 1776, d.y.; Stephen, b 25 Dec 1777; Abigail, b 4 Dec 1781, poss. spouse of William Hutchins; Peter+, b 29 Apr 1784; and Samuel, b 6 Jul 1787. (ME I.G.I.; Census York Co., 1790, p71; 1800, p1017; Bragdon & Frost's York V.R., p405)

ROWLAND, b ca 1760, of York, antecedents not evident. The following court case was brought by this Rowland Young of York against John Young Jr. of York: on 22 Mar 1799 J.P. Daniel Sewall, Esq. awarded Rowland, as creditor, damages in the amount of $190.00, plus $2.99 for cost of suit against John Young Jr. who had defaulted on a loan; John was to be detained in jail until the full sum was paid; witness William Frost, rec'd 5 May 1799 [York Deed 62:269-270].

RUFUS, b ca 1785, of York, joiner, filed (Ints.) 3 Jan 1810, York, Nancy Perkins [b ca 1790, of same town]. Rufus was listed head of household in the 1810 census for York, age 16-26, containing a spousal figure of the same age, and one female under ten years of age. One land deed was found for Rufus up through 1810: he bought from Josiah Gilman of York, physician, for $30.00, one-half of a pew in the Meeting House in the First Parish of York, it being the same Gilman bought from Sewell by deed dated 28 Jan 1808 [York Deed 83:245]. (Bragdon & Frost's York V.R., p196; Census York Co., 1810, p822)

RUTH, b ca 1825, of Ossipee, N.H., m 9 May 1845, Waterboro, Elias Carpenter [b ca 1820, of Waterboro]. (**Reg.** 91:35, 1937)

SALLY, b ca 1790, Sanford, m 15 Mar 1810, Sanford, Richard W. Ricker [b ca 1785]. (ME I.G.I.; Mormon/ME V.R., Wright-Zitkov; MH&G **Rec.**, V2, p110)

SALLY, b 1790, York, d/o John and Hannah (Banks) Young, alive 7 Jun 1847, native town; filed (Ints.) 4 Mar 1814, m 18 Mar 1814, York, Ivory Sherman [b ca 1785, of same town]. Sally Sherman's sister Perthenia appointed her sole Exec. of her will dated 15 Sep 1829, and devised to her real and personal estate in York after the demise of their widowed mother Hannah Young. But after Sally's death, it was Perthenia's wish that Sally's daughters Perthenia Sherman and Sally Sherman [Jr.] become her residuary legatees. Sally Sherman filed probate papers on Perthenia's estate 7 Jun 1847. See Perthenia for full documentation. Sherman ch. b York: Perthenia Sherman, b ca 1815; Sally Sherman, b ca 1817. (ME I.G.I.; Bragdon & Frost's York V.R., p201)

SALLY, b 17 Dec 1795, Limington, d/o David and Elizabeth (Smith) Young, d 29 Sep 1833, age 37-9-12, filed (Ints.) 10 Sep 1820, m 17 Oct 1820, Limington, Benjamin Moody [b 1797, d 2 Dec 1867, South Limington, age 70]. Both were buried at the Davis Cemetery, Boothby Road, South Limington. (Hale's Cems., n.p.; Taylor's **Limington**, TMs, pp60, 83, 134)

SALLY A., b 6 Feb 1840, Sanford, youngest d/o Joseph and Edna M. (Huston) Young, d 13 Jun 1910, native town; m 2 Jan 1859, Sanford, Christopher Hammond Cram [b 24 Sep 1838, Sanford, s/o David and Laura J. (Bennett) Cram, d 16 Mar 1920, native town, lumberman and farmer]. Cram ch. b Sanford: Hannah J. Cram, b 7 Feb 1859, d 20 Mar 1930, age 71-1-14; Nathaniel Bennett Cram, b ca 1861; Laura A. Cram, b ca 1865; Ozro L. Cram, b 1869; Dana C. Cram, b Jan 1878; and Joseph Young Cram, b 11 Oct 1880. (F. R. Boyle's **Sanford**, pp76-77, 330-332; Mormon/ME V.R., Wright-Zitkov)

SAMUEL, b ca 1630, of York. In York Court Case 3:46, dated 12 Jun 1666, the Jury found for plaintiff Robert Knight on behalf of Samuel Young in an action of the case against

John Andrews, defendant, to the value of 300 pounds. (ME
Prov. & Court Recs., V1, p260)

SAMUEL, b 1650s, York, s/o Rowland Sr. and Joan (Knight)
Young, killed 1691/2 in the Candlemas Day massacre; m ca 1680,
Elizabeth Masterson [b ca 1660, d/o Nathaniel and Elizabeth
(Cogswell) Masterson, alive 1712, Ipswich, MA, widow]. Samuel
received land in York by deed of gift from his parents on
18 Apr 1682, rec'd 23 Nov 1685: ten acres land lying and
being in part of a tract of land granted to Rowland by the
Town of York at a town meeting held 15 Sep 1667, and laid out
to Rowland on 9 Apr 1679; it was situated behind Rowland's
dwelling house. This same acreage was disposed of after
Samuel's death by sons Jonathan and Ichabod when they reached
their majority, selling it to their uncle Job Young of York,
Samuel's sibling, by deed signed 28 Nov 1712, rec'd 7 Jul
1720. For details and documentation on these deeds, please
see son Jonathan.

Ch. b York: Rowland, b 1680s; Jonathan+, 1680s; Icha-
bod+, b 1687; Elizabeth+ (Young) Greeley, b ca 1690. (Noyes
et al, pp467, 776-777)

SAMUEL, b 21 Jul 1704, York, s/o Lt. Joseph and Abigail
(Donnell) Young, gr.s/o Rowland Young, d 2 Dec 1730, native
town, age 26-4-11, predeceased his father; filed (Ints.)
13 Nov 1725, Mehitable Beane aka Bane [b 21 Sep 1705, York,
d/o Lewis and Mary (Austin) Beane, aka Mehitable Haines, w/o
Aquilla Haines, alive 17 Apr 1753, native town].

A few years before his father's will was written, Samuel
received a deed of gift from him dated 30 Apr 1729, rec'd
5 Feb 1730, a tract of land in York, "it being the same land
whereon Samuel's grandfather Rowland Young and great grandfather Rowland Young once lived." This deed of gift reserved to
Joseph himself "a certain two acres of land on the N.E. side
thereof to be laid out...as I shall think fit."

Upon Samuel's death in 1730, his father Joseph was
appointed Admin. of Samuel's estate [York Probate #20985].
Joseph submitted his first accounting of costs and disbursements which came to 171-18-3, attested to and allowed 10 May
1732; this included sundries allowed the widow in bringing up
two small children. Another accounting by Joseph, attested to
17 Jul 1733, gave costs and distributions in the amount of 20-
5-6. In May 1732, Joseph, acting with license to sell in
order to pay debts, sold by deed signed 12 Apr 1734, rec'd
12 Jul 1734, to Benaiah Young of York, kinsman, for 25-6-0,
land that was adjacent to Benaiah's property; witnesses
Jeremiah Moulton, Samuel Bragdon Jr. [York Deed 16:201]. An
additional four acres of Samuel's land was sold at public
auction to Henry Simpson Jr. of York by deed signed 25 Jun
1733, rec'd 27 May 1734, the acreage abutting the corner of
John Bradbury's fence and the bank of the river, for 35 pounds
in good Bills of Credit; witnesses John Carlisle and Benaiah
Young [York Deed 17:185]. Apparently Joseph, in being Admin.,
could not act for himself in this sale for we find that he

purchased these exact same four acres the very next day from grantee Henry Simpson Jr. and then resold them to his son-in-law and neighbor John Bradbury for 40 pounds on 16 Apr 1734, rec'd 27 May 1734; witnesses John Carlisle, Benaiah Young [York Deed 18:185-186].

On 15 Oct 1734, the Judge of Probate notified Joseph Young that Samuel's estate appeared to be insolvent: inventory was established at 148-17-0; costs and disbursements 37-18-6; widow's necessaries 46-18-6; balance undistributed 64-0-0. The Judge directed that distribution be made to creditors in allotted amounts [York Probate 4:264].

The will drawn up by Samuel's father Joseph on 1 May 1734, probated 4 Jun 1734, spoke of three generations: it indicated that not only had Samuel predeceased his father Joseph, but also Samuel had two children, Abigail and Joseph Jr. Samuel's son Joseph was to become residuary legatee of his grandfather Joseph's estate, provided the latter lived to the age of majority. Samuel's daughter Abigail was also heir-at-law of her grandfather Joseph, and was to receive three pounds when her sibling Joseph inherited the estate.

Samuel's widow Mehitable filed (Ints.) 26 Jan 1733, m2 24 Feb 1733/4, York, Aquilla Haines Jr. [b 17 Jul 1702, s/o Thomas and Mehitable (Freethy) Haines of Amesbury, MA, d 2 Mar 1750, native town]. In 1732 Aquilla was listed in the final division of lands in York; he was also a witness to the will of Samuel's father Joseph Young, dated 1 May 1734, proved 4 Jun 1734.

The third generation was represented by Joseph Jr., a minor when his father Samuel died. Petition for Guardianship of Joseph Jr. was filed by Jonathan Sayward of York, mariner, 5 Jan 1746. Sayward announced on 24 Nov 1746 that he would act upon Joseph's share of the estate of his grandfather Joseph Young of York; witnesses Hannah Moulton, Daniel Moulton [York Probate #20953]. Joseph Jr. went on to become mariner, an heir-at-law of both his paternal grandfather Joseph and his father Samuel; he died in 1752, a young man in his twenties.

Mehitable Haines of York, Joseph's widowed mother who had remarried in 1733/4, was granted Letters of Admin. on his estate 17 Oct 1752, with instructions to have inventory taken before 17 Jan next, and an accounting returned by 17 Apr 1753 [York Probate #20954]. Inventory was submitted and approved 15 Nov 1752, by appraisers Daniel Moulton, Paul Nowell and Norton Woodbridge, total value 30 pounds, attested to 1 Jan 1753, by Mehitable. The estate included about four acres land fronting York River, part of the homestead formerly belonging to Lt. Joseph Young [York Probate 8:346]. By deed signed and rec'd 31 Jul 1753, Mehitable Haines sold at public auction to Cotton Bradbury of York for 20 pounds lawful money in order to pay just debts, four acres land fronting S.W. on the York River, bounding upon the lands of the late John Bradbury, with the exception of the one-third Dower Rights; witnesses Jeremiah Moulton Jr., George Goodin [York Deed 31:76].

Inasmuch as the estate was represented as insolvent 16 Oct 1753, attested to same date, the court ordered that distribution of the balance of 9-3-6 be made proportionately among the creditors who included Joseph's and Abigail's grown daughters Mary, Abigail, Bethulah and Bethia, and granddaughter Abigail, viz daughter of Joseph, deceased [York Probate 8:462].

Ch. b York: Abigail+ (Young) Grow, b 30 Jun 1727; Joseph Jr., b ca 1728, d 1752. (Noyes et al, pp85, 295, 776; Bragdon & Frost's York V.R., pp121, 392, 486)

SAMUEL, b ca 1710, of Wells and Biddeford, laborer, filed (Ints.) 6 Mar 1735, Biddeford, m 16 Apr 1735, Wells, Dorcas Day [b ca 1715, of Wells]. The two earliest deeds found for Samuel of Biddeford were deeds of purchase signed before his marriage in 1735. The first of these was purchase from Robert and Susanna Whipple of Biddeford on 8 Jan 1734/5, rec'd 28 Apr 1736, of five acres in Biddeford, 140 poles from the county road above the brook by lands of Edward Proctor; witnesses Samuel Willard, Jonathan Emery [York Deed 19:11]. The other purchase was from neighbors Edward and Abigail Proctor, of nine acres land for 25 pounds lawful money, beginning at the brook that comes out of Mr. Hill's land, by the S.E. corner of Samuel's land which he bought of Whipple; by deed signed 10 Mar 1734/5, rec'd 28 Apr 1736; witnesses Samuel Willard, Robert Whipple [York Deed 19:10].

Shortly after his marriage to Dorcas, Samuel bought from Abraham Townsend of Biddeford for 35 pounds in good bills of credit, 40 acres land which the town of Biddeford granted him at a town meeting on 21 Mar 1721, but not laid out to him until 9 May 1728; by deed signed 28 Nov 1735, rec'd 28 Apr 1736, witnesses Isaac Townsend, John Gray [York Deed 19:10]. In his next deed, Samuel sold some shares of Common Lands in York, for two pounds current money, to Jeremiah Moulton 3rd, Gent. of York, being two full shares which were granted him at a legal town meeting held 25 Sep 1732; witnesses John Webber, William Davis, by deed signed and rec'd 17 Feb 1736 [York Deed 18:110-111].

Thereafter, Samuel concentrated his land holdings to Biddeford. The following deposition was sworn to by Samuel Smith, lot layer for the Town of Biddeford, on 29 Sep 1736, that "he measured out to Samuel Young eight acres land adjoining Young's former lot on the N.E. end of said lot...then upon a S.W. line to said Young's lot as before, which eight acres the said Samuel Young purchased of Robert Whipple and Edward Proctor as may appear by a deed to Young by me [said Samuel Smith]"; rec'd 9 Apr 1737 [York Deed 18:168].

With spouse Dorcas ceding Dower Rights, Samuel next sold to Edward Proctor of Biddeford, for 250 pounds old Tenor, 50 acres land in Biddeford beginning at the western corner of Edward Proctor's lands, lately bought of Robert Whipple, and by lands which Proctor bought of Nathaniel Whitney; deed signed 29 Sep 1743, rec'd 2 Mar 1747; witnesses Wyatt Moore, Benjamin Gooch [York Deed 26:276].

Two deeds of purchase were then made: **(1)** by first deed signed 29 Jun 1743, rec'd 15 Jun 1748, Samuel bought some 45 acres land in Biddeford from Edward and Abigail Proctor of the same town, for 250 pounds old Tenor, situated by lands of Wyatt Moore and "the land I lately bought of Nathaniel Whitney," witnesses Wyatt Moore, Benjamin Gooch [York Deed 27:95]; **(2)** by second deed dated 29 Nov 1760, rec'd 5 Jan 1764, Samuel bought from Wyatt Moore of Biddeford for eight pounds money, a parcel of land situated on the S.W. side of Biddeford River, on the west corner of the twelve acres sold formerly to Nathan Whitney, and east of the land of said Samuel; witnesses John Davis, Jonathan Emery [York Deed 38:180].

Ch. bp First Congregational Church, Biddeford: Job, bp 11 Mar 1744; John, bp 4 May 1746. (ME I.G.I.; MH&G. **Rec.**, V6, pp336, 338)

SAMUEL, Capt. aka Gent., b 27 Feb 1727, York, mariner, s/o Jonathan Jr. and Abigail (Came) Young, gr.s/o Samuel Came of York, d 25 May 1816, age 89, native town; filed (Ints.) 23 Sep 1763, m1 12 Oct 1763, York, Patience Came [b ca 1735, York, d/o Joseph and Keziah (McIntire) Came, maternal gr.d/o Samuel and Elizabeth (   ) Came, Esq., d pre 26 Feb 1773, native town]. Samuel m2 late 1773, Mary (   ) [b ca 1750, of York, alive 18 Aug 1806].

The 1810 census for York indicated Samuel was resident there at age 45 plus: the family profile included a maternal figure of same age bracket with three other males, two age 10-16, one 26-45, and two other females, both ages 26-45. A household of such size could signify a grown child or two living at Samuel's home with their spouses and families in 1810.

Before Samuel married, he became shareholder in Lots No. 3, 1st Div. and No. 4, York Common Lands that were adjacent to lands of Ebenezer Young, Jonathan Young, Joshua Young and Lydia Young Haines of York, later to become the spouse of Samuel Bragdon in 1754. Four deeds of purchase were found for Samuel who bought into Lot No. 3, 1st Division, York, for a total of 25 shares at a cost of 20 pounds lawful money. **(1)** Bought from Samuel Bragdon of York, mariner, by deed dated 10 Oct 1753, rec'd 12 Oct 1753, five shares for four pounds lawful money, granted to Bragdon by Samuel Bragdon Jr. [York Deed 31:130]. **(2)** Bought by deed dated 15 Oct 1753, rec'd 26 Nov 1753, eight shares from Christopher Pottle of York for six pounds, eight shillings, four shares of which were granted to John Baker, the other four, bought from Jonathan Sayward, three of which were originally granted to Joseph Leavitt and the other one from Acquilla Haines from whom the said Sayward bought [York Deed 31:41]. **(3)** By third deed signed and rec'd 18 Jun 1754, purchased from Benjamin Holt of York, mariner, 10 shares for the price of eight pounds, six shares of which were granted to Elias Weare, the other four shares to Jeremiah Bragdon [York Deed 31:250]. **(4)** And the fourth deed, signed and rec'd 13 Apr 1758, bought two shares of Common Lands from Daniel Moulton, Esq. of York, that were originally laid out to Nathaniel Lewis, for 32 shillings [York Deed 33:190].

The deed which confirmed Samuel's share holdings was signed 18 Oct 1753, rec'd 6 Nov 1753: Samuel was a member of a consortium whose members included Benjamin Holt, Joseph Junkins and Daniel Johnston who petitioned the court to partition the lands so that they could start settling and improving the same; witness Alexander MacIntire [York Deed 32:20]. The court verified that Samuel held 25 shares in Lot No. 3, 1st Div., which equalled out to 33 acres, 22 rods, as well as 13 shares in Lot No. 4, 2nd Div., which credited him with 20-1/2 acres land.

Recently married in 1763, Samuel and sibling Masterson, both of York, were granted Letters of Admin. on Samuel's father's estate dated 2 Apr 1764. They were given instructions to make inventory on or before 2 July next, and a true and complete account be submitted by 2 Oct 1764 [York Probate #20945]. The estate was sizeable as attested to by the appraisers on 11 Jul 1764, containing over 130 acres in and around Old York: inventory included the homestead of 24 acres land and marsh with the house and barn, about 22-1/2 acres land called the Rocky Pasture, 30 acres land at Birch Hill, one acre salt marsh at same, about 23 acres land where he lived, about 7 acres land at the head of Scituate Millpond, 8 acres land in No. 8, 2nd Div. of the Inner Commons, about 16 acres fresh meadow near Groundnut Hill, and a pew in the Meeting House Gallery [York Probate 11:250].

One of Samuel's land deeds before he married was signed 28 Nov 1762, rec'd 28 Dec 1769, when he was yeoman: he bought from his wife-to-be Patience's grandfather Samuel Came, for 4-16-0 lawful money, shares of land in Lot No. 4, 1st Div. of the Commons in York; witnesses George Simpson, Edward Ingraham [York Deed 40:207-208]. Then when married, his next deed involved the sale of 10 acres land in York for 36 pounds lawful money, to Ebenezer Sayward, yeoman of York, signed 26 Jul 1764, rec'd 6 Aug 1764; wife Patience relinquished her Thirds; witnesses Daniel and Mary Bragdon [York Deed 40:22]. Samuel bought this acreage on 2 Apr 1758 from James Sayward, for a certain consideration, Sayward's wife Bethulah ceding Dower Rights; witnesses Edward Grow, David Bane, by deed signed 22 Apr 1758, rec'd 18 Sep 1762 [York Deed 34:191].

Samuel's grandfather Samuel Came, Esq. had his will drawn up 28 Jun 1764, probated 2 Jan 1769. Although other Came grandchildren received bequests, Came's grandson Samuel Young and wife Patience Young [Samuel Came's granddaughter, viz. his son Joseph Came, deceased, and spouse Kezia ( ) Came] were virtually residuary legatees. They were to receive "my homestead, land and marsh, dwelling, barn, mills and other buildings, one acre of upland adjacent to his late father's

marsh and that part of the salt marsh on the N.E. side of the
N.W. branch of York River which he bought from Nathaniel
Donnell, Esq., and his silver tankard, they paying from all of
it my just debts, funeral charges and legacies." They were
also to provide annually for Came's wife, covering all her
reasonable necessaries and a decent and Christian burial.
Son-in-law Arthur Bragdon was named Exec. of the will;
witnesses Cotton Bradbury, Henry Sewall, David Moulton [York
Probate #2477].

Samuel turned a profit in the following two sales of Lot
No. 3, 1st Div. and Lot No. 4, 2nd Div., both lots having been
laid out to him by York Deed 32:20 [see above]. (1) He sold
to Joseph Austin Jr., mariner, for 60 pounds lawful money, all
those 25 shares in Lot No. 3, 1st Div. of the Commons in York
by deed signed and rec'd 26 Feb 1765; witnesses Daniel
Moulton, Matthew Austin [York Deed 34:280]. (2) He sold to
John Carlisle, 20-1/2 acres land set off to him in Lot No. 4,
2nd Div., of the Commons adjoining to Cape Neddick Road, for
12 pounds lawful money by deed signed and rec'd 26 Aug 1772;
witnesses Daniel Moulton, William Moulton [York Deed 40:299].

In 1766, by deed signed the 9 Jul, rec'd 24 Oct 1772,
Samuel bought from his married sisters and their husbands
Abigail and William Grow, Eunice and John Junkins, and
Patience and John Stover, the sisters' shares in their
father's estate, excepting their mother Abigail's dower
rights, for 80 pounds lawful money. See sisters for documentation.

Next, by deed signed 27 Mar 1767, rec'd 30 Mar 1767, he
and Samuel Moulton bought 55 acres of pasture and meadow land
with dwelling house and buildings in York, from neighbor
Jeremiah Paul of York for five pounds lawful money; this
acreage abutted lands of Robert Cutts, John Frost, the late
Joseph Junkins, Samuel Came, Esq. and Thomas Rogers, and the
S.W. branch of the York River; witnesses Daniel and Hannah
Moulton Jr. [York Deed 41:14].

By deed of gift the following month, signed and rec'd
8 Apr 1767, Samuel's wife's grandfather Samuel Came, Esq.
ceded his entire estate to Samuel, for the sum of five
shillings; actually this was more or less a duplication of his
will drawn up in 1764. Came's estate included the homestead
where he then dwelt, the barns, mills and uplands adjacent to
his late father, and his silver tankard; the one stipulation
of the deed of gift being that Samuel was to pay all Samuel
Came's just debts and funeral charges; witnesses Daniel
Moulton, Jonathan Nowell [York Deed 41:21].

Kezia Came of York, widow of Joseph, and mother-in-law of
Samuel Young, had her will drawn 26 Feb 1773, probated 14 Apr
1773; among the many provisions made for children and grandchildren was a bequest to Samuel's daughter, i.e., her
granddaughter Abigail Young by her daughter Patience, deceased, a three-year old heifer; witnesses Jonathan Sargent,
Phebe Came, Job Lyman. [York Probate #2470]. As will be

noted, Samuel's wife Patience Came Young was deceased by this date.

In the following deed signed and rec'd 25 Nov 1778, it was shown that Samuel had remarried inasmuch as wife Mary ceded Dower Rights in the sale of some property. Samuel and siblings Abigail Grow, Eunice Junkins and Patience Stover, along with their husbands, quitclaimed to sibling Jonathan Young all their shares and interest in the house, lands and marsh originally belonging to their parents Jonathan Jr. and Abigail Came Young, excepting land that was their mother's Thirds, for 26-13-4; witnesses Daniel Moulton, John Holman [York Deed 45:141].

By deed signed 29 Jan 1794, rec'd 21 Mar 1803, Samuel purchased 7 acres land of Lot No. 4 in the 1st Div. of the Inner Commons of York from Thomas Norman and spouse Elizabeth of York for the price of four pounds legal money, bounded by lands of Capt. Abel Moulton; mother Martha Norman ceded dower rights; witnesses William Frost, Shadrach Nowell [York Deed 69:86].

There were four deeds of late vintage between 1800-1810, that neither adds nor subtracts substantially from Samuel's extensive land holdings in York. Upon reflection on the growth and wealth of Samuel's real and personal estate, one realizes that a great deal of his estate was inherited over the years, from the time of his first marriage onward. With his purchases of land, the estate visibly grew. He became shrewd; this could be seen in the way he prepared his sons to manage the estate after his demise. Witness the following deed of gift to his two eldest sons Samuel and Noah, signed 10 May 1811, rec'd 11 May 1811 [York Co. Deed 84:163]. In consideration of the following services to be performed by Samuel Jr. and Noah, sons of Samuel Young of York--providing particular care and every necessity for the comfort, support and maintenance of their father and mother, as well as a christian burial, and in consideration of providing for Joseph Young Jr., son of said Samuel, $800.00 within four years, or in lieu, to take the same $800.00 for the purchase of a farm for Joseph, along with Joseph's board and room while he is single, then for the cost of $1.00 each paid by Samuel and Noah, they shall receive the remainder of his real estate in York; witnesses Alexander McIntire, Joel Young.

Ch. b York by first wife Patience: Patience (Young) Love aka Lowe, b ca 1763; Abigail, b 2 Nov 1764, alive 26 Feb 1773. Ch. b York by second wife Mary (   ): Samuel+ Jr., b ca 1773; Noah+, b 11 Feb 1775; and Joseph+, b 1791. (ME I.G.I.; Bragdon & Frost's York V.R., pp25, 83, 146 412; Census York Co., 1810, p822)

SAMUEL, b ca 1735, of Biddeford, m 10 May 1761, Bidde-ford, Elizabeth Joy [b ca 1740, of Biddeford]. Ch. bp First Congregational Church, Biddeford: Sarah, bp 31 Jul 1763; Elizabeth, bp 24 Jun 1764; Mary, bp 9 Feb 1766; Samuel Jr., bp

4 Sep 1768; and Benjamin, bp 22 Jul 1770. (ME I.G.I.; MH&G **Rec.**, V7, pp83-85, 87)

SAMUEL, b ca 1740, of York, filed (Ints.) 30 Mar 1767, York, m 5 Apr 1767, Kittery, Mary Fernald [b ca 1745, of Kittery]. (Bragdon & Frost's York V.R., p150; Kittery V.R., p228)

SAMUEL, b ca 1745, of York, listed as head of a large family of eleven besides himself in the 1790 census, including three other males over 16, four males under 16, and four females living at home. (Census York Co., 1790, p72)

SAMUEL, b pre 1755, of York, head of household in York in 1800, age 45 plus, family containing a spousal figure of the same age bracket, four males, one under 10, one age 10-16, and two age 16-26, and two females, age 16-26. (Census York Co., 1800, p1034)

SAMUEL, b ca 1765, listed as resident of York in the 1820 census, age 45 plus, with five other members in the family: a spousal figure 45 plus, three males, one each under 10, 16-18, and 16-26, and one other female age 16-26. This Samuel was probably a little older and more "settled" by the year 1820 than the Samuel listed just below with six children under the age of sixteen in 1820. (Census York Co., 1820, p604)

SAMUEL, b ca 1765, lived in York in 1820, age 45 plus, with possibly a spousal figure in the household, age 26-45. There were two other male family members, one under 10, the other age 10-16, and four females, three under 10, and one age 10-16. (Census York Co., 1820, p593)

SAMUEL Jr., b ca 1765, resident of York in 1800, age 26-45, widower, with one young male under 10 in the household. (Census York Co., 1800, p1035)

SAMUEL Jr., b 1770, York, Gent., d 22 Dec 1845, native town, age 75; filed (Ints.) 4 Feb 1796, m1 22 Feb 1796, York, Dorcas Lowe [b 1773, York, d 21 Jan 1802, age 29, native town]; filed (Ints.) 7 Jan 1803 (2nd marr.), York, Mary Lowe [b ca 1775, of same town].

Samuel was listed as resident of York in 1810 and 1830-1840 census reports. In 1810 his age was 26-45, with household containing a spousal figure of same age bracket, and three young children under 10, two males and one female. In the 1830 census, his age and that of a maternal figure was 50-60, the family containing two males, one each 15-20 and 30-40, and one female age 20-30. And in 1840, he was then age 70-80, with household containing a female parental figure of the same age, two other males ages 20-30 and 30-40, and two other females, one each 20-30 and 30-40.

Admin. Papers on the estates of both sons of Samuel and Dorcas (Lowe) Young, i.e., Oliver and Edward, were found which indicated each had died possessed of goods and chattels of more than twenty dollars, and according to petition made by kinsman Samuel P. Young of York "the estate should be administered." For full details on Samuel P. Young's two separate petitions to the court for probate, please see main entry on Samuel's son Edward+ [b 1797].

Samuel and sibling Noah Young, their wives and families were buried at the Young lot on the east side of Route 91, next to the road and adjoining driveway of 204 Cider Hill Road, York. Ch. b York by first wife Dorcas: Edward+, b 1797; Charlotty, b 1798, d 1 Feb 1850, of consumption, single, age 52. Ch. b York by 2nd wife Mary: Oliver, b 1809, bur. 18 Nov 1858, York, age 49, see entry on Edward for details on Letters of Admin. mentioned above. (Bragdon & Frost's York V.R., pp180, 187, 437, 621; ME I.G.I.; Hale's Cems., n.p.; Census York Co., 1810, p822; 1830, p250; 1840, Reel B, p259; Picton's ME Cem. Inscrips., V3, p2373; 1850 Mort. Sched., York Co.)

SAMUEL, b ca 1785, of York, listed as resident of York in 1810 and 1830 census reports. In 1810 his age was 16-26, with a family profile of a spousal figure of the same age group, a maternal figure age 45 plus, two children under 10, male and female, and one other female age 26-45. In 1830, Samuel, still known as Jr., and a spousal figure were both age 40-50, their family containing five males and five females, the eldest age 30 down to age 5. (Census York Co., 1810, p821; 1830, p238)

SAMUEL aka 3rd, b 6 Jul 1785, York, d 26 Feb 1839, native town, widower; filed (Ints.) 9 Feb 1805, York, Grace Hutchins [b 2 Jul 1785, York, d/o Enoch and Mary ( ) Hutchins, d 16 Jun 1837, native town, age 52-11-0, married]. Both Samuel and Grace were buried at Hutchins' Lot #64, York Cemetery. This citation on Grace's father Enoch Hutchins appeared in Nathan Hale's **Cemeteries, Series** I: "Patriot of the Revolution, he having served as an officer in the American Army throughout the whole campaign."

Ch. b York: Samuel+, b 1806; Mary, b 14 Jan 1809; George E., b ca 1810, alive 19 May 1885, East Boston, MA, participant in the probate of sibling Samuel's estate that year; Hannah, b 27 Jan 1812; prob. Peter+, b 29 May 1815; Olive Ann+ (Young) Hutchins, b 19 Jan 1818. (ME I.G.I.; Bragdon & Frost's York V.R., pp190, 257, 632; Hale's Cems., n.p.)

SAMUEL 3rd, b 1806, York, master mariner, s/o Samuel and Grace (Hutchins) Young, d 16 Sep 1885, native town, testate, age 79-5-0, widower; filed (Ints.) 11 Sep 1835, m 26 Sep 1835, York, Martha Ann Crosby [b 1811, N.H., of Portsmouth, d 24 Jan 1884, York, age 73, married]. Samuel 3rd and family were listed as residents of York in three census reports from 1840-1860 inclusive. In 1840, his age was 30-40, with family containing a female parental figure age 20-30, and two young children under 5, one male, one female. In 1850, his age was 44, the estate valued at $1,000. His household included spouse Martha and children Martha, Charles, George and John. In 1860 his occupation was master mariner; at home were spouse Martha and four children Charles E., George S., John C. and William N.

Samuel was widower when he drew up his will 19 May 1885, naming brother George E. Young of East Boston, MA and Edward P. Kimball of Portsmouth, N.H. as Co-Execs. Probate papers were filed 6 Oct 1885, with bond of $10,000 posted by the Co-Execs. as well as Edward E. Young and Eastman Hutchins, both of York, on 3 Nov 1885; witnesses Samuel W. Junkins, J. Howard, Louise M. Bragdon [York Probate #20986]. Samuel made these bequests: to son John C., all his real estate; to married daughter Annie Grant, w/o John P. Grant, $1,000; to granddaughter Abigail Young, d/o Charles Young, deceased, $100; to single daughters Abigail and Olivia, each $200; to grandson George Samuel Grant, s/o Annie Grant, the money deposited in the East Boston Savings Bank by his deceased son George S. Young; to [sister] Olive Ann Hutchins, w/o John Hutchins, $500; to brother Peter Young, $500; and to Mary Caswell, w/o of George Caswell, $300. The residue was to be equally divided among the heirs-at-law.

Ch. b York: Annie M.+ (Young) Grant, b ca 1835; Charles E., b 1840; George S., b 1846, mariner, lost at sea Lat. 32 North, Long. 74'20 West, on 24 Feb 1873, age 26-6-0; John C., b 1848; Olivia, b 1850s; Abigail, b 1850s; and William Newman, b 1851, d 1 Mar 1878, age 26-3-0. (Bragdon & Frost's York V.R., p244; Frost's York Cem., p522; Census York Co., 1840, Reel B, p259; 1850, Reel A, p199; 1860, Reel C, p914)

SAMUEL, b 1810, Canada, head of household in the 1860 census for Biddeford, age 50. His spouse was Mathilda ( ) Young [b 1820]. The three oldest of seven children were operatives at a mill, Philomon, Celesta and Alphonso. Ch. b Canada: Philamon+, b 1838; Celeste, b 1844; Alphonso, b 1846; Napoleon, b 1850; Eliza, b 1851; Louisa, b 1853; and Joseph, b 1856. (Census York Co., 1860, Reel A, p237)

SAMUEL N., b 9 Nov 1828, of Berwick, d 2 May 1898, age 70, Berwick, buried at the Richard and Rebecca Young family plot at Evergreen Cemetery, Berwick. (Hale's Cems., n.p.)

SAMUEL P., b 1845, Acton, s/o Peter and 2nd wife Deborah M. (Berry) Young, d 1925, native town, married, age 80; m ca 1870, Acton, Ella M. ( ) [b 1855, MA, d 1934, Acton, age 79, widow]. In 1900 Samuel, age 55, lived in Acton with spouse Ella M.; they lived alone. Both were buried at the Young cemetery on Youngs Ridge Road, Acton. (Hale's Cems., n.p.; 1900 ME Soundex)

SAMUEL PREBLE, b 22 Apr 1823, York, s/o Joseph and Susannah (Preble) Young, d 9 Mar 1903, native town, age 80. In 1860 Samuel P. was head of household in York per the 1860 census that year, single, with an estate valued at $14,300. At home were his widowed mother Susan, age 76, and kinswoman Mary Young, age 86 [b 1774]. From 1865-1868, he served in the elected position of Town Clerk; in 1868, he was reelected to serve up through 1873 in this position. His household contained a young domestic Eliza P. Jenkins, age 15 [b 1845], and Charles Hutchins, farm hand, age 16 [b 1844]. In 1900 Samuel P. maintained his home in York with household containing Rebecca Smith, servant [b Jun 1836, Canada/English], and boarders Willie and Jeremiah Lewis [b Dec 1868 and Apr 1877, respectively]. (Bragdon & Frost's York V.R., pp280, 312; Frost's York Cem., p526; Census York Co., 1860, Reel C, p920; 1900 ME Soundex)

SAMUEL T., b 1846, of York, d 1920, York, age 74, married; spouse was Hannah (   ) [b 1856, d 1936, York, age 80, widow]. (Bragdon & Frost's York V.R., p542)

SAMUEL T., b 10 Aug 1852, Rochester, N.H., shoemaker, s/o Thomas and Sabrina (Wentworth) Young [no main entry], alive 1888, Portsmouth, N.H., shoemaker; m 17 Sep 1872, Lebanon, by Rev. Thomas Keniston, Dorcas J. Furbush [b 1851, Lebanon, alive 1882, Rochester, N.H.]. Samuel m2 30 Sep 1888, Portsmouth, N.H., Nellie M. Foss [b 1858, Madbury, d/o Horace and Betsey (   ) Foss]. For additional family background, please see Youngs of Strafford County, N.H., Vol. I.

Ch. by Dorcas, b Lebanon, not traced further: Sidney S., b 1874. Born Farmington, N.H., dau., b 2 Jan 1875. Born Rochester, N.H., dau. M. C., b 2 Jan 1878. Born Lebanon, Winnie L., b 17 Jul 1882, d 1 Nov 1884, age 2-3-15, Rochester. (Lebanon Marr, p224, Deaths, p149; NHVR-Marr, Births, Deaths; Mormon/ME V.R., Wright-Zitkov; Rochester Deaths, p45; LDS I.G.I. BR)

SARAH (   ), b ca 1729, of York, d 6 Jun 1818, York, widow, age ca 89 years. (Bragdon & Frost's York V.R., p414)

SARAH, b 1681, York, d/o Deacon Rowland and Susanna (Matthews) Young, m ca 1715, York, Henry Brookin [b ca 1675, of York]. Brookin ch. b York: Elizabeth Brookin, b 19 May 1717; Samuel Brookin, b 19 Aug 1719; Joseph Brookin, b 1 Nov 1720; Sarah Brookin, b 4 Nov 1722; and Mercy Brookin, b 3 Mar 1723/4. (ME I.G.I.; Bragdon & Frost's York V.R., p21)

SARAH, b ca 1702, York, d/o Job and Sarah (Austin) Preble Young, alive 1734, native town; m ca 1722, York, Joseph Favour [b ca 1700, of York]. Sarah Favour was one of the witnesses to the will of Joseph Young of York, signed 1 May 1734, probated 4 Jun 1734; Joseph was the husband of Abigail Donnell Young. Favour ch. b York: Sarah Favour, b 30 Aug 1724; Mary Favour, b 10 May 1726; Ruth Favour, b 15 Feb 1727. (ME I.G.I.; Bragdon & Frost's York V.R., p34)

SARAH, b ca 1730, of Biddeford, m 8 Aug 1751, York, dual entry same date, First Congregational Church, Biddeford, Ebenezer Redlon aka Ridlen [b ca 1725, of same town]. (ME I.G.I.; MH&G Rec., V6, p295; Marshall's Buxton, ME, p152)

SARAH, b ca 1750, of York, filed (Ints.) 26 Mar 1774, m 29 Jun 1774 at First Parish Church, York, Isaac Perkins [b ca 1745, of same town]. (Bragdon & Frost's York V.R., pp157, 359)

SARAH, b pre 1775, of York, listed as resident of York in 1820 census, single, age 45 plus; she lived alone. (Census York Co., 1820, p604)

SARAH, b 1836, of Saco, domestic, per 1860 census for Saco; she lived at the home of Joseph and Jane J. Hobson [b

1817 and 1819, respectively]. (Census York Co., 1860, Reel C, p762)

SARAH ANN, b 14 Sep 1815, Lebanon, d/o Joseph and Patience (Wentworth) Young; filed (Ints.) 27 Jan 1838, Lebanon, by Rev. James Weston, m 15 Feb 1838, Somersworth, N.H., Samuel Clements [b ca 1810, Somersworth, d 28 Apr 1838, same town]. For full N.H. bibliography, please see Youngs of Strafford County, N.H., Vol. I. Clements ch. b Somersworth, N.H.: Charles A. Clements, b 2 Dec 1838; Frank P. Clements, b 26 Nov 1850; Mary E. Clements, b 30 Sep 1852, d 11 Apr 1872, Somersworth; and Almira A. Clements, b 29 Sep 1854. (Wentworth Gen., V1, pp456-457; ME I.G.I.; Lebanon Marr, p224)

SARAH ANN, b ca 1815, of York, filed (Ints.) 25 Oct 1834, m 8 Nov 1834, York, Benjamin Donnell [b ca 1810, of same town]. (Bragdon & Frost's York V.R., p243)

SARAH F., b ca 1855, of Barrington, N.H., filed (Ints.) 14 Oct 1878, Lebanon, cert. issued 19 Oct. 1878, Allen Hall [b ca 1850, of Lebanon]. (Lebanon Marr, p224)

SARAH H., b 1802, Acton, d/o Jonathan and Mehitable (Moody) Young, alive 19 Dec 1870, native town, m after 1838, William B. Green [b ca 1795, of Acton]. Sarah H. was mentioned as single daughter in her father Jonathan's will signed 8 Oct 1838, proved 7 Jan 1839. Sibling Peter's will signed 19 Dec 1870, proved 3 Dec 1872, revealed that she was then w/o William B. Green. (ME I.G.I.)

SARAH SEMANTHA, b 12 Nov 1840, Rollingsford, N.H., d/o James M. and Susan P. (Henderson) Young of South Berwick; m May 1859, prob. South Berwick, George W. Luke [b ca 1835, of South Berwick]. They took up residence in Fitchburg, MA. Luke ch. b Fitchburg: Emma Susan Luke, b Dec 1859. (Mormon/ME V.R., Wright-Zitkov; Wentworth Gen., V1, pp456-457)

SHERMAN, b 1852, N.H., resident of Waterboro, d 1934, same town, widower, age 82. His spouse was Sarah C. (   ) [b 1852, d 1928, Waterboro, age 76, married]. In 1900 Sherman, spouse Sarah C., and son Frank lived at a boarding house in Waterboro, Sherman's y-o-b given as 1845 and Sarah C.'s as 1853. He, Sarah and son Frank G. were buried at Pine Grove Cemetery, opposite the high school, Waterboro. Ch. b Waterboro, not traced further: Frank Gilman, b 7 Oct 1880, d 25 Jul 1942, native town. (Hale's Cems., n.p.; 1900 ME Soundex)

SILAS H., b 1826, North Berwick, farmer; m 17 Oct 1847, Berwick, Julia Ann Grant of South Berwick [b 1825]. He and wife Julie A. were listed as residents of Berwick in the 1860 census, their real estate valued at $2,000. As married man Silas enlisted in the Civil War as Pvt. on 29 Feb, 1864, mustered in 3 Mar 1864, Augusta, in the 32nd Infantry, Co. A, and was killed in action 11 Jul 1864. Another military record stated that Silas H. died from disease on same date. His complexion and eyes were dark, his hair black, and he stood 5', 8" tall. (Census 1860, Reel B, p925; Civil War res. by T. E. Brooks of Maine)

SILAS P., b 1835, of North Berwick, farmer, alive 1890, same town. Silas was listed as resident of North Berwick in the 1890 ME Vets, Census Index of Civil War Vets or Their Widows for York Co., District SD#1, Enum. #223.

SIMEON, n.d., of Kennebunk, d 21 Nov 1840, same town. (Thompson's Recs. of York Co., TMs, p417)

SIMON M., b Apr 1833, N.H., of Parsonsfield, listed as resident in the 1900 census, age 67. His spouse was Ella N. (   ), age 60 [b Dec 1840, MA]. They lived alone. (1900 ME Soundex)

SOLOMON, b 25 Apr 1742, York. (ME I.G.I.)

SOLOMON, b ca 1755, of Wells, listed as head of household in the 1790 census for Wells, his family containing one other male, under 16 years of age, and one female. (Census York Co., 1790, p71)

SOLOMON T., b 1827, N.H., farmer, cabinet maker, resident of Biddeford in 1850 per census that year, d Jul 1859, age 32, drowned. His household contained spouse Lydia A. (   ) [b 1830], and two children Tobias and Emma. Ch. b ME: Tobias, b 1847; Emma, b 1849. (Census York Co., 1850, Reel A, p60; 1860 ME Mort. Sched., p26)

SOPHIA J., b ca 1843, of Lebanon, filed (Ints.) 19 Dec 1863, Lebanon, John F. Wildes [b ca 1840, of same town]. (Lebanon Marr, p224)

STEPHEN, b ca 1735, Biddeford, m 26 Jul 1759, First Congregational Church, Biddeford, Jerusha Smith [b ca 1740]. This was probably the Stephen Young family listed as residents of Biddeford in the 1790 census, household containing one other male under 16 and three females. Until more data is in, Stephen could be considered a likely contender as progenitor of the Youngs in Biddeford, along with David Young and Thomas Young. (ME I.G.I.; Census York Co., 1790, p55; MH&G **Rec.**, V6, p297)

STEPHEN, b ca 1755, resident and head of household in Waterboro per 1800 census, age 26-45, household containing a spousal figure of same age, and 8 children: one male and five females all under ten, and one male and one female each age 10-16. (Census York Co., 1800, p956)

STEPHEN, b 1770s, of York, mariner, d pre 12 Jun 1810, York. Admin. Papers on his estate in York were filed on that date by widow Sally (   ) Young [b 1770s, of York], who was instructed that inventory should be presented within three months. Bond of $200 was paid by William Gunnison, surety. Inventory of his estate was appraised and presented to the court 14 Jun 1810 by Joseph Gilman and Samuel Moody, and attested to by widow Sally; total amount of estate was set at $37.21 [York Probate #20993].

STEPHEN, b ca 1780, of York, filed (Ints.) 3 Jun 1803, York, Sally Robey [b ca 1785, of same town]. (ME I.G.I.; Bragdon & Frost's York V.R., p187)

STEPHEN, b ca 1780, of York, filed (Ints.) 15 Aug 1807, York, Sally Gullison [b ca 1785, of same town]. (Bragdon & Frost's York V.R., p193)

STEPHEN, b ca 1785, resident of Sanford in the 1830 census, age 40-50. At home was a spousal figure of the same age bracket and two young females, both under age of 10. (Census York Co., 1830, p344)

STEPHEN, b ca 1795, of Berwick, filed (Ints.) 18 Oct 1819, Berwick, m 4 Nov 1819, Shapleigh, Abigail Ricker [b 1797, of same town, prob. d/o William and Amy (Hobbs) Ricker, d 14 Apr 1831, Wells, age 34, buried at Wells Branch Cem., Rte. 9A]. Ch. poss. b Kennebunk: Eliza Jane+ (Young) Pike, b 1829. (F. R. Boyle's **Sanford**, p265; ME I.G.I.; Hale's Cems., n.p.; Picton's ME Cem. Inscrips., V3, 2171)

STEPHEN, b 1825, of Biddeford, head of household in Biddeford per the 1860 census. Spouse was Mehitable (   ) [b 1825]. They lived alone. (Census York Co., 1860, Reel A, p229)

STEPHEN, b ca 1840, Shapleigh, m 24 Aug 1866, Shapleigh, Hannah Ann Challies [b ca 1845, of same town]. (ME I.G.I.)

STEPHEN, b ca 1855, Cornish, m 8 Jan 1879, Cornish, Elizabeth H. Sawyer [b ca 1860, of same town]. (ME I.G.I.)

STEPHEN E., b 28 Nov 1838, Waterboro, d 14 Oct 1909, Limerick, of heart disease, age 71-11-0, married; m ca 1875, Hannah E. (   ) [b 23 Dec 1853, d 6 May 1924, Limerick, age 70, widow]. Stephen served in the Civil War, Co. D, 1st Battalion, ME Volunteer Infantry, with the rank of Pvt., date of enlistment 5 Apr 1865 at Shapleigh, date of discharge 5 Apr 1866. A personal profile was given for Stephen: complexion, light; eyes blue; hair dark; stood 5', 5".

In the 1890 Maine Vets, Census Index of Civil War Vets or Their Widows, Stephen was listed for the town of Limerick, York Co., District SD#1, Enum.#219. The 1900 Soundex for Limerick also listed him as head of household, with wife Hannah at home; their ages then were 60 and 46 respectively. Children at home were Bertha, Delia F., Alice E., Reuben W. and Lillian R. Stephen, Hannah E. and daughter Delia F. were buried at Highland Cemetery on Rte. 5, Limerick.

Ch. b Limerick, not traced further: Bertha, b Oct 1879; Delia F., b Jul 1881; Alice E., b Feb 1883; Reuben W., b May 1895; and Lillian R., b Jan 1897. (Hale's Cems., n.p.; 1900 ME Soundex; Picton's ME Cem. Inscrips., V2, p1191; Civil War research by T. E. Brooks of ME)

STEPHEN H., b 1794, N.H., long-time resident of Kittery, ship's carpenter, d 21 Jan 1862, age 66-7-0, Kittery, married; m 12 Jun 1833, Kittery, Eunice L. Fernald [b 1793, Kittery, d 1 Nov 1888, age 95, native town, widow].

It is believed that Stephen H. was the earliest Young to settle in Kittery, and could very well have been progenitor of the Youngs in this town. He was listed as head of household in Kittery in four census reports for 1820, 1840-1860. In the 1820 census for Berwick, Stephen's age was 16-26, as was the

146

spousal figure; at home were two young females age under 10. In 1840 his age was 40-50, family containing elderly parental figures, ages 70-80 [male] and 80-90 [female]. Other family members were Stephen's spouse age 40-50, two males, one under 5, the other under 10, and five females, and seven children: one age 40-50, one under 5, one under 10, and two age 10-15.

In 1850, Stephen's spouse was named Eunice, age 57; four children at home were Elizabeth, Abbie, Eunice and Stephen. In 1860, both Stephen and Eunice were age 65, their household containing three young adults, Maria E., Stephen A. and Abbie A., operative in a mill.

Stephen, Eunice and two of their children were buried at Orchard Grove Cemetery on Rogers Road, Kittery. Ch. b Kittery: Elizabeth, b 1829; Abbie A.+, b 26 Nov 1834; Eunice aka Maria E. (Young) Tilton, b 1838; Stephen A., b 1840; Augustus D.+, b 6 Jan 1841. (Hale's Cems., n.p.; Census York Co., 1820, p656; 1840, Reel B, p283; 1850, Reel B, p281; 1860, Reel C, p867; 1900 ME Soundex; Picton's ME Cem. Inscrips., V2, p1103; Kittery V.R., p290)

SUSAN, b ca 1835, of Sanford, m 3 Sep 1854, Sanford, John Chapman [b ca 1830, of same town]. (ME I.G.I.)

SUSAN A., b 1859, York, d/o Moses C. and Lydia E. (Trafton) Young; filed (Ints.) 19 Dec 1881, York, m 30 Dec 1881, South Berwick, Charles E. Scruton [b 1851, Rollingsford, N.H. at age 30, s/o Darius K. and Harriet R. (Speed) Scruton]. (Bragdon & Frost's York V.R., p349)

SUSANNA (   ), b 1780, of York, widow of ____ Young, d 1870, York, age 90, of old age. (Bragdon & Frost's York V.R., p441)

SUSANNA (   ), b 1784, of York, listed as head of household in the 1840-1850 census reports for York, widow of ____ Young. In 1840 Susanna's age was 50-60. Members of family included a female age 30-40 (daughter probably), and one male age 10-15. In 1850 her age was 66, her estate valued at $5,000. At home were son Samuel and boarders Mary Bradbury [b 1775], Susan Bradbury [b 1805] and John Hutchins [b 1830]. Ch. b York: Samuel, b 1823, farmer. (Census York Co., 1840, Reel B, p259; 1850, Reel A, p227)

SUSANNA, b 1677, York, d/o Deacon Rowland and Susanna (Matthews) Young, m ca 1705, York, John MacIntire [b ca 1670, York]. MacIntire ch. b York: Joseph MacIntire, b 25 Mar 1707; Susanna MacIntire, b 16 May 1709; John MacIntire, b 25 Feb 1710/11; Hannah MacIntire, b 6 Nov 1712; Ebenezer MacIntire, b 16 Apr 1714; Daniel MacIntire, b 5 Sep 1717; and Samuel MacIntire, b 20 Sep 1721. (Noyes et al, p472; ME I.G.I.; Bragdon & Frost's York V.R., p37)

SUSANNA, b 3 Nov 1696 or 1701, York, d/o Matthews and Eleanor (Haynes) Young, alive 20 Nov 1750, married, native town; m1 1717, York, Ichabod Austin [b ca 1695, York, s/o Matthew and Mary (Littlefield) Austin, d 19 Sep 1718, native town]. Widow Susanna m2 1720, York, Magnus Redlon [b ca 1695, of York], by whom she had four children. Susanna Redlon was

147

named daughter and heir-at-law of Matthew Young by will drawn 20 Nov 1750, probated 1 Apr 1751. Austin ch. b York: Ichabod Austin Jr., b 29 Mar 1717/8. (Noyes et al, pp69, 776; ME I.G.I.; Bragdon & Frost's York V.R., p35)

SUSANNA aka Susannah, b ca 1738, York, filed (Ints.) 9 Sep 1758, m 27 Sep 1758, York, Ebenezer Hall [b ca 1735, originally of Pemaquid, later of York]. (ME I.G.I.; Bragdon & Frost's York V.R., p142)

SUSANNA, b ca 1764, of York, filed (Ints.) 16 Feb 1784, m 1 Mar 1784 at First Parish Church, York, James McDaniel [b ca 1760, of same town]. (Bragdon & Frost's York V.R., pp165, 362)

SUSANNAH (   ), b pre 1775, of York, widow of ___ Young, listed as resident of York in 1820 census with a household of nine other individuals: five males, two under 10, one age 16-18, and two age 26-45, and four other females, one under 10, and three age 10-16. This would seem to indicate a family unit or two by Susan's grown children and their spouses. (Census York Co., 1820, p367)

SUSANNAH, b ca 1750, of York, filed (Ints.) 30 Dec 1769, m 16 Jan 1770, at First Parish Church, York, Ichabod Austin [b ca 1745, of same town]. (Bragdon & Frost's York V.R., pp152, 357)

TABITHA, b 6 Oct 1705, York, d/o Matthews and Eleanor (Haynes) Young, alive 20 Nov 1750, native town; filed (Ints.) 23 Jul 1726; m Aug 1726, York, William Murch [b ca 1700, of same town]. Tabitha Murch was named married daughter of Matthews and an heir-at-law by will signed 20 Nov 1750, proved 1 Apr 1751.

Murch ch. b York: Joanna Murch, b 9 Sep 1726; Tabitha Murch, b 12 Aug 1728; and John Murch, b 2 May 1730. (Noyes et al, p776; Bragdon & Frost's York V.R., pp46, 117)

THEODORE, b ca 1745, of York. Two land deeds were found for Theodore: (1) as grantee, bought for 125 pounds legal tender from Job Layman of York, one part of the house formerly belonging to Manwarren Beale, part of the land 4 rods square, execution upon 30 Apr 1777, and one part of the dwelling house where Samuel Simpson lived, execution of this same date. Layman's spouse Abigail ceded Dower Rights; witnesses Timothy and Hannah Frost, by deed signed 17 Jun 1778, rec'd 23 Jul 1778 [York Deed 45:93]. (2) The other deed attributed to Theodore was dated 15 Feb 1779, rec'd the day after: for 125 pounds current money, Theodore sold to John Savage of York, merchant, "the whole of the house and land bought of Job Lyman, Esq., witnesses Daniel Moulton and Daniel Moulton Jr. [York Deed 45:186].

THEODORE T., b Oct 1854, Saco, s/o Daniel L. and Olive Ann (Tripp) Young, m pre 1890, Freda F. (   ) [b May, 1854, of Saco]. The 1860 census for Saco listed his parents as residents when he was five years old. In the 1900 census for Saco, Theodore was head of household, age 45, and lived on Elm Street with spouse Freda F. Child then at home was Ruth M., age 8. Ch. b Saco, not traced further: Ralph, b 1890, d 1891; Ruth M., b May 1892, alive 1900, and Olive B., b 1898, d 1899. (Picton's ME Cem. Inscrips., V2, p1503; 1900 ME Soundex)

THOMAS, b ca 1725, of Biddeford and Saco, laborer, m ca 1750, Biddeford, Eunice (   ) [b ca 1735, of same town]. Thomas' name was found on the list of "the more prominent early townsmen who were settled [in Saco] before the beginning of the present century," as was kinsman David Young, b ca 1695 [Ridlon's Saco, p119]. There was, however, an area of uncertainty as to Thomas' kinship to Jonathan Young of Biddeford. Lacking vital records, it was assumed that Thomas was a close kinsman--perhaps son, sibling, or father--of Jonathan Young of Biddeford based upon Letters of Admin. on Jonathan's estate filed by Thomas, himself, on 6 Oct 1753. He was to render an inventory of the estate by 6 Jan next, submitting a true account by 6 Oct 1754 [York Probate #20944].

Thomas bought land on the west side of the Saco river above the township of Biddeford, from Ebenezer Ayer of same town, 231 acres in all situated at the S.E. corner of Abraham Townsend's land, S.E. 112 poles to John Gordon Sr., excepting a road four rods wide that Thomas indicated he would allow to be built on the property, by deed signed 3 Aug 1761, rec'd 30 Oct 1765; witnesses Francis Tucker, John Armstrong [York Deed 40:13]

Ch. bp First Congregational Church, Biddeford: Mary, bp 29 Sep 1751; Hezekiah+, bp 24 Jun 1753; John+, bp 11 May 1755; Eunice, bp 17 Mar 1757; Anna, bp 10 Jun 1759; Thomas Jr., bp 8 Mar 1761; and Sarah, bp 30 May 1762. Ch. b Saco: Daniel+, b 2 Nov 1765; and David, b 4 Aug 1770. (ME I.G.I.; MH&G Rec., V6, pp494, 497-498; V7, pp9, 11, 13, 82)

THOMAS aka 2nd, b ca 1770, most likely s/o Thomas and Eunice (   ) Young, of Hollis aka Littlefalls. He was listed as resident of Littlefalls as of the 1790 census; one female was at home. The earliest land deed found for Thomas of Littlefalls was signed 26 Aug 1783, rec'd 4 Jun 1794, in which he bought from John Gordon of the same town for 12 pounds lawful money, one-third of a certain tract of land in Coxhall, 60 acres called Jacobs Green, it being the two-thirds of the one moiety which he purchased from John Lathrop and his wife Elizabeth; Elizabeth Lathrop was the Exec. of the last will of Ebenezer Sayer, Esq., deceased; witnesses Jeremiah Hill, Peter Page [York Deed 55:402].

Thomas' next deed of record was signed 5 Oct 1793, rec'd 2 Apr 1801, and was significant in that it held dealings with three sons of Thomas and Eunice: he sold to John Young of Littlefalls, yeoman, for 195 pounds lawful money, part of his land with the house and barn situated on 105 acres, 43 rods, adjoining land of Hezekiah Young in Littlefalls, on a S.E. line running from Smith's High Landing which was at the foot of Young's lot; witnesses Joseph Chadbourne, Daniel Young [York Deed 65:253].

Thomas' name reappeared in the 1830-1840 census reports for Hollis after Littlefalls had been renamed. In 1830 his age was 50-60, widower, with a family containing one male and female, both ages 20-30, probably a married son and his wife, and two small children, one boy and one girl both under five. In 1840 his age was 70-80, household of four other males, two under 5, one 5-10, and one 40-50; one female age 30-40, two females age 5-10, and one female 10-15. These ages profile a married son or daughter and their young family living in with Thomas. (Census York Co., 1790, p64; 1830, p169; 1840, Reel B, p321)

THOMAS, b ca 1790, of Lebanon, poss. s/o Eliphalet Young, d pre 1891, prob. Dover Neck, N.H., married; filed (Ints.), Lebanon, 4 Jul 1818, m 8 Aug 1818, York, Anna Furbush [b 1798, Kittery, d/o Joseph and Martha (Lord) Furbush, d 30 Jan 1891, Dover Neck, N.H., widow, age 93]. For further details, see Youngs of Strafford Co., N.H. (ME I.G.I.; Lebanon V.R., pp168, 224; Lebanon Marr., p224; NHVR-Deaths)

THOMAS, b 1794, of Dayton and Lyman, farmer, s/o Daniel and Abigail (Dyer) Young of Hollis, d 18 Jun 1868, Dayton, buried at family plot, age 74; m 29 Nov 1827, Lyman, Abigail Cousens [b 1801, of same town, alive 1860, Dayton, married]. Daniel Young's will signed 8 Jan 1848 and filed for probate 6 Mar 1848, named Thomas as an heir-at-law.

Thomas, Abigail and family lived in that part of Hollis that became Dayton in 1854. He was resident of Hollis according to census reports from 1830-1860, excluding 1840. In 1830 his age was given as 30-40, household containing a spousal figure age 20-30 and two children, one male age 10-15 and a female under 5 years. In 1850 Thomas' age was 56, Abigail's, 49. Their large household contained children Julia Ann, Martha, Seth, Abigail, Henry and George. In 1860 Thomas was listed as farmer at age 66; spouse Abigail, age 59; children at home had dwindled down to daughter Julia Ann and sons Seth S. and George.

Ch. b Dayton: Julia Ann, b 1828, d 21 Jan 1861, native town, age 32-5-0; Martha Jane, b 1831, d 26 Oct 1856, age 25-10-0; Seth S., b 1834; Abigail, b 1836; Henry J.+, b 1837; and George A.+, b 1839. (ME I.G.I.; Mormon/ME V.R., Wright-Zitkov; Census York Co., 1830, p170; 1850, Reel B, p111; 1860, Reel C, p991)

THOMAS, b 1815, N.H., machinist, resident of Saco per the 1860 census. He and spouse Aurora (   ) [b 1816, MA] lived alone, real estate valued at $1,500. (Census York Co., 1860, Reel 3, p758)

THOMAS, b ca 1815, resident of York in the 1840 census, age 20-30, a bachelor. (Census York Co., 1840, Reel B, p259)

THOMAS, b 1819, N.H., of Newfield per the 1860 census, farmhand. Thomas lived alone, age 41. (Census York Co., 1860, Reel C, p641)

THOMAS, b Dec 1823, of Farmington, N.H., shoemaker, resident of Lebanon in 1860, but by 1900 had relocated in

Rochester, N.H.; m 9 Jun 1850, Somersworth, Sabrina Wentworth [b Jan 1826, Berwick, d/o Samuel and Lydia (Thompson) Wentworth of Rochester, one of ten children, alive 1900, Rochester]. Note that **Wentworth Genealogy** gave Sabrina's d-o-b as 3 Jan 1827. Thomas and Sabrina lived in Farmington in 1850 when eldest daughter Martha A. was born; the child died young.

Within the next decade, Thomas had relocated from Farmington, N.H. to Lebanon. In 1860 Thomas was listed head of household in Lebanon, age 35; spouse Sabrina was age 34. Four children lived at home, Samuel F., Eliza A., Mary and Susan. Another member of household was Samuel E. Kimball, age 14 [b 1846, MA]. The 1860 Maine census listing for the family would appear not complete when compared with listings from NHVR-Births and Marriages: lacking from these listings were Clara A., b 1851 and Lovina A., b 1858, both of whom lived to marriageable age. The family later moved to Rochester. For background information on Thomas and the marriages of son and daughters, please see full entry on him in the Youngs of Strafford County, N.H., Vol. I.

Ch. b Farmington, N.H.: Martha A., b Aug 1850, d 28 Dec 1853, Farmington. Ch. b Rochester, N.H.: Clara A. (Young) Furbush, b 2 Aug 1851; Samuel F., b 10 Aug 1852; Eliza A., b 12 Jan 1854; Mary L. (Young) Willand, b 3 Jul 1855; and Lovina A. (Young) Hayes, b 19 May 1858. (NHVR-Births, Marr, Brides, Deaths; Census Strafford Co., 1850, p644; Wentworth Gen., V2, pp583-584; LDS I.G.I. BR; Rochester TR, Marr; Census York Co., 1860, Reel A, p83)

THOMAS aka Ithamer, b 1824, Sanford, s/o Joseph and Edna M. (Huston) Young, alive 1870, native town; m 17 Jan 1854, Alfred, Congregational Church, Adeline Willard [b 17 Feb 1825, Sanford, d/o Stephen and Louisa (Tripp) Willard, d 1856, native town]. Thomas m2 7 Dec 1858, Alfred, Louisa Tripp [b 1 Dec 1833, Sanford, d/o John and Anna (Littlefield) Tripp, alive 1860]. The 1860 census report listed Thomas as head of household in Sanford, age 36, spouse Louisa's age 25. They were newlyweds at this point in time. His real estate was valued at $800. Ch. b Sanford by 2nd wife Louisa: Mabella, b ca 1866; Mary A., b Jan 1870. (ME I.G.I.; F. R. Boyle's **Sanford**, pp330-332; Census York Co., 1860, Reel A, p433; MH&G **Rec.**, V4, p268)

THOMAS W., b 1867, of Saco, d 1937, age 70, same town, m ca 1890, Rose E. (   ) [b 1866, d 1926, Saco, age 60]. Thomas, Rose, two sons and their wives were buried at Saco. Ch. b Saco, not traced further: Roy O., b 1887, d 1962, his spouse Annie N. (   ) Young, b 1893, d 1967; Stanley W., b 1893, d 1958; his spouse Cora B. (   ) Young, b 1892, d 1958. (Picton's ME Cem. Inscrips., V3, pp1656-1657)

TIMOTHY, b ca 1745, of York, filed (Ints.) 8 Apr 1772, m 20 Apr 1772, at First Parish Church, York, Hannah Sargent [b ca 1750, of same town]. (Bragdon & Frost's York V.R., pp155, 358)

TIMOTHY, b 13 Apr 1776, of York Co., s/o Jonathan and Mercy (   ) Young of England [no main entry], d 10 Apr 1841, Effingham, N.H.; (Ints.) 25 Apr 1802, Parsonsfield, m 27 Apr 1802, Effingham, Molly aka Mary D. Hobbs [b 1775, Effingham, sister of Jonathan Hobbs, d 6 May 1845, native town, age 70, widow]. For extensive background information on Timothy's family and property in Effingham inherited from his father, please see Youngs of Strafford County, N.H., Vol. I. (Parsonsfield V.R., Town Clerk, p84)

TIMOTHY aka Capt., b 25 May 1813, York, carpenter, s/o Jonathan and Joanna (Nowell) Young, d 13 Nov 1892, native town, age 79, married; filed (Ints.) 20 Jan 1843, York, m 23 Feb 1843, Kennebunkport, Mary Ann Simpson [b 16 Sep 1822, York, d 10 Jul 1901, native town, age 79, widow]. After the death of his father Jonathan on 14 Nov 1827, guardianship of Timothy and his three brothers was awarded to George Grant of York 6 Dec 1830, when Timothy was but a minor of fourteen years plus.

In the 1850 and 1860 census reports he was listed as head of family in York: in 1850 his age was 37, occupation carpenter, his home immediately adjacent to his brother Jonathan's. At home were Timothy's spouse Mary, sons David and Joseph, and Woodbury Simpson, presumed to be brother-in-law [b 1812]. In 1860 Timothy was farmer with real estate valued at $2,500; spouse Mary A. was age 38, and four children were at home, David W., Joseph Y., Mary H. and Charles H.

The 1900 census report indicated that Mary Ann, age 77, was widow and head of household in York. Members of family living at home were son George H., his wife Mary A., their son Arthur S. and daughter Louella. Timothy and Mary Ann, son George H. and his wife Mary A., son Charles H. and spouse Mariette, and their children were buried in the Young Lot, No. 25, York Cemetery, York.

Ch. b York: David, b 1843; Joseph Timothy+, b Feb 1847; Mary H., b 1851; Charles H.+, b Feb 1854; George H.+, b May 1861. (ME I.G.I.; Bragdon & Frost's York V.R., pp258, 352, 393; Frost's York Cem., p614; **Plaisted Private Recs.**; Mormon-ME V.R., Wright-Zitkov; Hale's Cems., n.p.; Census York Co., 1850, Reel A, p215; 1860, Reel C, p959; 1900 ME Soundex; Picton's ME Cem. Inscrips., V3, p2367)

VICTOR, b Sep 1846, Canada/French, head of household in Kennebunk per 1900 census report, age 53, living with wife Celina (   ) [b Jan 1850, Canada], two sons, Alfred [b Mar 1877, Canada], a naturalized citizen, Wilfred [b Feb 1886, MA], and their stepson Napoleon, age 13 [b Dec 1886, ME]. (1900 ME Soundex)

VOLTAIRE, b ca 1805, of Biddeford, mariner, deceased by 6 Nov 1837, intestate. Elder brother James L. Young of Exeter, N.H. petitioned on 6 Nov 1837 "that Letters of Admin. upon Voltaire's estate be granted to him, with the request of all the remaining heirs, which was also presented," and added that the parents were not living. On same date, petition was allowed and the court appointed as appraisers, Ichabod Jordan, William Hoppin, and Wetherly Smith, all of Biddeford [York Probate #20997].

WARREN, triplet, b 11 Dec 1817, Gloucester, MA, fisherman, farmer, s/o Daniel and Hannah (Lane) Young [no main entry], d 13 Nov 1887, native town, age 69-11-0. Warren filed (Ints.) 2 Nov 1845, Gloucester, Betsey Woodbury Dodd [b 26 Jan 1824, Gloucester, d/o John and Tamesin (   ) Dodd, d 24 Jan 1864, native town, married, age 40]. Warren m2 (dual entry) 1 May 1865, Gloucester, MA and York, Sarah S. Blaisdell [b 1819, York, d/o Theodore and Mary (   ) Blaisdell, alive 1865, Gloucester, MA]. See Youngs of Essex County, MA, Vol. II for full particulars on the parentage of Warren and family. Ch. b York by first wife Betsey: Georgianna, b 7 Nov 1849. (ME and MA I.G.I.; Bragdon & Frost's York V.R., pp303, 305)

WILLIAM, b 1663, York, s/o Rowland and Joan (Knight) Young, glazier. The only document to turn up on William was a deed signed 11 Feb 1684, when he bought from Benjamin Curtis of Wells, carpenter, for 15-10-0 in current money, twenty acres land with a small house or tenement upon it, situated on the S.W. side of the N.W. branch of York River above York Bridge, bounded by lots of Phillip Frost on the S.W., and by John Hoys' house and land on the N.W.; witnesses Will Gowen alias Smith, Daniel Livingston; rec'd 12 Feb 1684 [York Deed 4:30-31]. (ME I.G.I.)

WILLIAM, b ca 1700, of Boston, Suffolk Co., cordwainer, was granted power of attorney from John Cotton of Boston, "a well beloved friend and relation" by deed signed 18 Feb 1740, rec'd 7 Apr 1741; witnesses E. Lawrence, J. Whitley, J. S. Lawrence [York Deed 22:90]. In the following month, William, acting for John Cotton of Boston, sold for 240 pounds lawful money, 92 acres land in Kittery, which belonged to John Cotton, late of Portsmouth, father of said John above, which had lately been divided by the Probate Count among his heirs by deed signed 16 Mar 1740, rec'd 19 Jun 1741; witnesses Edmund Coffin, William Park [York Deed 22:192].

WILLIAM, b 1746, of York, ME and Newburyport, Essex County, MA. William enlisted 27 Jul 1775, mustered in 1 Aug 1775, as Pvt. For additional details on military service please see Youngs of Essex County, MA, Vol. II, p268. (Revol. Soldiers & Sailors, p1037)

WILLIAM, b ca 1785, of Salem, Essex County, MA, glazier, purchased from Peter Nowell of York for 30 pounds in money, fifty acres situated in "Crickson in York" bounded with the lands of John Haines to the N.E. and the bounds of William Shaw to the S.W. at the foot of Thompson's land, William Young holding the estate of inheritance, by deed signed 13 Oct 1720, rec'd 21 Oct 1720; witnesses Samuel Hayward, Richard Milberry, Samuel Shattock [York Deed 10:85]. It is noteworthy that Richard Milberry was a neighbor of Job and Sarah Young of York.

WILLIAM, b ca 1810, of Kennebunk; filed (Ints.) 19 Apr 1834, Waterboro, Sarah Peirce [b ca 1815, of Waterboro]. (**Reg.** 90:333, 1936)

WILLIAM, b Nov 1816, sole resident of Lyman by the name of Young in the 1900 census for that town; he lived alone at age 83 as a boarder at the home of David Waterhouse [n.d.]. (1900 ME Soundex)

WILLIAM, b 1844, of Waterboro, farm hand, age 16, lived at the home of John and Chanty Sayward [b 1814 and 1813, respectively]. (Census York Co., 1860, Reel B, p970)

WILLIAM, b ca 1845, of Biddeford, alive same town 1890, listed in the 1890 ME Vets, Census Index of Civil War Vets or Their Widows, York Co. for Biddeford, District SD#1, Enum.-#208)

WILLIAM A., b 1805, N.H., of South Berwick, d 18 Mar 1883, South Berwick; m Oct 1838, Vassalboro, Dorcas A. Nichols [b 1815, of Vassalboro, d 9 Oct 1874, age 59, South Berwick]. William A. and spouse Dorcas were listed as residents of this town in the 1850-1860 census reports, his estate valued at $3,000 in 1850, $4,500 in 1860. At home in 1850 were five young children: John W., Mary E., Anna K., Rebecca and Lydia E. In 1860 the list of children was the same, less Anna, and toddler Augustus; sibling John had become farmer, sibling Mary E., a teacher.

William A., Dorcas, and children John W., Rebecca, Anna R., Hannah K. and Charlotte were buried at the family plot in South Berwick. Ch. b ME: John W.+, b 27 May 1840; Mary E., b 1842; Anna K., b 1844, twin, d.y; Charlotte, b 1844, twin, d 10 Aug 1846, aged 2 mos, 11 days; Rebecca O.+, b 31 Oct 1847; Lydia E., b Feb 1850; and Augustus, b 1853. (Census York Co., 1850, Reel C, p319; 1860, Reel B, p783; Picton's ME Cem. Inscrips., V3, p2047; J. P. Thompson, Recs. of York Co., TMs, p417)

WILLIAM BABB, b ca 1735, of York, filed (Ints.) 2 Jan 1762, York, Betty York [b ca 1740, of same town]. (Bragdon & Frost's York V.R., p144)

WILLIAM E., b 1820, VT, resident of Kittery in 1850 census, age 30, member of the U.S. Marine Corp. (Census York Co., 1850, Reel B, p281)

WILLIAM H., b 23 Mar 1847, Waterboro, farmer, s/o John Young, d 23 Oct 1888, native town, age 41-7-0; m 22 Feb 1870, Biddeford, Clara J. Rhodes [b ca 1850, of Waterboro, alive 1890, widow, same town]. At age 18, William H. mustered in 2 Sep 1862, at Augusta, for three years, where he served in the 1st Reg. Calvary. Due to the fact that his age was just 18, his father John had to certify that William's age was indeed 18, and give his consent to son William enlisting as a soldier. His personal profile showed that William's complexion was light, eyes were gray, hair was light; he stood 5' 7".

In the 1890 Maine Veterans' Census Index of Civil War Vets or Their Widows, Clara J. Young of Waterboro was listed as widow of a Civil War veteran. William and Clara J. were buried [n.d.] at Pine Grove Cemetery, Waterboro. (ME I.G.I.; Hale's Cems., n.p.; 1890 Census Index, District SD#11, Enum. #233; Civil War research by T. E. Brooks of Maine)

WILLIAM H. CUMMINGS, b Jul 1859, York, s/o Charles and Eliza Ann ( ) Young, d 1937, York, age 78. William H. was listed as member of Charles' and Eliza Ann's family in the 1860 census for York, and as a resident there in the 1900 census, age 40, married. His family then included spouse Laura H. ( ) [b Aug 1861] and son George H. [b May 1880]. (Bragdon & Frost's York V.R., p548; 1900 ME Soundex)

WILLIAM M., b 19 Apr 1804, Acton, farmer, s/o Jonathan and Mehitable (Moody) Young, d 19 Jan 1877, native town, married, age 72-9-0; m ca 1830, Grace S. ( ) [b 27 Feb 1810, d 27 Mar 1885, age 75, native town, widow]. William M. and sibling Peter were named Co-Execs. and residuary legatees of their father's estate by will drawn 8 Oct 1838, probated 7 Jan 1839. Jonathan devised the dwelling house equally among son William and those sisters who remained unmarried.

William lived in York per the 1840-1860 census reports. In 1840 his age was 30-40; his household was quite large, with twelve other family members at home: four males, one each under 5, 10-15, 15-20, and 20-30; one female under 5, six females, five of whom were age 20-30, believed to be his unmarried sisters, one 30-40 believed to be his spouse, and an elderly female figure age 60-70, poss. his spouse's mother. In both the 1850 and 1860 reports, Grace was named his wife. Nephew Joshua M. Young [b 1836] lived with them during his youth; he was the s/o William's sibling Peter Young of Acton. In 1860 a domestic by the name of Louisa Witlaw lived in [b 1814].

William and Grace S. were buried at the Young plot on Young's Ridge Road, Acton. (Hale's Cems., n.p.; Census York Co., 1840, Reel B, p298; 1850, Reel B, p8; 1860, Reel B, p644)

WILLIAM N., b ca 1805, head of household in South Berwick per 1840 census, age 30-40. A spousal figure was age 20-30, and three young males were at home, one age 15-20 and two under ten years. (Census York Co., 1840, Reel B, p210)

WINFIELD SCOTT, b 15 Sep 1848, Parsonsfield, s/o George and Jane (Keazer) Young; m 1 Jan 1874, Parsonsfield, Mrs. Ella H. ( ) Eastman [b ca 1850, of same town]. In 1850 Winfield S. was listed as an infant of one year in his parents' household, the youngest of four born to George and Jane. (Mormon-ME V.R., Wright-Zitkov)

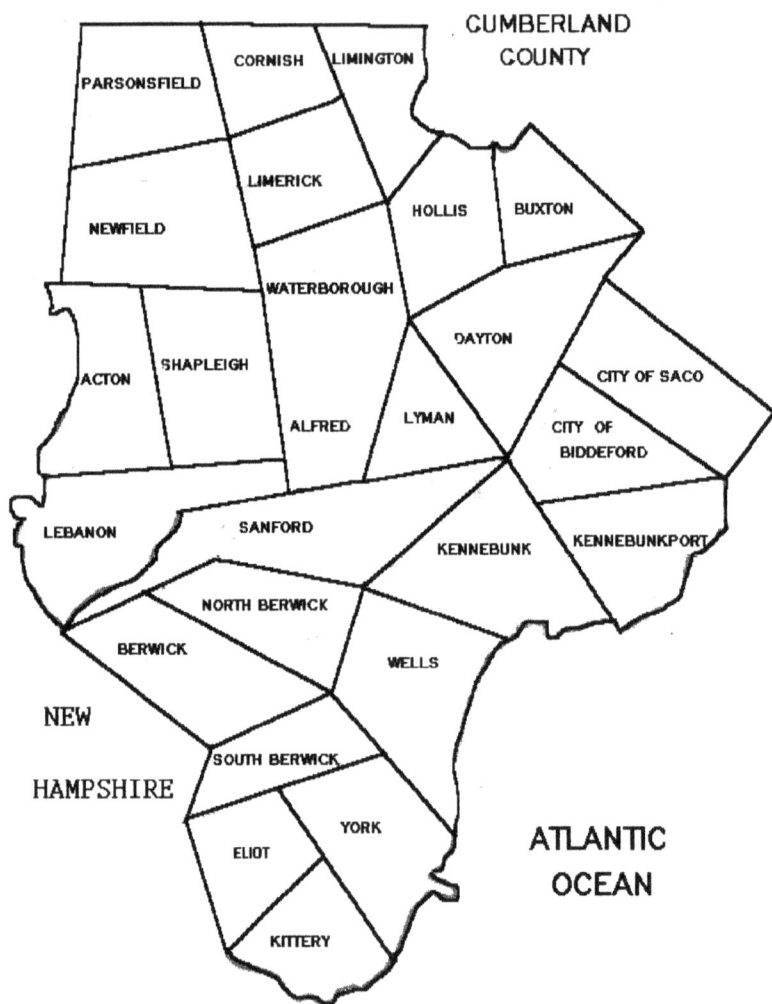

OXFORD COUNTY

CUMBERLAND COUNTY

PARSONSFIELD

CORNISH LIMINGTON

LIMERICK

NEWFIELD

HOLLIS BUXTON

WATERBOROUGH

DAYTON

ACTON SHAPLEIGH

CITY OF SACO

ALFRED LYMAN

CITY OF BIDDEFORD

LEBANON SANFORD

KENNEBUNK

KENNEBUNKPORT

NORTH BERWICK

BERWICK

WELLS

NEW

SOUTH BERWICK

HAMPSHIRE

YORK

ATLANTIC OCEAN

ELIOT

KITTERY

YORK COUNTY, MAINE
in 1872

Appendix A

OLD YORK COUNTY, MAINE

Appendix B

ANNOTATED BIBLIOGRAPHY OF YORK COUNTY, MAINE

NATIONAL - REGIONAL

A Census of Pensioners for Revolutionary or Military Services, 1840, and A General Index to a Census of Pensioners. 2 Vols. in 1. Baltimore: Genealogical Publishing Co., 1989.

House, Charles J. Names of Soldiers of the American Revolution Who Applied for State Bounty under Resolves of March 17, 1835, March 24, 1836, and March 20, 1836, as Appears of Record in Land Office. Augusta: Burleigh & Flynt, 1893.

Paige, Lucius R. List of Freemen of Massachusetts, 1630-1691. With Index by Elizabeth Petty Bentley. Baltimore: Genealogical Publishing Co., Inc., 1988.

Massachusetts and Maine Direct Tax Census of 1798. Microfilm Edition, Reel No. 2, Vol. 3, York County, edited by Michael H. Gorn. Boston: New England Historic Genealogical Society, 1979. The census for Assessment District No. 10 listed names of occupants of dwelling homes, their "reputed owners," currant valuations and taxes due. These listings did not include the name of Young.

Massachusetts Soldiers and Sailors of the Revolutionary War. Boston: Wright & Potter Printing Co., 1908.

Noyes, Sybil, Charles Thornton Libby, and Walter Goodwin Davis. Genealogical Dictionary of Maine and New Hampshire. 1928-39. Reprint. Baltimore: Genealogical Publishing Co., 1983.

Pope, Charles Henry. The Pioneers of Maine and New Hampshire, 1623 to 1660. 1908. Reprint. Baltimore: Genealogical Publishing Co., 1973.

Savage, James. A Genealogical Dictionary of the First Settlers of New England. 4 Vols. 1860-62. Reprint. Baltimore: Genealogical Publishing Co., 1986.

Sperry, Kip. New England Genealogical Research, A Guide to Sources. Bowie, MD: Heritage Books, Inc., 1988.

Steuerwald, Emma Neal, comp. Inscriptions From Some Homestead Cemeteries and Other Burial Places in Strafford County, in and Around Dover, New Hampshire, and a Few From the Adjoining County of York, Maine. TMs filmed by Genealogical Society of Utah, Microfilm No. 1004509, item 9.

Thaxter, Celia. <u>Among the Isles of Shoals</u>. Boston: Hought-on Mifflin Co., ca 1901.

Torrey, Clarence Almon. <u>New England Marriages Prior to 1700</u>. Baltimore: Genealogical Publishing Co., 1985.

United States. Bureau of the Census. <u>Heads of Families at the First Census of the United States Taken in the Year 1790</u>: Maine. National Archives, Washington, D.C.

_____. <u>Heads of Families at the Second Census of the United States Taken in the Year 1800</u>: Maine.

_____. <u>Heads of Families at the Third Census of the United States Taken in the Year 1810</u>: Maine.

_____. <u>Heads of Families at the Fourth Census of the United States Taken in the Year 1820</u>: Maine.

_____. <u>Heads of Families at the Fifth Census of the United States Taken in the Year 1830</u>: Maine.

_____. <u>Heads of Families at the Sixth Census of the United States Taken in the Year 1840</u>: Maine.

_____. <u>Heads of Families at the Seventh Census of the United States Taken in the Year 1850</u>: Maine.

_____. <u>Heads of Families at the Twelfth Census of the United States Taken in the Year 1900</u>: Maine.

_____. <u>Mortality Schedule Showing a Census of Deaths in the Seventh Census from June 1849-June 1850</u>. Filmed by the Genealogical Society of Utah, Microfilm No. 0009739.

_____. <u>Mortality Schedule Showing a Census of Deaths in the Eighth Census from June 1859-June 1860</u>. Filmed by the Genealogical Society of Utah, Microfilm No. 0009740.

_____. <u>Mortality Schedule Showing a Census of Deaths in the Ninth Census from June 1869-June 1870</u>. Filmed by the Genealogical Society of Utah, Microfilm No. 0009741.

_____. <u>United States Direct Tax Census For Maine and Massachusetts Massachusetts for 1798</u>. York County, Reel #2. New England Historic Genealogical Society, Film #M2-87302.

STATE OF MAINE

Daughters of the American Revolution. <u>Revolutionary Soldiers'</u>
<u>Graves Marked by the Maine Daughters of the American</u>
<u>Revolution</u>. (1940)

Fisher, Major Gen. Carleton and Sue G. Fisher. <u>Soldiers,</u>
<u>Sailors, and Patriots of the Revolutionary War: Maine</u>.
Picton Press, Camden, ME, 1982.

Frost, John Eldridge. <u>Maine Probate Abstracts: 1687-1800</u>.
Vol. 1:1687-1775; Vol. 2: 1775-1800.

_____. "Maine Genealogy: Some Distinctive Aspects."
Register, 131 (1977):243-66.

Gray, Ruth. <u>Maine Families in 1790</u>. Camden, ME: Picton
Press, 1988-1992, 4 Vols.

Hall, Mabel G. <u>Maine Ancestors in the American Revolution</u>.
(Index of Maine Men in the Rolls of Honor of the Lineage
Books of the National Society of the Daughters of the
American Revolution). Vols. 1-70.

<u>Heads of Families at the First Census of the United States</u>
<u>Taken in the Year 1790, Maine</u>. Baltimore: Genealogical
Publishing Co., 1973.

Little, Geoerge Thomas. <u>Genealogical and Family History of</u>
<u>the State of Maine</u>. New York: Lewis Historical Publish-
ing Company, 1909, Vol. 4.

Maine <u>Mortality Schedules for 1850, 1860 and 1870</u> - please see
United States, Bureau of the Census.

Maine Cemeteries, Maine State Library. <u>Nathan Hale Cemetery</u>
<u>Collection, Surname Index</u>, Series 1: Wyman, Eunice to
Young, Ellis H.; Young, Elmer E. to Zwicker, Charles
Edwin. Filmed by the Genealogical Society of Utah.
Microfilm Nos. 1316337 and 1316338.

_____. Series 2. Wellman, Samuel B. - Zelkan, Otto B.
Microfilm No. 1316354.

Maine <u>Cemetery Inscriptions, York County</u>, Maine Old Cemetery
Associates, Special Publications, Vols. 1-4. Camden, ME:
Picton Press.

Maine Court Records - Indexes: Massachusetts, County Court,
Suffolk County, up through 1820. <u>County Court Files</u>

Index Sec-Zw, 1629-1795. Filmed by the Genealogical Society of Utah, Microfilm No. 0909871.

_____. County Court Files Index I - Z, 1629-1729, Microfilm No. 0909873.

_____. County Court Files Index S - Z, 1730-1799, Microfilm No. 0909877.

Maine, Division of Vital Statistics. Index to Vital Records Prior to 1892 of...80 Towns: Wright (1871) to Zitkov. Filmed by the Genealogical Society of Utah, 1953. Filmed by the Genealogical Society of Utah, 1953, Microfilm No. 0009883.
      Records of births (including delayed births), deaths, and marriages are arranged alphabetically by surname, then by year within surname.

Maine Historical Society. Province and Court Records of Maine. Vol. I, from 1636 - 1668 (until taken away by the Colony of Massachusetts Bay). Portland, Maine Historical Society (1931).

_____. Vol. II. York County Court Records, Colony of Massachusetts Bay. County Court, Vol. I, 1653 - 1672; County Court, Vol. II, 1672 - 1679; Court of Associates, 1658 - 1679. Portland, Maine Historical Society (1931).

_____. Vol. III. Province of Maine Records, 1680 - 1692. Portland, Maine Historical Society (1947).

_____. Vol. IV. The Court Records of York County, Maine, Province of Massachusetts Bay, November, 1692 - January, 1710-11. (1958)

_____. Vol. V. The Court Records of York County, Maine, Province of Massachusetts Bay, April, 1711 - October, 1718. (1964)

_____. Vol. VI. The Court Records of York County, Maine, Province of Massachusetts Bay...The Records of the Court of General Sessions of the Peace, January 1718/19 - October 1727. (1976)

Maine Revolutionary Soldiers' Graves, Golden Jubilee Project, 1940, Daughters of the American Revolution of Maine.

Maine State Archives. Delayed Returns for Births, Deaths and Marriages, 1670? to 1891: Woodman, 1850 to Z. Filmed by the Genealogical Society of Utah, Microfilm No. 1205259.

_____. Veterans Cemetery Records. Revolutionary War: Cushman, T. to Young, filmed by Photographic Science Corp., 1975?, Microfilm No. 1001838.

Sargent, William M., comp. Maine Wills, 1640-1760. 1887. Reprint. Baltimore: Genealogical Publishing Co., 1972.

Sylvester, Herbert M. Maine Pioneer Settlements. Old York. Vol. 2 (1909)

Varney, George J. A Gazetteer of the State of Maine. Boston: B. B. Russell, 1881. Bowie, MD: Heritage Books, Inc., 1991, Reprint, 2 Vols.

Watson, S. M., Ed. The Maine Historical and Genealogical Recorder, Nine Vols. in Three. Baltimore: Genealogical Publishing Co., 1973.

YORK COUNTY

Chamberlain, George W. "York County, Maine, Marriage Returns, 1771-1794," Register 63 (April 1909).

"Docket of Marriages Solemnized by the Rev. Hugh G. Carley," Register 117 (July 1963).

Thompson, Joseph P. Records of York County, Maine. Copied by Samuel D. Rumery for the Maine Historical Society, TMs, 1926. Two Vols. in One.

York County. History of York County, Maine, With Illustrations and Biographical Sketches of its Prominent Men and Pioneers. (1880)

York County Deeds, 1642-1737. 18 vols. Portland, Maine: Maine Historical Society, 1887-1910 (publisher varies). Transcription of deeds, 1642-1737.

TOWNS OF YORK COUNTY

Acton

Fullonton, Joseph. The History of Acton, Maine. Dover: William Burr, 1847.

Alfred

Church of Jesus Christ of Latter-Day Saints. <u>Congregational Church, Alfred, Maine</u>. Maine Computer Printout: Births or Christenings, 1806-1870. Filmed by the Genealogical Society of Utah, 1977, Microfilm No. 1002590, item 17.

Daughters of the American Revolution. <u>Alfred, Maine, Congregational Church Records</u>, Vols. 1-3, 1782-1895. Members, baptisms, marriages and deaths in the custody of the Parson's Memorial Library, Alfred, Maine. Copied by Benapeag Chapter D.A.R., Sanford and Springvale, Maine. 1949. TMs filmed by the Genealogical Society of Utah, 1982, Microfilm No. 1033845, item 2.

Parsons, Dr. Usher and Samuel M. Came. <u>A Centennial History of Alfred, York County, Maine</u>. Philadelphia: Sanford, Everts & Co., 1872.

Town Clerk. <u>Town Records of Alfred, Maine, 1796-1895</u>. Contains Intentions of Marriage ca. 1797-1895 and Marriage Records ca 1796-1891. Filmed by the Genealogical Society of Utah, 1956, Microfilm No. 0010469.

Berwick

Frost, John Eldridge. <u>Berwick, Maine Vital Records</u>. TMs filmed by Genealogical Society of Utah, Microfilm No. 1597554, item 1. Includes Index.

Scates, Hon. John C. "Records of the First Church of Berwick (South Berwick), Maine." **Register** 82 (Jan. 1928) - 83 (April 1929).

Spencer, Wilbur D. <u>Burial Inscriptions and Other Data of Burials in Berwick, York County, Maine to the Year 1922</u>. Filmed by the Genealogical Society of Utah, Microfilm No. 1033825, item 1.

Town Clerk. <u>Town and Vital Records of Berwick, Maine, 1701-1776</u>. Family records listing births and deaths; lands. Filmed by the Genealogical Society of Utah, Microfilm No. 0010551.

_____. 1701-1891. Family records listing births and deaths; marriages 1713-1734, 1789-1812; intentions of marriage 1790-1813; births 1770; deaths to 1812. Microfilm No. 0010552.

_____. Deaths 1813-1886. Microfilm No. 0010553.

Biddeford

City Clerk. <u>Vital Records of Biddeford, Maine, 1779-1895</u>. Filmed by the Genealogical Society of Utah. Marriage records 1779-1818, 1836-1844; family records listing births; deaths 1805-1843; intentions of marriage 1815-1844-; depositions of birth. Microfilm No. 0010601.

_____. Marriage Records 1854-1895; Deaths 1855-1895. Microfilm No. 0010602.

Please see also **Saco**.

Buxton

Goodwin, William F. <u>Records of the Proprietors of Narragan-set Township, No. 1, Now the Town of Buxton, York County, Maine, from August 1, 1733 to January 4, 1811, With a Documentary Introduction</u>. Concord, N.H., 1871.

Marshall, Joel M. <u>A Report of the Proceedings at the Celebra-tion of the First Centennial Anniversary of the Incorp-oration of the Town of Buxton, Maine, Held at Buxton, August 14, 1872</u>. Portland: Dresser, McLellan & Co., 1874.

<u>The Records of the Church of Christ in Buxton, Maine, 1763-1817: During the Pastorate of Rev. Paul Coffin, D.D.</u> 1989. Picton Press, Camden, ME.

Town Clerk. <u>Vital Records of Buxton, Maine, 1773-1891</u>. Filmed by the Genealogical Society of Utah, Microfilm No. 0010594. Intentions of marriage, 1773-1804; 1847-1891; marriage records 1787-1802; 1847-1861; a copy of marriage records 1787-1891; family records listing births, deaths, and marriages; another copy of the family records; depos-itions of births.

Cornish

Cole, Albert. <u>Baptismal, Marriage, and Funeral Records of Rev. Albert Cole (1818-1881) of Cornish, Maine</u>. 1983. Very helpful inasmuch as there were no town records.

Taylor, Robert L. <u>Early Families of Cornish, Maine</u>. 1985.

Eliot

Benton, Alice H., comp. <u>Cemetery at Eliot, Maine</u>. Included are church records, vital records, marriage records, wills, Revolutionary soldiers and family bibles of founders and Patriots of America. Vol. 2. Microfilm of Leaves 42-50, No. 0165996.

Fogg, William. <u>Early Families of Eliot and Kittery, Maine</u>. No. VI, 1902. Filmed by the Genealogical Society of Utah, Microfilm No. 1033880.

Frost, John Eldridge. <u>Eliotiana</u>, I, Marriages, 1810-1891, TMs, 1984.

Willis, John Lemuel Murray. <u>Old Eliot, a Magazine of the History and Biography of the Upper Parish of Kittery, now Eliot, Maine</u>. 1985. Picton Press, Camden, ME. Vol. 2. (1897-1909, reprint 1985)

Please see also **Kittery**.

Groveville

Daughters of the American Revolution. <u>Gorham, West Hollis and Groveville, Maine Cemetery Records</u>, copied by Mr. and Mrs. Percy L. Tate. Rebecca Emery Chapter, D.A.R. TMs filmed by the Genealogical Society of Utah, 1971, Microfilm No. 0855268, item 6.

Hollis

Gould, Emma, Comp. <u>Marriages Between 1784-1831 in Hollis, Lyman and Next Towns</u>, by Rev. Simon Lock, Second Baptist Church. 1906.

Town Clerk. <u>Town and Vital Records of Hollis, Maine, 1781-1893</u>. Filmed by the Genealogical Society of Utah, 1956. Microfilm No. 0011028.
Intentions of marriage 1799-1892; marriage records 1812-1892; family records listing births to 1891; delayed births; list of men who died in service 1861-1865.

Please see also **Groveville** and **West Hollis**.

Kennebunk

Town Clerk. <u>Town and Vital Records of Kennebunk, Maine, 1727–1892</u>. Filmed by the Genealogical Society of Utah, Microfilm No. 0011326.
Family records listing births 1729-1891; depositions and delayed births; marriage records 1727-1892; deaths 1773-1891; intentions of marriage 1820-1857; marriage records 1820-1856.

Please see also **Wells**.

Kennebunkport

Remick, Daniel. <u>History of Kennebunk From its Earliest Settlement to 1890, Including Biographical Sketches</u>. (1911)

Town Clerk. <u>Town and Vital Records of Kennebunkport, Maine, 1678-1891</u>. Filmed by the Genealogical Society of Utah, Microfilm No. 0011328.
Intentions of marriage 1790-1891; marriage records 1768-1891; family records listing births and deaths; births and deaths 1856-1891.

Kittery

Anderson, Joseph Crook and Lois Ware Thurston, Ed. <u>Vital Records of Kittery, Maine to the Year 1892</u>. Maine Genealogical Society Special Publication No. 8.

Daughters of the American Revolution. <u>First Parish Church, Kittery Point: Congregational Records from the First Church in Kittery, Maine, 1715-1797 (1820)</u>. TMs filmed by the Genealogical Society of Utah, 1981, Microfilm No. 1035868, item 4.

Fogg, William. <u>Early Families of Eliot and Kittery, Maine</u>. No. VI, 1902. Filmed by the Genealogical Society of Utah, Microfilm No. 1033880.

Remick, Oliver Philbrick. <u>A Record of the Services of the Commissioned Officers and Enlisted Men of Kittery and Eliot, Maine</u>.

Stackpole, Everett S. <u>Old Kittery and Her Families</u>. Somersworth, N.H.: New England History Press, 1903. Reprint 1985, Picton Press, Camden, ME.

Steuerwald, Mrs. Louis J. Cemetery Inscriptions From New Castle and Gilmanton, N.H. and from Kittery, Maine. TMs filmed by the Genealogical Society of Utah, Microfilm No. 0015566, item 13.

Lebanon

Chamberlain, George Walker. Lebanon - Maine Genealogies, 1750-1892. 1892.

_____. Vital Records of Lebanon, Maine, to the Year 1892. Vol. 1, Births, 1922; Vol. 2, Marriages rec'd, 1922; Vol. 3, Deaths, Rec'd, 1923. Filmed by the Genealogical Society of Utah, Microfilm No. 1033822, items 1-3.

Frost, John Eldridge. Addenda to Record Books of Towns, Lebanon, TMs, July 1989.

Limerick

Grant, Stephen A., comp. History, Town and Vital Records of Limerick, Maine. Filmed by the Genealogical Society of Utah, Microfilm No. 0011542.

Swasey, William, Town Clerk, Old Families of Limerick, Maine. between 1805-1807. TMs.

Limington

Taylor, Robert Lewis. Early Families of Limington, Maine. Danville, ME: Author, 1984.

_____. History of Limington, Maine, 1668-1900. Norway, ME: Oxford Hills Press, 1975.

Vital Records of Limington, Maine (Including Proprietors Records of the Ossipee Towns), reproduced by Ancient Landmarks Society of Parsonsfield, 1991.

Lyman

Town Clerk. Town and Vital Records of Lyman, Maine, 1783-1893. Filmed by the Genealogical Society of Utah, Microfilm No. 0011539.
    Marriage records 1783-1892; intentions of marriage 1783-1888; family records listing births.

_____. Microfilm No. 0011540.
  Deaths, 1865, 1892; births 1864-1865; family records
listing births.

North Berwick

Town Clerk. Town and Vital Records of North Berwick, Maine,
  1829-1883. Filmed by the Genealogical Society of Utah,
  Microfilm No. 0011585.
    Contains births, ca 1829-1883; family records
  listing births; intentions of marriage 1831-1877;
  marriage records 1831-1878; deaths ca 1832-1878.

Parsonsfield

A History of the First Century of the Town of Parsonsfield,
  Maine: Incorporated August 29, 1785, and celebrated with
  impressive ceremonies at North Parsonsfield, August 19,
  1885. Portland, ME: Brown Thurston, 1888. Filmed by
  the Genealogical Society of Utah, Microfilm No. 1421816,
  item 8.

Hobbs, Constance. Cemetery Records, Parsonsfield, ME. (1982)

Town Clerk. Vital Records of Parsonsfield, Maine, 1771-1897.
  (1988).
    Contains marriage records 1785-1860; family records
  listing births and deaths; deaths 1785-1799, 1864-1897;
  school district records; intentions of marriage 1806-
  1862; deposition of births; births 1864-1897.

Saco

City Clerk. First Book of Records of the Town of Pepperell
  borough, Now the City of Saco. Filmed by the Genealogical Society of Utah, 1956, Microfilm No. 0012243, item 1.
    Contains intentions of marriage 1796-1831; family
  records listing births.

_____. Vital Records, 1840-1900. Filmed by the Genealogi-
  cal Society of Utah, 1956. Microfilm No. 0012243, items
  2-6.
    Contains deaths 1840-1891; family records listing
  births and deaths; adoption of a child; marriage records
  1851-1867, 1881; intentions of marriage 1851-1891; births
  ca 1865-1900; delayed births.

Folsom, George. History of Saco and Biddeford, with Notices of Other Early Settlements, and of the Proprietory Governments in Maine, including the Provinces of New Somersetshire and Lygonia. Bowie, MD: Heritage Books, Inc., 1984, Reprint.

Ridlon, Gideon Tibbetts. Saco Valley Settlements and Families. 1895. Somersworth, N.H.: New England History Press, 1984, Reprint.

Sanford

Boyle, Frederick R. Early Families of Sanford-Springvale, Maine. Portsmouth, N.H.: Peter E. Randall, Pub., 1988.

Emery, Edwin, ed. by William M. Emery. The History of Sanford, Maine, 1661-1900. Fall River, Mass.: W. M. Emery, 1901.

Perkins, Rachel Bean. Index of Names in the History of Sanford, Maine, 1661-1900 by Edwin Emery. Sanford, ME: Sanford-Alfred Historical Society, 1985.

Town Clerk. Vital Records of Sanford, Maine, 1769-1892. Filmed by the Genealogical Society of Utah, Microfilm No. 0012232, Items 1-1; No. 0012233, Items 1-3.
    Contains births, deaths, marriages; intentions of marriages.

Shapleigh

Loring, Rev. Amasa. History of Shapleigh, Maine. Portland: B. Thurston, 1854.

Town Clerk. Vital Records of Shapleigh, Maine. Filmed by the Genealogical Society of Utah, Microfilm Nos. 0012237-0012239.
    Contains marriage, birth and scattered death records; intentions of marriage.

South Berwick

Benton, Alice H. Oldfields Cemetery, South Berwick, Maine. Filmed by the Genealogical Society of Utah, Microfilm No. 0165996 (leaves 53-57).

Town Clerk. Vital Records of South Berwick, Maine, ca 1774-1924. Filmed by the Genealogical Society of Utah, Microfilm Nos. 0012240 and 0012241.

Birth, death and marriage records; intentions of
marriage; family records listing births; delayed births;
deaths to 1924.

Waterboro

Town Clerk. Vital Records of Waterboro, ME, 1787-1891.
Filmed by the Genealogical Society of Utah, Microfilm No.
0012325 and 0012327.
Birth, marriage and death records; intentions of
marriage; some scattered deaths.

"Vital Records of Waterborough, Maine," **Register** 90:333, 335
(October 1936) - 91:35, 126 (January 1937).

Wells

Bourne, Edward E. The History of Wells and Kennebunk From the
Earliest Settlement to the Year 1820, at Which Time Ken-
nebunk Was Set Off and Incorporated, with Biographical
Sketches. Portland, ME: B. Thurston & Co., 1875.
Bowie, MD: Heritage Books, Inc., Reprint.

Bragdon, Lester MacKenzie. "Inscriptions from Gravestones at
Wells, Maine," **Register** 92 (July 1938) - 94 (October
1940).

Town Clerk. Town and Vital Records of Wells, 1715-1895.
Filmed by the Genealogical Society of Utah, 1956, Micro-
film Nos. 0012622 and 0012623.
Births, marriages and deaths; freeholders records.

West Hollis

Town Clerk. Cemetery Records of West Hollis and Groveville,
Maine. Filmed by the Genealogical Society of Utah.
Microfilm No. 08552668.

York

Banks, Charles Edward. History of York, Maine: Successively
Known as Bristol (1632), Agamenticus (1641), Gorgeana
(1642), and York (1652). Boston: The Calkins Press, ca
1931-35. 2 Vols. [Vol. 3 never published]

Bragdon, Lester MacKenzie and John Eldridge Frost. Vital
Records of York, Maine. Rockport, ME: Picton Press
(1982).

"Name Index of Births and Marriages in York, Maine," **Register** 109 (1955).

Battin
  Abraham 24, 82
  Mary (Young) 82
  Mary+ (Young), b 1681 121
  Sarah, b ca 1705 24
Beal
  Anna 14
  Anna, b 1850 38
  Etta+ (Young), b 22 Nov
    1856 30
  George G., b 1823 14, 38
  George, Jr. 14
  George, Jr., b 1855 38
  Hannah W.+ (Young), b 1829
    14, 38
  Joseph, b 13 Jun 1843 30
  Minnie, b 1884 30
  Roscoe E., b Jun 1898 21
  Sidney R., b Jan 1900 21
Beale
  Alfreda F. (   ), b Dec
    1873 21, 120
  Ansel, b Jun 1871 21, 120
  Bethulah+ (Young), b 25 Feb
    1707/8 81
  Levi, b ca 1838 120
  please see Beal 21
  Rhoda+ (Young), b Aug 1843
    21, 120
  Roscoe E., b Jun 1898 21,
    120
  see Bale 12
  Sidney R., b Jan 1900 21,
    120
Beane
  Lewis 133
  Mary (Austin) 133
  Mehitable, b 21 Sep 1705
    133
Beattle
  see Beedle 11
Beedle
  Esther, b ca 1765 11
Bennett
  Daniel, b 1802 14
  Ebenezer 15
  Mary, b 1794 14
Berry
  Deborah M., b 4 Jan 1806
    117
  Hosiah, b 1801 93
  Sally, b 1802 93

Blaisdell
  Mary (   ) 153
  Sarah S., b 1819 153
  Theodore 153
Bone
  see Beane 133
Booker
  Hannah+ (Young), b 25 Dec
    1733 10, 37
  James, b ca 1700 109
  Mercy+ (Young), b 15 Jul
    1728 10, 109
  Nicholas, b ca 1730 37
Bourne
  Clara E.+ (Young), b ca
    1850 16
  Jonathan Avander, b ca 1845
    16
Boynton
  Mathilda+ (Young), b ca
    1800 107
  William, b ca 1795 107
Bradbury
  Abigail, b 12 Aug 1731 2
  Abigail+ (Young), b 22 Aug
    1699 2, 81
  Anne, b 2 Jun 1743 2
  Bethulah, b 20 Mar 1726/7
    2
  Cotton, b 4 Oct 1722 2
  Elizabeth, b 5 Jan 1733/4
    2
  Elizabeth, b 6 Jul 1738
    119
  Jacob, b 8 May 1736 119
  John Jr., b 18 Sep 1736 2
  John Jr., b ca 1695 2
  Joseph, b 23 Oct 1740 2
  Lucy, b 18 Jan 1724/5 2
  Maria (Cotton) 2
  Maria, b 5 Apr 1729 2
  Mary (Donnell), b ca 1710
    119
  Mary, b 1775 147
  Mary, b 30 Apr 1734 119
  Phebe+ (Young), b 25 Jan
    1702 81, 119
  Samuel, b 26 Mar 1731 119
  Sarah (Pike) 119
  Susan, b 1805 147
  Susanna, b 26 Jan 1728/9
    119

Bradbury, continued
  Thomas, b 8 May 1736 119
  Wymond 2, 119
  Wymond Jr., b 13 May 1669
    119
Bragdon
  Hannah+ (Young), b ca 1775
    37, 104
  Lucy+ (Young), b ca 1760
    96
  Lydia+ (Young) Haines, b
    1672 97, 124
  Mercy+ (Young), b ca 1725
    109
  Nancy+ (Young), b ca 1800
    111
  Patience 29
  Samuel, b 1682 97
  Samuel, b ca 1720 109
  Simeon, b ca 1795 111
  Thomas Jr., b ca 1770 37
  Warren, b ca 1755 96
Bray
  Mary (Sayward) Young, b ca
    1660 121
  Mary Young 121
  Rebecca (   ) 121
  Richard Jr. 121
  Richard Jr., b ca 1655 121
  Richard, b ca 1655 121
Bridges
  Salome, b ca 1825 13
Brock
  Elijah 94
  Julia A.+ (Young), b 1855
    94
  Nancy H. (   ) 94
Brookin
  Elizabeth, b 19 May 1717
    143
  Henry, b ca 1675 143
  Joseph, b 1 Nov 1720 143
  Mercy, b 3 Mar 1723/4 143
  Samuel, b 19 Aug 1719 143
  Sarah, b 4 Nov 1722 143
  Sarah+ (Young), b 1681
    125, 143
  Brown
  Benjamin 100
  John, b ca 1685 100
  Martha (Maxwell), b Apr
    1736 100

Brown, continued
  Mary+ (Young), b ca 1690
    100
Came
  Abigail, b 18 Sep 1700 29,
    66
  Arthur 29
  Elizabeth (   ) 136
  Elizabeth+ (Young) Webber
    Stover 29
  Elizabeth+ (Young) Webber
    Stover, b 1679 125
  Joseph 136
  Patience (Bragdon) 29, 66
  Patience, b ca 1735 136
  Samuel 66, 136
  Samuel, b ca 1675 29
  Samuel, Esq. 136
  Violet 29
Card
  Betty, b ca 1725 64
  Elizabeth, see Betty 64
  Mary, b ca 1745 106
  William 64
Carlisle
  Mary, b ca 1765 85
Carpenter
  Elias, b ca 1820 132
  Elizabeth, b ca 1735 84
  Ruth+ (Young), b ca 1825
    132
Chadbourne
  Alice, b 1663 99
  Caroline A., b ca 1835 6
Chadwick
  Elizabeth (Goodwin) 110
  Mary, b 23 Nov 1769 110
  Molly, see Mary 110
  William 110
Challies
  Hannah Ann, b ca 1845 146
Chapman
  George, b ca 1770 101
  Israel, b ca 1732 110
  John, b ca 1735 110
  John, b ca 1830 147
  Mary (Hodgdon) 110
  Mary (Wilborne) 110
  Mary, b ca 1733 110
  Mary+ (Young), b ca 1776
    101
  Miriam, b 1728 110

Dearborn
  Eveline, see Mary E.   63
  Mary E., b Oct 1841   63
Dill
  Hannah, b ca 1735   41
  Hannah, b ca 1740   50
  Mary, b ca 1740   122
Dixon
  Abigail, b ca 1715   128
  Elizabeth (   )   128
  Peter   128, 130
  Sarah, b ca 1725   55
Dodd
  Betsey Woodbury, b 26 Jan
    1824   153
  John   153
  Tamesin (   )   153
Donnell
  Abigail, b ca 1675   78
  Alice (Chadbourne), b 1663
    99
  Benjamin, b ca 1810   144
  Daniel Bragdon, b ca 1810
    37
  Hannah+ (Young), b ca 1815
    37
  Mary, b ca 1710, York   119
  Sarah Ann+ (Young), b ca
    1815   144
Dow
  Eunice (Young), b 1800s   19
  Jeremiah, b ca 1800   119
  Miriam (   ), b Dec 1772
    18
  Phoebe+ (Young), b 1802
    19, 119
Downs
  Lydia, b ca 1795   77
Duran
  Mary+ (Young), b 17 May
    1793 23, 101
  Nathaniel, b ca 1790   101
Durgin
  Benjamin, b 1836   12
    J., b 1843   12
  Sally, b 1827   12
Durning
  Margaret, b 1841   31
Dyer
  Abigail, b 1767   18
  Lydia (   ), b 1804   1
  Lydia, b 1804   1

Dyer, continued
  Thomas, b 1802   1
Eastman
  Ella H. (   ), b ca 1850
    155
Edgecomb
  Mary, b ca 1700   21
  Rachel (   )   21
  Robert   21
Elliot
  Margery   Batson   Kendall
    Young, b ca 1635   120
  Robert, b ca 1631   120
Ellis
  Lavina J. (Young), b 1828
    111
Elwell
  Abigail   28
  Abigail, b ca 1695   40
Emery
  Daniel, b ca 1815   101
  Hiram, b ca 1803   98
  Margaret+ (Young), b ca
    1808   98
  Mary+ (Young), b 8 Feb 1819
    101
  Rebecca, b 11 Aug 1838   64
  Sally, b ca 1770   92
Estes
  James M., b 1848   60
Favour
  Joseph, b ca 1700   143
  Mary, b 10 May 1726   143
  Ruth, b 15 Feb 1727   143
  Sarah, b 30 Aug 1724   143
  Sarah+ (Young), b ca 1702
    49, 143
Fernald
  Benjamin Ayres Jr., b ca
    1815   13
  Benjamin Chandler, b 25 Feb
    1842   13
  Benjamin Marvin, b 14 Feb
    1847   13
  Caroline Elizabeth, b 2 Dec
    1855   13
  Caroline   Elizabeth+
    (Young), b 24 Nov 1821
    13, 87
  Eunice L., b ca 1810   146
  James Alvah, b 25 Nov 1852
    13

Fernald, continued
  John Franklin, b 6 Dec 1839
    13
  Mary, b ca 1745 140
  Salome (Bridges), b ca 1825
    13
  Sedelia Adeline, b 25 Jan
    1845 13
Flanders
  Alice C., b Jul 1851 89
  Charlotte E., see Lottie E.
    89
  Lottie E., b 1847 89
Fletcher
  Anna+ (Young), b ca 1728 6
  Brian, b ca 1725 6
  Bryan, see Brian 6
Fogg
  Irene, b 1827 61
  William, b 1828 61
Folsom
  Olive, b ca 1785 86
Forbush
  David, b ca 1810 96
  Louisa+ (Young), b ca 1815
    96
Foss
  Betsey (   ) 143
  Ella A. (Young), b 1858 32
  Horace 143
  Nellie M., b 1858 143
Frost
  Hester Ann+ (Young), b ca
    1820 38
  James R., b ca 1815 38
  Katherine, b ca 1685 41
  Lydia, b 31 Mar 1787 112
  Nicholas 41
  William, Esq. 112
Furbish
  Martha (Lord) 150
Furbush
  Anna, b 1798 150
  Clara A. (Young), b 2 Aug
    1851 151
  Dorcas J., b 1851 143
  Joseph 150
  Martha (Lord) 150
Garvin
  Mary, b 31 May 1809 117
  Sarah (Wentworth) 117
  Wentworth 116, 117

Gatchell
  Abel 100
  Miriam (Maxwell), b Mar
    1729 100
  Susannah, b ca 1730 55
Getchell
  Albert F., b ca 1850 113
  Olive A.+ (Young), b ca
    1855 113
Gibbins
  James 21
Glidden
  Miriam (Chapman), b 1728
    110
Gooch
  Ruth 97
Goodale
  Abigail+ (Young), b ca 1800
    4
  Abner, b ca 1795 4
Goodall
  Elizabeth, see Rhoda E. 32
  Rhoda E., b 1823 32
Goodwin
  Abigail+ (Young), b ca 1800
    4
  Alice+ (Young), b 21 Apr
    1859 5
  Betsey (Bennett) 62
  Elizabeth (   ), b ca 1740
    22
  Fred H., b 2 Aug 1858 5
  George, b ca 1795 4
  Jane A., b 4 Jan 1842 62
  Joseph, b ca 1735 22
  Jotham Young, b ca 1825 94
  Nathaniel 62
Gordon
  Hannah E., b ca 1805 114
Gorman
  Hugh J., b ca 1810 108
  Mehitable H.+ (Young), b
    1810s 76, 108
Gowen
  Hazel, b Sep 1892 5
Grant
  Annie M.+ (Young), b ca
    1835 7, 142
  Daniel, b ca 1710 29
  David 31
  Elizabeth+ (Young) Sayward,
    b 25 Feb 1715 10, 29

Grant, continued
  Elizabeth+ (Young) Saywood,
    b 25 Feb 1715 29
  Frank Topliff, b ca 1865
    90
  George Samuel, b ca 1860 7
  Joanna, b 1778 42
  John P., b ca 1830 7
  Josephine+ (Young), b 10
    Oct 1868 90, 93
  Joshua 31
  Julia Ann, b 1825 144
  Lydia, b 8 Jun 1756 29
  Mirabah A. (Young), b 1860
    7
  Olive+ (Young), b ca 1764
    104, 113
  Philomalea, b 30 Mar 1759
    29
  Stephen, b ca 1760 113
Greeley
  Elizabeth+ (Young), b ca
    1690 29, 133
  Joseph, b ca 1685 29
Green
  Sarah H.+ (Young), b 1802
    76, 144
  William B., b ca 1795 144
Griffin
  Sarah J., see Susan J. 1
  Susan J., b ca 1825 1
Grover
  Abigail, b ca 1740 25
  Andrew 25
  Matthews 25
Grow
  Abigail, b 2 Dec 1760 3
  Abigail+ (Young), b 11 Jul
    1729 3
  Abigail+ (Young), b 30 Jun
    1727 2, 135
  Dorcas, b 18 Jul 1763 3
  Eunice, b 12 Jan 1757 3
  Henry, b ca 1725 2
  John, b 14 Jul 1767 3
  Joseph, b 25 Apr 1765 3
  Sally, see Sarah 42
  Sarah, b 1789 42
  Timothy, b 13 Jul 1769 3
  William 2
  William Jr., b 9 Mar 1755
    3

Grow, continued
  William, b ca 1730 3
Gullison
  Sally, b ca 1785 146
Haines
  Aquilla 133
  Aquilla Jr., b 17 Jul 1702
    134
  Eleanor, b ca 1675 107
  Lydia+ (Young), b 1672 97,
    124
  Mehitable (Beane) Young
    134
  Mehitable (Beane), b 21 Sep
    1705 133
  Mehitable (Freethy) 134
  Thomas 134
  Thomas, b 27 May 1670 97
Haley
  Miriam, b ca 1790 60
  Olive, b 1798 61
Hall
  Allen, b ca 1850 144
  Ebenezer, b ca 1735 148
  Esther, b 10 May 1790 60
  Sarah F.+ (Young), b ca
    1855 144
  Susanna+ (Young), b ca 1738
    148
Ham
  Charles 40
  Mary (Shaw) 40
  Mary M., b 1854 40
Hanson
  Mary A., b 1810 98
  Moses, b 1810 98
Harriman
  Nancy Elizabeth+ (Young), b
    1836 112
  Warren, b 1833 112
Harris
  Daniel B., b Sep 1830 15
Hart
  James, b ca 1785 97
  Lydia+ (Young), b ca 1790
    97
Hatch
  Hannah (Sawyer), b ca 1710
    47
  Jerusha+ (Young), b 15 Mar
    1711 47, 66
  Joseph, b 8 May 1709 47

Hatch, continued
  Mary (Littlefield) 47
  Samuel 47
Hayes
  Fannie J. (Young), b 11 Mar
    1856 32
  Lovina A. (Young), b 19 May
    1858 151
  Sarah, ba 14 Feb 1751 116
Haynes
  see Haines 107
Hellins
  James, b 1815 60
Henderson
  Hannah+ (Young), b ca 1805
    37
  Joseph, b ca 1800 37
  Susan P., b 1815 46
Hicks
  Daniel 114
  Pamelia A.+ (Young), b ca
    1830 76, 114
  Robert E., b ca 1825 114
  Sarah ( ) 114
Higgins
  Jerusha, b 1780 95
Hill
  Elizabeth, b ca 1740 56
  James 56
  Naomi, b ca 1735 115
  Pamela+ (Young), b 1 Feb
    1763 56, 114
  Parmela, see Pamela 56
  Theodore, b ca 1760 114
Hobbs
  Fanny C., b 10 Jun 1819 11
  Jenny C., see Fanny C. 11
  Jonathan 152
  Mary (Chadbourne) 11
  Mary D., b 1775 152
  Molly, see Mary D. 152
  William 11
Hobson
  Jane J., b 1819 143
  Joseph, b 1817 143
Hodgdon
  Mary 110
Hodsdon
  Jerusha+ (Young), b 1802
    47
  Marcy, see Mercy+

Hodsdon, continued
  Mercy+ (Young), b 19 Dec
    1768 109
  Moses Jr., b ca 1765 109
  Moses, b ca 1797 47
Holman
  Eliza Ann ( ), b 1829 14
Holt
  Rachael, b 1787 28
Hood
  John, b 1846 40
Horn
  Nancy, b 1795 60
Huff
  Eunice+ (Young), b ca 1805
    31
  Thomas, b ca 1800 31
Huston
  Abraham 88
  Edna M., b 7 Jun 1801 88
  Sarah (Littlefield) 88
Hutchins
  Abigail+ (Young), b ca 1780
    3
  Charles, b 1844 142
  Eastman, b ca 1800 101
  Enoch 141
  Grace, b 2 Jul 1785 141
  John, b 1830 147
  John, b ca 1815 113
  Mary ( ) 141
  Mary, b ca 1680 81
  Mary+, b ca 1808 101
  Olive Ann+ (Young), b 19
    Jan 1818 113, 141
  Rebecca, b 1757 62
  William 131
  William, b ca 1775 3
Ingraham
  Aaron, b 15 Sep 1737 12
  Abraham, b 15 Oct 1739 12
  Alice, b ca 1715 128
  Bethiah+ (Young), b 9 Feb
    1717/8 12, 83
  Henry, b ca 1710 12
Jackson
  Caroline+ (Young), b ca
    1820 13
  Mary Caroline+ (Young), b
    ca 1820 102
  William, b ca 1815 13, 102

Jellison
  Abigail+ (Young), b ca 1750
    3
  Betsy (   ) 38
  Esther+ (Young), b ca 1765
    30, 104
  Ichabod, b ca 1745 3
  Joel, b ca 1760 30
  Leland 38
  Sarah E., b 1846 38
Jenkins
  Eliza P., b 1845 142
Jillison
  see Jellison 3
Johnson
  Amanda (Fernald) 26
  Anna, b ca 1750 16
  Anne, see Anna 16
  Elizabeth (Adams) 8
  Elizabeth, b 23 Feb 1757
    37
  Ellen F.+ (Young), b ca
    1850 30
  Gilbert, b ca 1845 30
  Hannah, b 20 Mar 1761 37
  Hannah+ (Young), b ca 1734
    37, 128
  Humility, b 5 Dec 1762 37
  John Jr., b 29 Dec 1754 37
  John, b ca 1730 37
  Jonathan 16
  Maria F., b Nov 1857 26
  Mary, b ca 1745 84
  Nathaniel, b 12 May 1764
    37
  Ruth, b ca 1795 8
  Samuel 8
  Samuel, b 8 Aug 1759 37
  Sarah (Babb) 16
  Susanna, b ca 1720 84
  Theodore 26
Joy
  Elizabeth, b ca 1740 139
Junkins
  Abigail, b 6 Aug 1761 31
  Alexander 31
  Clara J., b Jun 1886 90
  Elijah, b 30 Aug 1763 31
  Eunice, b 27 Feb 1766 31
  Eunice+ (Young), b ca 1734
    31, 68
  Hannah, b 1769 31

Junkins,   continued
  John Jr., b 15 Sep 1759 31
  John, b 19 Jul 1733 31
  Mary Abigail, b 1815 61
  Susanna, b 24 Jun 1757 31
Keazer
  Jane, b 5 Oct 1805 35
Kelly
  Louisa Augusta (Young), b 7
    Apr 1847 11
Kendall
  Margery (Batson), b ca 1635
    120
  William 120
Kezer, see Keazer 35
Kimball
  Aaron, b ca 1785 119
  Abigail+ (Young), b ca 1795
    3, 19
  Amos, b 18 Aug 1790 3
  Daniel, b ca 1816 3
  Emma J., b 1858 101
  Esther, b ca 1814 93
  Martha, b ca 1818 3
  Polly+ (Young), b ca 1790
    119
  Samuel E., b 1846 151
  Sarah L. 114
King
  Abigail (Elwell) Young, b
    ca 1695 40
  John, b ca 1700 40
  Mary (Lydston) 81
  Patience, b ca 1700 50
  Richard 81
  Sarah, b 17 May 1687 81
Knight
  Joan, b ca 1625 122
  Robert 122
Knowlton
  Rachael (   ) 110
Knox
  Mary E., b 11 Feb 1878 110
Land
  Rosanna, b ca 1845 32
Larrabee
  Esther+ (Young), b ca 1705
    30
  Stephen, b ca 1700 30
Leach
  Alice P., b 1855 15
  Andrew 15

Leavitt
  Andrew J., b 1829 28
  Susanna, b 1832 28
LeBreton
  Elizabeth (   ) 54
  Elizabeth, b ca 1695 54
  Philip 54
Lewis
  Jeremiah, b Apr 1877 143
  Willie, b Dec 1868 143
Libby
  Arena, b 1847 62
  Hannah+ (Young), b ca 1750
    37
  Stephen, b ca 1745 37
Littlefield
  Alice P., b 27 Mar 1821 78
  Augustus T., b ca 1845 108
  Eliza Jane, b 14 Feb 1836
    28
  Eliza U. 28
  Joseph 28
  Melissa O.+ (Young), b ca
    1850 108
  Miriam, b 1819 88
  Roger 100
  Susanna (Maxwell), b Mar
    1734 100
Livingston
  Asa, b 1819 96
  Dorothy, b 1819 96
Long
  Mary, b ca 1786 117
Longfellow
  Patience+ (Young), b ca
    1752 115
  Stephen, b ca 1745 115
Lord
  John Calvin, b ca 1825 114
  Olive Esther+ (Young), b 29
    Mar 1829 60, 114
Love
  Patience (Young), b ca 1763
    139
Lowe
  Dorcas, b 1773 140
  Mary, b ca 1775 140
Lucas
  see McLucas 36
Luke
  Emma Susan, b Dec 1859 144
  George W. 144

Luke, continued
  George W., b ca 1835 144
  Sarah Semantha+ (Young), b
    12 Nov 1840 46, 144
MacIntire
  Daniel, b 5 Sep 1717 147
  Ebenezer, b 16 Apr 1714
    147
  Hannah, b 6 Nov 1712 147
  John, b 25 Feb 1710/11 147
  John, b ca 1670 147
  Joseph, b 25 Mar 1707 147
  Samuel, b 20 Sep 1721 147
  Susanna, b 16 May 1709 147
  Susanna+ (Young), b 1677
    147
Main
  Dorothy (Trafton) 105
  Mercy, b ca 1710 105
Marston
  Aurelia, b 1803 45
Mason
  Frank, b 1852 33
  George E., b ca 1825 101
  Ham 59
  Mary+ (Young), b ca 1830
    101
Masterson
  Elizabeth (Cogswell) 133
  Elizabeth, b ca 1660 133
  Nathaniel 133
Maston
  Eunice+ (Young), ca 1805
    31
  John, b ca 1775 31
Mathias
  Hannah, b 1831 112
Matthews
  Mary (   ) 124
  Susanna, b ca 1650 124
  Walter 124
Maxwell
  Abigail, b Mar 1720 100
  Barak, b Jan 1732 100
  Daniel F., Capt. 100
  David, b Jun 1724 100
  Gershom Jr., b Mar 1740
    100
  Gershom, b ca 1696 100
  John, b Mar 1722 100
  Martha, b Apr 1736 100

Maxwell, continued
  Mary+ (Young), b ca 1698
    100
  Miriam, b Mar 1729 100
  Susanna, b Mar 1734 100
Maybury
  Eliza C. (Young), b 25 May
    1860 89
McDaniel
  James, b ca 1760 148
  Susanna+ (Young), b ca 1764
    148
McDonald
  Betty, b 1 Aug 1754 47
  Daniel, b 23 Feb 1757 47
  James, b 25 Apr 1759 47
  Joan+ (Young), b 10 Mar
    1731/2 47, 50
  Michael, b ca 1725 47
McGowan
  Sarah, b ca 1860 26
McInnes
  Mary, b ca 1725 4
  William 4
McIntire
  Daniel 69
  Martha+ (Young), b ca 1790
    98
  Nancy, b ca 1776 69
  Susanna (Simpson) 69
  Susanna+ (Young), b 1677
    125
  Timothy, b ca 1785 98
McLaughlin
  John 24
McLucas
  Benjamin, b ca 1765 24
  Dorcas+ (Young), b ca 1770
    24
  Hannah (   )+, b ca 1760
    36
  Oliver, b ca 1760 36
Mighel
  Daniel, b 1790 35
Milgate
  Alice A., b ca 1860 11
Milliken
  Rebecca, b Jan 1850 89
Mitchell
  Alfred M., b Sep 1857 94
  Daniel T., b ca 1835 96
  Isaac, b 1828 94

Mitchell, continued
  Julia M.+ (Young), b Sep
    1829 53
  Lucy E.+ (Young), b 1840
    96
Moody
  Benjamin, b 1797 132
  Elizabeth (Scannan) 75
  Mehitable, b 4 Dec 1775 75
  Sally+ (Young), b 17 Dec
    1795 23, 132
  William Pepperell 75
Morrill
  Hannah, b ca 1790 86
Moulton
  Abigail+ (Young), b ca 1776
    3
  Alice (Chadbourne) Donnell,
    b 1663 99
  Daniel Jr., b ca 1770 3
  Eunice+ (Young), b ca 1800
    31
  George 109
  George C., b 1855 109
  George D., b 29 Feb 1824
    112
  George M., b 1849 109
  Harriet E.+ (Young), b ca
    1820 38
  Herbert H., b 1858 109
  James Heber 3
  Jeremiah, b ca 1795 31
  Jeremiah, Esq., b ca 1650
    99
  Jonathan, b 19 Jul 1820
    109
  Joseph, b 18 Jan 1679/80
    99
  Joshua, b ca 1815 38
  Mary, b 14 Jan 1681/2 99
  Mary+ (Young), b 1653/4
    99, 124
  Mercy+ (Young), b 7 Sep
    1818 77
  Nancy (   ) 109
  Nancy A., b 1853 109
  Nancy C., b 1847 109
  Nancy Frost+ (Young), b 28
    Mar 1828 112, 113
  Olive, b 3 Jun 1820 78
  Persis (Young), b ca 1758
    92

Mudgett
  Dorcas+ (Young), b 26 Jun
    1833 24, 35
  Jacob D., b ca 1828 24
Murch
  Joanna, b 9 Sep 1726 148
  John, b 2 May 1730 148
  Tabitha, b 12 Aug 1728 148
  Tabitha+ (Young), b 6 Oct
    1705 108, 148
  William, b ca 1700 148
Murphy
  James, b 1827 38
  Mary, b 1830 38
Nason
  Batholomew 59
  Caleb 59
  Daniel 59
  David 59
  John 59
  Molly 59
  Nathaniel 59
Nelson
  Mary F. (Young), b 30 Sep
    1839 11
Newman
  Abigail (Young), b 24 Oct
    1718 41
  Thomas 41
Nichols
  Dorcas A., b 1815 154
Norton
  John 130
  John Jr., b ca 1720 100
  Mary, b ca 1749 130
  Mary+ (Young), b ca 1723
    100, 128
  Olive+ (Young), b ca 1770
    113
  William, b ca 1765 113
  William, b ca 1771 55
Nowell
  Dorcas C., b 1794 78
  Dorcas, b 1785 105
  Joanna, b 1774 73
  Katherine 69
  Marcy, see Mercy 69
  Mercy, b 1736 69
  Peter 69
Nutter
  Mary K., b 1808 102

Palmer
  Alfred, b 1859 12
  Lucy A., b 1840 12
  Sarah E., b May 1860 12
  William, b 1835 12
Peabel
  see Preble 5
Peare
  Abigail+ (Young), b ca 1790
    3
  Jacob, b ca 1780 3
Peavey
  Alice, b 8 Oct 1800 110
  Daniel 111
  Dorothy, b 1789 110
  Mary (   ) 111
Peirce
  Sarah, b ca 1815 154
Perkins
  Abner F. 30, 102
  Alexander, b 1835 78
  Edmund Trafton, b 11 Jun
    1836 102
  Edward M., b 1854 114
  Emma+ (Young), b Jun 1859
    30, 36
  Grenville, b ca 1815 114
  Isaac, b ca 1745 143
  James Mills, b 10 Sep 1842
    30
  Mary H. (Allen) 30, 102
  Mary Jane+ (Young), b 17
    Dec 1836 88, 102
  Nancy, b ca 1790 132
  Olive B.+ (Young), b ca
    1820 114
  Sarah L. (Kimball), b 1850s
    114
  Sarah+ (Young), b ca 1750
    143
Phelps
  Theodora (Wheelock), b ca
    1735 56
Phillips
  Hannah, b 1800 53
Phinney
  Leonard S., b Jan 1870 14
Pike
  Ambrose, b 1829 28
  Eliza Jane+ (Young), b 1829
    28, 146
  Eunice, b Dec 1815 14

Row
  Ransey, b ca 1770 33
Runnels
  Sarah, b ca 1830 62
Ryan
  Mary S., b 24 Jun 1852 45
Sadler
  Mary, b 17 Mar 1841 99
Sargent
  Daniel, b ca 1770 101
  Hannah, b ca 1750 151
Sawyer
  Anna L., b ca 1850 98
  Elizabeth H., b ca 1860
    146
  Hannah, b ca 1710 47
Sayward
  Chanty, b 1813 154
  Elizabeth+ (Young), b 25
    Feb 1715 10, 29
  Hannah, b ca 1795 47
  Henry 81, 82, 121
  John 82
  John, b 1814 154
  Joseph 82
  Mary (Peasley) 81, 121
  Mary, b ca 1660 121
  Susan, b 1805 53
Saywood
  Joseph, b ca 1720 29
Scruton
  Charles E., b 1851 147
  Darius K. 147
  Harriet R. (Speed) 147
  Susan A.+ (Young), b 1859
    111, 147
Sedgeley
  Betsey+ (Young), b ca 1790
    12
  Elizabeth+ (Young), b ca
    1760 29, 104
  John, b ca 1785 12
  Joseph, b ca 1755 29
Shamber
  John, b 1816 119
  Sophia, b 1820 119
Shapleigh
  Myra S. (Prescott), b 11
    Oct 1846 21
  Oliver Waldron 21

Shatswell
  Ellen Jane (Young), b 31
    May 1841 11
Shaw
  Huldah+ (Young), b ca 1750
    40
  Samuel, b ca 1745 40
Shedd
  Mabel L., b 25 Feb 1861 35
Sherman
  Hannah, b ca 1785 94
  Ivory, b ca 1785 132
  Perthenia, b ca 1815 132
  Sally, b ca 1817 132
  Sally+ (Young), b 1790 57,
    132
Shorey
  Charlotte+ (Young), b ca
    1825 15, 77
  Daniel, b ca 1820 15
Simpson
  Abigail, b 17 Jul 1722 108
  Abigail, b Dec 1723 108
  Ann L. (Plaisted) 101
  Charles E., b 1841 101
  Ebenezer, b 8 Jan 1736/7
    109
  Edward, b ca 1810 102
  Henry Jr., 8 Jul 1732 109
  Henry, b ca 1680 108
  Ivory, b 1794 101
  John, b Nov 1724 108
  John, ca 1718 108
  Mary Ann, b 16 Sep 1822
    152
  Mary Elizabeth+, b ca 1813
    102
  Mary+ (Young), b ca 1800
    53, 101
  Mercy, b 27 Feb 1741 109
  Mercy+ (Young), b 1685
    108, 125
  Paul, b 1 Jan 1723/4 108
  Samuel, b 30 Nov 1726 108
  Tabitha, b 22 Jul 1730 109
  Thomas, b 9 Oct 1738 109
  Woodbury, b 1812 152
Sinnot
  Joseph 19
  Sally (Young), b 1790s 19

Thombs
  see also Alice Boulter
  Thomas 44
Thompson
  Charles Standish, b 1801
    30
  Elizabeth S.+ (Young), b
    1806 30, 76
  Rhoda ( ), b ca 1785 86
Tibbetts
  Lurana+ (Young), b ca 1735
    96
  see Tebbetts 88
  William, b ca 1730 96
Tilton
  Maria E. (Young) 2
  Maria E. (Young), b 1838
    147
Todd
  Andrew W. 13
  Anna (Beale), b 1850 38
  Caroline M.+ (Young), b
    1852 13, 111
  George A. 38
  George A., b 1848 13
  Phebe K. (Littlefield) 13
Townson
  Betsey, b ca 1795 20
Trafton
  Benjamin, b ca 1825 95
  Ebenezer 30
  Ellen F.+ (Young), b 21 Apr
    1861 30, 111
  Josiah 105
  Julie Ann+ (Young), b ca
    1830 95
  Lydia Elizabeth, b 1827
    111
  Phebe P. (Osgood) 30
  William L., b 1849 30
Tripp
  Anna (Littlefield) 151
  John 151
  Louisa, b 1 Dec 1833 151
  Mary G. (Clark) 21
  Olive Ann, b 15 Oct 1832
    21
  Theodore 21
Tucker
  Dorcas+ (Young), b 21 Apr
    1771 24, 73
  Samuel, b ca 1765 24

Turnbow
  Mary Caroline 29
Tuttle
  Hannah Jane+ (Young), b
    1836 20, 38
  John Henry, b ca 1830 38
Twombly
  Asenith (Young), b 1810s
    77
Wadleigh
  Robert 53
  Sarah (Smith) 53
  Sarah, b 1655 53
Wagner
  Eunice, b ca 1815 20
Walker
  Joshua, b 1800 7
  Susan ( ), b 1803 7
Wallace
  Elizabeth, b ca 1765 92
Wallett
  Ida E., b Jul 1856 16
Wallingford
  Alice+ (Young), b ca 1818
    5
  Henry, b ca 1815 5
  Susannah, b ca 1765 27
Ware
  see Weare 97
Warren
  Anna+ (Young), b ca 1760 6
  Benjamin 96
  Dominicus, b 1782 7
  Edmund, b 1800 7
  Eunice (Weymouth) 96
  Eunice, b 20 Aug 1822 96
  Francis G., MD, b 4 Mar
    1828 96
  Hezekiah, b 1785 7
  Joseph, b 18 Sep 1797 7
  Joshua Jr., b 1781 7
  Joshua, b 14 Apr 1758 6
  Lovinia+ (Young), b 1803
    96
  Mary A., b ca 1845 64
  Stephen, b 12 Dec 1800 96
  Thomas, b 16 Jul 1788 7
  Weymouth, b 6 Jul 1803 7
Waterhouse
  David 154
Watt
  Alexander, b 1797 6

187

Watt, continued
  Ann+ (Young), b 1801   6
Weare
  Hopewell, b ca 1690   97
  John, b 9 Sep 1720   97
  Joseph, b 25 Oct 1718   97
  Lydia+ (Young), b ca 1700
    49, 97
  Mary (Purington)   97
  Mary Purington   97
  Peter   97
  Ruth (Gooch)   97
  Ruth Gooch   97
Webber
  Elizabeth, b 12 Oct 1705
    29
  Elizabeth+ (Young), b 1679
    28, 125
  Gershom, b ca 1710   109
  Joseph, b 24 Jul 1727   29
  Mercy+ (Young), b 25 Jan
    1714   108, 109
  Nathaniel, b 9 Sep 1722   29
  Paul, b 7 Oct 1729   29
  Samuel   28
  Samuel Jr., b ca 1675   28
  Sarah, b 31 Jan 1719/20   29
Wells
  Job, b 17 Jan 1729/30   97
  John Jr., b ca 1680   99
  John, b ca 1695   97
  Lydia, b 22 Jan 1727/8   97
  Lydia+ (Young) Weare, b ca
    1700   49, 97
  Mary+ (Young) Stover, b
    1676   99, 125
  Nehemiah, b 1737   97
  Sarah, b 25 Aug 1733   97
Wentworth
  Abbie   46
  Asenith D.+ (Young), b ca
    1825   7
  Cynthia Delana+ (Young), b
    ca 1823   16
  Jane, b Dec 1820   46
  Lydia (Thompson)   151
  Nathaniel, b ca 1820   7, 16
  Patience (Downs)   87
  Patience, b 9 Aug 1790   87
  Rosanna (Hill)   87
  Sabrina, b Jan 1826   151
  Samuel   87, 151

Wheeler
  Mercy, b ca 1840   73
  Rachel, b ca 1685   7
Wheelock
  Theodore, b ca 1735   56
Whitehouse
  Herbert L.   94
Whiting
  Florence S. (Young), b 1855
    89
Whitney
  Lydia+ (Young), b 15 Oct
    1711   97, 108
  Nathan, b ca 1705   97
  Ruth, b 1804   101
Whitten
  Eunice, b Jul 1817   20
Whittum
  Mary, b ca 1820   120
Wiggins
  Alice (Peavey) Young, b 8
    Oct 1800   111
  Joseph, b 1804   111
Wildes
  John F., b ca 1840   145
  Sophia J.+ (Young), b ca
    1843   145
Wilkinson
  Grace, b Feb 1879   89
Willand
  Mary L. (Young), b 3 Jul
    1855   151
Willard
  Adeline, b 17 Feb 1825   151
  Louisa (Tripp)   151
  Stephen   151
Williams
  Frances A., b ca 1845   7
Wilson
  Catherine, b ca 1715   13
  Ruth, b ca 1770   59
Winn
  Martha, b 1840   98
Witham
  Jeremiah   20
  Sarah, b ca 1780   20
Witlaw
  Louisa, b 1814   155
Wright
  Narsis Albra, b ca 1865   14
York
  Betty, b ca 1740   154

INDEX II. THE YOUNGS
(+ signifies main entry)

Young

Alice P. (Leach), b 1855 15

Alice P. (Littlefield), b 27 Mar 1821 78

Alice+, b 21 Apr 1859 5

Alice+, b ca 1818 5

Almira+, b 1842 5

Almon G., b 9 Jun 1874 34

Almon, b 10 Dec 1831 20

Alphonso, b 1846 142

Alphonsus B., b Jun 1879 93

Althea F., b Dec 1887 12

Alvah, b 19 Jul 1818 111

Amaziah ( )+, b ca 1765 5

Amelia A., b 3 Sep 1842 20

Amelia, b 1819 13

Ammi+, b 1800 6

Amos Jr., b 1861 6

Amos+, b 1828 6

Amos+, b 1831 6, 34

Amy ( ), b ca 1855 34

Amy S., b Mar 1893 47

Andrew G., b Dec 1893 41

Ann (Babb), b ca 1805 20

Ann J., b 1854 28, 112

Ann L.+, b 1853 6

Ann+, b 1801 6

Ann+, b ca 1720 6

Anna ( )+, b 1715 6

Anna (Furbush), b 1798 150

Anna (Johnson) 1, 20, 35

Anna (Johnson), b ca 1750 16

Anna Bell, b 1854 62

Anna K., b 1844 154

Anna L. (Sawyer), b ca 1850 98

Anna L., b 1846 105

Anna, bp 10 Jun 1759 6, 149

Anna+, b 23 Feb 1775 7

Anna+, b ca 1728 6

Anna+, b ca 1760 6

Anne (Barton), b ca 1730 112

Anne (Johnson) 86

Annette, b 19 Apr 1846 20

Annie M.+, b ca 1835 7, 142

Young

Annie N. ( ), b 1893 151

Anthony+, b ca 1680 7

Ariana, see Anna 38

Arthur Stuart, b 13 Aug 1885 35

Asenith D.+, b ca 1825 7

Asenith, b 1810s 77

Augusta+, b 1835 7

Augustus D.+, b 6 Jan 1841 7, 147

Augustus, b 1853 154

Aurelia (Marston), b 1803 45

Aurora ( ), b 1816 150

Benaiah 11, 29, 37, 64, 109

Benaiah+, b 1670s 125

Benaiah+, b 1690s 8

Benaiah+, b 1763 11

Benaiah+, Jr., b 9 Feb 1724 10, 11

Benjamin 15

Benjamin F. 32

Benjamin F. Jr., b Jan 1890 12

Benjamin F., b 26 Jul 1843 11

Benjamin F., b 9 Jun 1838 34

Benjamin F.+, b ca 1855 11

Benjamin F.+, Jul 1855 11

Benjamin, b 21 Oct 1724 126

Benjamin, bp 22 Jul 1770 140

Benjamin+, b 19 Nov 1810 11

Bertha A., b 25 May 1848 20

Bertha, b Oct 1879 146

Bessie M., b 1876 15

Bethiah+, b 5 Sep 1709 12, 81

Bethiah+, b 9 Feb 1717/8 12, 83

Bethulah+, b 25 Feb 1707/8 12, 81

Betsey ( )+, b ca 1785 12

Betsey (Cook) 101

Young

Betsey (Townson), b ca 1795
  20
Betsey H. (   )+, b 1801
  12
Betsey Woodbury (Dodd), b
  26 Jan 1824 153
Betsey, b 12 Nov 1790 23
Betsey, b 1756 63
Betsey, b 3 Apr 1834 93
Betsey+, b ca 1790 12
Betty (Small), b ca 1765
  23
Betty (York), b ca 1740
  154
Brigham 7, 27
Caleb Hammond+, b ca 1710
  13
Caleb+, b ca 1710 12
Caleb+, b ca 1712 13
Carl F., b Aug 1892 95
Carmela, see Pamela 13
Caroline (Smith) 16
Caroline (Smith), b 1 Jan
  1836 27
Caroline A. (   ), b 15 Mar
  1852 64
Caroline A. (   ), b Mar
  1852 64
Caroline A. (Chadbourne), b
  ca 1835 6
Caroline Elizabeth+, b 24
  Nov 1821 13, 87
Caroline M.+, b 1852 13,
  111
Caroline+, b 16 Jan 1838
  13
Caroline+, b 1849 13, 26
Caroline+, b ca 1820 13
Catherine (Wilson), b ca
  1715 13
Catherine, b 1850 26
Celeste, b 1844 142
Celina (   ), b Jan 1850
  152
Charles 155
Charles A., b 1849 24
Charles E., b 1840 142
Charles F. 38
Charles F., b 1843 28
Charles F.+, b 18 Apr 1819
  14, 113

Young

Charles F.+, b 1800 14
Charles H., b 10 Mar 1838
  20
Charles H.+, b 1846 14
Charles H.+, b Feb 1854
  15, 152
Charles Henry+, b 26 Jul
  1843 11, 15
Charles M. H.+, b 1856 15,
  105
Charles P., b Apr 1855 105
Charles P.+, b ca 1805 15
Charles S., b Apr 1852 105
Charles W., b 28 Jul 1865
  64
Charles, b 1838 21
Charles, b 1848 87
Charles, b 25 Apr 1855 119
Charles, b Jan 1888 90
Charles+, b 1795 13
Charles+, b 1818 14
Charles+, b 1821 14
Charles+, b 1839 14
Charles+, b ca 1860 14
Charles+, b Jun 1812 14
Charles+, b Sept 1838 14
Charlotte Emma, b 17 Mar
  1892 89
Charlotte, b 1844 154
Charlotte+, b 1801 15
Charlotte+, b ca 1825 15,
  77
Charlotty, b 1798 141
Claiborne A.+, b ca 1855
  16
Clara A., b 2 Aug 1851 151
Clara A., b 31 Jul 1846 32
Clara C., b 1848 111
Clara E.+, b ca 1850 16
Clara J. (Rhodes), b ca
  1850 154
Clara, b 1848 64
Clara, b 1857 89
Clara, see Clarissa A. 89
Clarence L.+, b May 1856
  16, 27
Clifford H., b Oct 1894 15
Cora B. (   ), b 1892 151
Cora C. (   ), b Feb 1868
  95
Cora E., b Nov 1879 27

Young

Coral O. (   ), b 1857 5
Cynthia Delana+, b ca 1823
    16
Cyrena (Thinnell), b 1810
    15
Daisy E., b Jul 1894 46
Daniel 1, 3, 16, 20, 26,
    35, 38, 40, 86, 101, 109,
    119, 120, 150, 153
Daniel 2nd+, b ca 1765 19
Daniel L. 148
Daniel L.+, b Mar 1828 21,
    88
Daniel, b 14 Dec 1725 83
Daniel, b 15 Jun 1842 24
Daniel, b 1785 59
Daniel, b 1790s 19
Daniel, b 26 Aug 1764 22
Daniel+, b 14 Jan 1800 20,
    23
Daniel+, b 1747 16
Daniel+, b 2 Feb 1812 60
Daniel+, b 2 Nov 1765 18,
    149
Daniel+, b 3 Feb 1814 20
Daniel+, b 7 Sep 1753 18
Daniel+, b ca 1680 54
Daniel+, b ca 1725 16
Daniel+, b ca 1750 18
Daniel+, b ca 1760 18
Daniel+, b ca 1785 20
Daniel+, b ca 1795 20
Daniel+, b ca 1805 23
Daniel+, b ca 1810 20
Daniel+, Jr., b ca 1780
    18, 20
Daniel+, Jr., b ca 1790 20
David 5, 20, 23, 32, 44,
    101, 132
David aka Jr., b ca 1735
    22
David Jr., b 23 Oct 1763
    22
David Jr., b 7 May 1832 24
David W., b Jan 1883 15
David, b 1808 40
David, b 1843 152
David, b 4 Aug 1770 149
David+, b 1809 24
David+, b 1810 24
David+, b 1822 24

Young

David+, b ca 1695 21
David+, b ca 1735 22
David+, b ca 1760 23
David+, b pre 1775 23
David+, Jr., b 24 Jun 1798
    23
David+, Jr., ba 23 Oct 1763
    23
Deborah (Furber) 32
Deborah M. (Berry) 142
Deborah M. (Berry), b 4 Jan
    1806 117
Delia F., b Jul 1881 146
Delphina, b 1833 32
Dora M., b 28 Dec 1878 45
Dorcas (   ), b 1700s 8
Dorcas (   ), b ca 1728 16
Dorcas (Babb), b ca 1730
    84
Dorcas (Babb), b ca 1745
    25
Dorcas (Crocet), b ca 1765)
    18
Dorcas (Day), b ca 1715
    135
Dorcas (Lowe) 26
Dorcas (Lowe), b 1773 140
Dorcas (Young), b ca 1730
    41
Dorcas A. (Nichols), b 1815
    154
Dorcas J. (Furbush), b 1851
    143
Dorcas N. (   ) 64, 120
Dorcas, b 26 Jun 1833 35
Dorcas, b 9 Oct 1750 50
Dorcas, b ca 1730 41
Dorcas+, b 21 Apr 1771 24,
    73
Dorcas+, b Apr 1852 24
Dorcas+, b ca 1770 24
Dorothy (Peavey), b 1789
    110
Dwight G., b 1881 27
Ebenezer 25
Ebenezer, b 1699 108
Ebenezer+, b 24 Aug 1729
    25
Ebenezer+, b 5 Apr 1701
    24, 108
Ebenezer+, b ca 1740 25

Young

Ebenezer+, b ca 1745   25
Edgar J.+, b 26 Nov 1856
   26
Edmund   95
Edmund J.+, b 1855   26
Edmund J.+, b ca 1838   26,
   76
Edmund, b 1844   118
Edmund, b 1849   45
Edna F., b Sep 1896   27
Edna M. (Huston)   21, 35,
   102, 132, 151
Edna M. (Huston), b 7 Jun
   1801   88
Edna, b 19 Mar 1832   88
Edward C.   13
Edward C. Jr., b 1843   26
Edward C.+, b ca 1818   26
Edward D.+, b Apr 1855   26,
   78
Edward E.+, b 5 Apr 1852
   27, 119
Edward, b 1800   99
Edward, b Feb 1884   93
Edward+, b 1797   26, 141
Edwin R., b Feb 1886   46
Edwin, b 1846   120
Eleanor (Haines)   97, 105
Eleanor (Haines), b ca 1675
   107
Eleanor (Haynes)   24, 27,
   36, 109, 147, 148
Eleanor J. (Allard)   26
Eleanor, b 12 Jan 1750   55
Eleanor, b 1810s   96
Eleanor+, b 6 Jan 1717/8
   27, 108
Eleanora E. (   ), b Nov
   1859   111
Eleazer+, bp 25 Apr 1742
   27
Elijah   16
Elijah, b ca 1790   19
Elijah+, b 14 Feb 1830   27
Eliphalet   77, 87, 150
Eliphalet+, b ca 1760   27
Eliza (   )   112
Eliza (   ), b 1810   112
Eliza (Roberts)   6
Eliza (Roberts), b 1807   33

Young

Eliza A. (   ), b Apr 1847
   46
Eliza A., b 12 Jan 1854
   151
Eliza Ann (   )   155
Eliza Ann (   ) Holman, b
   1829   14
Eliza B., b 23 Jan 1830   20
Eliza C., b 25 May 1860   89
Eliza Jane+ (Littlefield),
   b 14 Feb 1836   28
Eliza Jane+, b 1829   28,
   146
Eliza, b 1814   40
Eliza, b 1844   119
Eliza, b 1851   142
Eliza+ (   ), b 1810   28
Eliza+ (   ), b 1821   28
Eliza+, b 1813   28
Eliza+, b 1836   28
Eliza+, b 1842   28
Elizabeth (   ) Goodwin, b
   ca 1740   22
Elizabeth (Carpenter), b ca
   1735   84
Elizabeth (Hill)   58, 114
Elizabeth (Joy), b ca 1740
   139
Elizabeth (LeBreton), b ca
   1695   54
Elizabeth (Masterson)   29,
   40, 66, 102
Elizabeth (Masterson), b ca
   1660   133
Elizabeth (Nason)   109
Elizabeth (Smith)   5, 20,
   23, 32, 44, 101, 132
Elizabeth (Smith), b 1764
   23
Elizabeth (Trafton)   13
Elizabeth (Wallace), b 8
   Apr 1762   92
Elizabeth C.+, b Dec 1824
   30
Elizabeth Garvin, b 3 Apr
   1834   118
Elizabeth H. (Sawyer), b ca
   1860   146
Elizabeth S.+, b 1806   30,
   76

Young

Elizabeth, b 13 May 1834 24

Elizabeth, b 14 May 1731 25

Elizabeth, b 1829 147

Elizabeth, b 1834 34

Elizabeth, b 1849 89

Elizabeth, b 5 Oct 1766 22

Elizabeth, b 8 Feb 1759 56

Elizabeth, bp 24 Jun 1764 139

Elizabeth+, b 10 May 1721 29, 68

Elizabeth+, b 14 May 1741 29

Elizabeth+, b 1679 28, 125

Elizabeth+, b 1828 30

Elizabeth+, b 23 Apr 1710 29, 66

Elizabeth+, b 25 Feb 1715 10, 29

Elizabeth+, b ca 1690 29, 133

Elizabeth+, b ca 1740 29

Elizabeth+, b ca 1760 29, 104

Ella A., b 1858 32

Ella H. ( ) Eastman, b ca 1850 155

Ella M. ( ), b 1855 142

Ella N. ( ), b Dec 1840 145

Ellen F.+, b 21 Apr 1861 30, 111

Ellen F.+, b ca 1850 30

Ellen Jane, b 31 May 1841 11

Ellen, b Dec 1888 15

Elmer E., b Jan 1853 27

Elmer R., b Aug 1897 15

Elsie M., b Jun 1895 64

Emily, b 1838 31

Emma A., b 1858 64

Emma E., b 7 Mar 1865 38

Emma Elizabeth, b 26 Mar 1873 93

Emma, b 1849 145

Emma+, b Jun 1859 30, 36

Enos, b 8 Feb 1837 24

Esther (Beedle), b ca 1765 11

Young

Esther (Hall) 114

Esther (Hall), b 10 May 1790 60

Esther (Kimball), b ca 1814 93

Esther P., b Oct 1893 16

Esther+, b ca 1705 30

Esther+, b ca 1765 30, 104

Ethel M., b Dec 1888 46

Etta M. (Alley), b Apr 1860 26

Etta M.+, b ca 1869 31

Etta+, b 22 Nov 1856 30

Eunice ( ) 6, 18, 38, 57, 149

Eunice ( ), b ca 1735 149

Eunice (Wagner) 38

Eunice (Wagner), b ca 1815 20

Eunice (Whitten) 40, 120

Eunice (Whitten), b Jul 1817 20

Eunice D., b 6 Apr 1828 20

Eunice L. ( ) 1

Eunice L. ( ), b 1793 146

Eunice L. (Fernald) 7

Eunice L. (Fernald), b ca 1810 146

Eunice, b 1800s 19

Eunice, bp 17 Mar 1757 149

Eunice, see Maria E. 147

Eunice+, b 1836 31

Eunice+, b ca 1734 31, 68

Eunice+, b ca 1780 31

Eunice+, b ca 1800 31

Eunice+, b ca 1805 31

Eva M., b ca 1838 26

Fannie A.+, n.d. 31

Fannie J., b 11 Mar 1856 32

Fannie J., b 1857 111

Fanny ( ), b 1793 32

Fanny (Bacon), b 1793 32

Fanny C. (Hobbs), b 10 Jun 1819 11

Florence S. ( ), b Nov 1864 41

Florence S., b 1855 89

Florence, b 1 Nov 1862 93

Young

Florence, b Nov 1886   47
Frances A. (Williams), b ca
1845   7
Frances, b 11 Mar 1850   32
Frances, b 1836   14
Frances, b 1841   21
Francis   100
Francis H., b 1827   61
Francis Jr., b 1831   32
Francis, b 1832   13
Francis+, b 14 Jul 1788
23, 32
Francis+, b ca 1650   31
Frank Gilman, b 7 Oct 1880
144
Frank, see John F.   89
Franklin P., b 1883   90
Fred R., b May 1887   46
Freda F. (   ), b May, 1854
148
Freddie E., b May 1891   63
Frederic C., b 1889   90
Frederic L.+, b ca 1840   32
Frederick, b 1858   27
Freeth, b 1856   21
Furber+, b 19 Jan 1827   32
Garth Galbraith, b 1892   16
George   6, 24, 35, 63, 155
George A., b 1847   21
George A., b 23 Jun 1875
64
George A.+, b 1839   34, 150
George A.+, b ca 1850   34
George A.+, b Jan 1840   34
George E.   142
George E., b ca 1810   141
George H.   34, 90
George H., b 30 Jun 1841
34
George H., b May 1880   155
George H.+, b 11 Feb 1808
120
George H.+, b May 1861   34,
152
George Johnson, b 17 Jun
1883   27
George M., b 1853   61
George R.+, b 3 Dec 1799
35
George R.+, b 7 Apr 1843
35

Young

George S.   7
George S., b 1846   142
George W.   30, 89
George W., b 1885   90
George W.+, b 1866   36
George W.+, b 7 Jul 1821
35, 88
George W.+, b ca 1840   36
George, b 1844   26
George+, b 11 Feb 1808   34
George+, b 11 Jun 1786   33
George+, b 1802   33, 77
George+, b 3 Dec 1799   63
George+, b ca 1755   5, 32
George+, b ca 1766   33
George+, b ca 1780   33
George+, b ca 1805   34
Georgianna (Ricker)   90
Georgianna (Ricker), b 16
Jan 1845   93
Georgianna (Summ), b ca
1850   45
Georgianna, b 7 Nov 1849
153
Grace (Hutchins)   113, 118,
141
Grace (Hutchins), b 2 Jul
1785   141
Grace S. (   ), b 27 Feb
1810   155
Habijah see Abijah   4
Hannah (   )   37, 55, 100
Hannah (   ), b 1856   143
Hannah (   ), b ca 1675   49
Hannah (   ), b ca 1695
126
Hannah (   )+, b ca 1755
36
Hannah (   )+, b ca 1760
36
Hannah (Banks)   94, 115,
132
Hannah (Banks), b 1758   56
Hannah (Chick), b 28 Jul
1821   89
Hannah (Dill), b ca 1735
41
Hannah (Dill), b ca 1740
50
Hannah (Lane)   153

Young

Hannah (Mathias), b 1831 112

Hannah (Morrill), b ca 1790 86

Hannah (Preble), b 7 Feb 1694 125

Hannah (Sargent), b ca 1750 151

Hannah (Sayward), b ca 1795 47

Hannah (Sherman) 4

Hannah (Sherman), b ca 1785 94

Hannah Ann (Challies), b ca 1845 146

Hannah E. (   ), b 23 Dec 1853 146

Hannah E. (Gordon), b ca 1805 114

Hannah F., b 11 Jul 1834 88

Hannah Jane+, b 1836 20, 38

Hannah W.+, b 1829 14, 38

Hannah, b 1836 60

Hannah, b 20 Apr 1826 20

Hannah, b 24 Sep 1717 25

Hannah, b 25 Mar 1829 60

Hannah, b 27 Jan 1812 141

Hannah, b 6 Jun 1803 23

Hannah, b 7 Jul 1850 24

Hannah+, b 1829 37

Hannah+, b 1830 38

Hannah+, b 1836 38

Hannah+, b 25 Dec 1733 10, 37

Hannah+, b 5 Jan 1698 36, 108

Hannah+, b 8 Feb 1745 37, 129

Hannah+, b ca 1734 37, 128

Hannah+, b ca 1750 37

Hannah+, b ca 1775 37, 104

Hannah+, b ca 1805 37

Hannah+, b ca 1815 37

Harriet Augusta, b 7 Apr 1835 87

Harriet E.+, b ca 1820 38

Harriet M., b 11 Jan 1830 33

Harriet, b 1843 14

Young

Harry M. E., b 9 Jun 1874 34

Harry M., b 5 Apr 1881 34

Henry J.+, b 1837 38, 150

Henry, b 19 Jul 1818 111

Henry+, b ca 1735 38

Herberta+, b 1842 38

Hester Ann+, b ca 1820 38

Hezekiah 40

Hezekiah+ Jr., b 1789 40

Hezekiah+, b 1753 38

Hezekiah+, b 1789 23, 39

Hezekiah+, b 1792 40

Hezekiah+, bp 24 Jun 1753 57, 149

Hiram H. 62

Hiram, b 1800s 19

Hiram+, b 1852 40

Hiram+, b May 1854 21, 40

Honora (   )+, n.d. 40

Horace J., b 25 Aug 1878 90

Huldah+, b ca 1750 40

Ichabod Jr., b 4 Aug 1722 41

Ichabod+, b 15 Mar 1728 41, 50

Ichabod+, b 1687 40, 133

Ichabod+, b ca 1730 41

Ida E. (Wallett), b Jul 1856 16

Ida M., b Sep 1873 46

Inez M., b 1870 34

Irena, b May 1850 62

Irene, b 1849 62

Irene, b 20 May 1830 88

Isaac J.+, b May 1853 41

Isabel F. (   ), b 1877 36

Israel+, b ca 1677 54

Israel+, b ca 1680 41

Ithamer, see Thomas+, b 1824 41

J. Bradford, b 1851 78

Jabez+, b 1772 73

Jabez+, b 1778 42, 72, 73

Jabez+, b ca 1775 42

Jacob E., see Edgar J. 26

James 5, 45, 98

James L. 152

James M. 97, 144

James M., b 19 Feb 1836 20

Young

James Madison+, b 4 Jun
  1849 45, 46
James Morrill 45
James Morrill+, b 6 May
  1813 45, 87
James W. Brock [b 1851 94
James W., b May 1851 46
James W., see John W.+ 64
James W.+, b 1870 46
James W.+, b Feb 1856 46,
  64
James, b 1685 54
James+, b 1800 45
James+, b 1837 45
James+, b 19 May 1786 23,
  44
James+, b ca 1845 45
Jane ( )+, b Feb 1821 46
Jane (Keazer) 24, 35, 63,
  155
Jane (Keazer), b 5 Oct 1805
  35
Jane (Wentworth)+, b Dec
  1820 46
Jane, b 24 Nov 1752 129
Jasper S.+, b Sep 1847 46
Jennie K., b 25 Nov 1866
  45
Jenny C. (Hobbs) 15
Jerusha (Higgins), b 1780
  95
Jerusha (Smith), b ca 1740
  145
Jerusha, b 19 Apr 1809 96
Jerusha+, b 15 Mar 1711
  47, 66
Jerusha+, b 1802 47
Jesse S., b Aug 1890 41
Jesse+, b 1780s 47, 53
Joan (Knight) 47, 78, 97,
  99, 121, 124, 133, 153
Joan (Knight), b ca 1625
  122
Joan+, b 10 Mar 1731/2 47,
  50
Joanna (Banks), b 1789 50
Joanna (Grant), b 1778 42
Joanna (Nowell) 78, 105,
  152
Joanna (Nowell), b 1774 73

Young

Joanna Billings, b 11 Aug
  1792 63
Joanna, b 20 Apr 1723 83
Joanna, b ca 1800 47
Joanna, b Jan 1815 44
Job 5, 41, 47, 50, 69, 80,
  97, 122, 126, 143
Job Jr.+, b ca 1697 49
Job, bp 11 Mar 1744 136
Job+, b 1664 47, 124
Job+, b 1788 50, 58
Job+, b ca 1670 49
Job+, Jr., b 21 Apr 1739
  50
Job+, Jr., b ca 1697 49,
  50
Joel 5, 47, 53, 101, 104
Joel S. 94
Joel S. aka Jr., b 1837 53
Joel S.+, Jr., b 1790 53
Joel+, b ca 1758 51, 73,
  104
John 20, 50, 53, 58, 94,
  114, 115, 132, 154
John 3rd+, b 25 Oct 1767
  59
John A.+, b 1842 62
John C., b 1848 142
John F. 89
John F., b 1845 89
John F., b 1851 28, 112
John F., see Frank 89
John Henry+, b 10 May 1841
  62
John Howard, b ca 1891 89
John Jr., b 26 Jul 1807 59
John Jr., b ca 1745 55
John L., b 9 Oct 1841 24
John M. 46, 113
John M., b 1845 61
John M., b 1856 62
John R. 35
John R.+, b 1760s 62
John R.+, b 5 Dec 1836 35,
  63
John S.+, b 1868 63
John W., b 31 Oct 1864 93
John W.+, b 21 Jun 1820 63
John W.+, b 27 May 1840
  64, 154

Young

John W.+, b 30 May 1851 46, 64
John W.+, b Jan 1870 64
John Wesley+, b 12 Jul 1838 64
John William, b 7 May 1838 118
John, b 11 Dec 1723 66
John, b 1810s 23
John, b 1815 6, 62
John, b 1828 13
John, b 1839 24
John, b 9 Feb 1824 60
John, b Sep 1881 15
John, bp 4 May 1746 136
John+, b 11 May 1755 39
John+, b 1720 55, 128
John+, b 1726 55
John+, b 1787 60
John+, b 1788 60
John+, b 1794 61
John+, b 1815 61, 77
John+, b 1823 62
John+, b 1824 62
John+, b 1840 62
John+, b 2 Nov 1649 53
John+, b 25 Oct 1767 131
John+, b ca 1672 54
John+, b ca 1690 54
John+, b ca 1700 54
John+, b ca 1725 55
John+, b ca 1735 56
John+, b ca 1750 56
John+, b ca 1755 58, 63
John+, b ca 1760 58
John+, b ca 1761 58
John+, b ca 1785 60
John+, b ca 1800 61
John+, b ca 1835 62
John+, b pre 1755 56
John+, bp 11 May 1755 57, 149
John+, Jr., b 15 Sep 1757 56, 58
John+, Jr., b ca 1755 56
John+, Jr., b ca 1777/8 60
John+, Jr., b ca 1825 62
Johnson+, b 7 Jan 1722 10, 64
Jonathan 4, 24, 26, 28-30, 33, 42, 47, 69, 75, 78,

Young

Jonathan, continued
85, 90, 93, 102, 105, 108-110, 114, 116, 117, 129, 144, 152, 155
Jonathan 3rd+, b 11 Jul 1729 69
Jonathan 3rd+, b 12 Dec 1773 73
Jonathan aka John, b ca 1755 56
Jonathan Jr. 2, 3, 29, 31, 115, 136
Jonathan Jr.+, b ca 1696 69
Jonathan Jr+., b 16 Jan 1809 74
Jonathan, b 1744 111
Jonathan, b 1774 109
Jonathan, b 1840s 118
Jonathan, n.d. 61, 66
Jonathan+ Jr., b 1773 44
Jonathan+, 1680s 133
Jonathan+, 3rd, b 12 Dec 1773 75
Jonathan+, b 1674 65, 125
Jonathan+, b 1680s 29
Jonathan+, b 1763 73, 104
Jonathan+, b 1821 78
Jonathan+, b ca 1675 65
Jonathan+, b ca 1696 49
Jonathan+, b ca 1710 69
Jonathan+, b ca 1735 73
Jonathan+, b ca 1760 75
Jonathan+, b ca 1765 74, 75
Jonathan+, b ca 1770 75
Jonathan+, b ca 1775 77
Jonathan+, b ca 1790 28, 77
Jonathan+, Esq., b 1774 15, 33, 61, 77, 109, 111
Jonathan+, Jr. 78
Jonathan+, Jr., b 1680s 66
Jonathan+, Jr., b 1763 104
Jonathan+, Jr., b ca 1770 75
Jonathan+, Jr., b ca 1775 77
Jonathan+, Lt., b ca 1765 74

Young

Joseph   5, 12, 13, 16, 21, 35, 45, 84, 88, 94, 102, 132, 142, 144, 151
Joseph 2nd+, b Oct 1821   89
Joseph A.+, b Oct 1846   89
Joseph Charles Wentworth, b 9 Oct 1824   87
Joseph Gilman, b 1820s   88
Joseph H., b Jul 1898   89
Joseph Jr.   84
Joseph Jr., b ca 1728   135
Joseph M., b 1848   61
Joseph Timothy+, b Feb 1847 90, 152
Joseph, b 16 Jun 1826   23
Joseph, b 1764   73
Joseph, b 1800s   19
Joseph, b 1806   23
Joseph, b 1836   53
Joseph, b 1856   142
Joseph, b 31 Oct 1744   84
Joseph, b ca 1690s   49
Joseph, see Johnson+   64
Joseph+, b 1 Dec 1715   83
Joseph+, b 11 Apr 1800   86
Joseph+, b 1671   125
Joseph+, b 1758   84
Joseph+, b 1770   86
Joseph+, b 1770s   18
Joseph+, b 1786   87
Joseph+, b 1791   87, 139
Joseph+, b 18 Jan 1849   36, 89
Joseph+, b 1814   88
Joseph+, b 31 Oct 1744   84
Joseph+, b 7 Aug 1788   87
Joseph+, b 8 Feb 1766   73, 85
Joseph+, b ca 1675   54
Joseph+, b ca 1700   84
Joseph+, b ca 1715   84
Joseph+, b ca 1725   84
Joseph+, b ca 1730   84
Joseph+, b ca 1740   84
Joseph+, b ca 1745   84
Joseph+, b ca 1765   85
Joseph+, b ca 1780   86
Joseph+, b ca 1785   86
Joseph+, b ca 1795   88
Joseph+, b pre 1765   85

Young

Joseph+, Jr., b 1 Dec 1715 84
Joseph+, Jr., b 11 Apr 1800 88
Joseph+, Jr., b 31 Oct 1744 84
Joseph+, Jr., b ca 1680 81, 121
Joseph+, Lt.   2, 12, 119, 133
Joseph+, Lt., b 1671   78
Joseph+, n.d   78
Josephine+, 10 Oct 1868   90
Josephine+, b 10 Oct 1868 93
Joshua Jr., b ca 1770   92
Joshua M.   90
Joshua M., b 1836   155
Joshua Moody+, b 29 Oct 1808   76, 93
Joshua Moody+, b 9 Apr 1836 93, 118
Joshua+, b ca 1730   66, 90
Joshua+, b ca 1765   92
Joshua+, b ca 1810   93
Joshua+, Jr., b ca 1760   92
Josiah T.+, b 1831   93
Josue Maria, see Joshua Moody+, b 29 Oct 1808   93
Josue, see Joshua Moody+ 76
Jotham   4
Jotham+, b ca 1782   57, 94
Jotham+, b pre 1775   94
Julia A., b 1833   34
Julia A.+, b 1855   94
Julia A.+, b Mar 1823   94
Julia Ann (Grant), b 1825 144
Julia Ann, b 1828   150
Julia E., b 1865   111
Julia M.+, b Sep 1829   5, 53, 94
Julie A. (   ), b 1825   144
Julie Ann+, b ca 1830   95
Katherine (Frost), b ca 1685   41
Keziah (McIntire)   136
Laura A. (Rhodes), b 27 Oct 1847   15
Laura A.+ (   ), b 1861   95

Young

Maria F. (Johnson), b Nov 1857 26

Marietta+, b ca 1855 98

Mariette (   ), b 1857 15

Mark A.+, b ca 1845 98

Mark R., b 1821 74

Martha (   ) 88

Martha (   ), b 1763 89

Martha (   ), b 1825 45

Martha (   ), b ca 1762 84

Martha (Winn), b 1840 46, 98

Martha A. (Thomas), b ca 1825 5

Martha A., b Aug 1850 151

Martha Ann (Crosby) 7

Martha Ann (Crosby), b 1811 141

Martha C., b 1820s 76

Martha Jane, b 1830 45

Martha Jane, b 1831 150

Martha, 1760s 92

Martha, b 1 Mar 1839 24

Martha+, b ca 1790 98

Martin+, b 1803 98

Mary K. (Nutter), b 1808 102

Mary (   ) 6, 87, 94, 95

Mary (   ) , b ca 1750 136

Mary (   ), b 1819 62

Mary (Adler), b ca 1845 35

Mary (Allen) 47, 53, 101, 104

Mary (Allen), b ca 1760 51

Mary (Card), b ca 1745 106

Mary (Carlisle), b ca 1765 85

Mary (Chadwick), b 23 Nov 1769 110

Mary (Cram), b 9 Mar 1781 1

Mary (Dill), b ca 1740 122

Mary (Edgecomb), b ca 1700 21

Mary (Fernald), b ca 1745 140

Mary (Garvin) 93

Mary (Garvin), b 31 May 1809 117

Mary (Hutchins), b ca 1680 81

Young

Mary (Johnson), b ca 1745 84

Mary (Kimball) 45

Mary (Long), b ca 1786 117

Mary (Lowe), b ca 1775 140

Mary (McInnes)+, b ca 1725 4

Mary (Norton) 3, 59, 117

Mary (Norton), b ca 1749 130

Mary (Preble), b ca 1845 5

Mary (Sayward) 81, 99, 121

Mary (Sayward), b ca 1660 121

Mary (Tebbetts), b ca 1800 88

Mary (Whittun), b ca 1820 120

Mary (Young) 40

Mary (Young), b 1769 38

Mary (Young), b ca 1735 90

Mary A. (   ) 46, 113

Mary A. (   ), b 1827 24

Mary A. (   ), b 8 Jan 1822 63

Mary A. (Plaisted), b 1866 34

Mary A. (Warren), b ca 1845 64

Mary A., b Jan 1870 151

Mary A.+, b 1830 101

Mary Abigail (Junkins), b 1815 61

Mary Ann (Simpson) 15, 34, 90

Mary Ann (Simpson), b 16 Sep 1822 152

Mary B., b Apr 1880 47

Mary Caroline+, b ca 1820 101

Mary Clark (Smith), b Jun 1852 90

Mary D. (Hobbs), b 1775 152

Mary D., b 29 Sep 1824 20

Mary E. (   ), b Oct 1841 63

Mary E. (Crosby) 27

Mary E. (Dearborn), b Oct 1841 63

Young

Mehitable (Beane), b 21 Sep
  1705 133
Mehitable (Moody) 26, 30,
  93, 108, 114, 144, 155
Mehitable (Moody), b 4 Dec
  1775 75
Mehitable H.+, b 1810s 76,
  108
Melissa O.+, b ca 1850 108
Melissa, b Sep 1849 46
Mercy ( ) 152
Mercy (Main) 106
Mercy (Main), b ca 1710
  105
Mercy (Nowell) 42, 75, 85,
  109, 116, 117
Mercy (Nowell), b 1736 69
Mercy (Wheeler) 42
Mercy (Wheeler), b ca 1840
  73
Mercy, b 1766 73
Mercy+, b 15 Jul 1728 10,
  109
Mercy+, b 1685 108, 125
Mercy+, b 19 Dec 1768 109
Mercy+, b 25 Jan 1714 108,
  109
Mercy+, b 7 Sep 1818 77,
  109
Mercy+, b ca 1718 109
Mercy+, b ca 1725 109
Mercy+, b ca 1795 109
Mercy+, b ca 1825 109
Mildred, b Nov 1891 15
Millie E., b Aug 1885 16
Milton L.+, b 9 Feb 1869
  110
Miriam ( ) Dow, b Dec
  1772 18
Miriam (Haley), b ca 1790
  60
Miriam (Littlefield), b
  1819 88
Miriam, b 1846 89
Miriam+, b 1773 110
Miriam+, b 31 Jan 1707 66,
  110
Molly+, b pre 1755 110
Montague, b May 1896 41
Moses C. 13, 30, 102, 147
Moses C.+, b 1822 105, 111

Young

Moses M.+, b Oct 1823 111
Moses+, b 1766 110
Moses+, b 1778 110
Moses+, b ca 1725 110
Myra S. (Prescott)
  Shapleigh, b 11 Oct 1846
  21
Nancy ( ) Cutts, b ca
  1830 105
Nancy (Horn) 20
Nancy (Horn), b 1795 60
Nancy (McIntire), b ca 1776
  69
Nancy (Perkins), b ca 1790
  132
Nancy Elizabeth+, b 1836
  112
Nancy Frost+, b 28 Mar 1828
  112, 113
Nancy, b 1835 34
Nancy, b 23 Mar 1828 23
Nancy+, b 8 Jul 1810 77,
  111
Nancy+, b ca 1800 111
Naomi ( ) 50
Naomi ( ), b 1760s 58
Naomi (Hill), b ca 1735
  115
Naomi, b 1805 86
Napoleon, b 1850 142
Napoleon, b Dec 1886 152
Narsis Albra (Wright), b ca
  1865 14
Nathan, b 1 Feb 1776 131
Nathaniel, b 10 Oct 1728
  83
Nathaniel, b 12 Oct 1743
  129
Nathaniel, b 1716 126
Nathaniel, b 21 Oct 1742
  129
Nathaniel, b ca 1806 59
Nathaniel+, b 1828 28
Nathaniel+, b ca 1725 112
Nathaniel+, b ca 1750 112
Nathaniel+, b ca 1805 112
Nellie M. (Foss), b 1858
  143
Nellie, b Dec 1848 46
Nettie, 1870s 34
Nettie, b 17 Sep 1856 112

Young

Newell H.+, b ca 1850 112
Noah 14, 112
Noah+, b 11 Feb 1775 112,
  139
Olive (   ) Curtis 111
Olive (   ) Curtis, b ca
  1800 104
Olive (   ), b 1803 61
Olive (Folsom), b ca 1785
  86
Olive (Haley), b 1798 61
Olive (Moulton) 26
Olive (Moulton), b 3 Jun
  1820 78
Olive A. (   ), b Feb 1863
  11
Olive A., 1853 64
Olive A., b Mar 1888 27
Olive A.+, b ca 1855 113
Olive Ann (Tripp) 148
Olive Ann (Tripp), b 15 Oct
  1832 21
Olive Ann+, b 19 Jan 1818
  113, 141
Olive B., b 1898 149
Olive B.+, b ca 1820 114
Olive Esther, b 20 Mar 1820
  114
Olive Esther+, b 29 Mar
  1829 60, 114
Olive M., b 1849 111
Olive S., b 1839 33
Olive, b 1819 99
Olive+, b 1780 113
Olive+, b ca 1760 113
Olive+, b ca 1764 104, 113
Olive+, b ca 1770 113
Oliver Martin, b ca 1830
  114
Oliver, b 1809 141
Oliver, b 1811 99
Oliver+, b 1802 114
Oliver+, b 1804 114
Olivia, b 1834 120
Olivia, b 1850s 142
Orrin, b 6 Jun 1851 36
Pamela+, b 1 Feb 1763 56,
  114
Pamelia A.+, b ca 1830 76,
  114
Parmela, see Pamela 114

Young

Parthena, see Perthenia
  115
Patience (Came), b ca 1735
  136
Patience (King) 5, 41, 47,
  50, 122
Patience (King) b ca 1700
  50
Patience (Wentworth) 13,
  45, 144
Patience (Wentworth), b 9
  Aug 1790 87
Patience Adeline, b 30 May
  1831 87
Patience, b 5 Dec 1745 50
Patience, b ca 1763 139
Patience+, b ca 1741 68,
  115
Patience+, b ca 1752 115
Patience+, b ca 1770 115
Patience+, b ca 1790 115
Patty, see Martha 84
Patty+, b ca 1805 115
Perley B., n.d. 95
Persis, b ca 1758 92
Perthenia+, b 1788 57, 115
Peter 27, 93, 142
Peter B., b 18 Oct 1833 20
Peter, b 12 Dec 1737 129
Peter, b ca 1750 116, 118
Peter+, b 14 Jan 1800 76,
  116, 117
Peter+, b 1746 115
Peter+, b 1823 119
Peter+, b 29 Apr 1784 117,
  131
Peter+, b 29 May 1815 118,
  141
Peter+, b ca 1730 115
Peter+, b ca 1750 116, 118
Phebe (Young), b 8 May 1744
  5
Phebe, b 8 May 1744 5
Phebe, see also Phoebe 119
Phebe+ (Young), b 8 May
  1744 50
Phebe+, b 25 Jan 1702 81,
  119
Philamon, b 1847 14
Philamon+, b 1837 119

Young

Ruth (Ramsdell) 88
Ruth (Ramsdell), b ca 1780
  86
Ruth (Wilson), b ca 1770
  59
Ruth M., b May 1892 149
Ruth, b 2 Sep 1720 10
Ruth, see Abigail 10
Ruth+, b ca 1825 132
Sabrina (Wentworth) 143
Sabrina (Wentworth), b Jan
  1826 151
Sally (   ), b 1770s 145
Sally (   ), b 1822 62
Sally (Emery), b ca 1770
  92
Sally (Gullison), b ca 1785
  146
Sally (Robey), b ca 1785
  145
Sally (Small), b ca 1805
  23
Sally A.+, b 6 Feb 1840
  88, 132
Sally S. (   ), b 1803 40
Sally, b 1790s 19
Sally, b 1835 32
Sally+, b 17 Dec 1795 23,
  132
Sally+, b 1790 57, 132
Sally+, b ca 1790 132
Samuel 2, 7, 26, 29, 31,
  37, 40, 66, 87, 89, 102,
  112, 113, 118, 119, 141
Samuel F., b 10 Aug 1852
  151
Samuel Jr., bp 4 Sep 1768
  139
Samuel N.+, b 9 Nov 1828
  142
Samuel P. 26
Samuel P., b 1846 53
Samuel P.+, b 1845 118,
  142
Samuel Preble+, b 22 Apr
  1823 88, 142
Samuel T.+, b 10 Aug 1852
  143
Samuel T.+, b 1846 143
Samuel, b 16 Mar 1719 41
Samuel, b 1650s 124

Young

Samuel, b 1823 147
Samuel, b 21 May 1740 50
Samuel, b 6 Jul 1787 131
Samuel+ Jr., b ca 1773 139
Samuel+, 3rd, b 1806 141
Samuel+, 3rd, b 6 Jul 1785
  141
Samuel+, b 1650s 133
Samuel+, b 1806 141
Samuel+, b 1810 142
Samuel+, b 21 Jul 1704 81,
  133
Samuel+, b 27 Feb 1727 68,
  136
Samuel+, b ca 1630 132
Samuel+, b ca 1710 135
Samuel+, b ca 1735 139
Samuel+, b ca 1740 140
Samuel+, b ca 1745 140
Samuel+, b ca 1765 140
Samuel+, b ca 1785 141
Samuel+, b pre 1755 140
Samuel+, Jr., b 1770 140
Samuel+, Jr., b ca 1765
  140
Sarah (   ) Young 53
Sarah (   ), b 1814 120
Sarah (   ), b 1815 24
Sarah (   ), see Sally S.
  40
Sarah (   )+, b ca 1729
  143
Sarah (Adams), b ca 1730
  11
Sarah (Austin) Preble 50,
  69, 97, 126, 143
Sarah (Austin) Preble, b ca
  1667 47
Sarah (Battin) 25
Sarah (Battin), b ca 1705
  24
Sarah (Curtis) 30, 37, 51,
  73, 113
Sarah (Curtis), b ca 1740
  102
Sarah (Davis), b ca 1795
  44
Sarah (Dixon), b ca 1725
  55
Sarah (Grow), b 1789 42
Sarah (Hayes) 116, 118

Young

Sarah (Hayes), ba 14 Feb
  1751 116
Sarah (King) 12, 16, 84
Sarah (King), b 17 May 1687
  81
Sarah (McGowan), b ca 1860
  26
Sarah (Peirce), b ca 1815
  154
Sarah (Preble) 80
Sarah (Ricker), b 1802 87
Sarah (Runnels), b ca 1830
  62
Sarah (Saunders) 89
Sarah (Wadleigh), b 1655
  53
Sarah (Witham), b ca 1780
  20
Sarah A. (   ), b 1854 112
Sarah A., b 23 Mar 1840 20
Sarah Ann+, b 14 Sep 1815
  87, 144
Sarah Ann+, b ca 1815 144
Sarah C. (   ), b 1852 144
Sarah E. (Jellison), b 1846
  38
Sarah F., see Florence S.
  89
Sarah F.+, b ca 1855 144
Sarah H.+, b 1802 76, 144
Sarah Hayes, b 8 Jun 1840
  118
Sarah Jane, b 1 Feb 1831
  35
Sarah S. (   ), b 1801 40
Sarah S. (Blaisdell), b
  1819 153
Sarah Semantha+, b 12 Nov
  1840 46, 144
Sarah, b 1 May 1814 33
Sarah, b 13 Apr 1830 23
Sarah, b 1767 104
Sarah, b 18 Feb 1730 50
Sarah, b 19 Feb 1749 55
Sarah, b 20 Aug 1750 129
Sarah, b 20 Dec 1724 68
Sarah, b 20 Oct 1760 56
Sarah, b 22 Mar 1723 22
Sarah, b 23 Jul 1734 50
Sarah, bp 21 Sep 1773 22
Sarah, bp 30 May 1762 149

Young

Sarah, bp 31 Jul 1763 139
Sarah+, b 1681 125, 143
Sarah+, b 1836 143
Sarah+, b ca 1702 49, 143
Sarah+, b ca 1730 143
Sarah+, b ca 1750 143
Sarah+, b pre 1775 143
see Thomas+, b 1824 151
Seth S., b 1834 150
Shadrach H., b 29 Apr 1832
  87
Shadrach Hill, b 15 Jul
  1827 87
Sherman+, b 1852 144
Sidney S., b 1874 143
Silas H.+, b 1826 144
Silas P.+, b 1835 145
Silva H., b Feb 1886 15
Simeon+, n.d. 145
Simon M.+, b Apr 1833 145
Solomon+, b 1827 145
Solomon+, b 25 Apr 1742
  145
Solomon+, b ca 1755 145
Sophia J.+, b ca 1843 145
Sophia, b 1836 13
Sophia, b 1846 87
Sophia, b 28 Jul 1818 87
Sophronia, b 11 Jan 1847
  24
Stanley W., b 1893 151
Stephen 28, 101
Stephen A., b 1840 147
Stephen E.+, b 28 Nov 1838
  146
Stephen H. 1, 7
Stephen, b 10 May 1755 129
Stephen, b 1839 21
Stephen, b 22 Oct 1854 101
Stephen, b 25 Dec 1777 131
Stephen+, b 1770s 145
Stephen+, b 1794 146
Stephen+, b 1825 146
Stephen+, b ca 1735 145
Stephen+, b ca 1755 145
Stephen+, b ca 1780 145
Stephen+, b ca 1785 146
Stephen+, b ca 1795 146
Stephen+, b ca 1840 146
Stephen+, b ca 1855 146

Young
  William 18
  William A. 64, 120
  William A., b 3 Jan 1838
    11
  William A.+, b 1805 154
  William Albert, b 29 Dec
    1871 89
  William Babb+, b ca 1735
    154
  William E.+, b 1820 154
  William H. Cummings+, b Jul
    1859 14, 155
  William H.+, b 23 Mar 1847
    154
  William J., b 1 Aug 1824
    23
  William M.+, b 19 Apr 1804
    76, 155
  William N.+, b ca 1805 155
  William Newman, b 1851 142
  William P., b 10 Apr 1875
    93
  William P., b 8 Oct 1870
    93
  William, b 1843 60
  William, b 1846 28
  William+, b 1663 124, 153
  William+, b 1844 154
  William+, b ca 1700 153
  William+, b ca 1785 153
  William+, b ca 1810 154
  William+, b ca 1845 154
  William+, b Nov 1816 154
  Willis E., b 1871 63
  Wilson C., b 18 Mar 1880
    64
  Winfield H., b 1882 90
  Winfield Scott+, b 15 Sep
    1848 35, 155
  Winnefred M., b Jun 1892
    90
  Winnie L., b 17 Jul 1882
    143

www.ingramcontent.com/pod-product-compliance
Lightning Source LLC
Chambersburg PA
CBHW070907270326

41927CB00011B/2484